Interpretation of Contracts in Comparative and Uniform Law

International Arbitration Law Library

VOLUME 47

Editors

Professor Julian D.M. Lew QC has been involved with international arbitration for more than forty years as counsel, as arbitrator and as an academic. He is the founder and has been the Head of the School of International Arbitration, Centre for Commercial Law Studies, Queen Mary University of London since its creation in 1985. He is now an independent international arbitrator at 20 Essex Street, London.

Stavros Brekoulakis is Professor at Queen Mary University of London and an associate member of 3 Verulam Buildings (Gray's Inn). He is a leading academic in international arbitration and has led, or been involved in, several projects with ICCA, ICC Commission and ILA. He also acts as an independent arbitrator and has been appointed as chairman, sole arbitrator, co-arbitrator and emergency arbitrator under the rules of all the major arbitration rules.

Introduction

Since its first volume published in 1993, this authoritative practitioner-oriented series has published in-depth and analytical works on niche aspects of international arbitration, authored by specialists in the field.

Objective

This authoritative and established series covering in-depth analyses of niche areas appeals to both practitioners and academics. The series includes specific monographs and PhD dissertations of high quality, which are practical and cover issues not fully explored in general texts.

Frequency

A volume is published whenever an interesting topic presents itself.

The titles published in this series are listed at the end of this volume.

Interpretation of Contracts in Comparative and Uniform Law

Ahmet Cemil Yıldırım

Wolters Kluwer

Published by:
Kluwer Law International B.V.
PO Box 316
2400 AH Alphen aan den Rijn
The Netherlands
E-mail: international-sales@wolterskluwer.com
Website: lrus.wolterskluwer.com

Sold and distributed in North, Central and South America by:
Wolters Kluwer Legal & Regulatory U.S.
7201 McKinney Circle
Frederick, MD 21704
United States of America
Email: customer.service@wolterskluwer.com

Sold and distributed in all other countries by:
Air Business Subscriptions
Rockwood House
Haywards Heath
West Sussex
RH16 3DH
United Kingdom
Email: international-customerservice@wolterskluwer.com

ISBN 978-94-035-1130-6

e-Book: ISBN 978-94-035-1104-7
web-PDF: ISBN 978-94-035-1115-3

Table of Contents

Preface

The interpretation of contracts is and has always been one of the most fundamental subjects in private law. As a result, individual legal systems and uniform law texts contain a considerable body of legal literature and case law on the principles relating to the interpretation of contracts.

To illustrate the fundamental importance of this subject as recently as the early modern era, it may be sufficient to point out that when the Ottoman Empire was codifying civil law in the nineteenth century, several of the highest ranked principles among the 100 introductory principles of the *Mecelle-i Ahkâm-ı Adliyye* were those relating to the interpretation of contracts. The importance given to the principles of the interpretation of contracts in other national legal systems is reflected in the volumes of commentaries on civil law and the law of obligations that exclusively cover this subject. Likewise, the Working Group for the provisions on the interpretation of contracts was the second one to be established by the International Institute for the Unification of Private Law (UNIDROIT) in their work on *The Progressive Codification of International Trade Law.*

It has been widely acknowledged that many modern principles of the interpretation of contracts in contemporary legal systems are based on Roman law. Some of these are even cited in Latin and referred to as *Latin maxims*, but without specific reference to their origins. Nevertheless, the historical origins of these commonly used Latin expressions can be precisely determined in the *Digesta* (*Dig.*), the entire text of which and its English translation are now available on the Internet. A closer look at the *Digesta* reveals that the fact that to a greater degree than commonly thought most modern principles on the subject have historical origins in Roman law. Indeed, the modern evolution of these principles has been somewhat minor compared with their development during the Roman period. However, while there have been studies examining the Roman origins of the principles of the interpretation of contracts, the legal literature has been lacking a holistic study of the historical development of these legal principles as they are expressed in contemporary legal systems.

Provisions on the interpretation of contracts in modern codifications of law reflect the high degree of importance that legislators continue to give to this subject.

Some legislators, especially from Latin legal traditions, as well as legal academics in the United States (U.S.), have put more emphasis on this issue than legislators from other jurisdictions. Elevated legislative interest on this subject is also quite naturally reflected in a greater volume of legal literature on the subject in Latin jurisdictions and the U.S. In fact, it should be noted that the amount and quality of academic studies and discussion on this subject is so great specifically in Italy and the U.S. that it is incomparable with the legal literature on the subject in any other country. Conversely and in a certain parallelism with the lower volume of legislative provisions dedicated to this subject, there are notably fewer academic studies found in the Romano-Germanic legal systems that address the interpretation of contracts as compared with those addressing the subject in Latin legal systems, common law, and uniform law.

In spite of the high number of jurisdiction-specific studies on the interpretation of contracts that are available, the number of comparative law studies on the subject has remained quite limited. The lack of comparative law studies on this subject has contributed to a general absence of available information on the relative approaches of different legal systems to this issue, and therefore, further contributed to prejudices by local practitioners against foreign legal systems, some of which are explored in this study.

It can be further observed that detailed provisions have been drafted in uniform law texts reflecting the importance of the interpretation of contracts in cross-border transactions. In particular, the interpretation of contracts is one of the most highly studied subjects within the United Nations Convention on Contracts for the International Sale of Goods, the UNIDROIT Principles, and the various bodies of uniform law that have followed them, not only in terms of legislative drafting and the legal literature but also in judicial and arbitral decisions. The uniform law texts of the European Union also reflect the fundamental importance of this issue, and a gradual evolution may be observed in the relevant provisions of these texts.

As with individual legal systems, however, although there have been some studies on the relevant provisions of particular uniform law texts, there has remained a notable absence of a comparative study covering all major uniform texts.

For these reasons, the aim of this study is, within the context of their historical origins, to offer a comparative examination of the principles relating to the interpretation of contracts in individual legal systems and uniform law texts.

This study does not pretend to offer a complete examination of its subject matter under any single legal system. Rather, every legal system covered in this study is examined in general terms and on the basis of resources particular to it by presenting the discussions in the literature belonging to each legal system or uniform law text and ultimately making some determinations on the general tendencies in comparative law that can be drawn from all the common discussions.

List of Abbreviations

ABGB	Österreich Allgemeines Bürgerliches Gesetzbuch
ALI	American Law Institute
Art.	Article
BAG	Bundesarbeitsgericht
Batider	Banka ve Ticaret Hukuku Dergisi
BGB	Bürgerliches Gesetzbuch
BGE	Entscheidungen des Schweizerischen Bundesgerichts
BGer	Entscheiden des Schweizerischen Bundesgerichts
BGH	Bundesgerichtshof
BGHZ	Bundesgerichtshofs in Zivilsachen
Bull. Civ.	Bulletin des arrêts de la Cour de cassation: Chambres civiles
Cass.	Cour de Cassation
Cass.	Corte di Cassazione
CC. Fr.	Code Civil Français
CC. It.	Codice Civile Italiano
CENTRAL	Center for Transnational Law
CESL	Common European Sales Law
CFR	Common Frame of Reference
Chi.-Kent. L. Rev.	Chicago-Kent Law Review
CIF	Cost, insurance, and freight
CISG	United Nations Convention on Contracts for the International Sale of Goods (1980)
civ.	civil

CLOUT	Case Law on UNCITRAL Texts
com.	commercial
DCFR	Draft Common Frame of Reference
Dig.	*Digesta*
EC	European Commission
EU	European Union
FOB	Free on Board
GI	Giurisprudenza Italiana
HD	Hukuk Dairesi
HGK	Hukuk Genel Kurulu
IBLJ/RDAI	International Business Law Journal/Revue de droit des affaires internationales
ICC	International Chamber of Commerce
ICSID	International Centre for Settlement of Investment Disputes
INCOTERMS®	International Commercial Terms
Int'l & Comp. L.Q.	International and Comparative Law Quarterly
İÜHFD	İstanbul Üniversitesi Hukuk Fakültesi Dergisi
Law Mag. & L. Rev.	Law Magazine and Law Review
LGDJ	Librairie générale de droit et de jurisprudence
Mecelle	Mecelle-i Ahkâm-ı Adliyye
n.	note
NCCUSL	National Conference of Commissioners on Uniform State Laws
NJW	Neue Juristische Wochenschrift
OLG	Oberlandesgericht
OR	Obligationenrecht
PECL	Principles of European Contract Law
RDC	Revue des contrats
Rep. Foro it.	Repertorio generale annuale del Foro italiano
RGZ	Reichsgerichts in Zivilsachen
TBK	Türk Borçlar Kanunu
Tex. L. Rev.	Texas Law Review
TKK	Tüketicinin Korunması Hakkında Kanun
TMK	Türk Medeni Kanunu
TTK	Türk Ticaret Kanunu
TvR	Tijdschrift voor Rechtsgeschiedenis [Legal History Review]

U. Pa. L. Rev.	University of Pennsylvania Law Review
U.N.	United Nations
UCC	Uniform Commercial Code
UCP	Uniform Customs and Practice
ULVC	UNIDROIT Draft Law for the Unification of Certain Rules Relating to Validity of Contracts of International Sale of Goods
UNCITRAL	United Nations Commission on International Trade Law
UNIDROIT	Institut International pour l'Unification du Droit Privé
Unif. L. Rev.	Uniform Law Review/Revue de droit uniforme
US	United States of America
ZBJV	Zeitschrift des Bernischen Juristenvereins
ZGB	Zivilgesetzbuch
ZPO	Zivilprozessordnung

Acknowledgments

This research was supported by Altınbaş University in Istanbul, Turkey, to which I am grateful for this opportunity. I would like to thank, especially, Prof. Dr. Şükran Şıpka for her kind and continuous support. I have conducted this research at the Institute for Private International and Comparative Law of the University of Cologne. I would like to thank Prof. Dr. Heinz-Peter Mansel, the director of the institute, for his kind invitation and hospitality.

I am also immensely grateful to Mr. Todd Germain for his corrections and comments that greatly improved the manuscript.

I would also like to show my gratitude to Dr. Giuseppe Didonna for his invaluable support throughout my life, as well as his assistance in providing me with the UNIDROIT documents.

Nevertheless, I am also grateful to Prof. Dr. Klaus-Peter Berger and Prof. Dr. Martin Avenarius for their sincere and unconditional support, their intellectual discussions, and invaluable suggestions.

Last but not the least, I would like to thank my family: my parents, my wife Arzu, and my daughters Berfin and İdil for supporting me spiritually throughout writing this treatise and my life in general.

CHAPTER 1

Introduction

§1.01 PURPOSE, METHOD, AND LIMITATIONS

This is a comparative law study. Accordingly, individual legal systems and uniform law texts are examined from their own perspectives and on the basis of the resources peculiar to each legal system or set of uniform legislation. That said, the approaches, legislative texts, practices, and theoretical debates vary significantly from one legal system to another. In this study, all the elements of individual legal systems to be examined have been presented within the context of that system, and in particular, the terminology peculiar to each system has been preserved in its language. In this way, readers will have the opportunity to make more comparisons and draw their own conclusions beyond those provided by the author in cross-references.

A comparative study can certainly not be considered complete by merely providing the legislation, case law, and literature in individual legal systems and uniform law texts. In order to make accurate determinations and draw concrete conclusions, it is also necessary to examine the historical background of the subject matter of the study. This is a must in a field like the interpretation of contracts, where the influence of Roman law is strongly felt, not only in Latin or Romano-Germanic legal systems but also in common law countries.

For this reason, the second chapter will examine the "Historical Development of the Principles of the Interpretation of Contracts." The scope of this chapter will not be limited to the Roman basis of our subject. Rather, a light will be shed on the connection between Roman law and modern legislation, to the extent that today's knowledge of legal history allows.

In this way, the "Interpretation of Contracts in Comparative Law," which will be examined in the third chapter, can be explored in light of the historical reasons for basic differences in the approaches of individual legal systems. Through this methodology, the intention is to provide a more complete perspective to the reader.

As regards uniform law, this study examines all the uniform law texts relevant to the topic, both in practice and in the legal literature. In addition to texts intended to unify or harmonize the law at a global level, the uniform law texts of European Union (EU), which constitute an important reference model for regional codifications, have also been presented. Therefore, the "Interpretation of Contracts in Uniform Law," which constitutes the subject matter of the fourth chapter, has been assessed both in the light of the historical background of the issue and in the context of comparative studies of national models upon which uniform law texts are based.

Finally, the conclusions to be drawn from the entirety of this study are systematically summarized in the fifth chapter. Even though the discussions on the interpretation of contracts in individual legal systems are numerous and various, they have a high degree of common ground regarding the most basic issues. When the approaches to and solutions for these common issues by different legal systems are examined from a comparative point of view, it becomes possible to observe that there are some common trends and tendencies. In order to present general determinations pertaining to these common tendencies in comparative law, the outcome of this study is provided in the fifth chapter, entitled "Final Remarks on General Tendencies in Comparative and Uniform Law on the Interpretation of Contracts."

A comparative study on a comprehensive subject matter with a deep historical background has some natural limits. It is impossible for a study such as this to cover every legal system, or even every legal family. For this reason, this study will be limited to an examination of the Latin and Romano-Germanic legal families, where the Roman influence is felt most strongly, and the common law family, which is highly relevant in today's legal environment. In the context of these legal families, the legal systems that prevail, their historical backgrounds, their scientific features, and those representing different approaches within the same legal families will be studied.

Along with a limited selection of legal families, the scope of this study is also limited by its exclusive focus on the interpretation of contracts in its narrow meaning. In most legal systems, a distinction is made between the interpretation of contracts in the narrow sense or "explanatory interpretation," which aims at determining the content of a contract and/or the will of the parties, and in the broad sense or "complementary interpretation," by which any gaps in contracts are filled with complementary information.

The issue of whether the latter can be deemed an activity of interpretation is debated in most legal systems. However, even in the Romano-Germanic legal systems, where complementary interpretation is considered to be an interpretative activity, a sharp distinction is made between explanatory interpretation and complementary interpretation. This is because complementary interpretation requires a determination of the presumed intent of the parties on the issues they omitted in their agreements rather than an examination of the intent of the parties and the interpretation of their declarations. For this reason, complementary interpretation is not usually regarded as an interpretative activity and therefore has been left beyond the scope of this study entirely.

As this study is exclusively limited to an examination of the interpretation of contracts, the "interpretation of norms," although another important aspect of legal interpretation, will not be covered.

§1.02 THE PROBLEMATIQUE OF THE INTERPRETATION OF CONTRACTS

"Hermeneutics" is the science of interpretation, named after Hermes, the ambassador of the gods. In Greek mythology, Hermes is charged with transferring messages from the gods to human beings. To carry out this mission, Hermes must go beyond merely translating the messages into human words, and rather, provide an explanation of the will of gods underlying these messages, without which a mere translation of the messages would not make very much sense to humans.

Accordingly, Plato speaks of hermeneutics as the art of explaining the will of the gods in his work *Laws*. Meanwhile, in a chapter entitled *peri hermeneias* of the *Organon*, Aristotle uses the word in the sense of a logical and grammatical examination of propositions. The further development of the science of hermeneutics was first observed to a large extent in the fields of theology and linguistics, and then in the field of philosophy.[1]

The historical arguments in the legal literature on interpretation have a common core in the approaches of Plato and Aristotle: the purpose of interpretation is considered either to be the revelation of an internal, subjective will that belongs to another world, as Plato conceptualized it, or as the determination of an objective meaning of declarations on the basis of the rules of logic and linguistics, as argued by Aristotle. Throughout legal history, the subjective approach has prevailed at times and the objective approach has prevailed at other times, but there has always been a search for a balance between the two.

In modern comparative law, it can be observed that the objective approach prevails in some legal systems, while the subjective approach is more dominant in others. This basic choice by individual legal systems determines the definition of interpretation, the distinction and connection between subjective and objective interpretation, the systems of rules and principles of interpretation, their manner of application, and even different consequences arising out of the same rules in individual legal systems. For this reason, the choice between these two basic approaches constitutes the core issue in the interpretation of contracts.

Although belonging to the same legal family, different legal systems may also attribute different meanings to objective and subjective interpretation. For this reason, this comparative study will use the terms objective and subjective interpretation in the senses represented by the approaches of Plato and Aristotle and thus will be abstracted from their meanings in any individual legal system.

1. On this issue, *see* generally, Hans-Georg Gadamer, *Classical and Philosophical Hermeneutics*, 23(1) Theory, Culture and Society 29-56 (2006).

Accordingly, for the purposes of this study, subjective interpretation will be referred to as "subjective" because it relates to the will or intent of the parties to a contract, and objective interpretation will be referred to as "objective" since it is based on the meaning of the expressions used by the parties as understood in the external world, free from party intent.

In this sense, it is possible to find a definition of subjective interpretation in the writings of Goudsmit, the famous Dutch Romanist of the nineteenth century. According to Goudsmit, the purpose of interpretation is "to make every effort to ascertain what was the true intent of the parties, and to penetrate the spirit of clauses, the mere letter of which often expresses but imperfectly purports."[2] Likewise, the famous German lawyer of the nineteenth century von Lingenthal writes that the purpose of interpretation is "to reveal the will behind the declaration."[3]

These definitions of subjective interpretation are, indeed, based on the presumption that there is necessarily a difference between the declaration and the intent because the words used in the declaration cannot be sufficient for expressing the intent. According to authors who adopt a subjective approach in interpretation, the language (be it either verbal or written) is usually an insufficient tool for expressing thought. As texts having legal significance, an insufficiency of the language found in contracts leads to interpretation disputes in practice. This is because it is not always, or even usually, possible to expect the contracting parties to have perfect skills of legal expression. Likewise, it is not possible to expect all contracts to foresee every possible contingency that may arise in the future. Therefore contracts, by their nature, are insufficient texts in terms of the issues they cover and incomplete texts in terms of the issues they do not cover.[4]

For these reasons, the subjective approach defines interpretation as the "determination of the true intent of the parties."[5] Behind this definition, based on the intent of the parties, lies the principle of freedom of contract, which has been championed by liberal thought in the nineteenth century. Under this principle, the intent of the parties is to be taken as a basis for interpretation because the agreement of the parties has the force of law between the parties thereto.[6]

Nevertheless, according to the objective approach, the reasoning that underlies the subjective approach proceeds from a logical fallacy. This is because it is simply impossible to interpret an unexpressed intent, and therefore it is not possible to detach

2. Joel Emanuel Goudsmit, *The Pandects: A Treatise on the Roman Law and upon Its Connection with Modern Legislation*, 175-176 (Longmans/Green, 1873).
3. Karl Salomo Zachariä von Lingenthal, *Versuch einer allgemeinen Hermeneutik des Rechts Erbstein*, 92 (Meissen, 1805).
4. Konrad Zweigert, Hein Kötz, *Introduction to Comparative Law*, 400 (3rd ed., Clarendon Press, Oxford, 1998); *see also* François Terré, Philippe Simler, Yves Lequette, *Droit Civil—Les Obligations*, 495 (11th ed., Dalloz, 2013).
5. *See, inter alia*, Philippe Malaurie, Laurent Aynès, *Les Obligations*, 381 (10th ed., LGDJ, 2018); Claus-Wilhem Canaris, Hans Christoph Grigoleit, *Interpretation of Contracts*, in Hartkamp et al. (eds.), *Towards a European Civil Code*, 447 (Kluwer Law International, 2004); Marcel Fontaine, Filip de Ly, *Droit des contrats internationaux—Analyse et rédaction de clauses*, 120 (2nd ed., Bruylant-FEC, 2003).
6. Canaris, Grigoleit, *supra* n. 5, at 446-447; Fontaine, de Ly, *supra* n. 5, at 120-121; Terré, Simler, Lequette, *supra* n. 4, at 497-498.

the intent from the expression. According to this view, it is impossible to accurately determine subjective intent, and thus, intent can only be interpreted when it has been expressed in an objective manner.[7] If there is room for subjective interpretation, it is necessarily limited because a common or real intent of both parties does not always exist, and it would be unproductive to attempt to determine one since each party would reasonably tend to interpret the agreement according to its best interests. For this reason, when subjective interpretation remains unfruitful, the process of interpretation quite naturally leads to objective interpretation, where the objective meaning of the expressions of the parties are examined by using objective instruments such as good faith and fair dealing, equity, and commercial customs.[8]

According to the objective approach, the intent of the parties must be expressed in order to be the subject of interpretation. In fact, mere expression alone is sufficient by itself to make intent known for the purpose of interpretation. In the words of Monateri:

> While the parties declare their intents for a contract, they make declarations that can be used against themselves. Each party makes declarations that it cannot fulfill anymore (if it could, there would be no dispute), but the each party sees the other as bound. For this reason, each party is bound with its own declarations with which it does not anymore wish to be. The essence of objective interpretation lies here; in binging the author of the declaration with his declaration against his will. In this sense, declaration is ... a reality that is extrinsic in terms of time, and beyond the subjective sphere of control of the party.[9]

Even though the objective approach is derived from such a practical and realistic reasoning, the effect of this reasoning in most modern legislation and uniform law has been limited by the principle of freedom of contract, which underlies the subjective approach. The majority of legal systems and all uniform law texts take the position that the principle of freedom of contract requires a determination of the common and true intent of the parties, and where this is not possible, to then examine the objective meaning of the declarations of the parties. Some authors refer to this method as a "hybrid approach."[10] The present author is of the opinion that this term is somewhat misleading; however, since in legal systems where the subjective approach dominates, the objective interpretation is always accepted as the secondary method of interpretation. Nevertheless, it is fair to state that this "hybrid approach" implies a search for balance between subjective and objective interpretation.

Although the supremacy of subjective interpretation is usually recognized because of the importance traditionally attributed to its theoretical basis, it is evident that in practice, this method cannot always be sufficient by itself to solve the problem of interpretation in disputes. It is also evident that the adoption of a purely objective

7. Rodolfo Sacco, *Dell'interpretazione del contratto*, 234-235, in Paolo Cendon (ed.), *Commentatio al Codice Civile* (Giuffrè Editore, 2010).
8. Terré, Simler, Lequette, *supra* n. 4, at 498.
9. Pier Giuseppe Monateri, *L'interpretazione del Contratto*, 426-427, in Pier Giuseppe Monateri, Enrico del Prato, Maria Rosaria Marella, Alessandro Somma, Cristina Costantini (eds.), *Il Nuovo Contratto* (5th ed., Zanichelli, 2010).
10. Fontaine, de Ly, *supra* n. 5, at 120; Terré, Simler, Lequette, *supra* n. 4, at 497.

method would inevitably lead to unjust consequences. For these reasons, a general tendency to consider some subjective elements (such as the circumstances in which the parties were negotiating) in contract interpretation has been adopted by most legal systems, as well as all uniform law texts, even among those that have opted for an objective approach by default.

CHAPTER 2

Historical Development of the Principles of the Interpretation of Contracts

§2.01 ROMAN LAW

The question of interpretation has been rooted in a struggle between *verba* and *voluntas*, between the wording and the will, throughout Roman legal history going back 2,500 years. In considering this long process, it is possible to observe a shift in focus from *verba*, which can be considered to represent the objective approach in its strictest meaning, to *voluntas*, in the most subjective sense of the word.[11]

[A] The Archaic Period

Neither in the archaic period nor in the following periods of Roman law has there ever been a clear distinction between the interpretation of norms and the interpretation of contracts.[12] These two concepts always developed hand in hand.[13] However, the legislative activities of the archaic period brought about a particular need for interpretation of norms, and this need led to the first developments in the field of legal interpretation.

Until the third century B.C., *pontìfices* enjoyed a monopoly of power in the interpretation of legal norms. Later on, however, judges also began to interpret

11. Reinhard Zimmermann, *The Law of Obligations—Roman Foundations of the Civilian Tradition*, 622 (2nd ed., Oxford University Press, 1996).
12. James Williams, *Interpretation in Roman Law*, 15 The Law Magazine and Review of All Reported Cases, 5th ser. 223, 229 (1890). On the interpretation of norms in Roman law, *see* generally, Friedrich Karl von Savigny, *System of the Modern Roman Law*, Vol I, 166 et seq, translated by William Holloway (J. Higginbotham Publisher, 1867); Peter Stein, *Interpretation and Legal Reasoning in Roman Law*, 70 Chicago-Kent Law Review 1539 (1995).
13. Williams, *supra* n. 12, at 225; Giuseppe Gandolfi, *Lezioni sull'interpretazione dei negozi giuridici*, 113 (La Goliardica, 1966).

norms.[14] Then, with the emergence of the office of *praetor* in the Republic period, a new kind of activity of interpretation developed. In that period, the law that was distilled from interpretations of the *praetor*s was considered to be a different law from the one that existed before the interpretation of the *praetor*s. This activity of the *praetors* was based on *æquitas* (equity as understood in modern law).[15]

Legal interpretation of contracts in the practice of law, however, as opposed to the interpretation of legal norms, truly emerged in the written record for the first time after the fifth century B.C., by means of judges' use of discretion in applying the Law of Twelve Tables (450-451 B.C.).[16] Although today's knowledge from the authors and their works of this period is limited, Williams states that the first known interpreter was Consul *Sextus Ælius Pætus* and that his work on the interpretation of the Law of Twelve Tables, which dates from 198 B.C., was named *Tripertita.*[17]

From this period on, many interpretative activities were conducted on the meaning of the provisions of the Law of Twelve Tables, and some of these interpretations are also reflected in *Digesta* (*Dig.*), which came about ten centuries later. For instance, the meaning of *pauperies* (damage caused by domestic animals) mentioned in the Law of Twelve Tables was expanded to cover any quadruped animal through an interpretation made in this period and reflected in *Digesta.*[18]

In the archaic period, the scope of legal interpretation was not limited to the interpretation of the Law of Twelve Tables. The assembly of sacerdotes set about interpreting the will and orders of the *pontìfices*. Their activity, which was called *interpretatio pontìficum*, emerged as a source of law in the late fifth century B.C. and early fourth century B.C.[19] This source of law merged toward the end of the archaic period with the *ius quiritum* (old customary law) and *ius legitimum vetus* (the Law of the Twelve Tables) to create the *ius civile romanorum.*[20] Eventually, the activity of the *interpretatio pontìficum* was expanded to cover the interpretation of the whole *ius civile* for adaptation to current needs and referred to as the *interpretàtio prudèntium.*[21]

It should also be mentioned that in the archaic period, a strict formalism was used to characterize all legal and religious procedures. Legal transactions were being made with a strict *stipulatio* procedure, and a minimal mistake, even a speech defect or a cough, was sufficient to invalidate the whole transaction. This rigid formalism in transactions gave rise to a rigid formalism in the interpretation of transactions along

14. Sergio Beltrani, *Istituzioni di Diritto Romano*, 34 (4th ed., Simone, 2003) (Beltrani, Istituzioni); Williams, *supra* n. 12, at 231.
15. Williams, *supra* n. 12, at 224.
16. *Ibid.*, at 230; Stein, *supra* n. 12, at 1540-1541.
17. Williams, *supra* n. 12, at 231.
18. *Ibid.*, at 231-132, *Dig.* 9, 1, 1, 2.
19. Beltrani, *supra* n. 14, at 8-9. Williams argues that the terms *interpres*, *interpretatio*, *interpretator*, and *interpretari* come from the late period Latin and were not in use before Cicero (the first century A.D.), Williams, *supra* n. 12, at 227. Savigny points out that for jurists of the classical period, the term "*interpretatio*" did not mean interpretation, but it had a broader meaning covering theory, tradition, and the legal science; von Savigny, *supra* n. 12, at 241.
20. Beltrani, *supra* n. 14, at 9.
21. *Ibid.*, at 34.

with it. For this reason, the will of the parties during the archaic period did not have any significance, and what was relevant was the *verba* only.[22]

[B] Emergence of the Principles of Interpretation of Contracts in the Classical Period

[1] Generally

Toward the end of the Republic, the boundaries of the Roman state had spread to all the coasts of the Mediterranean Sea, leading to the expansion of trade and consequently, the emergence of most of the principles of the law of obligations, which are still reflected in today's legal systems. Most of the notions and principles in the field of the interpretation of contracts developed in this, the classical period, with the diversification of the forms of the *stipulatio* and the emergence of consensual contracts. Both written law texts and the interpretation of those laws developed considerably in this period, and the process of interpretation was largely examined in the works of the authors of at that time.[23] This being the case, the distinction between the interpretation of norms and the interpretation of contracts was not precise, nor was the distinction between the rules on interpretation and other substantive rules. This caused the principles of contractual interpretation to appear in the *Digesta* in a manner that was far from systematic.[24]

Consensual contracts focusing on the will of the parties developed in the classical period within the context of *ius gentium* and prevailed over the strict formalism of previous periods, which led to a flexible approach in the interpretation of party intent.[25] For this reason, it is possible to observe that legal interpretation considered not only *verba* but also *voluntas* by the end of the Republic.[26] However, neither *verba* nor *voluntas* enjoyed complete domination in the classical period. There was a certain balance between them, and strict formalism was abandoned, but it was not replaced by an absolute subjectivist approach.[27] Accordingly, when interpreting legal transactions, both objective criteria, such as the declared intents of the parties, and subjective criteria, such as the expectations of the parties and their internal wills, were being taken into consideration during the classical period.[28] Consequently, individual legal transactions were being interpreted to a large degree in the light of the circumstances specific to each case.[29]

22. Zimmermann, *supra* n. 11, at 622.
23. Williams refers to *Topica* by Cicero, *Regulae* and *ad Edictum* by Ulpianus, *Sententiae Receptae* and *ad Edictum* by Paulus, and *Definitiones* by Quintus Mucius Scaevola; Williams, *supra* n. 12, at 232-234.
24. Williams, *supra* n. 12, at 226.
25. Zimmermann, *supra* n. 11, at 627; Alan Watson, *Narrow, Rigid and Literal Interpretation in the Later Roman Republic*, 37 Tijdschrift voor Rechtsgeschiedenis 351, 352 (1969).
26. Zimmermann, *supra* n. 11, at 627; Williams, *supra* n. 12, at 225.
27. Zimmermann, *supra* n. 11, at 634.
28. *Ibid.*, at 633-634.
29. *Ibid.*, at 627.

Toward the end of the Republic, *voluntas* became so important that it could occasionally prevail over *verba* and be decisive in the outcome of cases. Treated by Gandolfi and Zimmermann, a case known as *Causa Curiana* is of particular relevance in demonstrating the importance attributed to *voluntas* during this period.[30] The case took place in 92 B.C. *Marcus Coponius* had written his last will and testament in which he appointed his "son" as his first heir, and *Curius* as *substitutio pupillaris*, to replace his son in the event that his son should die before reaching the age of maturity. This was a common practice in that period, based on the assumption that the testator would eventually have a son but balanced by the reasonable concern that if that son were to die without reaching the age of maturity, then the deceased's estate would remain ownerless. Having had no son, however, *Marcus Coponius* died leaving no clear heir because the wording of his last will and testament did not automatically lead to the conclusion that *Curius* would become heir under these circumstances.

In the proceedings, *Quintus Mucius Scaevola* argued from an objective theory that *Curius* could not be his heir according to a strict reading of the text of the last will and testament. Another famous *orator* of the era, however, *Lucius Licinius Crassus* argued that the intent of *Marcus Coponius* was to appoint *Curius* as a subsidiary heir that he could not foresee that he would die without ever having a son and that his last will and testament must be interpreted according to *Marcus Coponius*' intent and not to its wording. The judge agreed that the last will and testament should be interpreted according to the testator's intent rather than a strict reading of its text, ruling that *Curius* was the rightful heir.

Two centuries later, Marcellus laid the foundations of the principle of *benignior interpretatio* in the second century, according to which testamentary dispositions must be interpreted in accordance with the testator's intent.[31]

In Roman law, no distinction was made neither between the interpretation of legislative texts and that of contracts nor between the interpretation of contracts and that of testamentary dispositions.[32] For this reason, it is possible to observe some of the most basic principles of interpretation, such as *falsa demonstratio non nocet*, emerging from texts that deal with testamentary dispositions.[33]

Authors of the classical period did not regard contracts as a mutual meeting of the minds through a declaration of intent because the concept of a legal transaction had not yet been developed. They considered contracts in their integrity and as a common expression of the individual parties to it.[34] The *stipulatio* procedure was quite relevant in practice during this period, as it had also been during previous periods, and therefore the agreement being interpreted was often a verbal transaction.[35] Authors of the classical period primarily discussed the interpretation of *stipulatio* procedures, and the principles of interpretation generally developed on this basis. However, in a departure

30. Gandolfi, *supra* n. 13, at 113; Zimmermann, *supra* n. 11, at 628-631.
31. Martin Avenarius, *Benignior Interpretatio: Origin and Transformation of a Rule of Construction in the Law of Succession*, 6 Roman Legal Tradition 1, 5 et seq. (2010).
32. Zimmermann, *supra* n. 11, at 632.
33. Gandolfi, *supra* n. 13, at 113; Zimmermann, *supra* n. 11, at 632.
34. Zimmermann, *supra* n. 11, at 626-627.
35. Williams, *supra* n. 12, at 225-226.

from the archaic period, *stipulatio* became more subjective, owing to the diversification of the forms of these procedures in the classical period, and the will of the parties gained greater importance.[36]

[2] Principles of Interpretation That Emerged in the Classical Period

[a] *The Emergence of Principles of Subjective Interpretation in the Classical Period*

Along with the rise of the importance of party will, and in the context of the interpretation of *locatio conductio* (hire, construction, or employment) contracts, Papinianus wrote of a determination of the real intent of the parties without limitation to an examination of the meaning of the words they used: "*In conventionibus contrahentium voluntatem potius quam verba spectari placuit.*"[37] This phrase by Papinianus is not only one of the most cited expressions in legal literature,[38] but also it represents the most basic rule of subjective interpretation in comparative[39] and uniform law.[40] In legislation where provisions on the interpretation of contracts are limited to one paragraph, such as in the Swiss and Turkish codes of obligations, legislators chose to mention this principle only.

The principle of *falsa demonstratio non nocet* (false description does not void a contract), according to which the intent of the parties prevails over the words they used in the event of a divergence between them, is linked by some authors and in some jurisdictions to the abovementioned expression by Papinianus.[41] Although there is a logical connection between Papinianus' text in *Dig.* 50, 16, 219 and the principle of *falsa demonstratio non nocet*, the latter is actually based on a text by Gaius on the interpretation of false descriptions in last wills and testaments in accordance with the real intent of the deceased.[42] Even though this principle has been primarily applied in

36. *Ibid.*, at 228.
37. *Dig.* 50, 16, 219 (Pap. 2 resp.), http://www.thelatinlibrary.com/justinian/digest50.shtml (accessed December 7, 2018). Ulpianus repeated the same phrase in *Dig.* 2, 1, 15. Pothier argued that this rule only applies when the meaning of an expression in a contract is ambiguous, and if the meaning of the contract is clear, it cannot be interpreted. Robert Joseph Pothier, *Traité des obligations*, n. 84 (Orléans 1761). However, the origins of the "*in claris non fit interpretatio*" rule are unknown, and this rule is generally not accepted as a legal principle. Nonetheless, the following text by Paulus (*Dig.* 32, 25, 1) is worth mentioning: "*Cum in verbis nulla ambiguitas est, non debet admitti voluntatis quaestio*", http://www.thelatinlibrary.com/justinian/digest32.shtml (accessed December 7, 2018).
38. Pothier, *supra* n. 37, at n. 91; Williams, *supra* n. 12, at 251; Gandolfi, *supra* n. 13, at 124; Zimmermann, *supra* n. 11, at 622; Ernst A. Kramer, Bruno Schmidlin, *Kommentar zu Article 1-18 OR, Berner Kommentar, Das Obligationenrecht*, Band VI, 1, n. 3 (Stämpfli, 1986).
39. Article 1188 of the CC. Fr.; Art. 1362 of the CC. It.; § 133 of the BGB; Article 18/1 of the OR; Art. 19/1 of the TBK and § 914 of the ABGB are based on this phrase.
40. *See*, sections §4.02[D][1] Article 8(1) of the CISG—Subjective Interpretation; §4.03[B][1] Article 4.1 of the UPICC, *infra*.
41. Canaris, Grigoleit, *supra* n. 5, at 454; *See*, sections §3.02[B][6][a] Article 1362 of the CC. It.; §3.03[A][3][b] § 133 of the BGB; §3.03[B] [4] Article 18/1 of the OR; §4.02[D][1] Article 8(1) of the CISG—Subjective Interpretation, *infra*.
42. Gaius, *Dig.* 35, 1, 17.

the interpretation of testamentary dispositions,[43] a text by Pomponius on an agreement to appoint a judge illustrated this principle as follows: "Where a mistake is made in the name or surname of a judge, it was the opinion of Servius that if the judge was appointed by an agreement of the litigants, he must act as judge whom both litigants had in view."[44]

Referencing Labeo[45] in a text dealing with *emptio-venditio* (sell-purchase) contracts, Giavoleno wrote that *quid actum* (the will of the parties) is to be given more weight than *quod dictum* (the wording of the agreement).[46] Likewise, Pomponius wrote that when interpreting an *emptio-venditio* contract, the will of the parties must be examined, without being limited to the wording of the agreement.[47]

Another important text reflecting the subjective approach during the classical period is to be found in *Dig.* 50, 17, 34 (Ulp. 45 ad Sab.), where Ulpianus listed three principles in hierarchical order for the interpretation of *stipulatio*. According to this text:

> In all stipulations and other contracts, we follow the intent of the parties; and if it is not apparent what their intent was, we observe the custom of the place where the transaction was concluded. But what rule should be adopted if the custom of the place did not settle anything, because it varied? In this instance, the smallest amount should be exacted.[48]

Ulpianus not only stated the three basic rules of interpretation in this text but also identified the real intent of the parties (*quod actum est*) and recognized its priority in the hierarchical order of the principles he mentions.

[b] The Emergence of Principles of Objective Interpretation in the Classical Period

These texts demonstrate that the balance between objective and subjective interpretation started to shift in favor of subjective interpretation during the classical period. Nevertheless, some of the most important principles of objective interpretation

43. Gandolfi, *supra* n. 13, at 112.
44. *Dig.* 5, 1, 80 (Pomp. 2 ad Sab.) "*si in iudicis nomine prenomine erratum est, Servius respondit, si ex conventione litigatorum is iudex addictus esset, eum esse iudicem, de quo litigatores sensissent,*" http://www.thelatinlibrary.com/justinian/digest5.shtml (accessed December 7, 2018), translation taken from https://droitromain.univ-grenoble-alpes.fr/Anglica/D50_Scott.htm (accessed December 7, 2018); Gandolfi, *supra* n. 13, at 112-113.
45. *Dig.* 18, 1, 77 (Iav. 4 ex post Labeon), http://www.thelatinlibrary.com/justinian/digest18.shtml (accessed December 7, 2018).
46. Gandolfi, *supra* n. 13, at 115.
47. *Dig.* 18, 1, 6, 1 (Pomp. 9 ad Sab.), http://www.thelatinlibrary.com/justinian/digest18.shtml (accessed December 7, 2018); Gandolfi, *supra* n. 13, at 116.
48. *Dig.* 50, 17, 34 (Ulp. 45 ad Sab.) "*Semper in stipulationibus [et in ceteris contractibus] id sequimur, quod actum est: aut, si non pareat quit actum est, erit consequens, ut id sequamur, quod in regione in qua actum est frequentatur. quid ergo, si neque regionis mos appareat, quia varius fuit? ad id, quod minimum est, redigenda summa est,*" http://www.thelatinlibrary.com/justinian/digest50.shtml (accessed December 7, 2018), translation taken from https://droitromain.univ-grenoble-alpes.fr/Anglica/D50_Scott.htm (accessed December 7, 2018); Gandolfi, *supra* n. 13, at 100.

emerged in the classical period too, such as the *contra stipulatorem* rule mentioned in the text by Ulpianus quoted above.

Contra stipulatorem, as the name suggests, is a principle regarding the interpretation of *stipulatio*. *Stipulatio* is an oral procedure, where the *stipulator* (creditor) speaks first and the *promissor* (debtor) replies to him. Therefore, from a very strict point of view, it is possible to say that according to the *contra stipulatorem* principle, in the event of an ambiguity in the meaning of the words used in the agreement, these were to be interpreted against the creditor.[49]

The reason for a strict application of this principle is to be found in the formalism of the *stipulatio*: the *stipulatio* procedure was not a negotiation, the *promissor* could either accept or reject the *stipulator*'s words but without having the opportunity to bargain.[50] On the basis of the divergence of the meaning of this principle from Roman law to the present, Gandolfi rightly states that the meaning of the expression of *contra stipulatorem* in Roman law should be considered to be *favor debitoris*[51] and not the meaning attributed to it today.

This principle finds expression again in two other texts: first in Celsus Dig. 34, 5, 26[52] and second in Ulpianus Dig. 45, 1, 38, 18 (Ulp. 49 ad Sab.),[53] where Ulpianus confirms Celsus' text. Nonetheless, the rationale that underlies this principle is the idea that creditors should bear the consequences of not having better expressed their will. This idea finds its expression in *Dig.* 45, 1, 99 where Celsus writes "*fere secundum promissorem interpretamur.*" These words have been referred to by Pothier, together with *Dig.* 34, 5, 26 and *Dig.* 45, 1, 38, 18, and they constituted the foundation of former Article 1162 of the French Civil Code.[54]

Goudsmit, another Romanist who contributed the extension of this principle into today's legal systems, again refers to *Dig.* 45, 1, 38, 18, writing that in synallagmatic agreements, the party who takes the principal part in the agreement should take the responsibility of the consequences of any inaccurate or defective expression in it. Likewise according to Goudsmit, the interpretation most favorable to the debtor is to be preferred in unilateral transactions.[55]

The specific aspects of the general principle of *contra stipulatorem* emerged as early as the birth of consensual contracts. The rules of interpretation of *emptio-venditio* agreements against the *venditor* (seller) (*contra venditorem*)[56] and interpretation of

49. Williams, *supra* n. 12, at 251; Gandolfi, *supra* n. 13, at 82.
50. Gandolfi, *supra* n. 13, at 84.
51. *Ibid.*, at 83.
52. *Dig.* 34, 5, 26 "*Cum quaeritur in stipulatione quid acti sit, ambiguitas contra stipulatorem est*", http://www.thelatinlibrary.com/justinian/digest34.shtml (accessed December 7, 2018); Gandolfi, *supra* n. 13, at 82; Zimmermann, *supra* n. 11, at 639; Canaris, Grigoleit, *supra* n. 5, at 461.
53. *Dig*, 45, 1, 38, 18 "*In stipulationibus cum quaeritur, quid actum sit, verba contra stipulatorem interpretenda sunt,*" http://www.thelatinlibrary.com/justinian/digest45.shtml (accessed December 7, 2018); Gandolfi, *supra* n. 13, at 100; Zimmermann, *supra* n. 11, at 639.
54. Pothier, *supra* n. 37, at n. 90.
55. Goudsmit, *supra* n. 2, at 177.
56. Pomponius *Dig.* 18, 1, 33 (34) (Pomp. 33 ad Sab.), http://www.thelatinlibrary.com/justinian/digest18.shtml (accessed December 7, 2018); Papinianus *Dig.* 2, 14, 39 (Pap. 5 quaest.), http://www.thelatinlibrary.com/justinian/digest2.shtml (accessed December 7, 2018); Paulus *Dig.* 18, 1, 21 (Paul. 5 ad Sab.), http://www.thelatinlibrary.com/justinian/digest18.shtml

locatio conductio agreements against *locator* (landlord or employer) (*contra locatorem*)[57] were developed in the classical period. In these contracts, the parties who were in the position of *venditor* and *locator* were considered to be the *stipulator*.[58]

Although the principle of *contra stipulatorem* and its specific aspects (*contra venditorem* and *contra locatorem*) were understood as early as the classical period, the principle of *contra proferentem*, which has a broader meaning and is commonly used today,[59] emerged much later, during the Middle Ages and through the works of the *Commentators*.[60]

In his *Commentaria*, dating from the fourteenth century, Bartolus commented on the *contra venditorem* rule described by Pomponius in *Dig.* 18, 1, 34 and the *contra locatorem* rule described by Papinianus in *Dig.* 2, 14, 39 and from them extracted the *contra proferentem* rule.[61]

Bartolus' contribution to the development of this principle did not end there. In his *Commentaria*, Bartolus also commented on Ulpianus' text in *Dig.* 45, 1, 38, 18 where he states that "*in dubio fit interpretatio contra creditorem*" (when in doubt, interpretation against the creditor is to be preferred).[62] However, it is not possible to regard this expression as a general rule because it cannot be simply presumed that the debtor is always necessarily the weaker party, whose bargaining power is limited.[63]

Nonetheless, considering that Bartolus' pupil Baldus laid the foundations for the distinction between commercial and ordinary transactions,[64] it is also a possibility that Bartolus used this expression with the aim of protecting weaker parties. If interpreted in this way, it can be stated that this principle should apply in modern legal systems to contracts where one of the parties is weaker than the other, such as in standard term contracts or consumer contracts. It is true that this principle enables judges in modern

(accessed December 7, 2018) and *Dig.* 50, 17, 172 (Paul. 5 ad Plaut): "*in contrahenda venditione ambiguum pactum contra venditorem interpretandum est,*" http://www.thelatinlibrary.com/justinian/digest50.shtml (accessed December 7, 2018); Gandolfi, *supra* n. 13, at 118 et seq.; Williams, *supra* n. 12, at 251; Zimmermann, *supra* n. 11, at 639.

57. Papinianus, *Dig.* 2, 14, 39, http://www.thelatinlibrary.com/justinian/digest2.shtml (accessed December 7, 2018); Gandolfi, *supra* n. 13, at 122; Zimmermann, *supra* n. 11, at 639.
58. Zimmermann, *supra* n. 11, at 639.
59. *See* sections §4.03[B][6] Article 4.6 of the UPICC; §4.05[B][4] Trans-Lex Principle No. IV.5.4, *infra*.
60. Javier M. Rodriguez Olmos, *Contexto y construcción de la regla "interpretatio contra proferentem" en la tradición romanista*, Revista de Derecho Privado, N. 14, 78 et seq. (2008).
61. Bartolus described the *contra proferentem* rule in his *Commentaria* as follows: "*interpretatio fit contra proferentem seu contra eum, pro quo profertur,*" Zimmermann, *supra* n. 11, at 640; Olmos, *supra* n. 60, at 80 (referring to Bartolus, *Commentaria*, *Dig.* 2, 14, 39 and *Dig.* 18, 1, 34).
62. Zimmermann, *supra* n. 11, at 641 (referring to Bartolus, *Commentaria*, *Dig.* 45, 1, 38, 18); Pothier's comment on *Dig*, 45, 1, 38, 18 constituted the basis of Art. 1190 (former Art. 1162) of the CC. Fr.; Pothier, *supra* n. 37, at n. 90. This phrase reads as follows "*In stipulationibus cum quoeritur, quid actum sit, verba contra stipulatorem interpretanda sunt,*" http://www.thelatinlibrary.com/justinian/digest45.shtml (accessed December 7, 2018), "When the intention of a stipulation is examined, the language should be interpreted against the stipulator," translation taken from https://droitromain.univ-grenoble-alpes.fr/Anglica/D45_Scott.htm (accessed December 7, 2018).
63. Zimmermann, *supra* n. 11, at 641.
64. Baldus de Ubaldis, *Commentaria*, Cod. 4.44.2, No. 21; Ahmet Cemil Yıldırım, *Equilibrium in International Commercial Contracts with Particular Regard to UNIDROIT Principles of International Commercial Contracts*, 3 (Wolf Legal Publishers, 2011).

legal systems to reach a reasonable solution to protect the weaker party without expressly opposing the principle of freedom of contract.[65]

For this reason, there is an opinion in some continental legal systems according to which the principles of *contra stipulatorem* and/or *contra proferentem* are only applicable to standard terms.[66] However, it is more appropriate to base this opinion on the *contra creditorem* rule, a special aspect of the principle of *contra stipulatorem* developed by Bartolus, and not on the general principle of *contra stipulatorem* itself.

It is also possible to find the Roman grounds of some other objective rules of interpretation in the writings of authors from the classical period: The rule of interpretation according to good faith and fair dealing and customary law is based on a text by Papinianus in *Dig.* 50, 16, 219,[67] and the rule for the interpretation of ambiguous expressions according to the nature of the contract has its grounds in a text by Iulianus in *Dig.* 50, 17, 67.[68]

The principle of *ut res magis valeat quam pereat*, according to which an interpretation that would render the contract valid should be preferred,[69] is again expressed in a text by Iulianus on the *formula* procedure as follows: "Whenever there is any ambiguous clause in the phraseology of an action [*formula*] or an exception [*exceptio*], it is most convenient to understand it in such a way that the property to which it relates shall rather be preserved than be lost."[70]

A more specific aspect of this principle pertaining to the interpretation of contracts is stated in a text by Ulpianus,[71] and this text is mentioned as the grounds for

65. Zimmermann, *supra* n. 11, at 641.
66. *See* sections §3.02[B][6][h] Article 1370 of the CC. It.; §3.03[A][3][c] § 157 of the BGB; §3.03[B][5] Principles of Interpretation Developed Through Case Law; §3.03[C][2][e] Article 23 of the TBK and the *Contra Stipulatorem* Rule, *infra*.
67. Zimmermann, *supra* n. 11, at 622.
68. *Dig.* 50, 17, 67 (Iul, 87 *Dig.*) "*Quotiens idem sermo duas sententias exprimit, ea potissimum excipiatur, quae rei gerendae aptior est,*" http://www.thelatinlibrary.com/justinian/digest50.shtml (accessed December 7, 2018) "Whenever a sentence has two meanings, that should be accepted which is the better adapted to the case," translation taken from https://droitromain.univ-grenoble-alpes.fr/Anglica/D50_Scott.htm (accessed December 7, 2018); Goudsmit, *supra* n. 2, at 176; Gandolfi, *supra* n. 13, at 87; Zimmermann, *supra* n. 11, at 637-638; Pothier, *supra* n. 37, at n. 86.
69. Williams, *supra* n. 12, at 239; Stefan Vogenauer, *Chapter 4—Interpretation*, in Stefan Vogenauer, Jan Kleinheisterkamp (eds.), *Commentary on the UNIDROIT Principles of International Commercial Contracts (PICC)*, Art. 4.5, n. 1 (2nd ed., Oxford University Press, 2015); Arthur L. Corbin, *A Comprehensive Treatise on the Rules of Contract Law (Corbin on Contracts)*, Vol 3, 4 (West, 1960).
70. *Dig.* 34, 5, 12 (13) (Iul. 50 *Dig.*) "*Quotiens in actionibus aut in exceptionibus ambigua oratio est, commodissimum est id accipi, quo res de qua agitur magis valeat quam pereat,*" http://www.thelatinlibrary.com/justinian/digest34.shtml (accessed December 7, 2018), translation taken from https://droitromain.univ-grenoble-alpes.fr/Anglica/D34_Scott.htm#V (accessed December 7, 2018); Gandolfi, *supra* n. 13, at 112.
71. *Dig.* 45, 1, 80 "*Quoties in stipulationibus ambigua oratio est, commodissimum est id accipi quo res de qua agitur in tuto sit,*" http://www.thelatinlibrary.com/justinian/digest45.shtml (accessed December 7, 2018); Philippe Antoine Merlin de Douai, *Répertoire universel et Raisonné de jurisprudence*, Vol. 3, 158 (3rd ed., Garnery, 1807); Nicola Armellini, *Dizionario di Giurisprudenza per uso del Regno delle due Sicilie*, Vol. 2, 284 (1822); Francesco Sangermano, *L'interpretazione del contratto: profili dottrinali e giurisprudenziali*, 267 (Giuffrè Editore, 2007).

the principle of the interpretation of ambiguous contractual clauses according to the meaning that would render it valid.[72]

Another principle mentioned by Ulpianus once more in *Dig.* 50, 17, 34[73] is that questions that are not expressly settled in the contract should be construed according to local custom. According to another principle cited by Ulpianus in *Dig.* 21, 1, 31, 20,[74] customary rules are so important that they are considered to be a part of the agreement of the parties even if they were not included in the contract.

Celsus formulated in *Dig.* 1, 3, 24 the principle that the whole law or contract should be taken into consideration for the interpretation of single clauses, or the principle of "systematic interpretation" as it is known in comparative law, as follows: "It is not proper without taking into consideration an entire law, either to decide or give an opinion upon any particular portion of the same."[75]

In addition to the principle of systematic interpretation, another principle that emerged in the classical period holds that the terms of the agreement of the parties cannot be interpreted expansively to cover matters upon which the parties did not mean their contract to cover, no matter how broadly these terms are drafted. Ulpianus stated this principle in *Dig.* 2, 15, 9, 3.[76]

72. Zimmermann, *supra* n. 11, at 637; Karl Salomo Zachariä von Lingenthal, *Versuch einer allgemeinen Hermeneutik des Rechts Erbstein*, 122 (1805); Former Art. 1157 of the CC. Fr. is based on this text, *see* Pothier, *supra* n. 37, at n. 85.

73. *Dig.* 50, 17, 34 "*Semper in Stipulationibus et in cæteris contractibus id sequimur quod actum est, aut si non appareat quid actum est, erit consequens, ut id sequamur, quod in regione, in qua actum est, frequentatur,*" http://www.thelatinlibrary.com/justinian/digest50.shtml (accessed December 7, 2018); Pothier, *supra* n. 37, at n. 87; Sangermano, *supra* n. 71, at 267; Zimmermann, *supra* n. 11, at 638; Joseph Story, *Commentaries on the Law of Bills of Exchange, Foreign and Inland (1847)*, 161-162 (The Lawbook Exchange, 2005); Goudsmit points out that this rule may not apply if it has been established that the party making the declaration regularly deviates from local custom. Goudsmit, *supra* n. 2, at 176.

74. *Dig.* 21, 1, 31, 20 "*ea enim, quæ sunt moris et consuetudinis, in bonaefidei iudiciis debent venire,*" http://www.thelatinlibrary.com/justinian/digest21.shtml (accessed December 7, 2018), "As the stipulation for double damages is perpetual, it is therefore held that an action on sale can be brought, even if the vendor has not given security for double the value of the slave; for matters of usage and custom should always be included in *bona fide* actions," translation taken from https://droitromain.univ-grenoble-alpes.fr/Anglica/D21_Scott.htm (accessed December 7, 2018); Pothier, *supra* n. 37, at n. 88; Zimmermann, *supra* n. 11, at 638; Joseph Story, *Commentaries on the Law of Bailments, with Illustrations from the Civil and the Foreign Law*, 256 (Hilliard and Brown, 1832).

75. *Dig.* 1, 3, 24, "*Incivile est, nisi tota lege perspecta, una aliqua particula eius proposita, iudicare vel respondere,*" http://www.thelatinlibrary.com/justinian/digest1.shtml (accessed December 7, 2018), translation taken from https://droitromain.univ-grenoble-alpes.fr/Anglica/D1_Scott.htm#III (accessed December 7, 2018); Zimmermann, *supra* n. 11, at 637.

76. *Dig.* 2, 15, 9, 3 "*Iniquum est perimi pacto, id de quo cogitatum non est/docetur,*" http://www.thelatinlibrary.com/justinian/digest2.shtml (accessed December 7, 2018); Pothier, *supra* n. 37, at n. 91; Zimmermann, *supra* n. 11, at 638; Francesco Astone, *Art. 1364, Dell'interpretazione del Contratto*, in Emanuela Navarretta, Andrea Orestano (eds.), *Commentario al Codice Civile*, Vol. 2, *Contratti in Generale*, at 467 et seq. (UTET Giuridica, 2011).

[C] Postclassical Period

One of the two developments that characterized the general approach to interpretation in the postclassical period was the attempt of the emperors to establish their monopoly on legal interpretation. In this period, emperors became the only lawmakers and the only sources of legitimacy as the power of the senate and the assemblies was reduced. Concurrent with an increase in their political strength, the emperors of this period published orders and *constitutiones* aimed at establishing a monopoly over the interpretation of legal texts.[77]

This situation had adverse effects on the development of legal science generally, and the development of the principles of legal interpretation was no exception. According to von Savigny, legal science deteriorated from the third century A.D., existed mainly in the books of the authors of the classical period, was substituted by the will of the emperor as the only source of law, and consequently, judicial discretion for interpretation almost disappeared.[78] Cod. 1, 14, 1 by Constantine, which was discovered in the nineteenth century, can be considered the starting point of the limitations set by the emperors in the field of interpretation. According to this code, "It is part of Our duty, and is lawful for Us alone to interpret questions involving equity and law."[79]

The concern for legal security underlying the studies to collect the laws and orders of the emperors into *Codex* during the postclassical period appears to contradict the concerns of interpretation during the classical period, which were a driving force behind the development of the legal science. In the postclassical period, the real concern of the emperors was to ensure their monopoly over lawmaking and legal interpretation by means of the collection and codification of laws. Williams argued that the *corpus iuris civilis* also emerged as a consequence of this concern.[80]

According to an order by Justinian dating from A.D. 529 and cited by von Savigny, "[t]he Emperor alone can make laws so he alone can interpret them ... Hence-forth let therefore all doubts vanish, and it is the Emperor who is to be acknowledged not merely as sole law-giver, but also as sole interpreter."[81]

Once more from a Code by Justinian enacted in 533 A.D., it is reiterated that the emperor is the sole lawmaker and the sole interpreter, and judges were also ordered to consult the emperor in the event that they had doubts regarding the meaning of legislative texts.[82] In other words, judges were prohibited from interpreting the law and according to von Savigny, this prohibition negatively affected the development of the legal science in the following periods.[83]

77. Williams, *supra* n. 12, at 232-235.
78. von Savigny, *supra* n. 12, at 242-243.
79. Cod. 1, 14, 1 "*Inter aequitatem iusque interpositam interpretationem nobis solis et oportet et licet inspicere,*" http://www.thelatinlibrary.com/justinian/codex1.shtml (accessed December 7, 2018), translation taken from https://droitromain.univ-grenoble-alpes.fr/Anglica/CJ1_Scott.htm#14 (accessed December 7, 2018); von Savigny, *supra* n. 12, at 243; Williams, *supra* n. 12, at 240.
80. Williams, *supra* n. 12, at 234.
81. von Savigny refers to L. 12. S. 1. o. de leg. (1. 14.); von Savigny, *supra* n. 12, at 244-245.
82. von Savigny refers to L. 2. S. 21; von Savigny, *supra* n. 12, at 246.
83. von Savigny, *supra* n. 12, at 247.

With regard to the abovementioned order and Code by Justinian, it should be acknowledged that Williams' theory regarding the efforts of Justinian to collect the sources of law sounds very reasonable. What Justinian intended to do with the *corpus iuris civilis* was not to contribute to the development of the legal science in the future but to limit its future with its past. It is also true that his work had some adverse effects, as von Savigny suggested, on the development of legal science after this period.

That being the case, it is beyond any doubt that the most significant development regarding legal interpretation in the postclassical period was the collection of the sources of law in *corpus iuris civilis* under the auspices of Justinian, because future generations became aware of the abovementioned sources from the classical period thanks to it. Through his work, Justinian preserved the sources of the classical to the present day and made it possible for the principles that emerged from the classical period to be reflected in today's legal systems, as is the case with most other subjects of private law. In other words, *corpus iuris civilis* exceeded its purpose in the long term and constituted not the limits of but the grounds for the development of the legal science, perhaps in a manner completely unforeseen by Justinian.

Another important development in the field of legal interpretation from the postclassical period was that the balance between objective and subjective approaches to interpretation was further distorted in favor of the subjective approach. The emergence of the notion of *animus* in this period, which means the express or implied common intent of the parties regarding the purpose of their contract, represents the rise of the subjective approach to the interpretation of contracts. This notion emerged through *interpolatio* (interpretation and adaptation to contemporary needs) of the texts of the classical period.

The idea of the superiority of *animus* was even further developed in Byzantine law, becoming the essential element of the interpretation of contracts in the postclassical period.[84] *Animus*, meaning "spirit," constitutes the basis for legislative texts today, according to the presumption that legal texts have a "spirit," as is stated in the first articles of the Swiss and Turkish Civil Codes (*Türk Medeni Kanunu*, TMK).

The concept that party intent is not limited to what the parties have declared expressly but can also be understood by what has been implied is reflected in the codes and decisions of emperors where they contemplated contracts. In a Code by Emperors Valerianus and Gallienus from the third century A.D., a rule of interpretation specific to contracts is cited as follows: "In contracts, the truth of the matter should rather be considered than what is stated in writing."[85]

The theory of interpreting contracts according to the implied intent of the parties gave birth to the theory of "complementary interpretation." A *constitutio* by Justinian states in Cod. 8, 37, 15 holds that in a contract for building a house, there is an implied term according to which if the *stipulator* (employer) dies before the completion of the

84. Zimmermann, *supra* n. 11, at 624-625.

85. Cod. 4, 22, 1 "*In contractibus rei veritas potius quam scriptura prospici debet,*" http://www.thelatinlibrary.com/justinian/codex4.shtml (accessed December 7, 2018); translation taken from https://droitromain.univ-grenoble-alpes.fr/Anglica/CJ4_Scott.htm#22 (accessed December 7, 2018); Williams, *supra* n. 12, at 251.

work, his heirs would substitute him and be bound by the contract.[86] However, it is apparent that this situation would have voided the contract during previous periods.[87]

In another *constitutio* by Justinian in Cod. 5, 13, 1, 1, it is again stated that the existence of a tacit hypothecation is assumed on the deceased husband's estate in favor of his wife, for her living expenses (*dos*).[88] This *constitutio*, therefore, established the Roman grounds for the "reserved portion," which is found in the law of successions in continental legal systems.

§2.02 HUMANIST AND NATURALIST SCHOOLS OF LAW AND THE DIVERGENCE OF APPROACHES AMONG CONTINENTAL LEGAL SYSTEMS

The principles of interpretation that emerged in the Roman law were passed down through a historical process which started with the work of Iohannes Bassianus, a *Glossator* of the twelfth century. Bassianus proposed a hierarchy among the rules of interpretation,[89] and his work constituted a basis for the work of canon lawyers and humanists.[90] Bassianus' work served as a guide for two important representatives of the Humanist School, Hugo Donellus in the sixteenth century and Jean Domat in the seventeenth century.[91] A divergence emerged between the approaches of the Humanist and Naturalist Schools during the seventeenth century in the field of interpretation, and this divergence caused further divergence among the approaches of the modern continental legal systems.

In the seventeenth century, Hugo Donellus wrote that interpretation is what the interpreter makes and not what the lawmaker does, by objecting to the monopolist approach of the postclassical period.[92] Although Donellus dedicated a chapter in his Commentary to the rules of legal interpretation, he did not make a systematic study of these principles. Instead, he limited his work to stating the principles that he found in Roman sources.[93] Among these principles, the majority were ones on literal interpretation, such as the principle that the meaning obtained through interpretation must not be absurd and that the words must be interpreted in their context. Nonetheless,

86. *See* http://www.thelatinlibrary.com/justinian/codex8.shtml (accessed December 7, 2018); *See* https://droitromain.univ-grenoble-alpes.fr/Anglica/CJ8_Scott.gr.htm#37 (accessed December 7, 2018).
87. Williams, *supra* n. 12, at 252.
88. *See* http://www.thelatinlibrary.com/justinian/codex5.shtml (accessed December 7, 2018); Williams, *supra* n. 12, at 252.
89. Zimmermann, *supra* n. 11, at 638.
90. Williams, *supra* n. 12, at 236-237.
91. Hugo Donellus, *Commentarii de iure civili* (1642); Jean Domat, *Les lois civiles dans leur ordre naturel*, Vol. 1 (Jean Baptiste Coignard, 1689), for an English translation of this work, *see*, Jean Domat, *The Civil Law in Its Natural Order*, Vol. 1 (Charles C. Little and James Brown, 1850); Zimmermann, *supra* n. 11, at 638.
92. Jan Schröder, *Recht als Wissenschaft*, 57 (C.H. Beck, 2001); Donellus, *supra* n. 91, Caput 15. at 12.
93. Donellus, *supra* n. 91, Caput 15. at 12-13.

Donellus also acknowledged the principle that contracts should be interpreted in light of the circumstances specific to each case.[94]

Donellus' most valuable contribution to legal interpretation has probably been the establishment of a link between legal interpretation and the principle of good faith and fair dealing rather than on purpose, by relying on Gaius' text in *Dig.* 50, 17, 56[95] and Marcellus' text in *Dig.* 50, 17, 192, 1.[96] The limit to literal interpretation is thus the appropriateness of the meaning of the words; if the meaning obtained through interpretation is not appropriate, then no literal interpretation should be conducted, but interpretation should rather be made on the basis of good faith and fair dealing.[97] This valuable contribution by Donellus finds its expressions in Article 1366 of the Italian Civil Code (*Codice Civile Italiano*, CC. It.) and § 157 of the German Civil Code (*Bürgerliches Gesetzbuch*, BGB), where good faith and fair dealing is expressed as a rule of interpretation. However, in the two texts referred to by Donellus, the term used by Gaius and Marcellus was not bona fides, which constitutes the basis of the principle of good faith and fair dealing in today's continental legal systems, but *benignitas*, which means benevolence.

Furthermore, Jean Domat systematized the principles of interpretation of contracts and listed fifteen of them.[98] Domat's work influenced the French Civil Code through the works of Robert Joseph Pothier and therefore continues to be relevant today. In his work, Domat brought the expression "common intent of the contracting parties" to the literature.

According to Domat's first principle, "ambiguities and doubts should be interpreted according to the common intent of the contracting parties."[99] The author complements this principle in his fourth principle with reference to the abovementioned text by Papinianus in *Dig.* 50, 16, 219,[100] according to which "intent should be preferred to expression."[101] These two principles constitute the core of the most basic principles of contract interpretation in legal systems where the subjective approach has been adopted.

In the event of a failure to determine the common intent of the parties, the principle to interpret agreements according to local custom ranked second in Domat's

94. *Ibid.*; Schröder, *supra* n. 92, at 58.
95. *Dig.* 50, 17, 56 "*Semper in dubiis benigniora praeferenda sunt,*" http://www.thelatinlibrary.com/justinian/digest50.shtml (accessed December 7, 2018), "In questions which are doubtful, the more benevolent opinion should always obtain the preference," translation taken from https://droitromain.univ-grenoble-alpes.fr/Anglica/D50_Scott.htm#XVII (accessed December 7, 2018).
96. *Dig.* 50, 17, 192, 1 "*In re dubia benigniorem interpretationem sequi non minus iustius est quam tutius,*" http://www.thelatinlibrary.com/justinian/digest50.shtml (accessed December 7, 2018), "In questions which are doubtful, the more benevolent opinion should always obtain the preference," translation taken from https://droitromain.univ-grenoble-alpes.fr/Anglica/D50_Scott.htm#XVII (accessed December 7, 2018).
97. Donellus, *supra* n. 91, Caput 15. at 12-13.
98. Domat, *supra* n. 91, at §§ 167-181.
99. *Ibid.*, at § 167.
100. *See*, section §2.01[B][2][a], The Emergence of Principles of Subjective Interpretation in the Classical Period, *supra*.
101. Domat, *supra* n. 91, at § 170. This principle was adopted in Art. 1188 (former Art. 1156) of the CC. Fr.

list of fifteen principles.[102] According to his list, the principle of systematic interpretation ranks third, which dictates the interpretation of every single clause in the light of the whole contract.[103] The sixth and the seventh principles are the interpretation in favor of the debtor and interpretation against the creditor, respectively. By mentioning these principles in consecutive order, Domat laid the foundations of former Article 1162 of the CC. Fr., where these principles are stated together. While citing the principle of interpretation in favor of the debtor, Domat referred to the abovementioned[104] text by Celsus in *Dig.* 45, 1, 99. Another principle mentioned by Domat which found its expression in the CC. Fr. is the interpretation of contracts within the frame of the subjects dealt with by the parties in their contract and the prohibition on expanding the agreement of the parties through interpretation to subjects that they did not cover in their deal.[105]

As is apparent in the work of Donellus and in particular in the work of Domat, party intent is relevant in the approach of the Humanist School to the interpretation of contracts, and therefore the dominance of the subjective interpretation is strongly felt. For this reason, it can be observed that in the CC. Fr. and the other civil law codifications in the Latin legal family that are based on it, the Humanist School's subjective approach dominated in large part due to the influence of the work of Domat's follower, Pothier.

Also in the seventeenth century, however, the leading representative of the Naturalist School, Hugo Grotius from the Netherlands, made important studies in the field of legal interpretation and differentiated the approach of the Romano-Germanic legal systems in this field from that of the Latin legal systems.

Grotius' contribution to the rules of interpretation is not to be found in his work on civil law,[106] but rather in his work entitled *De lure Belli ac Pacis*,[107] which is considered to be the starting point of modern public international law, and therefore in the context of the interpretation of international treaties. In his work, Grotius listed the principles of interpretation under thirty-two titles, where he primarily explored the matters of public international law in a casuistic manner.

Although some part of the principles mentioned by Grotius was previously cited in *Digesta*, Grotius stated in his thirty-first principle that "the contracts of kings are not to be interpreted according to Roman law." Therefore, Grotius' influence on Romano-Germanic legal systems has been felt through the incorporation of his general approach, rather than the adoption of single principles.

102. Domat, *supra* n. 91, at § 168. This principle was adopted in former Art. 1159 of the CC. Fr.
103. Domat, *supra* n. 91, at § 169. This principle was adopted in Art. 1189 (former Art. 1161) of the CC. Fr.
104. *See* section §2.01[B][2][b], The Emergence of Principles of Objective Interpretation in the Classical Period, *supra*.
105. Domat, *supra* n. 91, at § 180. This principle was adopted in former Art. 1163 of the CC. Fr.
106. Hugo Grotius, *Commentaries on the Roman-Dutch Law*, translated by Simon van Leeuven (Joseph Butterworth and son, 1820).
107. Hugo Grotius, *De Jure Belli ac Pacis Libris Tres*, Vol. 2, Ch. XVI (1625); for an English translation of this work, *see* http://www.lonang.com/exlibris/grotius/gro-216.htm (accessed December 7, 2018).

Grotius was suspicious of the dominance of the subjective approach, which prevailed following the classical period of Roman law and has been reflected in modern legal systems through the works of the Humanist School. As expressed by Zimmermann, Grotius maintained that not only *voluntas* but also *signum voluntatis* (indications of intent) is relevant in interpretation and his ideas influenced German law in particular.[108]

Even though Grotius acknowledged the importance of the intent of the parties, he held that this intent could only be determined by the words used for expressing it, or other indications of this intent. Accordingly, among the thirty-two principles of interpretation listed by Grotius, the first one is that "The measure of correct interpretation is the inference of intent from the most probable indications ... These indications are of two kinds, words and implications; and these are considered either separately or together."

The concern for justice that underlies this approach by Grotius becomes even more evident in the illustration that Grotius provided for the principle that he ranked second. According to Grotius' second principle of interpretation, "[i]f there is no implication which suggests a different conclusion, words are to be understood in their natural sense, not according to the grammatical sense which comes from derivation according to current usage, to whose behest belong the law and rule of speech."[109] Grotius illustrates this principle by referring to Polybius, as follows:

> Locrians [a Greek tribe] ... took oath that they would keep the agreement as long as they should stand on that ground and should bear heads on their shoulders; then they threw away the earth which they had placed in their shoes, and the heads of garlic which they had laid on their shoulders, as if in that manner they could free themselves from the religious obligation.[110]

Contractual justice is so important for Grotius that some of his principles even exceed the limits of interpretation. For instance, pursuant to the principle that Grotius ranks twenty-seventh, "[a] second implication will become manifest if, while the literal interpretation may not in itself involve something unlawful, the obligation, in the view of one who judges the matter fairly, shall appear to be burdensome and unbearable, whether the condition of human nature is considered in the abstract, or the person and matter under consideration are brought into comparison with the result of the act itself."[111] According to the illustration that Grotius provides for this principle, "a man who has lent a thing for some days will be able to demand its return within those days, if he himself is greatly in need of it; for the nature of a generous act is such that it is not to be believed that any one has wished to obligate himself to his own great disadvantage."[112]

108. Zimmermann, *supra* n. 11, at 637.
109. Grotius, *supra* n. 107, at n. II, translation taken from http://www.lonang.com/exlibris/grotius/gro-216.htm (accessed December 7, 2018).
110. *Ibid.*
111. Grotius, *supra* n. 107, at n. XXVII, translation taken from http://www.lonang.com/exlibris/grotius/gro-216.htm (accessed December 7, 2018).
112. *Ibid.*

In accordance with the importance that Grotius adhered to the wording of the agreement, he listed many principles of literal interpretation, which are recognized today by Romano-Germanic legal systems. In the author's third principle, it is stated that "[t]echnical terms are to be explained according to their technical use."[113]

Pursuant to the author's fourth principle, "[r]esort is to be had to conjectures in the case of ambiguous and contradictory expressions, or if conjectures naturally suggest themselves ... But at times the conjectures themselves are so evident that they naturally suggest themselves, even against the more commonly accepted interpretation of the words."[114] In the seventh principle, which seems to be linked with the latter, Grotius states that conjectures should be drawn "from elements that are connected either in origin, or also in place."[115] As an illustration, Grotius mentions the agreement between Paris and Menelaus in Homer's Iliad, according to which Helen should belong to the victor and where "the victor" should be understood as the one who killed the other.[116]

Grotius emphasizes the importance of the motive (reason or *causa*) of the agreement in the principle he ranked the eighth by stating that motive is one of the elements of the conjecture, albeit the strongest one.[117] According to the author, for instance, "a present made by reason of a wedding will not be valid if the wedding does not take place."[118]

Because of the importance that Grotius adheres to the wording of the agreement, he also considers the possibility that the latter would be meaningless: Pursuant to the principle that he ranks the twenty-second:

> A restrictive interpretation, outside of the natural meaning of the words containing the promise, is derived either from an original defect in the intent, or from the incompatibility with the intent of a case occurring. A defect inherent in the intent is recognized from the absurdity which evidently would otherwise result, or from the cessation of the reason which alone furnished the full and effective motive for the intent, or from a defect in the subject-matter. The first case has its foundation in this principle, that no one ought to be believed to wish absurdities.[119]

As we arrive at the eighteenth century, Robert Joseph Pothier came on the scene and shaped the codification of French Civil Law to a great extent through his work. Pothier was influenced by Jean Domat and by the Humanist School. He examined and systematically listed the principles relating to the interpretation of contracts in his two important works. First, in his work titled *Pandectæ Justinianæ in novum ordinem*

113. Grotius, *supra* n. 107, at n. III, translation taken from http://www.lonang.com/exlibris/grotius/gro-216.htm (accessed December 7, 2018).
114. Grotius, *supra* n. 107, at n. IV, translation taken from http://www.lonang.com/exlibris/grotius/gro-216.htm (accessed December 7, 2018).
115. Grotius, *supra* n. 107, at n. VII. translation taken from http://www.lonang.com/exlibris/grotius/gro-216.htm (accessed December 7, 2018).
116. *Ibid.*
117. Grotius, *supra* n. 107, at n. VIII.
118. *Ibid.*
119. Grotius, *supra* n. 107, at n. XXII, translation taken from http://www.lonang.com/exlibris/grotius/gro-216.htm (accessed December 7, 2018).

digestæ (*Pandectæ Justinianæ*), which he wrote between the years 1748 and 1752,[120] Pothier examined the interpretation of contracts. Then in 1761, in his work entitled *Traité des obligations*,[121] he further developed and systematized his study. His latter work in particular has been a source of inspiration for the provisions of the CC. Fr. pertaining to the interpretation of contracts. The eleven principles listed by the author in his latter work (*Traité des obligations*) are so comprehensive that Williams stated that to extract the rules of contract interpretation from the *corpus iuris civilis* and to lay them down once more "would be simply to repeat what has already been so excellently done by Pothier."[122]

Nevertheless, there are some significant differences between the principles of interpretation in Pothier's two treatises, which were written on a ten-year interval. In *Pandectæ Justinianæ*, various principles are provided in five paragraphs and in an unsystematic order. Here, the principle ranked first by Pothier is that "in case of an ambiguity in the meaning of the words in a contract, the interpretation that will keep the contract valid should be preferred."[123] Just after this principle, the author stated the principle according to which, "besides the words used in the contracts, the intent of the parties should be taken into consideration."[124] In *Traité des obligations*, it can be observed that the order of priority of these principles is reversed, the relevance of the common intent of the parties is emphasized, and this principle was ultimately reflected in Article 1188(1) (former Article 1156) of the CC. Fr. in its latter form.[125]

Moreover, in *Traité des obligations*, Pothier inserted two principles that he had not mentioned in his previous work and placed them in the third and sixth places. These are the principles that "when the terms in a contract are doubtful to have two meanings, they should be understood in the sense which conforms better to the nature of the contract"[126] and "what seems ambiguous in a contract should be interpreted according to the custom of the land."[127]

Nevertheless, although in *Pandectæ* Justinianæ, Pothier had cited the principle of interpretation according to *benignitas*,[128] which was revealed by Hugo Donellus with reference to *Dig.* 50, 17, 56 and *Dig.* 50, 17, 192, 1, he did not include this principle in his latter work, and he probably prevented this principle from appearing in the CC. Fr. as a specific aspect of the general principle of good faith and fair dealing.

120. Robert Joseph Pothier, *Pandectæ Justinianæ in novum ordinem digestæ* (1748-1752).
121. Pothier, *supra* n. 37.
122. Williams, *supra* n. 12, at 237-238.
123. Pothier, *supra* n. 120, at n. 984.
124. *Ibid.*
125. Pothier, *supra* n. 37, at n. 84.
126. *Ibid*, n. 86.
127. *Ibid*, n. 89.
128. Pothier, *supra* n. 120, at n. 984.

CHAPTER 3

Interpretation of Contracts in Comparative Law

§3.01 GENERALLY

The divergence among the approaches by individual legal systems resulted from the divergence in legal interpretation between the humanist and naturalist schools. German and English legal systems, where the objective approach is dominant, are influenced by the Naturalist School, which criticizes the subjective interpretation. However, the rules of interpretation determined by the humanist authors have been reflected in the legislation of Latin legal systems.

Nonetheless, it is impossible to strictly state that Latin legal systems prefer a subjective interpretation, while Romano-Germanic legal systems and common law countries opt for an objective interpretation. Although there is a certain parallelism between the provisions of French and Italian laws on the interpretation of contracts, the basic approaches of these two legal systems differ considerably from one another, and this difference amounts to quite different legal consequences in the application of the same provisions.

Likewise, although Romano-Germanic legal systems share the common feature of containing very few provisions on the interpretation of contracts, they do not have a common approach to this subject. The objective approach dominates German law, whereas the subjective approach is more prominent in Swiss law, bringing it closer to the French law's liberal conception. Common law, however, is almost like a laboratory environment, where approaches to the interpretation of contracts developed much faster than they did in continental legal systems, making it possible to observe all the phases of this development simultaneously.

Despite all their differences, individual legal systems have a common feature in their approaches to the interpretation of contracts: every legal system seeks a balance between subjective and objective interpretation. In legal systems where the subjective approach dominates, principles and theories of objective interpretation redress the balance. Alternatively, in legal systems where the objective approach is preferred, it remains possible to find all the elements and principles of subjective interpretation.

The consequence of this common trend in contemporary legal systems is that they adopt similar or even the same methodologies for interpretation, they bring similar solutions to the same problems, and their practice is ultimately similar, no matter how different are the provisions contained in their legislation.

§3.02 THE LATIN LEGAL FAMILY

[A] French Law

[1] Generally

The provisions of the French Civil Code of 1804 (*Code Civil Français*, CC. Fr.) covering the law of obligations were completely reformed through an *ordonance* issued on February 10, 2016, which took effect on October 01, 2016.[129] Through this *ordonance*, the French legislators also revised and changed the provisions on the interpretation of contracts and totally abrogated some of them.[130]

Former Articles 1156-1164 of the CC. Fr., which remained in effect until 2016, were the oldest and the most detailed provisions on the interpretation of contracts in

129. Ord. n° 2016-131 du 10 févr. 2016, www.legifrance.gouv.fr (accessed December 7, 2018).

130. The French legislators revised former Arts 1156, 1161, 1162, and 1157 which will be examined below; whereas they abrogated Arts 1158, 1159, 1160, 1163, and 1164, which used to read as follows:

> Article 1158
>
> Words susceptible of two meanings must be taken in the meaning that best suits the subject matter of the contract.
>
> Article 1159
>
> What is ambiguous shall be interpreted according to what is the usage in the region where the contract was made.
>
> Article 1160
>
> Clauses which are commonly used in a contract shall be filled in, even though they have not been inserted.
>
> Article 1163
>
> However general the terms in which an agreement is worded, it includes only the things on which the parties appear to have intended to contract.
>
> Article 1164
>
> When in a contract a case was mentioned to give an explanation of the obligation, it shall not be deemed that the parties thereby intended to restrict the scope of their contract which, as a matter of right, shall apply to the cases not expressed.

Translation by Davis W. Gruning, *Civil Code*, 129, https://www.legifrance.gouv.fr/Traductions/en-English/Legifrance-translations (last updated July 1, 2013, accessed December 7, 2018).

comparative law. These provisions were also the second most detailed regulation on the interpretation of statements and contracts in legal history after the *Allgemeines Landrecht für die Preußichen Staaten* (General State Laws for the Prussian States) of 1794, which contained twenty-eight articles on this issue.[131] The former provisions of the CC. Fr. were based on detailed studies of the *Digesta*, conducted by Jean Domat[132] and his follower Robert Joseph Pothier.[133]

A considerable body of literature and case law had developed on these now abrogated provisions. Although the 2016 reform brought significant changes to the provisions on the interpretation of contracts, the literature and case law that has been established on the abrogated articles will definitely continue to play a significant role in the application of the amended provisions. For this reason, this study will examine new and abrogated provisions of the CC. Fr. together and compare them.

[2] Classification of the Types of Interpretation and the Relationship Between Subjective and Objective Interpretation

The subjective approach to interpretation, which is based on the intent of the parties, prevails in French law. This is a natural consequence of the influence of liberalism, which enshrines the principle of freedom of contract (*liberté contractuelle*) in the French law of obligations.[134]

The influence of liberalism is also reflected in the basic distinction between the interpretation of norms and the interpretation of contracts. Since the former are products of a common will, the *Cour de Cassation* has the authority to review them. However, the *Cour de Cassation* does not have the authority, in principle, to review decisions relating to the interpretation of contracts, as contracts are the products of the will of private parties.[135]

The interpretation of contracts is twofold, including explanatory interpretation (*l'inteprétation explicative*) where courts determine the meaning of terms of contracts or contracts as a whole and complementary interpretation (*l'inteprétation supplétive* or *l'inteprétation créatrice*) where courts fill gaps in contracts.[136] As regards explanatory interpretation, French law does not regard the determination of the meaning of a contract and its legal consequences as different activities, as do the German[137] and United States (U.S.)[138] legal systems. The interpretation of contracts in the French legal system is an integral process that covers both.[139]

131. Stefan Vogenauer, *Interpretation of Contracts*, in Jürgen Basedow, Klaus J. Hopt, Reinhard Zimmermann, Andreas Stier (eds.), *The Max Planck Encyclopedia of European Private Law*, Vol. 1, 974 (Oxford University Press, Croydon, 2012).
132. Domat, *supra* n. 91; Zimmermann, *supra* n. 11, at 638.
133. Pothier, *supra* n. 37; Jacques Ghestin, Marc Billiau, *Traité de Droit Civil—Les obligations, les effets du contrat*, 31 (4th ed., Librarie Générale de Droit et de Jurisprudence, 2001).
134. Fontaine, de Ly, *supra* n. 5, at 120-121.
135. Ghestin, Billiau, *supra* n. 133, at 6; Terré, Simler, Lequette, *supra* n. 4, at 497.
136. Terré, Simler, Lequette, *supra* n. 4, at 495.
137. *See*, section §3.03[A][1] Generally, *infra*.
138. *See*, section §3.04[B][1] Generally, *infra*.
139. Ghestin, Billiau, *supra* n. 133, at 7.

French law classifies the rules on explanatory interpretation as the rules of subjective interpretation based on a determination of the intent of the parties and the rules of objective interpretation based on equity and usages. There is a hierarchical order between them in favor of the former.[140] Courts must first examine the common intent of the parties. If a common intent cannot be determined, then courts may apply the rules of objective interpretation. This hierarchy is also a consequence of the supremacy of the principle of party autonomy.[141]

A distinctive feature of French law is the absence of a distinction between objective and complementary interpretation.[142] The limits of subjective interpretation draw the line between explanatory and complementary interpretation. For this reason, French law considers interpretation according to good faith and fair dealing, equity, and usages as forms of complementary interpretation.[143]

Although the subjective approach prevails in French law, a purely subjective approach is considered outdated and has been criticized in the French literature since the early twentieth century, seeking to make the French approach more objective. For instance, Ghestin/Billiau argue that Article 1188 (former Article 1156) of the CC. Fr., which provides for an ascertainment of the common intent of the parties rather than stopping at the literal meaning of the words, should not be considered to be a mandatory provision.[144]

The limits of subjective interpretation are becoming increasingly more defined, and French literature and case law have likewise increasingly recognized that it is not always possible to determine the common intent of the parties. Therefore, courts must take into account the objective elements in the interpretation of a contract, such as good faith and fair dealing and usages. As a result, today the subjective and objective methods of interpretation are being applied together in French law.[145]

[3] Review of Decisions Relating to the Interpretation of Contracts

The question of whether the *Cour de Cassation* has the authority to review decisions relating to the interpretation of contracts has two dimensions: first, whether the interpretation of contracts is a question of law or facts and second, whether the provisions on this issue are mandatory or not.

As regards the first aspect of the question, it should be stated that according to the French law of civil procedure, the *Cour de Cassation* is not permitted to review the

140. Terré, Simler, Lequette, *supra* n. 4, at 498-499.
141. Ghestin, Billiau, *supra* n. 133, at 53.
142. Fontaine, de Ly, *supra* n. 5, at 120.
143. Ghestin, Billiau, *supra* n. 133, at 41 et seq.
144. *Ibid.*, at 8-9.
145. *Ibid.*, at 9.

merits of cases brought before it.[146] For this reason, decisions relating to the interpretation of contracts are reviewable if they relate to law, and they are not reviewable if they relate to facts.

Initially, following the promulgation of the French Civil Code, the *Cour de Cassation* ruled that since contracts and legal transactions in general have the force of law between the parties, decisions relating to them, including those relating to the interpretation of contracts, are reviewable.[147] However, the court changed this view shortly after that decision. In 1808, the *Cour de Cassation* held that the interpretation of a company contract was an issue of facts, the court that interpreted the contract in that case exercised sovereignty, and even if it was mistaken, the *Cour de Cassation* could not review the decision of the lower court.[148] Since then, the *Cour de Cassation* has not changed its position on this issue.[149]

As a result, French law currently considers the interpretation of contracts to be a question of facts and not a question of law.[150] Therefore, it has to be considered by lower degree courts,[151] and, as a rule, decisions of lower degree courts regarding issues of fact are not reviewable on appeal.[152]

There are some exceptions to this rule: the *Cour de Cassation* has the exclusive authority to interpret contracts that relate to public policy, the treasury, or taxes.[153] The court can also interpret collective agreements.[154] The *Cour de Cassation* also reviews decisions that relate to the interpretation of labor, insurance, and loan contracts, the limits of which are defined by law.[155] In addition, Ghestin/Billiau suggest that the *Cour de Cassation* should also have the authority to review decisions relating to the interpretation of standard contracts.[156]

The second aspect of the question of reviewability of decisions relating to the interpretation of contracts is about whether the provisions on this issue are mandatory. The *Cour de Cassation* is of the opinion that they are not,[157] unlike Italian law where they are deemed to be mandatory.[158]

This opinion is based on very old case law. In 1807, the *Cour de Cassation* held that the provisions on this issue are not mandatory and left a great deal of space for

146. Article 3(3) of the law dated November 27—December 1, 1790 "*la Cour de cassation ne reconnait pas du fond des affaires, sauf disposition législative contraire*"; Ghestin, Billiau, *supra* n. 133, at 12.
147. Civ., 4 brumaire An VII, S. chron. cited by Terré, Simler, Lequette, *supra* n. 4, 508.
148. Malaurie, Aynès, *supra* n. 5, at 419; Ghestin, Billiau, *supra* n. 133, at 11; Terré, Simler, Lequette, *supra* n. 4, at 508, these authors refer to Cass., sect. réun., 2 févr. 1808, S. chron., Grands arrêts, t. 2, n° 160.
149. Malaurie, Aynès, *supra* n. 5, at 419; Ghestin, Billiau, *supra* n. 133, at 11; Terré, Simler, Lequette, *supra* n. 4, at 508.
150. Vogenauer, *supra* n. 131, at 957.
151. Terré, Simler, Lequette, *supra* n. 4, at 497.
152. Canaris, Grigoleit, *supra* n. 5, at 456.
153. Ghestin, Billiau, *supra* n. 133, at 14-15.
154. *Ibid.*, at 16.
155. *Ibid.*, at 17.
156. *Ibid.*, at 18 et seq.
157. Cass, civ., 19.12.1995, *Bull. civ.*, I, n° 466, section 324, www.legifrance.gouv.fr (accessed December 7, 2018); Canaris, Grigoleit, *supra* n. 5, at 455.
158. *See*, section §3.02[B][1] Generally, *infra*.

judicial discretion to lower degree courts.[159] In this decision, the *Cour de Cassation* ruled that former Articles 1157 (new Article 1191), 1158, and 1161 (new Article 1189) of the CC. Fr. were not mandatory but directory. In 1981, the *Cour de Cassation* also confirmed that former Articles 1162 (new Article 1190) and 1163 were not mandatory either.[160]

Although there has been well-established case law regarding the directory nature of most of the provisions on the interpretation of contracts, the position of former Article 1156 (new Article 1188(1)) remained unclear for a long time. In 1970, the *Cour de Cassation* held that the courts must examine the common intent of the parties in the sense of former Article 1156 of the CC. Fr., and the fact that a court examined the intent of only one of the parties was a reason for reversal.[161]

In a 1988 decision, the *Cour de Cassation* reversed a decision by referring to former Articles 1134, 1156, and 1159 of the CC. Fr., where a court had interpreted a contract on the basis of usages, without examining whether the parties intended to incorporate them into their contract.[162] In addition, two separate decisions of the *Cour de Cassation* also held that former Article 1161 was mandatory; the court then reviewed the merits of those decisions and reversed them on the basis of erroneous qualification by omission (*dénaturation par omission*).[163]

As demonstrated above, the exceptions to the rule according to which decisions relating to the interpretation of contracts are not reviewable are rooted in the rule, even though interpretation is considered to be a question of facts and most of the provisions on the interpretation of contracts are deemed directory.

[4] Provisions of the French Civil Code Relating to the Interpretation of Contracts

[a] Article 1188 (Former Article 1156) of the CC. Fr.

Former Article 1156 of the CC. Fr. reads as follows:

> One must in agreements seek the common intention of the contracting parties, rather than stop at the literal meaning of the words.[164]

In 2016, this article was revised in Article 1188 as follows:

159. Cass. Req., 18 mars 1807, S. 1807. 1. 361; D. 1807. 1. 241, www.legifrance.gouv.fr (accessed December 7, 2018); Ghestin, Billiau, *supra* n. 133, at 34-35.
160. Cass. com., 19 janvier 1981, *Bull. civ.*, IV, n° 34, 25, www.legifrance.gouv.fr (accessed December 7, 2018); Ghestin, Billiau, *supra* n. 133, at 35.
161. Cass. civ., 1re, 20 janvier 1970, *Bull. civ.*, I. n° 24, 20, www.legifrance.gouv.fr (accessed December 7, 2018); Ghestin, Billiau, *supra* n. 133, at 36.
162. Cass. com., 17 mai 1988, *Bull. civ.*, IV. n° 167, 116, www.legifrance.gouv.fr (accessed December 7, 2018).
163. Cass. civ. 5 janvier 1948, D. 1948, 265; Cass. civ. 29 juin 1948, D. 1948, 554, www.legifrance.gouv.fr (accessed December 7, 2018).
164. "*On doit dans les conventions rechercher quelle a été la commune intention des parties contractantes, plutôt que de s'arrêter au sens littéral des termes*", www.legifrance.gouv.fr (accessed December 7, 2018), translation by Gruning, *supra* n. 130, at 129.

> A contract is to be interpreted according to the common intention of the parties rather than stopping at the literal meaning of its terms. Where this intention cannot be discerned, a contract is to be interpreted in the sense which a reasonable person placed in the same situation would give to it.[165]

In *Traité des obligations*, Pothier ranks the principle stated in Article 1188(1) (former Article 1156) of the CC. Fr. as the first principle.[166] He illustrates this principle with the example of a landlord who rents a small apartment in his building where he lives but writes "my house" instead of "my apartment" in the contract. Since the parties do not intend the rent of the whole house, the subject of the contract is only the apartment.

Pothier also states that this rule only applies when the meaning of a term is ambiguous and that when the meaning of a contract is "clear" it cannot be interpreted.[167] His approach is an expression of the *in claris non fit interpretatio* rule, which is generally not recognized as a principle in today's legal systems, and which was not adopted by the French legislators in 1804. However, the new Article 1192, which will be studied below, represents an outdated trend toward recognizing this rule in French law.

Article 1188(1) (former Article 1156) of the CC. Fr. differs significantly from other provisions on the interpretation of contracts. This article lays down general principles of interpretation; it is the "rule of the rules,"[168] whereas the other provisions of the CC. Fr on this issue are only directory rules for judges.[169]

This article addresses two basic principles of the interpretation of contracts. First, the common intent of the parties must be ascertained and not the intent of only one of the parties. Second, the spirit (*l'esprit*) of a contract prevails over its wording.[170]

Interpretation of a contract requires, first of all, a determination of the common intent of the parties. As mentioned above, if a court examines the intent of only one of the parties, this is a reason for the reversal of that decision.[171] In another decision of the *Cour de Cassation* mentioned above, the court reversed a decision where a lower court had interpreted a contract on the basis of usages, without examining whether it was the intent of the parties to adopt that usage.[172]

165. "*Le contrat s'interprète d'après la commune intention des parties plutôt qu'en s'arrêtant au sens littéral de ses termes. Lorsque cette intention ne peut être décelée, le contrat s'interprète selon le sens que lui donnerait une personne raisonnable placée dans la même situation.*" www.legifrance.gouv.fr (accessed December 7, 2018), translation by John Cartwright, Bénédicte Fauvarque-Cosson, Simon Whittaker, *The Law of Contract, The General Regime of Obligations, and Proof of Obligations*, 17, http://www.textes.justice.gouv.fr/art_pix/THE-LAW-OF-CONTRACT-2-5-16.pdf (accessed December 7, 2018).
166. Pothier, *supra* n. 37, at n. 84; Pothier, *supra* n. 120, at n. 984.
167. Pothier, *supra* n. 37, at n. 84.
168. Ghestin, Billiau, *supra* n. 133, at 32.
169. Terré, Simler, Lequette, *supra* n. 4, at 499.
170. Malaurie, Aynès, *supra* n. 5, at 418.
171. *See* the above cited case Cass. civ., 1re, 20 janvier 1970, *Bull. civ.*, I. n° 24, s. 20, www.legifrance.gouv.fr (accessed December 7, 2018); Ghestin, Billiau, *supra* n. 133, at 36.
172. *See*, section §3.02[A][3] Review of Decisions Relating to the Interpretation of Contracts, *infra*; Cass. com., 17 mai 1988, *Bull. civ.*, IV. n° 167, s. 116, www.legifrance.gouv.fr (accessed December 7, 2018).

The court must determine the common intent of the parties at the time of the conclusion of a contract.[173] For an accurate interpretation of this common intent, the circumstances in which the parties found themselves at that time must also be taken into consideration.[174] Courts are allowed (but not obliged) to accept extrinsic evidence, such as the conduct of the parties before and after the conclusion of the contract, their previous agreements and statements, and their subsequent conduct.[175] This follows from the principle of circumstantial evidence.[176] This approach of the French law represents a middle point between the rules that prohibit the admittance of such evidence in U.S. law[177] and the continental approach that obliges courts to take extrinsic evidence into account.[178]

Some subsidiary rules of literal interpretation have developed in practice as French courts have applied former Article 1156 of the CC. Fr. According to these rules of literal interpretation, individually negotiated clauses prevail over standard clauses, handwritten clauses prevail over printed ones, special clauses prevail over general ones, and the main text of a contract prevails over its annexes.[179]

The second paragraph added to this article with the 2016 reform appears to be specifically inspired by Article 8 of the United Nations Convention on Contracts for the International Sale of Goods (CISG),[180] and it is also in accordance with the other uniform law texts that have followed the example of the CISG, such as Article 4.1 of the UNIDROIT Principles of International Commercial Contracts (UPICC) and Article 5:101(3) of the PECL.[181] Although the criterion of a "reasonable person" was not unknown to the Civil Code, this criterion was first introduced within the framework of contract interpretation in Article 1188(2) of the CC. Fr. Therefore, the CISG is the source of the criterion of a "reasonable person" in French law with respect to contract interpretation. Considering that it is because of common law jurists that the "reasonable person" standard was included in the CISG as a rule of objective interpretation, it is possible to say that the reference to this criterion in the CC. Fr. represents the indirect influence of common law.[182]

173. Ghestin, Billiau, *supra* n. 133, at 37.
174. Terré, Simler, Lequette, *supra* n. 4, at 500.
175. Ghestin, Billiau, *supra* n. 133, at 37; Alain Bénabent, *Droit des Obligations*, 231-232 (15th ed., LGDJ, 2016); Cass. civ., 1re, 13 décembre 1988, *Bull. civ.*, I. n° 352, s. 239, www.legifrance.gouv.fr (accessed December 7, 2018); Cass. civ., 3e, 5 février 1971, D. 1971, p. 281, www.legifrance.gouv.fr (accessed December 7, 2018). Cass. civ., 1re, 9 novembre 1993, *Bull. civ.*, I. n° 317; Com., 22 mars 2005, n° 02-15357.
176. Terré, Simler, Lequette, *supra* n. 4, at 500-501.
177. *See*, section §3.04[B][4][a] (Non)interpretation Rules: The Parol Evidence Rule, the Plain Meaning Rule, and the Four Corners Rule, *infra*.
178. *See*, sections §3.02[B][6][a] Article 1362 of the CC. It.; §3.03[A][3][b] § 133 of the BGB; §3.03[B][4][b] Objective Interpretation; §3.03[C][2][f] Principles of Interpretation Developed Through Case Law or Recognized in the Literature, *infra*.
179. Terré, Simler, Lequette, *supra* n. 4, at 500.
180. Ahmet Cemil Yıldırım, *Raisonnable et bonne foi: de nouveaux usages des standards juridiques? / Reasonable and Good Faith: New Usages for Legal Standards?*, 6 IBLJ/RDAI 549, 556 (2017).
181. Bénabent, *supra* n. 175, at 232; Barthélémy Mercadal, *Les principes généraux gouvernant l'interprétation du contrat/ The General Principles Behind Contract Interpretation*, 6 IBLJ/RDAI 541, 541-542 (2017).
182. Yıldırım, *supra* n. 180, at 556.

[b] Article 1189 (Former Article 1161) of the CC. Fr.

Former Article 1161 of the CC. Fr. reads as follows:

> All the clauses of an agreement are interpreted with reference to one another by giving to each one the meaning that results from the whole act.[183]

In 2016, this article was revised in Article 1189 as follows:

> All the terms of a contract are to be interpreted in relation to each other, giving to each the meaning which respects the consistency of the contract as a whole.
>
> Where, according to the common intention of the parties, several contracts contribute to one and the same operation, they are to be interpreted by reference to this operation.[184]

This article is an expression of the principle of systematic interpretation, ranked in sixth place by Pothier in his *Traité des obligations*.[185] According to this principle, a court must consider the purpose, spirit, and economic balance of a contract and use unambiguous provisions thereof in order to interpret ambiguous provisions in it.[186] According to Ghestin/Billiau, however, the techniques and methods used in contract drafting and the order of the provisions of a contract cannot be considered to be tools of interpretation but only as evidence to support a particular meaning of a term.[187]

Former Article 1161 of the CC. Fr. previously applied as if it was a mandatory provision, despite the abovementioned decision of the *Cour de Cassation* where the court declared that this article is of a directory nature.[188] The *Cour de Cassation* reverses decisions where lower courts do not apply this rule since this failure leads to an erroneous qualification by omission (*dénaturation par omission*) in the determination of whether the meaning of a term is clear.[189] In other words, if a court finds a term ambiguous and interprets it, or finds it clear and does not interpret it without considering the whole contract, it would have reached this conclusion through an incomplete examination, which is grounds for reversal.[190] This practice is also in

183. "*Toutes les clauses des conventions s'interprètent les unes par les autres, en donnant à chacune le sens qui résulte de l'acte entire,*" www.legifrance.gouv.fr (accessed December 7, 2018), translation by Gruning, *supra* n. 130, at 129.
184. "*Toutes les clauses d'un contrat s'interprètent les unes par rapport aux autres, en donnant à chacune le sens qui respecte la cohérence de l'acte tout entier. Lorsque, dans l'intention commune des parties, plusieurs contrats concourent à une même opération, ils s'interprètent en fonction de celle-ci.*" www.legifrance.gouv.fr (accessed December 7, 2018), translation by Cartwright, Fauvarque-Cosson, Whittaker, *supra* n. 165, at 17-18.
185. Pothier, *supra* n. 37, at n. 89; Ghestin, Billiau, *supra* n. 133, at 33.
186. Terré, Simler, Lequette, *supra* n. 4, at 501.
187. Ghestin, Billiau, *supra* n. 133, at 33.
188. Cass. com., 19 janvier 1981, *Bull. civ.*, IV, n° 34, 25, www.legifrance.gouv.fr (accessed December 7, 2018); Ghestin, Billiau, *supra* n. 133, at 35.
189. Ghestin, Billiau, *supra* n. 133, at 39-40.
190. Cass. civ., 5 janvier 1948, D. 1948, 265, www.legifrance.gouv.fr (accessed December 7, 2018); Cass. civ. 1re, 5 janvier 1956, *Bull. civ.*, I. n° 11, 9, www.legifrance.gouv.fr (accessed December 7, 2018).

accordance with other legal systems where the principle of systematic interpretation is deemed mandatory.[191]

The second paragraph added to this article refers to a group of contracts and provides that a group of contracts must also be interpreted as a whole. A similar reference can also be found in the Comments to Article 5:105 of the PECL,[192] and this new provision of the CC. Fr. appears to be inspired by this reference.

[c] Article 1190 (Former Article 1162) of the CC. Fr.

Former Article 1162 of the CC. Fr. reads as follows:

> In case of doubt, an agreement is interpreted against the party who has stipulated and in favor of the party who has contracted the obligation.[193]

This provision was revised in Article 1190 of the 2016 text as follows:

> In case of ambiguity, a bespoke contract is interpreted against the creditor and in favour of the debtor, and a standard-form contract is interpreted against the person who put it forward.[194]

According to Pothier, who ranked this principle in seventh place among his principles of contractual interpretation, the creditor should bear the risk of failure to express himself clearly.[195]

This article sets forth a purely objective rule of interpretation that does not consider the common intent of the parties, and which therefore may lead to a result contrary to it.[196] However, this rule is a subsidiary rule, and it only applies when the common intent of the parties cannot be determined.[197]

Article 1190 on the general principle of *contra proferentem* is not the only provision in the CC. Fr. on this rule. Article 1602 of the CC. Fr. also includes a special provision on the principle of *contra venditorem* that expresses the same principle in the context of sales contracts.[198] The main difference between Articles 1602 and 1190 (former Article 1162) of the CC. Fr. is that the former is a mandatory provision, whereas

191. *See*, sections §3.02[B][6][b] Article 1363 of the CC. It.; §3.03[B][4][b] Objective Interpretation; §3.03[C][2][f] Principles of Interpretation Developed Through Case Law or Recognized in the Literature; §3.04[A][4] Other Principles of Interpretation, *infra*.
192. The Commission on European Contract Law, Ole Lando, Hugh Beale (eds.), *Principles of European Contract Law Parts I and II*, 296 (Kluwer Law International, 2000); M.H. Wissink, *Interpretation*, in Danny Busch et al. (eds.), *The Principles of European Contract Law and Dutch Law*, 254 (Kluwer Law International, 2002); *see*, section §4.04[A][2][e] Article 5:105 of the PECL, *infra*.
193. "*Dans le doute, la convention s'interprète contre celui qui a stipulé et en faveur de celui qui a contracté l'obligation*", www.legifrance.gouv.fr (accessed December 7, 2018), translation by Gruning, *supra* n. 130, at 129.
194. "*Dans le doute, le contrat de gré à gré s'interprète contre le créancier et en faveur du débiteur, et le contrat d'adhésion contre celui qui l'a proposé.*" www.legifrance.gouv.fr (accessed December 7, 2018), translation by Cartwright, Fauvarque-Cosson, Whittaker, *supra* n. 165, at 18.
195. Pothier, *supra* n. 120, at n. 986; Pothier, *supra* n. 37, at n. 90.
196. Ghestin, Billiau, *supra* n. 133, at 33.
197. *Ibid.*, at 33-34. These authors refer to C. Civ., v. Reims, 7 janv. 2004, RDC 2004. 933.
198. Ghestin, Billiau, *supra* n. 133, at 34; Art. 1602 of the CC. Fr. reads as follows:

the latter is a directory. In addition to Article 1602 of the CC. Fr., Article L. 133-2 of the French Consumer Code also sets forth a special mandatory provision on the *contra proferentem* principle in favor of consumers.[199]

Former Article 1162 of the CC. Fr. previously addressed the interpretation "against the party who has stipulated" (the *contra stipulatorem* rule) first, and it then continued with an interpretation "in favor of the party who has contracted the obligation" (the *contra creditorem* rule). The former is a well-established principle of the Roman and civil traditions, whereas the latter is not recognized as a general principle in comparative and uniform law. This is because the *contra creditorem* rule is based on erroneous presumptions that there is a clear distinction between the creditor and the debtor and that the debtor is the weaker party.[200] Canaris/Grigoleit also criticized former Article 1602 of the CC. Fr. for this reason.[201]

It appears that while revising this article, however, the French legislators did not take into account this criticism or the general trends in comparative and uniform law. The first part of new Article 1190 of the CC. Fr. does not even refer to the principle of *contra stipulatorem* anymore and addresses only the questionable *contra creditorem* rule. In other words, the 2016 reform has sacrificed an important general principle and then adopted another principle that is not regarded as a real principle under uniform law and comparative law.[202]

The second part of new Article 1190 of the CC. Fr., however, accurately addresses the interpretation of standard form contracts, which are frequently used in today's business life.

[d] Article 1191 (Former Article 1157) of the CC. Fr.

Former Article 1157 of the CC. Fr. reads as follows:

> Le vendeur est tenu d'expliquer clairement ce à quoi il s'oblige.
>
> Tout pacte obscur ou ambigu s'interprète contre le vendeur.

("The seller must clearly express the extent of his obligations. Any obscure or ambiguous clause is interpreted against the seller." Author's translation) www.legifrance.gouv.fr (accessed December 7, 2018).

199. Malaurie, Aynès, *supra* n. 5, at 418-419; Bénabent, *supra* n. 175, at 232, 233; Art. L. 211-1, para. 2 of the Code de la Consommation reads as follows:

> Elles [Les clauses des contrats proposés par les professionnels aux consommateurs] s'interprètent en cas de doute dans le sens le plus favorable au consommateur.

("In the event of doubt, [contract terms proposed by professionals to consumers] are interpreted in the sense which is most favourable to the consumer." Author's translation) www.legifrance.gouv.fr (accessed December 7, 2018).

200. The *contra creditorem* rule was not part of Roman law. It was suggested by Bartolus in the Middle Ages; however, it did not stand because of the abovementioned reasons. *See*, section §2.01[B][2][b] The Emergence of Principles of Objective Interpretation in the Classical Period, *supra*.

201. Canaris, Grigoleit, *supra* n. 5, at 462.

202. *See also* Yıldırım, *supra* n. 180, at 559-560.

> When a clause is susceptible of two meanings, it shall be understood to mean that which may produce some effect, rather than according to the meaning which would produce none. [203]

Article 1191 of the CC. Fr. which corresponds to former Article 1157 of the CC. Fr. reads as follows:

> Where a contract term is capable of bearing two meanings, the one which gives it some effect is to be preferred to the one which makes it produce no effect.[204]

These articles reflect the principle that Pothier ranked second in his work *Traité des obligations*.[205] Although this principle was placed just after the main principle in former Article 1156 of the CC. Fr. in the 1804 version, it was placed among the last provisions on the issue in the 2016 reform.

Terré/Simler/Lequette point out that the principle stated in Article 1191 (former Article 1157) of the CC. Fr. is a natural consequence of the principle mentioned in Article 1188 (former Article 1156) of the CC. Fr. because this article is based on the presumption that the common intent of the parties should tend toward the sense that gives effect to their agreement.[206] Likewise, according to Ghestin/Billiau, Article 1191 (former Article 1157) and former Article 1158 of the CC. Fr., which provide for an interpretation in accordance with the subject matter of the contract, assume that the parties to a contract are reasonable persons.[207]

[e] Article 1192 of the CC. Fr.

The new Article 1192 of the CC. Fr. reads as follows:

> Clear and unambiguous terms are not subject to interpretation as doing so risks their distortion [*dénaturation*].[208]

Although this article is new to the CC. Fr., it must be read in the light of the case law underlying it. This article addresses first the doctrine of *clauses claires et précises*, which recalls the *in claris non fit interpretatio* rule, which is not recognized in comparative and uniform law. It then refers to the concept of erroneous qualification (*dénaturation*). The case law on this latter concept must be examined in order to have a more complete understanding of the doctrine of *clauses claires et précises*.

---

203. "*Lorsqu'une clause est susceptible de deux sens, on doit plutôt l'entendre dans celui avec lequel elle peut avoir quelque effet, que dans le sens avec lequel elle n'en pourrait produire aucun.*" www.legifrance.gouv.fr (accessed December 7, 2018), translation by Gruning, *supra* n. 130, at 129.
204. "*Lorsqu'une clause est susceptible de deux sens, celui qui lui confère un effet l'emporte sur celui qui ne lui en fait produire aucun.*" www.legifrance.gouv.fr (accessed December 7, 2018), translation by Cartwright, Fauvarque-Cosson, Whittaker, *supra* n. 165, at 18.
205. Pothier, *supra* n. 37, at n. 85; Pothier, *supra* n. 120, at n. 984.
206. Terré, Simler, Lequette, *supra* n. 4, at 501.
207. Ghestin, Billiau, *supra* n. 133, at 32.
208. "*On ne peut interpréter les clauses claires et précises à peine de dénaturation.*" www.legifrance.gouv.fr (accessed December 7, 2018), translation by Cartwright, Fauvarque-Cosson, Whittaker, *supra* n. 165, at 18.

Some comparatists present the doctrine of *clauses claires et précises* as the functional equivalent of the *in claris non fit interpretatio* rule, which prohibits the interpretation of contracts or terms that are "clear."[209] The present author is of the opinion that this equation risks oversimplifying the doctrine of *clauses claires et précises*. Although some authors in the French literature favor this narrow meaning of the doctrine,[210] and the *Cour de Cassation* exceptionally applied this doctrine in this sense,[211] the case law on the connection of this doctrine with erroneous qualification cannot be disregarded.

The application of this doctrine in the sense of *in claris non fit interpretatio* is exceptional, because according to the *Cour de Cassation* there is ambiguity in the meaning of a contract at a minimum doubt,[212] or in case of a contradiction between the literal meaning of the words and the intent of the parties.[213] Therefore, the doctrine of *clauses claires et précises* in its strict sense is also incompatible with Article 1188 (1) of the CC. Fr., which is a mandatory provision and provides for the determination of the intent of the parties.

The determination of whether a contract or a clause is *claire et précise* is also a result of an activity of interpretation. According to a 1975 decision of the *Cour de Cassation*, interpretation of an ambiguous act, contract, or term is a task for lower courts. If a court erroneously qualifies a clause as *claire et précise* without interpreting it, this erroneous qualification makes the decision subject to review of the *Cour de Cassation* and it is grounds for reversal.[214]

As to *dénaturation* or erroneous qualification, it should be stated that French law makes a clear distinction between qualification and interpretation of contracts. Interpretation of a contract includes determination of the meaning and legal consequences thereof, whereas qualification of a contract is a determination of the judicial category into which it falls and the rules to which it is subject. Courts must first interpret a contract in order to be able to qualify it.[215]

Courts are not bound by the qualification of the parties, and they can requalify a contract in order to determine the rules that will apply.[216] Qualification of a contract is a question of law, and decisions relating to qualification are reviewable on appeal.[217] Consequently, an important function of the concept of *dénaturation* is to provide an excuse for the *Cour de Cassation* to review these decisions.

209. Canaris, Grigoleit, *supra* n. 5, at 457-458; Fontaine, de Ly, *supra* n. 5, at 127-128.
210. Malaurie, Aynès, *supra* n. 5, at 419; Mercadal, *supra* n. 181, at 544; Pothier, *supra* n. 37, at n. 84.
211. Cass. Civ., 14 dec. 1942, D. 1944, 112; Cass. Civ. 23 avr. 1945, D. 1945, 261, Zweigert, Kötz, *supra* n. 4, at 403.
212. Civ. 1re, 13 juin 1979, *Bull. civ.*, I, n° 182; Bénabent, *supra* n. 175, at 233.
213. Civ. 3e, 15 janvier 2014, *Bull. civ.*, n° 12-27716; Bénabent, *supra* n. 175, at 233.
214. Cass. Com., 7 janvier 1975, D. 1975, s. 516, www.legifrance.gouv.fr (accessed December 7, 2018); Ghestin, Billiau, *supra* n. 133, at 29-30.
215. Bénabent, *supra* n. 175, at 234-235.
216. Terré, Simler, Lequette, *supra* n. 4, at 496. Bénabent, *supra* n. 175, at 235.
217. Cass. civ. 3e, 30 mai 1969, *Bull. civ.* III, n° 437, www.legifrance.gouv.fr (accessed December 7, 2018); Malaurie, Aynès, *supra* n. 5, at 420. However, the *Cour de Cassation* cannot review these decisions ex officio. One of the parties must allege that the court erroneously qualified the contract for the *Cour de Cassation* to consider this issue. Ghestin, Billiau, *supra* n. 133, at 24.

In 1872, the *Cour de Cassation* established the connection between *dénaturation* and the doctrine of *clauses claires et précises* by holding that if lower degree courts erroneously qualify contracts despite their clear wording, this is a reason for reversal.[218] The concern underlying this decision is to protect the binding force of contracts from the intervention of courts.[219]

Since that decision, the *Cour de Cassation* has reviewed decisions of lower degree courts in view of *dénaturation* and also reversed decisions in which courts erroneously qualify contracts as *claires et précises*.[220] Therefore, one may say that *dénaturation* also functions in the opposite direction of the narrow meaning attributed to the doctrine of *clauses claires et précises*. If a court erroneously qualifies a contract or a clause as *claire et précise*, the *Cour de Cassation* reverses such decision if it finds that the contract or clause is, indeed, not *claire et précise*.

The determination of whether a contract or a term is *claire et précise* also has some procedural consequences.[221] If a contract or a term is found to be clear, courts must apply the rules of evidence in a strict manner.[222] However, the *Cour de Cassation* ruled in a decision of 1886 that in cases where a contract needs to be interpreted, the apparent meaning of the wording of a contract can be refuted with any kind of evidence.[223]

In summary, the doctrine of *clauses claires et précises* is not simply the functional equivalent of the *in claris non fit interpretatio* rule. Together with the concept of *dénaturation*, it works not only as a rule prohibiting the interpretation of clauses which are found to be "clear" but also as a rule that serves to make possible the review and reversal of decisions in which courts erroneously qualified contract clauses as "clear." The first function of this doctrine is very limited, contradictory, and outdated, whereas its second function addresses a need.

The French legislators could have taken advantage of the 2016 reform to formulate the reviewability of decisions relating to the qualification of contracts in the CC. Fr. That would have been more compatible with comparative and uniform law and the case law on which Article 1192 of the CC. Fr. is based.[224] However, French legislators choose to formulate the doctrine of *clauses claires et précises* in the new Article 1192 and were satisfied with a simple reference to the concept of *dénaturation*, the functionality of which is questionable. This provision risks functioning as an *in claris non fit interpretatio* rule, and it is obviously inconsistent with the established principles of comparative and uniform law on the interpretation of contracts.

218. Cass. Civ., 15 avr. 1872, DP 72.1.176, S. 72.1.232, Grands arrêts, t. 2, n° 160, www.legifrance.gouv.fr; Terré, Simler, Lequette, *supra* n. 4, at 509; Ghestin, Billiau, *supra* n. 133, at 22; Zweigert, Kötz, *supra* n. 4, at 403.
219. Ghestin, Billiau, *supra* n. 133, at 22; Bénabent, *supra* n. 175, at 233.
220. Cass. Com., 7 janvier 1975, D. 1975, s. 516; Civ. 1re, 13 juin 1979, *Bull. civ.*, I, n° 182; Civ. 3e, 15 janvier 2014, *Bull. civ.*, n° 12-27716.
221. Ghestin, Billiau, *supra* n. 133, at 27-28.
222. *Ibid.*, at 27, these authors refer to V.J. Deveze's comment on Cass. Civ. 1er, 20 mai 1981, D. 1983 (at 289).
223. Cass. Req., 31 mars 1886, S. 86. 1. 260.
224. However, some authors welcome Art. 1192 as a codification of the case law. *See*, Mercadal, *supra* n. 181, at 544; Bénabent, *supra* n. 175, at 233.

[B] Italian Law

[1] Generally

As a member of the Latin legal family, Italian law like French law contains detailed provisions on the interpretation of contracts. Articles 1362-1371 of the Italian Civil Code (*Codice Civile Italiano*, CC. It.) cover the interpretation of contracts. The provisions of these articles are also used in the interpretation of the conduct of the parties[225] and unilateral transactions.[226] These provisions of the CC. It. are based on the corresponding provisions of the CC. Fr.[227] and overlap with them to a large extent in terms of their content.

Nevertheless, some of these overlapping provisions are conceived and applied very differently in Italian law than they are in French law. For this reason, it is impossible to speak of true unanimity within the Latin legal family regarding the interpretation of contracts.

A general study of the provisions of the CC. It. may give the impression that the subjective approach dominates Italian law, just as in other Latin systems. While this may be the case, if one considers the effect of Italian legal literature on practice, it may be concluded that the search for a balance between the subjective and objective approaches is more pronounced in Italian law than it is in French law.

Therefore, the definitions for the activity of interpretation proposed by Italian authors are not subjective definitions on the basis of a determination of the real intent of the parties, as is the case in the French,[228] Swiss,[229] and Turkish[230] legal systems. According to Bigliazzi Geri, "[i]t cannot be denied that the ambiguity is the reason for the activity of interpretation; likewise, getting over [the ambiguity] constitutes the basis of all the rules of interpretation, and therefore of the activity of interpretation."[231]

One of the most fundamental differences between Italian law and French law in the conception and application of the rules of interpretation is that these rules are deemed to be mandatory in Italian law.[232] Rules of interpretation are addressed to judges and are binding upon them.[233] Judges cannot avoid the application of these provisions, nor can the parties derogate from their application.[234] On the basis of this feature of the rules of interpretation, Monateri defines the activity of interpretation as

225. Monateri, *supra* n. 9, at 425.
226. C. Massimo Bianca, *L'interpretazione*, in *Diritto Civile*, Vol. 3, *Il Contratto*, 408-409 (2nd ed., Giuffrè Editore, 2000); Monateri, *supra* n. 9, at 432.
227. Vogenauer, *supra* n. 131, at 974.
228. *See*, section §3.02[A][4][a] Article 1188 (Former Article 1156) of the CC. Fr., *supra*.
229. *See*, section §3.03[B][4][a] Subjective Interpretation, *infra*.
230. *See*, section §3.03[C][2][a] Article 19(1) of the TBK, *infra*.
231. Lina Bigliazzi Geri, *L'interpretazione del Contratto Artt. 1362-1371*, in *Il Codice Civile—Commentario*, 40 (Giuffrè Editore, 2013).
232. Aurelio Gentili, *Art. 1362, Dell'interpretazione del Contratto*, in Emanuela Navarretta, Andrea Orestano (eds.), *Commentario al Codice Civile*, Vol. 2, *Contratti in Generale*, 368 (UTET Giuridica, 2011).
233. Monateri, *supra* n. 9, at 425.
234. Cass. 30 gennaio 1960, n. 268, in *Rep. Foro it.*, 1969, voce "Obbligazioni e contratti", n. 275., www.foroitaliano.it. (accessed December 7, 2018).

a "determination of the legally relevant meaning of the declaration of intent, in accordance with the legal norms serving interpretation."[235] Likewise, according to Bianca, interpretation is "the operation to ascertain the legally relevant meaning of the contractual deal"[236] and that meaning "emerges from an objective assessment of the transaction under the rules of interpretation."[237]

Nonetheless, Italian law like French law[238] conceives of the interpretation of contracts as a whole, including a determination of both the content of the contract and its legal consequences, which differs from the German[239] and U.S.[240] legal systems. The aim of the interpretation of contracts in Italian law is to define the allocation of the interests of the parties in the contract, their rights and obligations, and therefore the legal consequences of their agreement. In this sense, interpretation is not only an activity of establishing past facts but also an attempt to define the legal significance of the contract.[241] However, Sacco argues that these two phases are separate from each other since the meaning to be obtained through the activity of interpretation is logically necessary for determining the legal consequences of the agreement.[242]

Also unlike common law, Italian law makes no distinction between written and unwritten contracts as regards their scope of application; the same rules of interpretation apply to both. Furthermore, the rules of interpretation apply, to the extent possible, to unilateral transactions as well (Articles 1324 of the CC. It. ff.).[243]

Italian law also distinguishes between the interpretation and classification of contracts.[244] According to Monateri and Bianca's view, in principle, interpretation precedes classification: party intent is first ascertained through interpretation, and then the legal framework for a relationship between the parties is determined.[245] This view has also been adopted in practice.[246] Nonetheless, according to Sacco, the sequence of these steps is not absolute and they may be reversed because it is reasonable for the parties to first decide on the type of the contract they want to make, before negotiating its terms.[247] Likewise, Capobianco states that classification and interpretation are

235. Monateri, *supra* n. 9, at 425-426.
236. Bianca, *supra* n. 226, at 407.
237. *Ibid.*, at 408.
238. *See*, section §3.02[A][1] Generally, *supra*.
239. *See*, section §3.03[A][1] Generally, *infra*.
240. *See*, section §3.04[B][1] Generally, *infra*.
241. Ernesto Capobianco, *La determinazione del regolamento—L'interpretazione*, in Giuseppe Vettori, Vincenzo Roppo (eds.), *Trattato del Contratto*, Vol. 2—*Regolamento*, 302 (Giuffrè Editore, 2006).
242. Sacco, *supra* n. 7, at 231.
243. Monateri, *supra* n. 9, at 432.
244. Sangermano, *supra* n. 71, at 25.
245. Monateri, *supra* n. 9, at 429; Bianca, *supra* n. 226, at 411.
246. Cass. 30 gennaio 1960, n. 268, in *Rep. Foro it.*, 1969, voce "Obbligazioni e contratti," n. 275., www.foroitaliano.it (accessed December 7, 2018); Cass. 10 febbraio 2003, n. 1928, *Rep. Foro it.*, 2003, 889, voce "Contratto in genere," n. 423, www.foroitaliano.it. (accessed December 7, 2018).
247. Sacco, *supra* n. 7, at 245-248.

inseparable, and the Court of First Instance is charged with both functions. Accordingly, these two steps cannot be separated logically or chronologically, since classification is also an outcome of the determination of party intent.[248]

CC. It. also includes special provisions for interpretation, along with those listed under the heading of "interpretation of contracts." Some of these special provisions are the first paragraph of Article 1342 relating to clauses inserted into standard form contracts, Article 1352 relating to the form of the contract, and Article 2223 relating to the determination of whether a contract is a sales or construction contract.[249]

[2] The Discussion on the **In Claris Non Fit Interpretatio** *Rule*

The rule of *in claris non fit interpretatio*, which is not considered to be a principle in comparative law or uniform law, has received different reactions from Italian authors. Alpa defines this rule in accordance with its conception in comparative law as a prohibition from interpreting a contractual clause where the judge finds its meaning to be "clear," but he objects to this rule. According to him, this rule is dangerous because in disputes arising out of contracts, it leaves it up to the exclusive discretion of the judge to decide the meaning of the parties' text. At the same time, it is inconsistent because a judge can only reach the conclusion that a contractual clause is "clear" through the process of interpretation. However, while a judge may interpret a contract and reach this conclusion, the parties to the contract or other relevant third parties are deprived of the possibility of expressing their interpretation. On the basis of this view, Alpa criticizes those courts that still apply this rule.[250]

Capobianco also objects to the *in claris non fit interpretatio* rule. According to him, one of the conclusions to be drawn from the first paragraph of Article 1362 of the CC. It., which states that when interpreting a contract one must find the common intent of the parties, and not limit oneself to the literal meaning of the words, is that *in claris non fit interpretatio* has not been adopted as a rule by legislators and that any contractual clause can be interpreted, even when it seems to be "clear."[251]

Nevertheless, Bigliazzi Geri and Sangermano conceive of the *in claris non fit interpretatio* rule in the same way as Alpa and Capobianco yet maintain that it is relevant. Even though the CC. It. of 1942 did not include this principle, in their view, it has been established through case law and it is being applied correctly by the courts.[252] Additionally, Gentili finds this rule legitimate, as it aims to prevent the manipulation of the statements or expressions of the parties.[253]

---

248. Capobianco, *supra* n. 241, at 304-305.
249. *Ibid.*, at 297-298.
250. Guido Alpa, *Istituzioni di Diritto Privato*, 342 (UTET, 2002).
251. Capobianco, *supra* n. 241, at 313.
252. Bigliazzi Geri, *supra* n. 231, at 102 et seq.; Sangermano, *supra* n. 71, at 79. An arbitral tribunal also applied this rule and rejected the application of Art. 1362 of the CC. It., *see*, ICC Interim Award in Case No. 9781, YCA 2005, at 22 et seq. at 28, https://www.trans-lex.org/209781 (accessed December 7, 2018), where the arbitral tribunal referred in its decision to Cass. 96/ 2372; 80/ 4864; 75/ 1314.
253. Gentili, *supra* n. 232, at 378.

However, Sacco conceives of the *in claris non fit interpretatio* rule in a very different manner. According to him, it does not direct the noninterpretation of contractual clauses when they seem to be clear, but the cessation of the gradual activity of interpretation when a satisfactory meaning has been reached, rather than proceeding with the other steps of the interpretation process. Within this meaning, *in claris non fit interpretatio* is an accurate[254] rule, well established in case law.[255] As will be explained below, it is generally accepted that the interpretation process is gradual, there is a hierarchy between the rules of interpretation that signify different phases of the process, and in particular, the rules of objective interpretation do not apply when the meaning can be determined through subjective interpretation.

[3] Review of Decisions Relating to the Interpretation of Contracts

As French law,[256] Italian law considers the interpretation of contracts to be a question of fact, and therefore decisions relating to the interpretation of contracts are not reviewable on appeal.[257] It is the judge's task to determine the underlying facts of the dispute while examining the common intent of the parties, and even if the facts are determined erroneously, these decisions cannot be appealed.[258]

Once again as in French law, however, this exclusion from appeal is only superficial. The *Corte di Cassazione* has developed very efficient methods for reviewing decisions that relate to the interpretation of contracts. Recognition of the mandatory character of the provisions dealing with the interpretation of contracts has strengthened the hand of the Italian *Corte di Cassazione* considerably in reviewing these decisions compared with the French *Cour de Cassation*. Because provisions on the interpretation of contracts are binding, it is impossible for judges to derogate from them. Judges are bound to apply these rules, and if they fail to do so, then it is a reason for the *Corte di Cassazione* to reverse the decision.[259]

According to a decision by the *Corte di Cassazione*,[260] although the interpretation of contracts is a question of fact and it is the Court of First Instance's task to determine the common intent of the parties, review on appeal is permissible in cases of inaccurate reasoning, or failure to observe the rules of interpretation set forth in Article 1362 of the CC. It. ff.[261] In this event, however, the *Corte di Cassazione* could not substitute the lower court's interpretation with the interpretation that it considers accurate, and it

254. Sacco, *supra* n. 7, at 257.
255. Cass. civ. Sez. lav. 23 novembre 1998, n. 11878, in *Rep. Foro it.*, 1998, 389, www.foroitaliano.it (accessed December 7, 2018); Cass. 28 aprile 1999, n. 4241, in *Rep. Foro it.*, 1999, www.foroitaliano.it (accessed December 7, 2018); Sangermano, *supra* n. 71, at 81.
256. *See*, section §3.02[A][3] Review of Decisions Relating to the Interpretation of Contracts, *supra*.
257. Monateri, *supra* n. 9, at 430; Gentili, *supra* n. 232, at 369; Bianca, *supra* n. 226, at 413.
258. Capobianco, *supra* n. 241, at 303; Sacco, *supra* n. 7, at 241; Bianca, *supra* n. 226, at 413.
259. Capobianco, *supra* n. 241, at 296 and 303; Sacco, *supra* n. 7, at 239; Gentili, *supra* n. 232, at 371.
260. Cass. 11 gennaio 2005, n. 367, in *Rep. Foro it.*, 2005, voce "Assicurazione (contratto)," n. 77, www.foroitaliano.it. (accessed December 7, 2018).
261. *See also*, Capobianco, *supra* n. 241, at 303.

would need to send the case back to the lower court.[262] In practice, therefore, review of the interpretation of contracts is not very different from review of a question of law, and the *Corte di Cassazione* exercises full judicial supervision over the decisions of lower courts in this regard.[263]

[4] Views Pertaining to the Objectivity of the Subjective Interpretation

As mentioned above,[264] although the wording of the provisions of the CC. It. relating to the interpretation of contracts gives the impression that the subjective approach is dominant, the search for a balance between subjective and objective interpretation characterizes the approach of Italian law.

The main reason for the apparent dominance of the subjective approach in Italian law is that the first paragraph of Article 1362 CC. It., which is the most basic provision relating to the interpretation of contracts, requires or rather commands a determination of "the common intent of the parties."

Nevertheless, differing from French,[265] Swiss,[266] and Turkish[267] laws, which contain similar provisions and where the subjective approach dominates, this provision is conceived of as a rule of objective interpretation in Italian law.[268]

One of the arguments upon which the objective approach is based is that when there is a dispute over interpretation, the person responsible for making the interpretation is the judge, i.e. a third person independent from the parties. According to Bigliazzi Geri, the interpretation of contracts is a subjective activity until a dispute arises, because the meaning of the contract is limited to what the parties attribute to it in their minds. However, interpretation turns into an objective activity when a dispute arises and the judge intervenes into the relationship of the parties.[269]

The fundamental reason why a rule of interpretation based on "the common intent of the parties" can be considered to be an objective rule in Italian law is the word "common." The emphasis on this word changes the whole character of this legal system's approach to the interpretation of contracts.

According to Alpa, the word "common" in the first paragraph of Article 1362 of the CC. It. implies that the intent to be interpreted must have been expressed. Therefore, this provision sets forth an objective criterion, and it simply cannot be classified as subjective.[270] The fact that not only "intent" but also "common intent" is to be determined requires that the intent to be interpreted must have been expressed by

262. Bianca, *supra* n. 226, at 413.
263. Monateri, *supra* n. 9, at 430.
264. *See*, section §3.02[B][1] Generally, *supra*.
265. *See*, section §3.02[A][4][a] Article 1188 (Former Article 1156) of the CC. Fr., *supra*.
266. *See*, section §3.03[B][4][a] Subjective Interpretation, *infra*.
267. *See*, section §3.03[C][2][a] Article 19(1) of the TBK, *infra*.
268. Sangermano, *supra* n. 71, at 51.
269. Bigliazzi Geri, *supra* n. 231, at 37-38.
270. Alpa Guido, *Il controllo giudiziale del contratto e l'interpretazione*, http://www.altalex.com/index.php?idnot=64932#_Toc369871176 (23.10.2013, accessed December 7, 2018).

at least one of the parties and to have been known by the other.[271] Likewise, according to Monateri, a statement is an objective phenomenon, beyond the subjective sphere of control of the parties. For this reason, by basing interpretation on the "common" intent of the parties, Italian law adopts an objective criterion, binding the parties against their own interests and their own true intents.[272]

Monateri takes this approach based on his reading of the first paragraph of Article 1362 of the CC. It.,[273] which is not at all clear according to him, even though this provision seems superficially clear. Pursuant to this provision, the common intent of the parties shall be sought in the interpretation of contracts, without limit to the literal meaning of the words. What stems from this provision is that a distinction is made between the literal meaning of the words and the intent of the parties, which is not reflected in their contract. However, since the parties must communicate in order to reach an agreement, any intent that is not reflected in their contract must be expressed in order to be "common." As a result, any divergence will not be between the expressed intent and an inherent intent, but rather between the literal meaning of the words and the expressed "common" intent of the parties. As a result, for an intent to be "common," it has to be an expressed intent and not merely one in the parties' minds. Only in this case it will be possible to speak of a meaning given by the parties to the words that is beyond the literal meaning of the words. In practice, however, there would hardly ever be a divergence between the expressed common intent of the parties and the wording of their contract.

In addition, while ascertaining the meaning given by the parties to the words they used, the appropriate meaning should be the one that would be understood by an average reasonable person of the same level of knowledge as the parties and in the same circumstances. For this reason, the criterion for an interpretation of the common intent of the parties is an objective one. The subject of interpretation should be what a reasonable addressee would understand and not what the author of the statement intended. In this sense, the law adopts an objective criterion that the understanding that will be taken as a basis for an agreement should be the one of a person in the same position with the addressee, also considering the addressee's specific knowledge and deficiencies, such as deafness, illiteracy, or ignorance. Statements, be they written or unwritten, are interpreted according to the objective understanding of a reasonable third person in the same circumstances with the addressee.[274]

Indeed, these approaches in Italian law are also relevant to other legal systems that have adopted the subjective approach, such as the French, Swiss, and Turkish legal systems, which refer to the "common" intent of the parties. One may say that this emphasis on a "common" intent of the parties and the approach developed on the basis

271. Capobianco, *supra* n. 241, at 301-302; Bianca, *supra* n. 226, at 408.
272. Monateri, *supra* n. 9, at 427.
273. *Ibid.*, at 434-435.
274. *Ibid.*, at 432.

of it is the functional equivalent[275] of the "principle of trust" found in Romano-Germanic legal systems.[276]

[5] *Classification of the Provisions of the Italian Civil Code Relating to the Interpretation of Contracts*

It is undisputed that the provisions of the CC. It. that deal with the interpretation of contracts reflect principles of both subjective and objective interpretation. It is also unanimously accepted in the Italian literature that there is a hierarchy and order of priority among these principles.[277] The dispute lies in the characterization and the place in this hierarchy of Article 1366 of the CC. It., which lays down the principle of good faith and fair dealing (*buona fede*) as a principle of interpretation.

CC. It. sets forth the rules of subjective interpretation in Articles 1362-1365 and the rules of objective interpretation in Articles 1367-1371. The *Corte di Cassazione* issued a decision that interprets Article 1366 as a rule of objective interpretation, holding that rules of objective interpretation only apply when the common intent of the parties cannot be determined through the rules of subjective interpretation.[278] Based on this opinion from the *Corte di Cassazione*, Monateri holds that the provisions of Articles 1362-1365 of the CC. It. are "strictly interpretative norms" (*norme strettamente interpretative*), and Articles 1366-1371 of the CC. It. are "integrative norms of interpretation" (*norme interpretative-integrative*). He further states that where the former provisions are sufficient for the determination of the common intent of the parties, the latter provisions cannot apply.[279]

However, the dominant view in the literature is that the principle of good faith and fair dealing set forth in Article 1366 of the CC. It. cannot be considered a subjective or objective principle.[280]

Capobianco and Bianca argue that the principle of good faith and fair dealing set forth in this article serves as a "*trait d'union*"[281] or a "point of suture"[282] between the subjective and objective principles of interpretation. Because of its position, this provision is superior to both groups of principles and applies to every phase of interpretation.[283]

275. Zweigert, Kötz, *supra* n. 4, at 34 et seq.; Arzu Oğuz, *Karşılaştırmalı Hukuk*, 68 et seq. (Yetkin, 2003).
276. *See*, sections §3.03[A][3][c] § 157 of the BGB; §3.03[B][4][b] Objective Interpretation; §3.03[C][2][b] The Will Theory, the Theory of Declaration, and the Trust Theory, *infra*.
277. Sacco, *supra* n. 7, at 265; Capobianco, *supra* n. 241, at 308; Monateri, *supra* n. 9, at 428; Bigliazzi Geri, *supra* n. 231, at 42; Bianca, *supra* n. 226, at 420.
278. Cass. 25 maggio 2000, n. 6874, in *Rep. Foro it.*, 2004, voce "Contratto in genere", n. 460, www.foroitaliano.it (accessed December 7, 2018).
279. Monateri, *supra* n. 9, at 428 et seq.
280. Sacco, *supra* n. 7, at 265; Capobianco, *supra* n. 241, at 307-308; Bigliazzi Geri, *supra* n. 231, at 42; Sangermano, *supra* n. 71, at 135. However, Bianca is in the opinion that this rule is the primary criterion of subjective interpretation. Bianca, *supra* n. 226, at 415, 423-424.
281. Capobianco, *supra* n. 241, at 336.
282. Bianca, *supra* n. 226, at 422.
283. Capobianco, *supra* n. 241, at 336; Bianca, *supra* n. 226, at 423.

Monateri, however, regards this article as an objective rule of interpretation, which can only apply when the common intent of the parties cannot be determined through subjective interpretation.[284] This view is also in accordance with the case law of the *Corte di Cassazione*.[285]

As for Bigliazzi Geri, although she concurs that Article 1366 of the CC. It. is situated between the subjective and objective principles of interpretation and does not belong to either of them, she argues that contrary to Capobianco's view, this rule is the last one to apply among the rules of interpretation. According to her, the principle of good faith and fair dealing is the last one to be considered for resolving a dispute because the aim of interpretation is to overcome ambiguity, and this principle only applies when an ambiguity cannot be overcome through the rules of subjective interpretation in Articles 1362-1365 of the CC. It. and the rules of objective interpretation in Articles 1367-1371 of the CC. It.[286]

[6] Provisions of the Italian Civil Code Relating to the Interpretation of Contracts

[a] Article 1362 of the CC. It.

Intent of the Contracting Parties

> That which is the common intent of the parties, not limited to the literal meaning of the words, shall be sought in interpreting the contract.
>
> In order to ascertain the common intent of the parties, the general course of their behavior, including that subsequent to the conclusion of the contract, shall be taken into account.[287]

Italian legislators first laid down the most basic principle of the interpretation of contracts in the first paragraph of Article 1362.[288] Sacco writes that the "common intent" criterion is appropriate, as it aims to prevent a result that would be contrary to the will of one or both of the parties. By this criterion, legislators made a choice for the judge to interpret an ambiguous contract in accordance with the intent of the parties, instead of rewriting it against the parties' will.[289]

---

284. Monateri, *supra* n. 9, at 447.
285. Cass. 27 maggio 2003, n. 8411, in *Rep. Foro it.*, 2003, voce "Contratto in genere", n. 415, www.foroitaliano.it (accessed December 7, 2018); Cass. 18 maggio 2001, n. 6819, in *Foro it.*, 2001, I, 3183, www.foroitaliano.it (accessed December 7, 2018).
286. Bigliazzi Geri, *supra* n. 231, at 42.
287. "*Art. 1362 Intenzione dei contraenti Nell'interpretare il contratto si deve indagare quale sia stata la comune intenzione delle parti e non limitarsi al senso letterale delle parole.*
    Per determinare la comune intenzione delle parti, si deve valutare il loro comportamento complessivo anche posteriore alla conclusione del contratto." www.jus.unitn.it (accessed December 7, 2018), translation by Mario Beltramo, Giovanni E. Longo, John Henry Merryman, *The Italian Civil Code*, 352 (Oceana, 1969).
288. Capobianco, *supra* n. 241, at 301.
289. Sacco, *supra* n. 7, at 233-234.

According to Bigliazzi Geri, the principle stated in this paragraph is a subjective one, because by the words "common intent" the legislators refer to the intent of the authors of the contract and not to the subject matter of it. This intent exists before the dispute arises. In this phase, interpretation can only be subjective.[290]

As explained above, however,[291] although the reference to the "common intent" of the parties appears to be a subjective criterion, it is generally conceived of as an objective one. In accordance with this conception, the first and the most relevant tool for ascertainment of the common intent of the parties is the wording of the contract.[292] The *Corte di Cassazione* also adopts this approach regarding the priority of this objective tool of interpretation.[293] Therefore, the first step to be taken in the determination of the common intent of the parties, or the first step of the interpretation, is to ascertain a presumed objective meaning to their statements.[294]

According to Monateri, if the objective meaning of the wording of the contract is linguistically clear, which is the first tool of interpretation pursuant to Article 1362/1, then the secondary tools of interpretation mentioned in the second paragraph of the same article (i.e., general course of behavior of the parties) cannot be used.[295]

On the contrary, Capobianco and Gentili contend that judges are bound to take into account of all the evidence other than the wording of the contract as per Article 1362/1 of the CC. It. and that they must do so without regard to whether or not the meaning obtained from a literal interpretation is clear.[296] In addition, Capobianco establishes a link between this article and the principle of systematic interpretation and writes that in order to ascertain the meaning of a contract, judges must examine and compare the words and provisions of whole contracts, instead of focusing only on a provision or a part of it.[297] Moreover, Gentili adds that an accurate interpretation in the sense of Article 1362 of the CC. It. is only possible by observing the principle of good faith and fair dealing.[298]

Several conclusions stem from the first paragraph of Article 1362 of the CC. It. As stated above, there is an argument that this provision demonstrates that *in claris non fit interpretatio* has not been adopted as a rule by the Italian legislature, as it would prohibit an interpretation based only on wording.[299] The conclusion can also be drawn from this provision that judges are not bound by the parties' characterization of a contract.[300]

---

290. Bigliazzi Geri, *supra* n. 231, at 116.
291. *See*, section §3.02[B][4] Views Pertaining to the Objectivity of the Subjective Interpretation, *supra*.
292. Sacco, *supra* n. 7, at 255; Capobianco, *supra* n. 241, at 310; Monateri, *supra* n. 9, at 438; Gentili, *supra* n. 232, at 395; Bianca, *supra* n. 226, at 423.
293. Cass., 13 maggio 1998, n. 4811, in *Rep. Foro it.*, 1996, voce "Contratto in genere", n. 1740, www.foroitaliano.it (accessed December 7, 2018).
294. Sacco, *supra* n. 7, at 256.
295. Monateri, *supra* n. 9, at 438 and 445; Cass., 19 maggio 2000, n. 6482, in *Rep. Foro it.*, 2000, voce "Contratto in genere", n. 469, www.foroitaliano.it (accessed December 7, 2018).
296. Capobianco, *supra* n. 241, at 311; Gentili, *supra* n. 232, at 397.
297. Capobianco, *supra* n. 241, at 311.
298. Gentili, *supra* n. 232, at 364.
299. Capobianco, *supra* n. 241, at 313.
300. *Ibid.*, at 315.

Another conclusion that emerges from the same provision is the rule that *falsa demonstratio non nocet*, according to which a false description does not void an agreement. As per this rule, once the common intent of the parties has been determined, this intent is to be preferred over all the other objective means of interpretation.[301] This common intent is even superior to the wording of the contract. Hence if there was a misstatement of the will of one of the parties, the other party should have understood what the former party intended. However, this is only true when a common intent exists. A misstatement that is not correctly understood by the addressee is not binding upon the parties.[302]

The second paragraph of Article 1362 of the CC. It. deals with nonliteral interpretation. Nonliteral interpretation would normally have a limited field of application, where the wording of the agreement lacks clarity but insufficient determination of the basic terms of the deal does not invalidate the agreement. However, nonliteral interpretation becomes more relevant in unwritten contracts.[303]

The use of party conduct and behavior as a tool of interpretation is only possible when literal interpretation and holistic interpretation of the contract are insufficient for determination of the common intent of the parties.[304] Monateri argues, in accordance with this subsidiary position of nonliteral interpretation, that the behavior of the parties can only serve as proof of the meaning of a contract alleged by them but cannot be used for changing the content of the contract.[305]

In order for behavior to be taken into consideration in the interpretation of a contract in the sense of this provision, it has to be bilateral. This is so because unilateral behavior does not reflect a "common" intent.[306] However, bilateral behavior can also be inferred through the acceptance by one of the parties of the behavior of the other.[307]

Article 1362/2 of the CC. It. requires taking into account all of the behaviors of the parties, including behavior before the conclusion of the contract, during the negotiations, and after its conclusion.[308] The law imperatively requires a chronological assessment of the behavior of the parties before and during the negotiations and after the conclusion of the contract,[309] because party statements and behavior should be interpreted in their chronological order.

301. Sacco, *supra* n. 7, at 253; Capobianco, *supra* n. 241, at 317.
302. Capobianco, *supra* n. 241, at 317.
303. Monateri, *supra* n. 9, at 439.
304. *Ibid.*, at 445; Cass., 19 maggio 2000, n. 6482, in *Rep. Foro it.*, 2000, voce "Contratto in genere", n. 469, www.foroitaliano.it (accessed December 7, 2018).
305. Monateri, *supra* n. 9, at 446.
306. Bigliazzi Geri, *supra* n. 231, at 134-135; Monateri, *supra* n. 9, at 445; Cass., 13 settembre 2004, n. 18352, in *Rep. Foro it.*, 2004, voce "Contratto in genere", n. 455, www.foroitaliano.it (accessed December 7, 2018).
307. Monateri, *supra* n. 9, at 445; Bianca, *supra* n. 226, at 430; Cass., sez., lav., 13 agosto 2001, n. 11089, in *Rep. Foro it.*, 2001, voce "Contratto in genere", n. 380, www.foroitaliano.it (accessed December 7, 2018).
308. Alpa, *supra* n. 250, at 342.
309. Monateri, *supra* n. 9, at 426.

[b] *Article 1363 of the CC. It.*

Comprehensive Interpretation of Clauses

> Every clause of the contract is interpreted with reference to all the others, attributing to each the meaning resulting from the act as a whole.[310]

This article addresses the principle known as "systematic interpretation" in legal literature.[311] Through this provision, the legislators aimed at consistency in the interpretation of contracts.[312] The principle of systematic interpretation requires a contract to be interpreted as a whole and not merely the interpretation of a provision or expression of the contract that is the subject of the interpretation dispute.[313] This results in a logical connection between the provisions of Article 1363 and the literal interpretation set forth in the first paragraph of Article 1362.[314] In the interpretation of even one single article, the interpretation must be carried through in such a systematic manner that a coherent meaning can be read of the whole text of the contract.[315]

According to Sacco, a consequence of the relationship between the provisions of these two articles is that the rule stated in Article 1363 of the CC. It. should logically apply before even the most basic rule of interpretation set forth in Article 1362/1 of the CC. It.[316] Monateri also adheres to this view, adding that even if a provision to be interpreted is not ambiguous, it still has to be interpreted together with the other provisions of the contract.[317] Bigliazzi Geri, however, states that Article 1363 of the CC. It. should only apply when the meaning of an agreement cannot be determined by the method stated in Article 1362 of the CC. It. Yet, Geri acknowledges that all provisions of the contract constitute indications of the "common intent" of the parties in the sense of Article 1362/1 of the CC. It.[318]

Article 1363 of the CC. It. does not mean that judges are bound to examine all the provisions of a contract in order to interpret one of them. However, the legislators did not set any limitations regarding the scope of the provisions to be examined. It is up to a judge's discretion to decide which provisions of a contract are relevant for the purposes of interpreting any given provision. The provisions to be examined do not necessarily have to be valid. The purpose of their examination is establishing the facts relating to the respective positions of the parties and contributing to the interpretation of the contract. For this reason, invalid provisions can also be used for the purposes of

310. "*Art. 1363 Interpretazione complessiva delle clausole Le clausole del contratto si interpretano le une per mezzo delle altre, attribuendo a ciascuna il senso che risulta dal complesso dell'atto.*" www.jus.unitn.it (accessed December 7, 2018), translation by Beltramo, Longo, Merryman, *supra* n. 287, at 352.
311. Sacco, *supra* n. 7, at 278-279; Bigliazzi Geri, *supra* n. 231, at 167.
312. Bigliazzi Geri, *supra* n. 231, at 167.
313. Alpa, *supra* n. 250, at 343; Monateri, *supra* n. 9, at 440; Astone, *supra* n. 76, at 452.
314. Monateri, *supra* n. 9, at 440.
315. *Ibid.*; Cass., 11 guigno 1999, n. 5747, in *Rep. Foro it.*, 1999, voce "Contratto in genere," n. 441, www.foroitaliano.it (accessed December 7, 2018).
316. Sacco, *supra* n. 7, at 278-279.
317. Monateri, *supra* n. 9, at 439.
318. Bigliazzi Geri, *supra* n. 231, at 169.

interpretation.[319] What counts in the determination of the provisions to be examined is their function as the elements that constitute the transaction.[320]

[c] *Articles 1364 and 1365 of the CC. It.*

Articles 1364 and 1365 of the CC. It. set forth two basic principles of literal interpretation. The first lays down a narrow rule of interpretation, whereas the second states an expansive rule of interpretation.[321] These provisions have been discussed in the literature but are hardly applied in practice.[322]

Article 1364 of the CC. It. reads that:

> **General expressions**
>
> No matter how general the expressions used in a contract, they only include the objects as to which the parties intended to contract.[323]

According to Article 1365 of the CC. It.:

> **Illustrative examples**
>
> When a case is mentioned in a contract in order to explain a clause, unmentioned cases to which the same clause could reasonably be extended are not presumed to be excluded.[324]

These provisions are, indeed, closely linked to the literal interpretation laid down in Article 1362/1 of the CC. It. These are more concrete provisions dealing with how to conduct literal interpretation intending to show how to determine the common intent of the parties without being limited to the literal meaning of the words.[325] According to Bigliazzi Geri, the criterion of reasonableness (*ragionevolezza*) could also perform the same function as these provisions.[326]

The rationale underlying these provisions is to protect the parties from their own deal. The parties to a contract may use general expressions with the aim of providing a remedy for every breach. The purpose of Article 1364 of the CC. It. is to secure the parties against excessive consequences of the general expressions that they used.[327]

---

319. Monateri, *supra* n. 9, at 441; Bianca, *supra* n. 226, at 432.
320. Capobianco, *supra* n. 241, at 319.
321. *Ibid.*, at 323.
322. Monateri, *supra* n. 9, at 444.
323. "*Art. 1364 Espressioni generali Per quanto generali siano le espressioni usate nel contratto, questo non comprende che gli oggetti sui quali le parti si sono proposte di contrattare.*" www.jus.unitn.it (accessed December 7, 2018), translation by Beltramo, Longo, Merryman, *supra* n. 287, at 352.
324. "*Art. 1365 Indicazioni esemplificative Quando in un contratto si è espresso un caso al fine di spiegare un patto, non si presumono esclusi i casi non espressi, ai quali, secondo ragione, può estendersi lo stesso patto.*" www.jus.unitn.it (accessed December 7, 2018), translation by Beltramo, Longo, Merryman, *supra* n. 287, at 352.
325. Capobianco, *supra* n. 241, at 322.
326. Bigliazzi Geri, *supra* n. 231, at 191-192 and 201-202.
327. Sacco, *supra* n. 7, at 285.

Article 1365 of the CC. It., however, is based on the assumption that the will of the parties is more comprehensive than an illustration they provided in their contract.[328] This is indeed a rule of logic of which the interpreter cannot be unaware. However, Italian legislators included these provisions into the CC. It. out of a concern that an interpreter might be reluctant to diverge from the wording of a contract, which might cause excessive consequences.[329]

[d] Article 1366 of the CC. It.

Interpretation of Good Faith

The contract shall be interpreted according to good faith.[330]

As mentioned above,[331] the use of the principle of good faith and fair dealing in the interpretation of contracts in today's legal systems is due to the work of Donellus. It should be emphasized however, that the principle stated in Article 1366 of the CC. It. is not a general principle of good faith and fair dealing but a specific aspect of it as a criterion of fair dealing (*lealtà*) in declarations of intent and reasonableness in the perception of them.[332] The *Corte di Cassazione* also applies the concept of "good faith" laid down in this article as a criterion of fair dealing and reasonableness. In this sense, good faith is a tool of interpretation that can only be used when the intent of the parties cannot be determined.[333] In accordance with this meaning, Bigliazzi Geri states that the title of this article "interpretation of good faith" ("*interpretazione di buona fede*") is misleading, and it should have been "interpretation according to good faith" ("*interpretazione secondo buona fede*").[334]

The rule of interpretation according to good faith requires an interpretation of the contract according to its economic purpose and therefore an understanding of the allocation of risks and benefits according to this purpose.[335] Furthermore, in the event of two contradictory provisions of a contract, the provision that is more beneficial for the parties should be preferred, without prejudice to Article 1367 of the CC. It. laying down the principle to opt for an interpretation that would render the contract valid.[336]

328. Bianca, *supra* n. 226, at 434-435.
329. Sacco, *supra* n. 7, at 288-289.
330. "*Art. 1366 Interpretazione di buona fede Il contratto deve essere interpretato secondo buona fede,*" www.jus.unitn.it (accessed December 7, 2018), author's translation.
331. *See*, section §2.02 Humanist and Naturalist Schools of Law and the Divergence of Approaches among Continental Legal Systems, *supra*.
332. Monateri, *supra* n. 9, at 447.
333. Cass. 27 maggio 2003, n. 8411, in *Rep. Foro it.*, 2003, voce "Contratto in genere," n. 415, www.foroitaliano.it (accessed December 7, 2018); Cass. 18 maggio 2001, n. 6819, in *Foro it.*, 2001, I, 3183, www.foroitaliano.it (accessed December 7, 2018).
334. Bigliazzi Geri, *supra* n. 231, at 209-210.
335. Alpa, *supra* n. 250, at 343.
336. Monateri, *supra* n. 9, at 460; Cass., 27 marzo 1996, n. 2773, in *Rep. Foro it.*, 1996, voce "Contratto in genere", n. 308, www.foroitaliano.it (accessed December 7, 2018).

As explained above, the position of this provision in the hierarchy of the rules of interpretation is controversial in Italian law, as opposed to German law where the principle of interpretation according to good faith holds a very strong position.[337]

However, it is not controversial that "good faith" means objective good faith or fair dealing rather than subjective good faith.[338] In other words, this provision does not direct the meaning as understood by a good faith addressee to be taken as a basis for interpretation.[339]

According to some authors, this provision must be read together with Article 1362/1 of the CC. It., providing for a determination of the "common intent" of the parties. In practical terms, there is no difference between a literal interpretation and an interpretation according to good faith, since the purpose of literal interpretation is to determine the intent of the parties in accordance with the principle of good faith and fair dealing.[340]

[e] Article 1367 of the CC. It.

Preservation of Contract

> In case of doubt, the contract or the individual clauses shall be interpreted in the sense in which they can have some effect, rather than in that according to which they would have none.[341]

As stated above, it is uncontroversial that this and the provisions that follow are subsidiary rules of objective interpretation.[342] One of the reasons for which this provision is subsidiary is that for this rule to apply, the meaning of the contract or its individual clauses must be "in doubt" (*nel dubbio*). In other words, the common intent of the parties must not have been determined in the sense of Article 1362 of the CC. It.[343] For this reason, recourse may only be had to the rule stated in Article 1367 of the CC. It. if it is not possible to ascertain the common intent of the parties through subjective rules of interpretation.[344]

As Bigliazzi Geri points out, although Article 1367 CC. It. states that in the event of doubt, a contract or its individual clauses shall be interpreted in the sense in which they can have some effect, it is possible to invalidate a contract or individual clauses under Article 1366 of the CC. It. For this reason, these two articles may seem

337. *See*, section §3.03[A][3][c] § 157 of the BGB, *infra*.
338. Bigliazzi Geri, *supra* n. 231, at 212; Capobianco, *supra* n. 241, at 337-338.
339. Bigliazzi Geri, *supra* n. 231, at 212.
340. Monateri, *supra* n. 9, at 448; Bigliazzi Geri, *supra* n. 231, at 212.
341. "*Art. 1367 Conservazione del contratto Nel dubbio, il contratto o le singole clausole devono interpretarsi nel senso in cui possono avere qualche effetto, anziché in quello secondo cui non ne avrebbero alcuno.*" www.jus.unitn.it (accessed December 7, 2018), translation by Beltramo, Longo, Merryman, *supra* n. 287, at 352.
342. *See*, section §3.02[B][5] Classification of the Provisions of the Italian Civil Code Relating to the Interpretation of Contracts, *supra*.
343. Bigliazzi Geri, *supra* n. 231, at 305; Capobianco, *supra* n. 241, at 347.
344. Monateri, *supra* n. 9, at 451; Cass., sez. lav., 20 novembre 1997, n. 11574, in *Rep. Foro it.*, 1997, voce "Contratto in genere," n. 398, www.foroitaliano.it (accessed December 7, 2018).

contradictory. In order to overcome any contradiction between these articles, Article 1366 of the CC. It. should be conceived as a general principle, whereas Article 1367 of the CC. It. is to be regarded as a specific rule. According to Geri, Article 1366 of the CC. It. aims at a determination of common intent. However, Article 1367 of the CC. It. applies only where common intent cannot be determined and the meaning of a contract (or its individual clauses) is in doubt.[345]

In practice, Article 1367 of the CC. It. is treated as a rule of interpretation based on the principle of good faith and fair dealing.[346] This is because, in practice, debtor parties typically rely on an interpretation of contracts that does not support the allegations that they undertook the obligation for which enforcement is being sought. In such cases, however, the law requires that the contract or its individual clauses be interpreted in the sense in which they can have some effect, as set forth in Article 1367 of the CC. It.[347]

According to Capobianco, Article 1367 of the CC. It. is the expression of a specific aspect of the general principle of *favor negotii* or *favor validitatis* in the field of interpretation of contracts. By this provision, it is enounced that ambiguous or erroneous expressions would not affect the validity of the contract, and for this provision to apply there must be a doubt between two possible meanings.[348]

[f] Article 1368 of the CC. It.

General Interpretative Practices

> Ambiguous clauses are interpreted according to the general practice in the place in which the contract was concluded.
>
> In contracts in which one of the parties is an enterpriser (2082), ambiguous clauses are interpreted according to the general practice of the place where the enterprise has its headquarters.[349]

This article lays down another subsidiary rule of objective interpretation, and recourse may be had to this rule only when the criterion of reasonableness is not sufficient to overcome an ambiguity in the meaning of the clauses or contracts.[350] For local practices to be taken as a basis for interpretation, these must reflect the "common" intent of the parties. In other words, the parties to the contract must be

345. Bigliazzi Geri, *supra* n. 231, at 314-316.
346. Cass., 1 settembre 1997, n. 8301, in *Rep. Foro it.*, 1997, voce "Contratto in genere", n. 450, www.foroitaliano.it (accessed December 7, 2018).
347. Monateri, *supra* n. 9, at 449-450.
348. Capobianco, *supra* n. 241, at 347.
349. "*Art. 1368 Pratiche generali interpretative Le clausole ambigue s'interpretano secondo ciò che si pratica generalmente nel luogo in cui il contratto è stato concluso. Nei contratti in cui una delle parti è un imprenditore (2082), le clausole ambigue s'interpretano secondo ciò che si pratica generalmente nel luogo in cui è la sede dell'impresa.*" www.jus.unitn.it (accessed December 7, 2018), translation by Beltramo, Longo, Merryman, *supra* n. 287, at 352.
350. Bigliazzi Geri, *supra* n. 231, at 337; Monateri, *supra* n. 9, at 455.

aware of these practices and must have expressly or impliedly declared their intent to be bound by them.[351]

When both parties are tradespeople and have their places of business at the same location, a conflict may arise between parties in different business sectors. According to Bianca, the practice of the sector of the provider of the goods or services prevails in this situation.[352]

Biglazzi Geri also points out the possibility of a contradiction between this article and the principle of *contra stipulatorem* laid down in Article 1370 of the CC. It. The author states that a possible contradiction can be avoided by considering that both articles lay down subsidiary rules, which can only apply in cases of a failure to determine the meaning through subjective interpretation and that the meaning to be determined through these provisions must comply with the criterion of objective good faith (fair dealing) set forth in Article 1366 of the CC. It.[353] According to Bianca, however, the rule laid down in Article 1370 prevails over the rule stated in Article 1368.[354]

[g] Article 1369 of the CC. It.

Expressions with Several Possible Meanings

> In case of doubt, expressions which can have more than one meaning shall be understood in the sense most suitable to the nature and object of the contract.[355]

The two prerequisites for this provision to apply are the presence of more than one possible meaning and the presence of a doubt between these meanings.[356] For this reason, this provision is an objective rule of interpretation aiming to overcome doubt. According to one view, the character of the contract is the subject matter of this provision.[357] According to another view, however, this provision is a reminder for the rule of interpretation according to the understanding of a reasonable third person.[358]

351. Monateri, *supra* n. 9, at 455.
352. Bianca, *supra* n. 226, at 439.
353. Bigliazzi Geri, *supra* n. 231, at 337.
354. Bianca, *supra* n. 226, at 441-442.
355. "*Art. 1369 Espressioni con più sensi Le espressioni che possono avere più sensi devono, nel dubbio, essere intese nel senso più conveniente alla natura e all'oggetto del contratto.*" www.jus.unitn.it (accessed December 7, 2018), translation by Beltramo, Longo, Merryman, *supra* n. 287, at 352-353.
356. Bigliazzi Geri, *supra* n. 231, at 345-346; Monateri, *supra* n. 9, at 456.
357. Bigliazzi Geri, *supra* n. 231, at 347.
358. Sacco, *supra* n. 7, at 312.

[h] *Article 1370 of the CC. It.*

Interpretation Against the Author of Provision

> Provisions contained in the standard conditions of a contract or in forms or formularies which have been prepared by one of the contracting parties, are interpreted, in case of doubt, in favor of the other.[359]

Contrary to Roman law, uniform law,[360] French law,[361] and the Romano-Germanic legal family,[362] the *contra stipulatorem* or *contra proferentem* rule dealt with by this provision is not regarded as a general principle in Italian law. For example, this provision of the CC. It. differs from Article 4.6 of the UPICC, because it applies only to standard conditions or forms.[363] This being the case, according to Capobianco, this is a general principle and it is superior to all the other rules of interpretation.[364] Considering that the principle of *contra stipulatorem* is based on the principle of good faith and fair dealing[365] and that there is already a provision in Italian law laying down a more specific aspect of this principle for consumer contracts,[366] Capobianco's view seems reasonable.

Nevertheless, Article 1370 of the CC. It. is an exceptional rule, because it provides a rule that can lead to a result contrary to the will and benefits of one of the parties, by contrast with the rules aiming at determination of the intent of the parties. This rule constitutes one of the limits to the freedom of contract. Therefore, this provision is one of the last resorts in the interpretation of contracts.[367]

According to Monateri, since the *contra stipulatorem* rule set forth in Article 1370 of the CC. It. is a last resort, it can also apply to contracts that are not standard form contracts when all the other rules of interpretation are insufficient to resolve the dispute, or when levels of education and expertise of one of the parties are higher than the those of the other party, and the former party prepared the contract and submitted it to the latter party for it to sign. However, in these cases, it is also possible to reach the solution of interpreting a contract against the party who drafted it through the principle

359. "*Art. 1370 Interpretazione contro l'autore della clausola Le clausole inserite nelle condizioni generali di contratto (1341) o in moduli o formulari (1342) predisposti da uno dei contraenti s'interpretano, nel dubbio, a favore dell'altro.*" www.jus.unitn.it (accessed December 7, 2018), translation by Beltramo, Longo, Merryman, *supra* n. 287, at 353.
360. *See*, section §4.03[B][6] Article 4.6 of the UPICC, *infra*.
361. *See*, section §3.02[A][4][c] Article 1190 (Former Article 1162) of the CC. Fr., *supra*.
362. *See*, sections §3.03[A][3][c] § 157 of the BGB; §3.03[B][5] Principles of Interpretation Developed Through Case Law; §3.03[C][2][e] Article 23 of the TBK and the *Contra Stipulatorem* Rule, *infra*.
363. Alpa, *supra* n. 250, at 343.
364. Capobianco, *supra* n. 241, at 360.
365. Monateri, *supra* n. 9, at 458; Bianca, *supra* n. 226, at 440.
366. Capobianco, *supra* n. 241, at 360. Capobianco refers to Art. 35(2) of the Italian Consumers Code that reads as follows: "*In caso di dubbio sul senso di una clausola, prevale l'interpretazione più favorevole al consumatore.*" ("In case of doubt about the meaning of a clause, an interpretation more favorable to consumer prevails." Author's translation) http://www.adusbef.veneto.it/normativa%20nazionale%20testi%20di%20legge/codice%20consumo%20%20approvato.pdf (accessed December 7, 2018).
367. Monateri, *supra* n. 9, at 457.

of interpretation according to good faith and fair dealing, without the need to resort to the *contra stipulatorem* rule.[368]

The application of this principle by the *Corte di Cassazione* has been very limited and exceptional in practice. It has been very limited because the *Corte di Cassazione* stated that this principle could apply only when the whole text of the contract is written by one of the parties for use in multiple transactions and has only been submitted to the other party for its approval.[369] It has also been very exceptional because the *Corte di Cassazione* ruled that the application of Article 1370 of the CC. It. is only possible when a determination of the common intent of the parties is not possible through the rules of subjective interpretation as laid down in Articles 1362-1365 of the CC. It. on the condition that a detailed reasoning for the insufficiency of a literal interpretation has been provided.[370]

[i] Article 1371 of the CC. It.

Final Rules

> When, notwithstanding the application of the rules contained in this chapter, the contract remains obscure, it shall be understood in the sense least burdensome for the debtor, if it is gratuitous, and in the case of a non-gratuitous contract, in the sense which equitably reconciles the interests of the parties.[371]

Article 1371 of the CC. It. is the very last resort in the interpretation of contracts, which may be also seen from its position as the final article among the rules of interpretation in the CC. It.[372] Therefore, the criterion of equity in this provision applies even after the criterion of good faith and fair dealing in Article 1366 of the CC. It.[373] Although the legislators distinguished between these two criteria, it is impossible to draw a sharp line between them.[374] Both criteria are expressions of the rules of objective interpretation. It can be stated that the main difference between these two provisions is that Article 1366 of the CC. It. aims at a determination of the intent of the parties, whereas the criterion of equity in Article 1371 of the CC. It. applies in the event of a failure to ascertain intent.[375]

368. *Ibid.*, at 458.
369. Cass., 27 maggio 2003, n. 8411, in *Rep. Foro it.*, 2003, voce "Contratto in genere", n. 414, www.foroitaliano.it (accessed December 7, 2018).
370. Cass. 28 gennaio 2005, n. 1754, in *Rep. Foro it.*, 2005, voce "Assicurazione (contratto)", n. 114, www.foroitaliano.it (accessed December 7, 2018).
371. "*Art. 1371 Regole finali Qualora, nonostante l'applicazione delle norme contenute in questo capo (1362 e seguenti), il contratto rimanga oscuro, esso deve essere inteso nel senso meno gravoso per l'obbligato, se è a titolo gratuito, e nel senso che realizzi l'equo contemperamento degli interessi delle parti, se è a titolo oneroso.*" www.jus.unitn.it (accessed December 7, 2018), translation by Beltramo, Longo, Merryman, *supra* n. 287, at 353.
372. Capobianco, *supra* n. 241, at 366.
373. Bigliazzi Geri, *supra* n. 231, at 232-233.
374. *Ibid.*, at 233.
375. *Ibid.*, at 234-235

According to a decision of the *Corte di Cassazione*, this provision is also a subsidiary rule of interpretation and applies only when the rules of literal interpretation (Articles 1362-1365 of the CC. It.) remain insufficient to ascertain the meaning of a contract.[376] For this reason, this provision is rarely applied in practice.[377]

Article 1371 of the CC. It. makes a distinction between gratuitous and non-gratuitous contracts. The *favor debitoris* rule applies in the former, while the interests of the parties are to be reconciled equitably in the latter.[378] In non-gratuitous contracts, the balance of interests of the parties should be considered as of the date of the conclusion of the contract and not on the date of the court's decision.[379] In cases where supervening circumstances fundamentally alter the balance of interests of the parties to a contract, the provision to be applied is Article 1467 of the CC. It. addressing hardship (*eccessiva onerosità*)[380] and not those on the interpretation of contracts.

The solution provided by this article for the interpretation of non-gratuitous contracts has been criticized in the literature. Bigliazzi Geri alleges that the purpose of the provision of Article 1371 of the CC. It. is unclear in light of the principle of interpretation according to good faith and fair dealing contained in Article 1366 of the CC. It.[381] According to Monateri, this provision was based on the assumption that the parties aimed at establishing a balance of interests while making their contract and applies when the meaning of the contract cannot be determined. However, if the contract is validly concluded and its essential terms are sufficiently clear, then there should be no obstacle to interpret it according to Article 1362 of the CC. It. Therefore, the practical function of Article 1371 of the CC. It. is in doubt.[382]

§3.03 ROMANO-GERMANIC LEGAL FAMILY

[A] German Law

[1] Generally

The history of German law has witnessed the dominance of both narrow and broad legislation regarding the interpretation of contracts, first laying down detailed provisions and subsequently limiting them to a few sentences. The latter policy emerged as a reaction to the former and has shaped today's German legislation on the question. The practice of reducing the provisions on the interpretation of contracts is based on the idea of leaving a great deal of space for judicial discretion.[383]

376. Cass. 16 febbraio 2005, n. 3099, in *Rep. Foro it.*, 2006, voce "Succesione ereditaria", n. 103, www.foroitaliano.it (accessed December 7, 2018).
377. Sacco, *supra* n. 7, at 321 and 324. Sacco refers only to one decision: Cass., 3 aprile 1979, n. 1891, in *GI*, 1980, I, 1, 1327.
378. Monateri, *supra* n. 9, at 459; Bigliazzi Geri, *supra* n. 231, at 375.
379. Sacco, *supra* n. 7, at 324.
380. Yıldırım, *supra* n. 64, at 61 et seq.
381. Bigliazzi Geri, *supra* n. 231, at 376.
382. Monateri, *supra* n. 9, at 458.
383. Vogenauer, *supra* n. 131, at 974.

General State Laws for the Prussian States (*Allgemeines Landrecht für die Preußichen Staaten*), also known as the Prussian Civil Code of 1794, included twenty-eight paragraphs on the interpretation of contracts and declarations of will. Besides these, there were also twelve more paragraphs regarding the interpretation of specific types of contracts. However, authors from the Romano-Germanic legal family started to question the appropriateness of the codification of the rules of interpretation starting in the mid-nineteenth century.[384] As a result of the discussions on this point and the efforts of the Historical School of Jurisprudence, in particular, the provisions on the interpretation of contracts and declarations of will were reduced to two very general paragraphs (§ 133 and § 157) in the BGB of 1900. This trend of limiting provisions on the interpretation of contracts continued with the Austrian and Greek Civil Codes and the Swiss[385] and Turkish[386] Codes of Obligations.

However, the principles of Roman law on the interpretation of contracts (such as *contra proferentem*, *favor negotii*, and *ut res mageat quam pereat*) continued to appear in the decisions of German courts. As will be shown in a later chapter, the trend of detailed and lengthy provisions on the interpretation of contracts has returned with the advent of uniform law texts, and the Historical School of Jurisprudence's position of addressing this issue in only a few provisions has remained limited to the Romano-Germanic legal family.[387]

The general approach by the Prussian Civil Code of 1794 was individualist, in accordance with the liberal thought underlying it. Therefore, this code adopted a subjective approach with respect to the interpretation of contracts. However, the BGB of 1900 adopted a more collectivist approach, focusing on the social aspects of law. Unlike the Prussian Civil Code, the BGB is not opposed to judicial intervention in contracts.[388] The doctrine of "*Treu und Glauben*" (good faith and fair dealing) underlies this shift in perspective. The Naturalist School of Law and in particular Hugo Grotius' criticism of the subjective approach of Roman law played an important role in this shift.[389]

The objective approach to the interpretation of contracts was adopted in German law as a result of this shift in perspective, differing not only from most Latin jurisdictions but also from the other Romano-Germanic jurisdictions.[390] In accordance with the objective theory, when interpreting declarations of intent, the focus is not on what the party making the declaration meant but on what a reasonable third person would understand from the declaration. If the meaning that the addressee understood from the declaration is afforded legal protection, then there is no room to determine the "real intent."[391]

384. Reinhard Zimmermann, *The New German Law of Obligations—Historical and Comparative Perspectives*, 8 et seq. (2nd ed., Oxford University Press, 2010).
385. *See*, section §3.03[B][1] Generally, *infra*.
386. *See*, section §3.03[C][2] Interpretation of Contracts in Modern Turkish Law, *infra*.
387. *See*, section §4.01 Generally, *infra*.
388. Zimmermann, *supra* n. 11, at 636-637; Vogenauer, *supra* n. 131, at 975.
389. *See*, section §2.02 Humanist and Naturalist Schools of Law and the Divergence of Approaches among Continental Legal Systems, *supra*; Zimmermann, *supra* n. 11, at 636-637.
390. Vogenauer, *supra* n. 131, at 975.
391. Zimmermann, *supra* n. 11, at 636.

Contrary to the other continental jurisdictions, but as is the case with U.S. law,[392] German law makes a distinction between the ascertainment of the meaning of a contract or a declaration of intent and the determination of its legal consequences. The meaning of contract or declaration of intent must be legally valid. In this sense, interpretation is a legal issue, and it is conducted ex officio by the judge.[393]

The distinction between the determination of the content of a contract or declaration of intent and its legal consequences bears important consequences pertaining to the reviewability of court decisions on these issues. Some issues in the content of the decisions are considered reviewable, while others are not.[394]

Since the determination of the content of a declaration of intent is a question of fact, decisions by the courts of first instance regarding this issue are not reviewable.[395] There is no doubt, however, that questions of law are reviewable pursuant to § 545 and § 546 of the Code of Civil Procedure (*Zivilprozessordnung*, ZPO).[396] Accordingly, appellate courts review the application of provisions on interpretation, generally recognized principles of interpretation, and the rules of logic.[397]

An error by the courts of first instance in the application of the general principles of interpretation, and in particular, erroneous interpretation of contract terms contrary to their usual meaning, is a legal question and important grounds for appeal.[398]

The burden of proof for facts lies on the party who relies on a particular interpretation of the contract or declaration of intent.[399] For this reason, the proof of facts underlying the real intent of the parties, or the fact that the addressee was aware of these facts, is considered to be an issue of fact and relies upon the party who asserts them.[400]

[2] Types or Methods of Interpretation in German Law

In German law, a basic distinction is made between explanatory interpretation (*einfache Auslegung*) and complementary interpretation (*ergänzende Auslegung*). Since the approach of German law is to interpret contracts based on the objective

392. *See*, section §3.04[B][1] Generally, *infra*.
393. Dirk Looschelders, *§ 133*, in Thomas Heidel, Rainer Hüßtege, Heinz-Peter Mansel, Ulrich Noack (eds.), *Nomos Kommentar, BGB Allgemeiner Teil/EGBGB, Band 1*, n. 99 (3rd ed., Nomos, 2016).
394. Looschelders, *supra* n. 393, at n. 105.
395. *Ibid.*, at n. 103.
396. *Ibid.*, at, n. 104; Bernhard Appelhoff, *Die Revisibilität der Auslegung von typischen Verträgen nach der Rechtsprechung*, PhD Thesis, 14 et seq. (University of Cologne, 1935).
397. Looschelders, *supra* n. 393, at n. 105.
398. *Ibid.*, at, n. 107 vd.; Reinhard Singer, *§ 133*, in Berg von J. Staudinger (ed.), *J. von Staudingers Kommentar zum Bürgerlichen Gesetzbuch: Staudinger BGB—Buch 1: Allgemeiner Teil*, n. 45 (15th ed., Sellier-De Gruyter, 2017); BGH LM [C] Nr. 17; RGZ 105, 417, 419 and BGH LM (Fb) Nr. 4. If the parties agreed upon a specific meaning of a term, that meaning prevails. BGH NJW 1999, 3191, 3191 f. = LM § 157 (C) Nr. 60; NJW-RR 1995, 364, 364 f.; 1994, 1008, 1009.
399. Jan Busche, *§ 133*, in Franz Jürgen Säcker, Rolan Rixecker (eds.), *Münchener Kommentar zum Bürgerlichen Gesetzbuch, Band 1 Allgemeiner Teil §§ 1-240, ProstG, AGG*, n. 66 (7th ed., C.H. Beck, 2015); Singer, *supra* n. 398, at n. 76; Looschelders, *supra* n. 393, at n. 100.
400. Looschelders, *supra* n. 393, at n. 100.

theory, complementary interpretation and objective interpretation are not considered to be identical, as is the case in French law.[401]

Explanatory interpretation can be either subjective or objective. Subjective interpretation is based on the will of the party making the declaration of intent as a psychological fact. In objective interpretation, however, what is at stake is how the addressee understood or should have understood the declaration of intent. If the interpretation pertains to the meaning of a declaration, normative interpretation (*normativ Auslegung*) is in question. If the interpretative activity departs from the elements that played a role in the transaction, this is a typological interpretation (*typisierende Auslegung*).[402]

Apart from these, some of the other types of interpretation mentioned in the literature are grammatical, historical, logical, systematic, and teleological interpretations.[403] These types of interpretation are laid down as "rules" (not types) of interpretation in the provisions of the French[404] and Italian[405] Civil Codes. Differing from French and Italian laws, German law does not provide for a hierarchy among these types of interpretation.[406] Judges can decide which of these methods to use according to the circumstances specific to each case and by using the broad discretion granted by § 133 of the BGB.[407]

The activity of interpretation begins with an ascertainment of the meaning of individual words used in a contract or declaration of intent.[408] The expressions of the parties are the first and most important basis for interpretation.[409] These are conceived in their normal, usual meaning.[410] Dictionaries may be employed for a determination of that meaning.[411] This method of interpretation, which is indeed a literal interpretation, is referred to as grammatical interpretation (*grammatische Auslegung*).[412]

Interpretation begins with a determination of the significance of one word but does not end there. Regard must be paid to the location of the word in the sentence and in the whole declaration of intent. This method of interpretation is known as systematic interpretation (*systematische Auslegung*).[413]

Apart from grammatical and systematic methods of interpretation, there is also the method of historical interpretation (*historische Auslegung*). The purpose of this

401. *See*, section §3.02[A][2] Classification of the Types of Interpretation and the Relationship Between Subjective and Objective Interpretation, *supra*.
402. Busche, *supra* n. 399, at n. 6.
403. Looschelders, *supra* n. 393, at nn. 67 et seq.; Busche, *supra* n. 399, at nn. 6-7.
404. *See*, section §3.02[A][4] Provisions of the French Civil Code Relating to the Interpretation of Contracts, *supra*.
405. *See*, section §3.02[B][6] Provisions of the Italian Civil Code Relating to the Interpretation of Contracts, *supra*.
406. Singer, *supra* n. 398, at n. 70.
407. Busche, *supra* n. 399, at n. 65.
408. Looschelders, *supra* n. 393, at, n. 30.
409. BGH LM [C] Nr. 7; LM [Fb] Nr. 4; OLG München NJW-RR 1996, 239; Busche, *supra* n. 399, at n. 56.
410. Singer, *supra* n. 398, at n. 45.
411. OLG München NJW-RR 1996, 239.
412. Looschelders, *supra* n. 393, at n. 68.
413. *Ibid.*, at n. 69; Busche, *supra* n. 399, at n. 7.

method is to determine the thought underlying a declaration of intent. In this method, courts consider the purpose of the party in making the declaration of intent, the particular circumstances of that party while making the declaration, and any previous declarations or negotiations to the extent that the addressee was aware of them.[414]

In teleological interpretation (*teleologische Auslegung*), a declaration of intent is instead interpreted according to the purpose or reason for the legal transaction. This is an objective method of interpretation, and it only applies when the subjective intent of the parties cannot be determined. Teleological interpretation departs from the presumption that fair parties would distribute their benefits in an equitable manner and aims instead at equitable interpretation.[415]

[3] Provisions of the BGB Relating to the Interpretation of Contracts (§ 133 and § 157 of the BGB)

The general provisions of the BGB regarding the interpretation of contracts are §133 dealing with the interpretation of declarations of intent and § 157 dealing with the interpretation of contracts. These read as follows:

§ 133 Interpretation of a Declaration of Intent

> When a declaration of intent is interpreted, it is necessary to ascertain the true intention rather than adhering to the literal meaning of the declaration.[416]

§ 157 Interpretation of Contracts

> Contracts are to be interpreted as required by good faith, taking customary practice into consideration.[417]

[a] Relationship Between the Two Paragraphs

It can be observed that the legislators intended to distinguish between the spheres of application of § 133 and § 157 of the BGB while enacting the BGB. The former was intended to apply to the interpretation of declarations of intent, whereas the latter would apply to the interpretation of contracts. However, the practice has shown that it

414. Looschelders, *supra* n. 393, at n. 71; Busche, *supra* n. 399, at n. 7.
415. Looschelders, *supra* n. 393, at nn. 72-73; Busche, *supra* n. 399, at n. 7.
416. "*§ 133 Auslegung einer Willenserklärung Bei der Auslegung einer Willenserklärung ist der wirkliche Wille zu erforschen und nicht an dem buchstäblichen Sinne des Ausdrucks zu haften.*" http://www.gesetze-im-internet.de/bgb/ (accessed December 7, 2018), translation taken from https://www.gesetze-im-internet.de/englisch_bgb/englisch_bgb.html#p0406 (accessed December 7, 2018).
417. "*§ 157 Auslegung von Verträgen Verträge sind so auszulegen, wie Treu und Glauben mit Rücksicht auf die Verkehrssitte es erfordern.*" yazarın çevirisi, http://www.gesetze-im-internet.de/bgb/ (accessed December 7, 2018), translation taken from https://www.gesetze-im-internet.de/englisch_bgb/englisch_bgb.html#p0406 (accessed December 7, 2018).

was not possible to clearly distinguish between the spheres of application of these provisions and that they could be applied together.[418] A sharp line cannot be drawn between the spheres of application of these paragraphs, because declarations of intent are the subject matter of § 133 of the BGB, but particular corresponding declarations of intent create a contract, which is the subject matter of § 157 of the BGB.[419]

Nonetheless, there is a difference between these two paragraphs in terms of the methodology they provide: while § 133 of the BGB is based on the true intent of the parties, which is a subjective criterion, § 157 of the BGB lays down an objective criterion by being based upon the principle of good faith and fair dealing.[420] Moreover, the fact that § 157 of the BGB limits the interpretation of contracts through the principle of good faith and fair dealing, customary practice seems to be a contradiction as it gives the impression that the true intent of the parties is not relevant.[421]

Another difference between § 133 and § 157 of the BGB lies in their fields of application in terms of the types of interpretation. § 133 of the BGB applies to explanatory interpretation, whereas § 157 of the BGB applies to complementary interpretation.[422]

Although it appears from the text of § 133 of the BGB that it might only apply to the interpretation of declarations of intent, it is generally recognized that this paragraph also applies to the interpretation of contracts.[423] In order to interpret a contract, these declarations of intent must be interpreted first since the contract is composed of corresponding declarations of intent.[424] Written contracts signed by the parties are also their common declarations of intent. Additionally, some Swiss authors find the system in § 133 of the BGB providing for ascertainment of the meaning of declarations of intent before the determination of the common intent to be more appropriate than the Swiss method set forth in Article 18/1 of the OR, which provides for the interpretation of a contract as a whole.[425]

As a result, both § 133 and § 157 of the BGB apply to the interpretation of contracts, and there are no differences between them in this regard. While interpreting declarations of intent pursuant to § 133 of the BGB, the principle of good faith and customary practice must be taken into consideration, as set forth in § 157 of the BGB.[426]

418. Looschelders, *supra* n. 393, at n. 2.
419. Jan Busche, *§ 157*, in Franz Jürgen Säcker, Rolan Rixecker (eds.), *Münchener Kommentar zum Bürgerlichen Gesetzbuch, Band 1 Allgemeiner Teil §§ 1-240, ProstG, AGG*, nn. 1-2 (7th ed., C.H. Beck, 2015); Dirk Looschelders, *§ 157*, in Thomas Heidel, Rainer Hüßtege, Heinz-Peter Mansel, Ulrich Noack (eds.), *Nomos Kommentar, BGB Allgemeiner Teil/EGBGB, Band 1*, n. 1 (3rd ed., Nomos, 2016).
420. Busche, *supra* n. 399, at n. 17; Nicole Kornet, *Contract Interpretation and Gap Filling: Comparative and Theoretical Perspectives*, 96 (Intersentia, 2006).
421. Kornet, *supra* n. 420, at 96-97; Kramer, Schmidlin, *supra* n. 38, at n. 21.
422. Looschelders, *supra* n. 393, at nn. 4-5; Looschelders, *supra* n. 419, at n. 2; Busche, *supra* n. 419, at n. 2.
423. Busche, *supra* n. 399, at nn. 1 and 17; Kramer, Schmidlin, *supra* n. 38, at n. 21.
424. Looschelders, *supra* n. 419, at n. 1; Kornet, *supra* n. 420, at 96.
425. Kramer, Schmidlin, *supra* n. 38, at n. 21.
426. Looschelders, *supra* n. 393, at n. 36; Busche, *supra* n. 399, at n. 17; Busche, *supra* n. 419, at n. 2.

Likewise, in the application of § 157 of the BGB for the purpose of explanatory interpretation, the same principles that apply to the interpretation of declarations of intent under § 133 must apply too.[427] Indeed, both paragraphs constitute the basis of explanatory interpretation and complement each other.[428] Both of them have the same level of importance, neither of them is superior to the other, and there is no order of priority between them in their application.[429]

[b] § 133 of the BGB

§ 133 of the BGB is a very general provision and in the absence of detailed provisions regarding the interpretation of contracts and declarations of intent, it provides a great deal of room for judicial discretion. In terms of content, this limited provision does not direct the judge but merely states that he is not bound to the wording of the declarations of intent while interpreting them.[430]

The text of § 133 of the BGB suggests that it is the most subjective provision of interpretation possible, as it is based on a "true intention," and not even on a "common intent" as is the case in French, Italian, Swiss, and Turkish legal systems. This is because while writing this provision of the BGB in 1900, the German legislators adopted the will theory (*Willenstheorie*) that considers the true intent as a mental fact. In the debates that followed, however, the declaration theory (*Erklärungstheorie*) prevailed, according to which the true intent is not an internal intent but an expressed, external intent.[431] Pursuant to this objective theory, unexpressed internal intent is no longer the subject of interpretation.[432] Internal intent can only be taken into consideration in disputes regarding the validity of a contract and for determination of the content of the declaration of intent.[433] Likewise, the circumstances affecting the declaration of intent (such as the time and place of the conclusion of the contract, the conduct of the parties prior and subsequent to the conclusion of the contract, their statements in the negotiations, the aim of the transaction, and so on) are not proper subjects for interpretation. These can be taken into consideration only to the extent that they contribute to the ascertainment of the true intent.[434]

In the interpretation of contracts, the objective theory views the "true intention" in the sense of § 133 of the BGB as the "common" intent of the parties and not only the intent of the party making the declaration.[435] This "common" intent becomes relevant only when it is declared, as is the case in Italian law.[436] For this reason, only the circumstances subsequent to the receipt of the declaration of intent by the addressee

427. Busche, *supra* n. 419, at n. 3.
428. Busche, *supra* n. 399, at nn. 17-18; Kornet, *supra* n. 420, at 97.
429. Looschelders, *supra* n. 393, at n. 3; Singer, *supra* n. 398, at n. 3; Busche, *supra* n. 399, at n. 18.
430. Busche, *supra* n. 399, at n. 65.
431. *Ibid.*, at n. 9; Kornet, *supra* n. 420, at 98.
432. Singer, *supra* n. 398, at n. 1; Looschelders, *supra* n. 393, at nn. 25-26.
433. Looschelders, *supra* n. 393, at n. 25; Busche, *supra* n. 399, at n. 9.
434. Looschelders, *supra* n. 393, at n. 26.
435. *Ibid.*, at n. 37.
436. *See*, section §3.02[B][4] Views Pertaining to the Objectivity of the Subjective Interpretation, *supra*.

are taken into consideration in interpretation, and the meaning of the declaration of intent cannot be changed through interpretation after it reaches the addressee.[437]

Nevertheless, there is a distinction between the declarations directed to another party and the declarations that are not. The latter are unilateral acts such as last wills and testaments, and only the true intent of the party making the declaration is taken into consideration in the interpretation of these.[438]

In the interpretation of the former, however, the activity of interpretation begins with the ascertainment of the true intent of the party making the declaration (§ 133 of the BGB). Then, pursuant to the "objective" declaration theory, the meaning that an addressee ought to have understood according to the principle of good faith and fair dealing and customary practices is examined (§ 157 of the BGB). While doing so, regard must be paid to all the circumstances affecting the declaration of intent. In the event of a discrepancy between the meaning given by the party making the declaration and the meaning understood by the recipient, the latter party's understanding will be given more weight. This is because declarants are responsible for their declarations and must consider how the recipients understand their expressions.[439]

The obligation for courts to not only rely on the wording, which is stated in the second part of § 133 of the BGB, is an important principle of the interpretation of contracts. The presence of this principle among the limited codification of the rules of interpretation in German law is owed to the influence of the Naturalist School of Law. According to this principle, a provision or an expression in a contract should not be interpreted on its own; rather, it must be interpreted in the context of the whole contract and in light of all the circumstances and behavior of the parties that are relevant in determining the intent of the parties.[440]

Even though internal intent is not to be the subject of interpretation, in the event of a discrepancy between the wording of a declaration of intent or contract and the meaning given by the parties, the latter prevails according to both § 133 of the BGB and the principle of *falsa demonstratio non nocet*. This is because, in such a case, the addressee does not have a legitimate interest worthy of protection.[441] For instance, if the parties agreed upon the sale of whale meat, by using the term "*hakjöringsköd*," which actually means "shark meat" in Norwegian, and if the seller supplied shark meat, he will be deemed to have breached the contract.[442] However, if the parties did not agree upon the same meaning of the term, the meaning that the addressee understood in good faith will be applied.

In order to determine this point, courts must examine the circumstances in which a declaration of intent has been received. First, courts must look to the circumstances of which the addressee was aware, and second, courts must determine whether or not

437. Busche, *supra* n. 399, at n. 5; Singer, *supra* n. 398, at n. 51.
438. Looschelders, *supra* n. 393, at n. 39; Busche, *supra* n. 399, at nn. 10 et seq.; Singer, *supra* n. 398, at n. 15; Kornet, *supra* n. 420, at 98.
439. Busche, *supra* n. 399, at n. 28; Kornet, *supra* n. 420, at 101-103.
440. Busche, *supra* n. 399, at n. 58, Kornet, *supra* n. 420, at 103.
441. Looschelders, *supra* n. 393, at, nn. 46-47.
442. RGZ 99, 47, Zweigert, Kötz, *supra* n. 4, at 404; Canaris, Grigoleit, *supra* n. 5, at 454; Kornet, *supra* n. 420, at 99-100.

the addressee could reasonably rely upon an alternative meaning which is now being claimed.[443] In interpretation, the conduct of the party making the declaration, the economic purpose of the contract, and the history of negotiations are taken into consideration to the extent that they aid in ascertaining the meaning of the declaration of intent.[444] Local practices are not to be taken into consideration, however, because they are not deemed to constitute objective criteria. Local practices are only taken into consideration when they become customary rules.[445]

In German law, unlike Italian law,[446] there is no discussion on the *in claris non fit interpretatio* rule: the literature unanimously agrees that the determination of whether a declaration of intent is "clear" can be made only through an interpretation process, and therefore the said rule is not accepted as a legal principle.[447] This has also been confirmed through case law.[448]

One of the principles that has developed through the application of § 133 of the BGB is the principle of *protestatio facto contraria non valet*. According to this principle, if there is a contradiction between the contract and subsequent conduct of the parties, the latter is to be taken into consideration.[449] This principle is a consequence of the principle of good faith and fair dealing.[450]

The German courts also apply the *contra proferentem* rule, which is another special aspect of the principle of good faith and fair dealing.[451] This is an objective rule of interpretation and does not aim to determine the true intent. For this reason, when this rule applies, § 133 of the BGB does not.[452] However, this rule is not accepted as a general principle, and its application is exceptional, as appears from the case law on § 157 of the BGB.[453]

[c] § 157 of the BGB

§ 157 of the BGB states that the interpretation of contracts has two bases: the principle of good faith and fair dealing, and customary practice. The influence of the Naturalist

443. Looschelders, *supra* n. 393, at, n. 48.
444. BGHZ 109, 19, 22 f. = NJW 1990, 441; BGHZ 63, 359, 362 = NJW 1975, 536; BGH NJW 2003, 2235, 2236; 1999, 3191 = LM § 157 (C) Nr. 60; NJW 1987, 2437, 2438; Busche, *supra* n. 399, at n. 55.
445. Looschelders, *supra* n. 393, at, nn. 59 et seq.
446. *See*, section §3.02[B][2] The Discussion on the *In Claris Non Fit Interpretatio* Rule, *supra*.
447. Busche, *supra* n. 399, at nn. 53-55; Singer, *supra* n. 398, at n. 9; Looschelders points out that § 133 of the BGB does not refer to a "clear" statement, Looschelders, *supra* n. 393, at n. 27.
448. BGHZ 86, 41, 46 mwN = NJW 1983, 672; BGH NJW 2002, 1260, 1261; NJW-RR 1996, 1458; BAG NJW 2005, 1144, 1144 f.; DB 1975, 1368; RGZ 163, 324, 328 f.; 158, 119, 124.
449. BGHZ 95, 395, 399; BGH NJW 1965, 387, 388; NJW 2000, 3429, 3431; BGH MDR 2000, 956, 957; RGZ 111, 310, 312; RG JW 1921, 1313; Looschelders, *supra* n. 393, at n. 33; Singer, *supra* n. 398, at n. 59; Busche, *supra* n. 399, at n. 56.
450. Looschelders, *supra* n. 393, at n. 33.
451. BGH LM § 157 [A] Nr. 14; VersR 1971, 172, 173; NJW 1981, 313, 315 f.
452. Busche, *supra* n. 399, at n. 64; Singer, *supra* n. 398, at n. 62.
453. Looschelders, *supra* n. 393, at, n. 23.

School of Law, and Hugo Donellus in particular, is strongly felt in this paragraph.[454] Through this provision, German legislators intended to give judges a great deal of discretion. According to Zimmermann, however, the appropriateness of this provision is doubtful since it is too general and abstract.[455]

Even though § 157 of the BGB is premised upon good faith and fair dealing, it has a different significance from the concept of good faith and fair dealing stated in § 242 of the BGB because § 157 of the BGB treats good faith and fair dealing as a specific rule of interpretation, whereas § 242 of the BGB lays it down as a general principle.[456] The concept of good faith and fair dealing is used indirectly when applying § 133 and § 157 of the BGB, as an objective criterion for a determination of the facts.[457] However, the general principle of good faith and fair dealing in the sense of § 242 of the BGB applies directly, as is the case with the presumption of good faith.

As mentioned above,[458] § 157 of the BGB differs from § 133 of the BGB in that it is used for complementary interpretation.[459] The basic condition for this paragraph to apply for the purpose of complementary interpretation is the presence of a gap in the contract.[460] In complementary interpretation, courts consider "presumed will" of the parties, which is based on the principles of good faith and fair dealing and an equitable distribution of benefits, rather than subjective will of the parties.[461]

However, it is disputed whether complementary interpretation can be qualified as "interpretation." German law is dominated by the opinion that it could because the purpose of complementary interpretation in German law is to validate a meaning pertaining to a given legal transaction. In this sense, complementary interpretation provides no general rule; rather it only serves to fill a gap in a given contract with a rule specific to that relationship.[462] For this reason, courts apply § 157 of the BGB for the purpose of complementary interpretation in light of the circumstances specific to each case.[463]

Although the prevalent view is that there is no order of priority or hierarchy between § 133 and § 157 of the BGB, a decision of the *Reichsgerichts in Zivilsachen* (RGZ) held that the principle of good faith and fair dealing in the sense of § 157 of the BGB cannot apply when it is possible to determine the meaning of a contract through other means of interpretation and that it only applies when an ambiguity in a contract cannot be overcome by any other means.[464]

454. Schröder, *supra* n. 92, at 58; *See also*, section §2.02 Humanist and Naturalist Schools of Law and the Divergence of Approaches among Continental Legal Systems, *supra*.
455. Zimmermann, *supra* n. 11, at 639.
456. Busche, *supra* n. 419, at n. 4.
457. Looschelders, *supra* n. 393, at, n. 17.
458. *See*, section §3.03[A][3][a] Relationship Between the Two Paragraphs, *supra*.
459. BGB § 157 applies not only to the interpretation of contracts but also to the interpretation of unilateral declarations of will, such as last wills and testament. Busche, *supra* n. 419, at nn. 26 et seq.
460. Busche, *supra* n. 419, at n. 38.
461. *Ibid.*, at n. 28, and nn. 47 et seq.
462. Busche, *supra* n. 419, at n. 27.
463. Zimmermann, *supra* n. 11, at 639.
464. RGZ 148, 81, 93; Busche, *supra* n. 419, at n. 11.

The general and abstract nature of § 157 of the BGB has led to the development of more specific principles in its application. The most important of these principles is the principle of trust (*Vertrauensprinzip*), which is itself based on the principle of good faith and fair dealing. Pursuant to this principle, declarations of intent must be interpreted according to the understanding of a reasonable addressee. This principle is also valid in the application of § 133 of the BGB.[465]

The principle of trust also requires the parties to look after each other's benefits.[466] For this reason, courts must consider contracts made with third parties when interpreting contracts in dispute.[467] Additionally, this duty also requires courts to interpret contracts in a way that equitably distributes the interests of the parties.[468]

Likewise, the *contra proferentem* rule can also be applied since the obligation to look after the counterparty's benefits is a consequence of the principle of good faith and fair dealing.[469] Nevertheless, differing from uniform law[470] but in alignment with Italian law,[471] the *contra proferentem* rule is not applied as a general principle in German law.[472]

The application of § 157 of the BGB has also led to the development of the principle that when there is more than one possible meaning of a contract term, the meaning that is not contrary to law and good morals is to be applied.[473]

[d] (Wide) Scope of Application of § 133 and § 157 of the BGB

The very limited nature of the provisions of the BGB pertaining to the interpretation of contracts necessitated their broad application.

The text of § 133 of the BGB gives the impression that the subject of interpretation is limited to the content of declarations of intent, and the purpose of interpretation is limited to the ascertainment of them. However, even the presence of a declaration of intent can only be determined through interpretation. Therefore, § 133 of the BGB also applies to the determination of whether or not a declaration of intent exists.[474]

As mentioned above,[475] although § 133 of the BGB appears to only deal with the interpretation of declarations of intent, it is unanimously accepted that it applies to the interpretation of contracts as well. Nonetheless, the scope of application of § 133 of the

465. Busche, *supra* n. 419, at n. 9.
466. Looschelders, *supra* n. 393, at, n. 53; Busche, *supra* n. 419, at n. 7.
467. BGH NJW 1955, 587, 588 ff.; Busche, *supra* n. 419, at n. 7.
468. Looschelders, *supra* n. 393, at, n. 53.
469. Busche, *supra* n. 419, at n. 8.
470. *See*, sections §4.03[B][6] Article 4.6 of the UPICC; §4.05[B][4] Trans-Lex Principle No. IV.5.4, *infra*.
471. *See*, section §3.02[B][6][h] Article 1370 of the CC. It., *supra*.
472. BGH LM (A) Nr. 14; VersR 1971, 172, 173; RGZ 131, 343, 350.
473. OLG DüsseldorfWuW/E OLG 1479, 1482; Busche, *supra* n. 419, at n. 14; Singer, *supra* n. 398, at n. 61.
474. Looschelders, *supra* n. 393, at, n. 24.
475. *See*, section §3.03[A][3][a] Relationship Between the Two Paragraphs, *supra*.

BGB is limited neither to declarations of intent nor to contracts, but it also applies to the interpretation of legislative texts.[476]

Moreover, § 133 of the BGB also applies to the interpretation of behaviors that constitute implied declarations of intent.[477] Therefore, silence that constitutes a declaration of intent is also subject to interpretation under this paragraph.[478]

Besides all these, Looschelders holds that § 133 and § 157 of the BGB must also apply to transactions that are required to be made in a certain form, general contract conditions, unilateral acts, automatic declarations of intent that are not addressed to a given addressee, collective agreements, and partnership agreements.[479] Case law shows that § 133 of the BGB is also used in the interpretation of party declarations made during court proceedings.[480] As a consequence of this expansive interpretation of the scope of application of the provisions relating to the interpretation of contracts, the requirement that a declaration of intent be made in a certain form does not entail a restriction of its interpretation.[481]

Likewise, established case law holds that § 133[482] and § 157[483] of the BGB also apply to the interpretation of contradictory or even incomprehensible provisions because it is precisely the purpose of interpretation to resolve contradictions and to clarify ambiguities.[484] For this reason, the possibility that the interpretation of a contract is impossible due to its being contradictory and meaningless (illogical) can only be considered in exceptional cases.[485]

As a result of the expansive interpretation of the scopes of application of § 133 and § 157 of the BGB, their limits are somewhat unclear. The decision of the German legislators to supply such limited provisions dealing with interpretation causes the relationship between interpretation and other related subjects, in particular gap-filling and "disappearance of the basis of the transaction" (*wegfall der geschäftsgrundlage*), to become ambiguous. According to Looschelders, recourse may be had to the remedy of adaptation of contract because of the disappearance of the basis of the transaction within the frame of complementary interpretation.[486]

Busche confirms the view that contracts are concluded on the basis of certain circumstances and their continuity depends on the continuity of these circumstances. The interpretation of contracts requires a determination of the circumstances upon which the contracts are based because the parties allocate their risks and benefits according to these circumstances. Therefore, the doctrine of disappearance of the basis

476. Busche, *supra* n. 399, at nn. 17-18.
477. BGHZ 186, 269, 290 Rn. 43 = NJW 2010, 3510; BGH NJW 2011, 1434, 1435 Rn. 14; OLG Saarbrücken NJW 1953, 1066; OLG Heilbronn NJW-RR 2004, 660; Looschelders, *supra* n. 393, at nn. 31-32; Busche, *supra* n. 399, at n. 33; Singer, *supra* n. 398, at n. 27.
478. Looschelders, *supra* n. 393, at nn. 31-32.
479. *Ibid.*, at nn. 74 et seq.
480. BGHZ 22, 267, 269 = NJW 1957, 383; BGHZ 63, 389, 392 = NJW 1975, 928; BGH NJW-RR 1999, 938; BAG NJW 2010, 956, 957 Rn. 12; Busche, *supra* n. 399, at n. 43.
481. Busche, *supra* n. 399, at nn. 29 et seq.
482. *Ibid.*, at n. 52; Singer, *supra* n. 398, at n. 10; Looschelders, *supra* n. 393, at nn. 28-29.
483. Busche, *supra* n. 419, at n. 6.
484. BGHZ 20, 109, 110; BGH NJW 1986, 1035; 1984, 721; 1981, 2745; *Biehl* JuS 2010, 195, 197.
485. BGHZ 20, 109, 110 = NJW 1956, 665.
486. Looschelders, *supra* n. 393, at n. 18.

of the transaction is not the only tool available for adaptation of contracts: according to Busche, a considerable proportion of cases referring to a change of circumstances can be resolved by contract interpretation.[487]

However, from the point of view of legal security, it seems more appropriate to precisely define the limits of possible court intervention into the contract by means of complementary interpretation or adaptation of the contract. In order to precisely define the limits between the remedy of adaptation of contracts (due to change of circumstances) and the interpretation of contracts, it can be argued that the subject of interpretation is only the determination of party intent at the moment of the conclusion of the contract, shaped by the circumstances up until that time. In the event of a change of circumstances, however, only the circumstances that were fundamentally altered after the conclusion of the contract are at stake.[488]

[B] Swiss Law

[1] Generally

As in the German BGB of 1900, the Swiss Code of Obligations (*Obligationenrecht*, OR) of 1911 contains very limited provisions on the interpretation of contracts in order to grant broad discretion to judges.[489] There are even fewer general provisions relating to the interpretation of contracts and declarations of intent in Swiss law than in German law. One may say that these general provisions are limited to the first paragraph of Article 18 of the OR on the interpretation of contracts (and simulation), and Article 2 of the Swiss Civil Code (*Zivilgesetzbuch*, ZGB), which sets forth the general principle of good faith and fair dealing.[490]

Nevertheless, unlike German law, the influence of the Humanist School has been less significant in Swiss law. Although the use of the objective principle of good faith and fair dealing in the interpretation of contracts developed by Hugo Donellus has been adopted to a greater degree, the criticisms by Hugo Grotius against the subjective approach have been adopted to a lesser degree. In other words, even though the interpretation of contracts is objectivized through the principle of good faith and fair dealing, the subjective theory is still dominant in Swiss law owing to the strong influence of liberal thought. Therefore, just as is the case with the Latin legal family, there is no unanimity within the Romano-Germanic legal family regarding the interpretation of contracts.

The approach of Swiss law to the interpretation of contracts is closer to that of French law, where the dominance of liberal thought led to a preference for the subjective approach, instead of German law where the objective approach is prevalent.

487. Busche, *supra* n. 399, at n. 22.
488. Yıldırım, *supra* n. 64, at 49 et seq.
489. Vogenauer, *supra* n. 131, at 974.
490. Viktor Aepli, *Art. 18 OR*, in Peter Gauch, Viktor Aepli, Hubert Stöckli, *Präjudizienbuch OR—Die Rechtsprechung des Bundesgerichts*, n. 1 (8th ed., Schulthess, 2012); Edward E. Ott, *Die Interpretation von Verträgen und Statuten*, 5 (Helbing & Lichtenhann 2000).

According to liberal thought, the principles underlying paragraph 1 of Article 18 of the OR are the freedom of contract and the private autonomy (*Grundgedanken der Privatautonomie*).[491] For this reason, considerable significance is attributed to this provision in Swiss law. Accordingly, and unlike Turkish law,[492] the subjective approach is mandatory, and interpretation on the basis of a third-party understanding is not allowed in principle.[493]

The influence of liberal thought is so strong in the literature that Kramer/Schmidlin purport that a "will-oriented approach to interpretation is the common feature of modern codifications," by seeing the provisions in comparative law through the lens of the subjective theory.[494] In order to support their thesis, they refer to former Article 1156 of the CC. Fr., § 914 of the Austrian Civil Code (*Österreich Allgemeines Bürgerliches Gesetzbuch*, ABGB), as well as Article 1362 of the CC. It. and § 133 and § 157 of the BGB, without addressing how the latter two are interpreted in Italian and German laws. However, an outsider may observe that a hybrid approach better represents the position of Swiss law, because of the use of Article 2/1 ZGB as a subsidiary tool of objective interpretation.[495]

Contrary to Kramer/Schmidlin's observation regarding the general tendency in comparative law, Honnold argues that "... current references to 'will' as the basis for contract resemble the echoes of distant thunder from a storm that has passed."[496] The opinion of the present author, however, is that a search for balance between the subjective and objective approaches better defines the general tendency of today's legal systems regarding the interpretation of contracts.

As will be seen below, [497] the process of ascertaining the true intent of the parties, or "subjective interpretation," is conducted to a large extent through literal interpretation in Swiss law, although literal interpretation is conceived of as "objective interpretation" in English law.[498] Therefore, the rules of literal interpretation are well established in Swiss law. For this reason, it might be more appropriate to hesitate in stating that the subjective approach to the interpretation of contracts dominates in this jurisdiction.

Once again, as the case with the German BGB of 1900, the legislators of the OR of 1911 preferred the will theory (*Willenstheorie*) and based the interpretation of contracts on the will of the parties.[499] Unlike German law, however,[500] the declaration

491. Wolfgang Wiegand, *Art. 18* in Heinrich Honsell, Nedim Peter Vogt, Wolfgang Wiegand, *Basler Kommentar—Obligationenrecht I, Art. 1-529 OR*, n. 1 (6th ed., Helbing & Lichtenhahn, 2015); Kramer, Schmidlin, *supra* n. 38, at n. 8.
492. *See*, section §3.03[C][2][b] The Will Theory, the Theory of Declaration, and the Trust Theory, *infra*.
493. Kramer, Schmidlin, *supra* n. 38, at n. 8.
494. *Ibid.*, at n. 3.
495. Fontaine, de Ly, *supra* n. 5, at 124.
496. John O. Honnold, *Uniform Law for International Sales under the 1980 United Nations Convention*, § 106 (3rd ed., Kluwer Law International, 1999).
497. *See*, section §3.03[B][4][a] Subjective Interpretation, *infra*.
498. *See*, section §3.04[A][2] Objective Approach, *infra*.
499. Wiegand, *supra* n. 491, at n. 1.
500. *See*, section §3.03[A][1] Generally, *supra*.

theory did not prevail in the interpretation of Article 18/1 of the OR thereafter; the prevalence of the will theory still continues in both theory and practice.

Nevertheless, the rules of objective interpretation are also well established in Swiss law. Differing once again from German law, however,[501] both literature and case law agree that there is a hierarchy between objective and subjective methods of interpretation and that the former is subsidiary to the latter.[502] Accordingly, the true (i.e., subjective) intent of the parties is first sought. Where it is not possible to determine the true intent, the objective theory of trust (*Vertrauenstheorie*) must be applied.[503]

In addition to the theory of trust, another tool of objective interpretation in Swiss law is the principle of interpretation according to good faith, based upon the general principle of good faith and fair dealing set forth in Article 2/1 of the ZGB.[504] Unlike German and Italian law, however, a special aspect of this general principle for the interpretation of contracts is not included in the OR, as it is in § 157 of the BGB and Article 1366 of the CC. It.

Kramer/Schmidlin, and Wiegand adhere to the opinion that for a declaration to be subject to interpretation, it must have been expressed,[505] as their colleagues in the Italian literature agree.[506] Therefore, the subject matter of Article 18/1 of the OR is the interpretation of objective facts and not unexpressed, inherent intent. Unsurprisingly, however, this opinion did not have broad repercussions in Swiss law because of the prevalence of the subjective theory in this jurisdiction.

"Implied terms" are another objective institution of Swiss law.[507] These are provisions that a court assumes were intended to be included in a contract but that are not expressly stated in it. Implied terms are used, in particular, in complementary interpretation, as in English law.[508] Regardless of the clarity of their wording, it is therefore always possible for contracts to include implied terms.[509]

501. *See*, section §3.03[A][3][a] Relationship Between the Two Paragraphs, *supra*.
502. BGE 92 II 347; 99 II 285; 101 II 331; 111 II 287, www.bger.ch (accessed December 7, 2018); Peter Gauch, Walter R. Schluep, *Schweizerisches Obligationenrecht Allgemeiner Teil*, 1,201 and 1,225 (9th ed., Schulthess, 2008); Peter Jäggi, Peter Gauch *(Zürcher) Kommentar zum Schweizerischen Zivilgesetzbuch—Obligationenrecht, Allgemeiner Teil, Band V 1b, Kommentar zu Art. 18 OR*, nn. 306 et seq. (3rd ed., Schulthess, 1980); Aepli, *supra* n. 490, at n. 3, 7-9.
503. Wiegand, *supra* n. 491, at n. 1 and 3; Aepli, *supra* n. 490, at n. 9.
504. BGE 95 II 437; 96 II 141; 99 II 285; 107 II 163; 110 II 146; 111 II 293, www.bger.ch (accessed December 7, 2018); Gauch, Schluep, *supra* n. 502, at 1,224.
505. Kramer, Schmidlin, *supra* n. 38, at n. 16; Wiegand, *supra* n. 491, at n. 2.
506. *See*, section §3.02[B][4] Views Pertaining to the Objectivity of the Subjective Interpretation, *supra*.
507. Nataša Hadžimanović, *Auslegung und Ergänzung von Verträgen—Vertragliche Nebenpflichten im englischen und schweizerischen Recht*, PhD Thesis, University of Zurich, 140 et seq. (Schulthess, 2006).
508. *See*, section §3.04[A][1] Generally, *infra*.
509. Kramer, Schmidlin, *supra* n. 38, at n. 45.

[2] The Use of the Principle of Trust in Disputes Regarding the Meeting of the Minds and "Pure Interpretation Disputes"

In Swiss law, a basic distinction regarding the subject matter of interpretation is made between disputes regarding a meeting of the minds and "pure interpretation disputes" (*reiner Auslegungsstreit*). At stake in the former is whether there has ever been a meeting of the minds and therefore whether or not the contract exists. The existence of the contract is not disputed in the latter, and instead, its meaning is sought through interpretation. In practice, "pure interpretation disputes" are more common.[510]

Disputes regarding a meeting of the minds are discussed more in Swiss law than in other jurisdictions, and the focus is on the applicability of Article 18/1 of the OR to the interpretation of declarations of intent in order to determine whether a contract was validly formed. Even though Article 18/1 of the OR appears to only deal with the interpretation of contracts, the majority opinion is that it applies to the interpretation of declarations of intent as well.[511] The *Bundesgericht* also adheres to this opinion.[512] According to this opinion, if the parties have a written contract, the question of whether their contract reflects their intent must be examined.[513] In this way, whether there is a meeting of the minds will be determined through an interpretation of the declarations of intent pursuant to Article 18/1 of the OR and therefore whether a contract has been validly formed.

The ascertainment of whether a contract has been validly formed through the interpretation of the declarations of intent creates an important field of application of the trust principle (*Vertrauensprinzip*) as a principle of objective interpretation. According to this principle, in situations where there has not been a meeting of the minds, it cannot always be presumed that the contract is nonexistent (without prejudice to Article 2 of the OR). What should be examined is whether the party requesting the interpretation of the contract is relying in good faith on the argument that a contract was validly formed. If this is the case, normative consensus (*normativer Konsens*) is at stake. This question must be answered according to Articles 1 and 2 of the ZGB, because it is beyond the scope of application of Article 18/1 of the OR.

Likewise, questions of failure of a meeting of the minds (*Dissens*) are also beyond the scope of this article. In any case, the real meaning of the parties' declarations of intent must be ascertained in order to determine whether there has, in fact, been a consensus (*Konsens*) between the parties but they have poorly expressed it their agreement, or they have actually never had a meeting of the minds (*Dissens*).[514]

The trust principle plays an important role in this determination, as it is a principle of objective interpretation based on the principle of good faith and fair dealing. According to the trust principle, in situations where there has not been a meeting of the minds regarding a given issue covered in a contract, the understanding

510. Gauch, Schluep, *supra* n. 502, at 1,197 et seq.; Jäggi, Gauch, *supra* n. 502, at nn. 324 et seq.
511. Jäggi, Gauch, *supra* n. 502, at n. 80; Aepli, *supra* n. 490, at n. 2; Wiegand, *supra* n. 491, at n. 10.
512. BGer 4C.16/2000 (24.1.01) E. 2a, www.servat.unibe.ch (accessed December 7, 2018).
513. Wiegand, *supra* n. 491, at n. 10.
514. Kramer, Schmidlin, *supra* n. 38, at n. 15.

of the good faith addressee should be taken as a basis for interpretation.[515] Gauch/Schluep argue, however, that there must have already been a meeting of the minds between the parties as to the formation of the contract in order for the trust principle to apply as a principle of interpretation. This is because there must be a contract in order for there to be a duty of good faith.[516]

[3] The Significance of the Distinction Between Subjective and Objective Interpretation for Reviewability of Decisions

Wiegand states that it is impossible to clearly distinguish between the processes of subjective and objective interpretation because they apply in progressive order and complement each other.[517] Nevertheless, the distinction between them has a practical significance for reviewability on appeal of court decisions relating to the interpretation of contracts. In principle, subjective interpretation is not subject to review on appeal because its purpose is to determine the intent of the parties, which is a question of fact.[518] However, objective interpretation[519] and the determination of presumed will of the parties[520] in particular are questions of law and are reviewable on appeal by the *Bundesgericht*. Accordingly, it is undisputed that normative interpretation of declarations of intent underlying a contract pursuant to the principle of good faith and fair dealing is a question of law, and reviewable on appeal.[521]

Another distinction made in Swiss law is between the aspects of court decisions relating to the interpretation of the terms of a contract and the aspects setting forth the legal consequences of the outcome of the interpretation,[522] as in the German[523] and U.S.[524] legal systems. The former are precluded from review on appeal in principle, in particular when the determination of party intent is involved, as they relate to the facts.[525] However, the latter relate to issues of law, and it is undisputed that they are reviewable on appeal.[526]

515. BGE 111 II 260; 113 II 50; 114 II 359; 117 II 492; 118 II 344, www.bger.ch (accessed December 7, 2018).
516. Gauch, Schluep, *supra* n. 502, at 1,226.
517. Wiegand, *supra* n. 491, at n. 14.
518. BGer 4C 108/2004, www.servat.unibe.ch (accessed December 7, 2018); Wiegand, *supra* n. 491, at n. 1.
519. BGE 126 III 29; 125 III 308; 118 II 366; 115 II 269; 110 II 292, www.bger.ch (accessed December 7, 2018); Wiegand, *supra* n. 491, at n. 15.
520. BGE 118 II 366, www.bger.ch (accessed December 7, 2018); BGer 4C.90 / 2002; 4C.286 / 2005, www.servat.unibe.ch (accessed December 7, 2018); Aepli, *supra* n. 490, at n. 15; Jäggi, Gauch, *supra* n. 502, at nn. 306 et seq.; Gauch, Schluep, *supra* n. 502, at 1,201.
521. BGE 96 II 325; 99 II 282; 107 II 417, www.bger.ch (accessed December 7, 2018); Kramer, Schmidlin, *supra* n. 38, at n. 80.
522. Kramer, Schmidlin, *supra* n. 38, at n. 75; Jäggi, Gauch, *supra* n. 502, at n. 414.
523. *See*, section §3.03[A][1] Generally, *supra*.
524. *See*, section §3.04[B][1] Generally, *infra*.
525. BGE 100 II 345; BGE 107 II 226; 84 II 418, www.bger.ch (accessed December 7, 2018).
526. BGE 85 II 97; 97 II 201, www.bger.ch (accessed December 7, 2018).

[4] *Article 18/1 of the OR*

Interpretation of Contracts, Simulation

> When assessing the form and terms of a contract, the true and common intention of the parties must be ascertained without dwelling on any inexact expressions or designations they may have used either in error or by way of disguising the true nature of the agreement.
>
> A debtor may not plead simulation as a defense against a third party who has become his creditor in reliance on a written acknowledgment of debt.[527]

Article 18 of the OR addresses three different issues under the same heading: the principle that the parties' intent prevails over the wording of their agreements, the principle of *falsa demonstratio non nocet*,[528] and applicability of simulation. The Swiss legislators did not only abstain from drafting detailed provisions regarding the interpretation of contracts but also did not even dedicate an independent provision to this important subject. Nonetheless, Kramer/Schmidlin state that the reason why the same article deals with the *falsa demonstratio non nocet* rule and simulation is that they are inseparable: in the former, the parties unconsciously give a different appearance to their contract, whereas in the latter they do so deliberately.[529]

As in German law, [530] the lack of detailed provisions on the interpretation of contracts results in an expansive interpretation of the scope of application of the only provision available on this subject in Swiss law.[531] Unlike § 133 of the BGB, Article 18/1 of the OR addresses the interpretation of contracts and not the interpretation of declarations of intent. According to some authors, this provision should also apply by analogy to the interpretation of unilateral declarations of intent[532] and unilateral

527. "Art. 18

D. Auslegung der Verträge, Simulation

1 Bei der Beurteilung eines Vertrages sowohl nach Form als nach Inhalt ist der übereinstimmende wirkliche Wille und nicht die unrichtige Bezeichnung oder Ausdrucksweise zu beachten, die von den Parteien aus Irrtum oder in der Absicht gebraucht wird, die wahre Beschaffenheit des Vertrages zu verbergen.

2 Dem Dritten, der die Forderung im Vertrauen auf ein schriftliches Schuldbekenntnis erworben hat, kann der Schuldner die Einrede der Simulation nicht entgegensetzen.

Article 18

D. Interprétation des contrats; simulation

1 Pour apprécier la forme et les clauses d'un contrat, il y a lieu de rechercher la réelle et commune intention des parties, sans s'arrêter aux expressions ou dénominations inexactes dont elles ont pu se servir, soit par erreur, soit pour déguiser la nature véritable de la convention.

2 Le débiteur ne peut opposer l'exception de simulation au tiers qui est devenu créancier sur la foi d'une reconnaissance écrite de la dette.

See http://www.zgbor.ch (accessed December 7, 2018), translation taken from www.admin.ch (accessed December 7, 2018).

528. Wiegand, *supra* n. 491, at n. 16.
529. Kramer, Schmidlin, *supra* n. 38, at n. 10.
530. *See*, section §3.03[A][3][d] (Wide) Scope of Application of § 133 and § 157 of the BGB, *supra*.
531. This article also applies to standard terms and insurance contracts, Aepli, *supra* n. 490, at n. 1.
532. Jäggi, Gauch, *supra* n. 502, at n. 80; Aepli, *supra* n. 490, at n. 2.

transactions.[533] Additionally, Kramer/Schmidlin state that this provision also applies to the interpretation of behaviors that constitute implied declarations of intent, because if the meaning of a behavior is ambiguous, it can be ascertained only through interpretation, as is the case with express declarations of intent.[534]

According to a dissenting opinion, this provision only applies to "pure interpretation disputes," and therefore it only applies when a contract has been validly formed in the sense of Article 1 of the OR. Otherwise, it would not be possible to speak of a "common intent" of the parties. According to this view, therefore, this provision only applies to the determination of the content of contracts and not to questions of their validity.[535] Even though this opinion appears to conform to the wording of the provision, the *Bundesgericht* applies Article 18/1 of the OR to the interpretation of unilateral declarations of intent by analogy in order to satisfy a practical need in the absence of detailed provisions on the subject of interpretation.[536]

Some authors observe that Article 18/1 of the OR is an insufficient text as it leaves certain issues unanswered; although this provision states that the aim of interpretation is to determine the true intent of the parties, it says nothing about how to do that and which criteria to apply to the determination of true intent.[537] Moreover, it does not say what will be done if the true intent cannot be determined.[538] The application of the trust principle to this situation has been developed through literature and case law.

Again, although Article 18/1 of the OR does not expressly deal with the burden of proof of the true intent of the parties, a party who alleges that a meaning is different from the apparent meaning of the contract bears the burden of proof in situations of both false statement and simulation.[539]

[a] Subjective Interpretation

There is a hierarchy between the methods of interpretation in Swiss law, as is the case in the French[540] and Italian[541] legal systems. Accordingly, the subjective method of interpretation applies first in order to determine the true intent of the parties, which can only be determined if there is sufficient evidence to demonstrate the real intent of the

533. BGE 115 II 323, www.bger.ch (accessed December 7, 2018). Peter Gauch, Viktor Aepli, Hugo Casanova, Schweizerisches *Obligationenrecht Allgemeiner Teil (Art. 1-183), Rechtsprechung des Bundesgerichts*, 31 (4th ed., Schulthess, 1996).
534. Kramer, Schmidlin, *supra* n. 38, at n. 45.
535. Wiegand, *supra* n. 491, at n. 2 and 8-9.
536. BGer 4C.16/2000 (24.1.01) E. 2a, *supra* n. 512.
537. Wiegand, *supra* n. 491, at n. 7; Gauch, Aepli, Casanova, *supra* n. 533, at 32.
538. *Ibid.*, at n. 3; Gauch, Aepli, Casanova, *supra* n. 533, at 32.
539. Kramer, Schmidlin, *supra* n. 38, at n. 13; Jäggi, Gauch, *supra* n. 502, at n. 33.
540. *See*, section §3.02[A][2] Classification of the Types of Interpretation and the Relationship Between Subjective and Objective Interpretation, *supra*.
541. *See*, section §3.02[B][5] Classification of the Provisions of the Italian Civil Code Relating to the Interpretation of Contracts, *supra*.

parties.[542] Where the real intent cannot be determined, the objective method of interpretation applies.[543]

The wording of contracts is a fundamental tool of subjective interpretation, albeit not the only one. Therefore, the process of interpretation requires verification of whether the meaning obtained from the wording is confirmed or contradicted by extrinsic evidence.[544]

As stated above, Swiss law attaches particular importance to the literal interpretation of the words used by the parties, even though the subjective theory prevails in this jurisdiction.[545] According to some authors, contracts must be interpreted according to their wording, unless other tools of interpretation leave no doubt that the meaning of the contract is different than its apparent meaning.[546] However, this view does not imply that interpretation is not needed if the wording is clear (*in claris non fit interpretatio*). Unlike Italian law,[547] legal theory and practice[548] in Switzerland view this rule as the expression of an outdated and over-formalistic approach that attributes absolute supremacy to the wording.[549]

In literal interpretation, words are interpreted according to their usual meaning at the time of the conclusion of the contract, unless proven otherwise.[550] This is their meaning in daily use usually found in dictionaries[551] and not their technical or scientific meaning.[552] If the usual meanings of the words differ from one place to another (which may be the case in a country with four official languages), words must be interpreted according to their usual meaning at the place of the conclusion of the contract.[553]

However, if the parties agreed upon a particular meaning of the word other than its usual meaning, that meaning prevails.[554] This is the case especially for technical, commercial, or legal terms that are used in a given sector or in a certain profession (such as International Commercial Terms (INCOTERMS), and banking or legal terms).

542. Wiegand, *supra* n. 491, at n. 12.
543. Jäggi, Gauch, *supra* n. 502, at nn. 306 et seq.; Gauch, Schluep, *supra* n. 502, at 1,201; Ott, *supra* n. 490, at 5.
544. BGE 111 II 287 and 99 II 285, www.bger.ch (accessed December 7, 2018); Wiegand, *supra* n. 491, at n. 25.
545. The wording of a statement or contract is the starting point of interpretation. BGE 118 II 366, www.bger.ch (accessed December 7, 2018); Gauch, Schluep, *supra* n. 502, at 1,206; Jäggi, Gauch, *supra* n. 502, at n. 347.
546. Gauch, Schluep, *supra* n. 502, at 1,220; Jäggi, Gauch, *supra* n. 502, at n. 369.
547. *See*, section §3.02[B][2] The Discussion on the *In Claris Non Fit Interpretatio* Rule, *supra*.
548. Gauch, Schluep, *supra* n. 502, at 1,221. These authors refer to BGE ZBJV 1995, 131, S. 241.
549. Gauch, Schluep, *supra* n. 502, at 1,221; Jäggi, Gauch, *supra* n. 502, at n. 368.
550. BGer 5C.87/2002, www.servat.unibe.ch (accessed December 7, 2018); BGE 97 II 74; 99 II 304; 115 II 329, www.bger.ch (accessed December 7, 2018); Wiegand, *supra* n. 491, at n. 19; Kramer, Schmidlin, *supra* n. 38, at n. 22; Jäggi, Gauch, *supra* n. 502, at n. 345; Gauch, Schluep, *supra* n. 502, at 1,207; Aepli, *supra* n. 490, at n. 5; Gauch, Aepli, Casanova, *supra* n. 533, at 31.
551. BGE 82 II 454; 85 II 348; 104 II 283; 118 II 345, 115 II 269, www.bger.ch (accessed December 7, 2018).
552. BGE 82 II 454, www.bger.ch (accessed December 7, 2018).
553. Kramer, Schmidlin, *supra* n. 38, at n. 22; Jäggi, Gauch, *supra* n. 502, at n. 345.
554. BGE 94 II 159; 95 II 533, 102 II 246, www.bger.ch (accessed December 7, 2018); Wiegand, *supra* n. 491, at nn. 21-22; Gauch, Aepli, Casanova, *supra* n. 533, at 31; Gauch, Schluep, *supra* n. 502, at 1,208-1,209.

For a term to be understood in its technical, commercial, or legal sense, all the parties must be aware of that meaning of the term or belong to a profession where that term is used in its specific meaning.[555] Otherwise, that term has to be interpreted in its usual sense.[556] In a determination of whether the parties attached a specific meaning to a term, the parties' or their representatives' education and the context and purpose of the contract must be taken into consideration.[557]

Another method used in subjective interpretation is systematic interpretation, which is also set forth in Article 1189 (former Article 1161) of the CC. Fr. and Article 1363 of the CC. It. This method is not an alternative but complementary to literal interpretation. Systematic interpretation requires the interpretation of the contract as a whole.[558] In other words, all the documents and all the clauses making up the contract must be taken into consideration in the interpretation of even one single term,[559] and the judge must interpret the contract by keeping in mind the whole context thereof.[560] In the interpretation of a single sentence or expression, the sentence structure, the structure of the contract, the documents exchanged by the parties, parties' statements in the negotiations, and their conduct subsequent to the conclusion of the contract must be considered.[561]

Systematic interpretation also requires an examination of the whole context in the interpretation of declarations of intent.[562] While doing so, all the circumstances that may shed a light on the true intent must be examined.[563] This includes both the circumstances that influenced the declaration of intent when it was made[564] and the circumstances that influenced the contract when it was concluded.[565]

In particular, the economic circumstances and market conditions underlying the contract must be taken into consideration.[566] Additionally, the time and place of the conclusion of a contract, the conduct of parties during negotiations, any previous drafts, the conduct of parties in the course of performance, the purpose of a contract, the balance of interest between the parties, and other relevant circumstances are other subjects of interpretation to be considered.[567]

---

555. Wiegand, *supra* n. 491, at n. 23; Kramer, Schmidlin, *supra* n. 38, at nn. 23-24; Jäggi, Gauch, *supra* n. 502, at nn. 349-350; Aepli, *supra* n. 490, at n. 5.
556. BGE 113 II 437; 104 II 283; 97 II 74; 82 II 445, www.bger.ch (accessed December 7, 2018).
557. BGE 101 II 325, 109 II 225, 115 II 348, www.bger.ch (accessed December 7, 2018).
558. BGE 113 II 50; 117 II 622, www.bger.ch (accessed December 7, 2018); Gauch, Schluep, *supra* n. 502, at 1,229.
559. Gauch, Schluep, *supra* n. 502, at 1,210.
560. BGE 128 III 267; 123 III 168, www.bger.ch (accessed December 7, 2018); Wiegand, *supra* n. 491, at n. 38.
561. Kramer, Schmidlin, *supra* n. 38, at nn. 26-28; Jäggi, Gauch, *supra* n. 502, at nn. 351, 357-359.
562. *Ibid.*, at n. 16; Gauch, Aepli, Casanova, *supra* n. 533, at 31.
563. Kramer, Schmidlin, *supra* n. 38, at n. 16.
564. Wiegand, *supra* n. 491, at nn. 12-13 and 18.
565. Kramer, Schmidlin, *supra* n. 38, at n. 44.
566. BGE 99 II 290, www.bger.ch (accessed December 7, 2018).
567. Jäggi, Gauch, *supra* n. 502, at nn. 370 et seq.; Gauch, Schluep, *supra* n. 502, at 1,212 et seq.

[b] Objective Interpretation

It is not always possible to determine a true common intent of the parties through the subjective method of interpretation. In this situation, a judge must resort to the objective method[568] and attempt to determine the presumed intent of the parties, in other words, what the parties' intent should have been and not what it was.[569] Recourse may only be had to the objective method of interpretation in Swiss law when the true intent of the parties cannot be determined.[570]

What is at stake here is not how the addressee subjectively understood the declaration of intent, but rather what reasonable parties should have meant by the words they used in their declarations of intent.[571] In order to determine that meaning, courts must examine what a reasonable person in the same circumstances as the addressee would understand from the declaration of intent.[572]

The trust principle[573] and the general principle of good faith and fair dealing set forth in Article 2/1 of the ZGB[574] constitute the basis of the objective method of interpretation. The principle of systematic interpretation also applies to objective interpretation; declarations of intent are to be interpreted in the context of the whole contract, and all relevant circumstances must be taken into consideration.[575] "All the relevant circumstances" is understood broadly to include all the tools of interpretation that may contribute to ascertaining the meaning of a contract.[576] Accordingly, the natural flow of life (*allgemeinen Lebenserfahrung*), purpose of the contract, circumstances at the time of the conclusion of the contract, previous drafts, parties' conduct in the negotiations and in the course of performance, and the balance of interests must be taken into consideration in the interpretation of a contract.[577] Again, the use of all of these secondary means of interpretation for the purpose of objective interpretation can only be possible if the meaning of the text of the contract, the primary means of interpretation, cannot be ascertained through subjective interpretation.[578]

568. BGE 92 II 347, www.bger.ch (accessed December 7, 2018); Jäggi, Gauch, *supra* n. 502, at nn. 306 et seq.; Gauch, Schluep, *supra* n. 502, at 1,201.
569. BGE 111 II 279; 115 II 268; 117 II 621; 118 II 344, www.bger.ch (accessed December 7, 2018).
570. Gauch, Schluep, *supra* n. 502, at 1,225; Gauch, Aepli, Casanova, *supra* n. 533, at 32; Aepli, *supra* n. 490, at n. 7.
571. BGer 4C.62/2004; 4C.107/2004, www.servat.unibe.ch (accessed December 7, 2018); Aepli, *supra* n. 490, at n. 3.
572. Wiegand, *supra* n. 491, at nn. 12-13.
573. Aepli, *supra* n. 490, at n. 3 and 9.
574. BGE 116 II 347; 111 II 293; 107 II 163; 105 II 16; 99 II 294; 88 II 498; 87 II 95, www.bger.ch (accessed December 7, 2018); Aepli, *supra* n. 490, at n. 7 and 9; Kramer, Schmidlin, *supra* n. 38, at nn. 29 et seq.; Wiegand, *supra* n. 491, at n. 35.
575. BGE 121 III 123, 122 III 108, 122 III 183, 122 V 146, 123 III 39, 125 III 308, 126 III 120, 126 III 379, 130 III 557, 131 III 592, www.bger.ch (accessed December 7, 2018); Aepli, *supra* n. 490, at n. 3.
576. BGE 101 II 325; 126 III 120; 125 III 437; 115 II 268; 113 II 51; 95 II 437; 90 II 454; 83 II 307, www.bger.ch (accessed December 7, 2018); Wiegand, *supra* n. 491, at n. 26.
577. Wiegand, *supra* n. 491, at nn. 27-31; Gauch, Aepli, Casanova, *supra* n. 533, at 32; Aepli, *supra* n. 490, at n. 7 and 9.
578. BGE 99 II 285, 101 II 331, 111 II 287, www.bger.ch (accessed December 7, 2018).

Commercial customs are a particularly important secondary tool of objective interpretation.[579] The common meanings of INCOTERMS in particular are taken into consideration in the interpretation of contracts since these terms are so well established that parties may reasonably expect each other to be aware of their meanings.[580] Moreover, the purpose of the contract and the balance of interests provided by the parties or in other words, "the economy of the contract" is also an important tool for the teleological interpretation of contracts.[581]

[5] Principles of Interpretation Developed Through Case Law

Even though Swiss law does not contain many provisions on the interpretation of contracts, some principles have developed through case law over time.[582] Some of these principles relate to the application of Article 18/1 of the OR, whereas some of them are more specific rules of interpretation.

One of the principles that relates to the application of Article 18/1 of the OR is that contracts should be interpreted *ex tunc*, not *ex nunc*. Accordingly, the judge should consider himself in the same circumstances with the parties at the time and place of the conclusion of the contract while interpreting it.[583] The events subsequent to the conclusion of the contract may be taken into consideration to the extent they help to clarify the circumstances at the time of the conclusion of the contract.[584]

The rule of *in claris non fit interpretatio* has not been generally adopted by Swiss law.[585] In a decision that does not expressly refer to this rule, however, the *Bundesgericht* has held that "[w]here the text of a contract is clear, there is no need to distort its meaning by seeking an interpretation based on elements extrinsic to the contract."[586] This decision has been criticized in the literature[587] for not being compatible with Article 18/1 of the OR because the legislators expressly acknowledged that a statement might have a meaning other than its apparent meaning, no matter how clear is the latter.[588] The *Bundesgericht* later clarified its position by issuing decisions to the effect that even contracts that appear to be clear can also be interpreted.[589]

579. Wiegand, *supra* n. 491, at n. 31; Kramer, Schmidlin, *supra* n. 38, at nn. 29 et seq.
580. Kramer, Schmidlin, *supra* n. 38, at n. 32.
581. *Ibid.*, at nn. 35 et seq.; Jäggi, Gauch, *supra* n. 502, at nn. 370 et seq.; Wiegand, *supra* n. 491, at n. 31.
582. Wiegand, *supra* n. 491, at n. 34.
583. *Ibid.*, at n. 36; Gauch, Schluep, *supra* n. 502, at 1,223; Jäggi, Gauch, *supra* n. 502, at n. 416., these authors refer to BGE 46 II 41, 461; 57 II 452.
584. BGE 107 II 418, www.bger.ch (accessed December 7, 2018).
585. Gauch, Schluep, *supra* n. 502, at 1,221, these authors refer to BGE ZBJV 1995, 131, S. 241; *see also* section §3.03[B][4][a] Subjective Interpretation, *supra*.
586. "*Lorsque le texte d'un contrat est clair, il n'y a pas lieu de dénaturer son sens par la recherche d'une interprétation fondée sur des éléments extrinsèques à la convention.*" BGE 99 II 282, www.bger.ch (accessed December 7, 2018), Author's translation.
587. Kramer, Schmidlin, *supra* n. 38, at n. 47.
588. *Ibid.*; Necip Kocayusufpaşaoğlu, Hüseyin Hatemi, Rona Serozan, Abdülkadir Arpacı, *Borçlar Hukuku Genel Bölüm*, Vol. 1, 333 (7th ed., Filiz, 2017).
589. BGE 127 III 444; 130 II 417, www.bger.ch (accessed December 7, 2018).

The *falsa demonstratio non nocet* principle implied under Article 18/1 of the OR[590] provides that when there is a discrepancy between the wording of the contract and the true intent of the parties, the latter prevails.[591] According to another principle developed on the basis of this principle, decisions on the interpretation of contracts cannot be based solely on the literal and grammatical interpretation of the contract.[592] In the words of the *Bundesgericht*, "[p]urely literal interpretation is ... prohibited."[593]

As regards more specific rules of interpretation developed through Swiss case law, these are indeed the rules that were codified in the Latin legal systems. One of these rules is the *favor negotii* rule, also set forth in Article 1191 (former Article 1157) of the CC. Fr. and Article 1367 of the CC. It., according to which, in the event of doubt, a contract should be interpreted in the sense in which it can have some effect.[594] Nonetheless, the *Bundesgericht* has also held that contract clauses deviating from dispositive rules should be interpreted narrowly.[595] For this reason, if the parties wish to deviate from dispositive rules, they have to do so with clear and explicit provisions.[596] Likewise, exemption of liability clauses should also be interpreted narrowly.[597]

Another rule developed through Swiss case law is the rule to interpret ambiguous clauses against the party who supplied them, which was also stated in Article 1190 (former Article 1162) of the CC. Fr. and Article 1370 of the CC. It. In Swiss law, this rule is referred to as the "*Unklarheitenregel*," which means the "ambiguity rule." According to this rule, if a contract or a clause thereof is written by one of the parties in an ambiguous manner, and if it is capable of bearing at least two meanings, the one against the party who wrote the contract prevails.[598]

In conformity with the liberal approach of Swiss law, *Unklarheitenregel* is also interpreted narrowly because to do otherwise would limit the application of Article 18/1 of the OR, which is based on the will of the parties. Therefore, Swiss literature considers it to be an exception that may apply to standard term contracts and insurance contracts in particular.[599] In conformity with the narrow interpretation and limited

590. Wiegand, *supra* n. 491, at n. 16.
591. *Ibid.*, at n. 44.
592. BGE 109 II 225, 92 II 349, www.bger.ch (accessed December 7, 2018); BGer 4C.290/2002, www.servat.unibe.ch (accessed December 7, 2018); Wiegand, *supra* n. 491, at n. 37; Gauch, Aepli, Casanova, *supra* n. 533, at 33.
593. "*L'interprétetation purement littéral est ... prohibée.*" BGE 127 III 444, www.bger.ch (accessed December 7, 2018), author's translation.
594. BGE 120 II 40; 117 II 621;115 II 268; 113 II 51; 110 II 160; 99 II 274, www.bger.ch (accessed December 7, 2018); Kramer, Schmidlin, *supra* n. 38, at n. 41; Jäggi, Gauch, *supra* n. 502, at nn. 441 et seq.; Wiegand, *supra* n. 491, at n. 40; Aepli, *supra* n. 490, at n. 9.
595. BGE 115 II 268, www.bger.ch (accessed December 7, 2018); Wiegand, *supra* n. 491, at n. 39.
596. BGE 122 III 121; 119 II 372; 117 II 621; 115 II 479; 115 II 268; 113 II 51, www.bger.ch (accessed December 7, 2018); BGer 5C.87/2002; 5C.36/2001, www.servat.unibe.ch (accessed December 7, 2018); Wiegand, *supra* n. 491, at n. 39; Aepli, *supra* n. 490, at n. 9; Gauch, Schluep, *supra* n. 502, at 1,230; Gauch, Aepli, Casanova, *supra* n. 533, at 33.
597. Kramer, Schmidlin, *supra* n. 38, at n. 39.
598. BGE 119 II 373; 118 II 344; 117 II 622; 115 II 479; 99 II 290, www.bger.ch (accessed December 7, 2018); Wiegand, *supra* n. 491, at n. 40.
599. Wiegand, *supra* n. 491, at n. 40; Kramer, Schmidlin, *supra* n. 38, at n. 48; Jäggi/Gauch, *supra* n. 502, at nn. 447 et seq.; Gauch, Schluep, *supra* n. 502, at 1,231-1,232.

scope of application of this rule, both the literature and the *Bundesgericht* agree that it can only apply when other means of interpretation are insufficient to ascertain the meaning of a contract.[600] Moreover, according to a decision of the *Bundesgericht*, if the meaning of the contract is not controversial between the parties, this rule cannot apply.[601]

The principle of *favor debitoris*, a more specific aspect of *Unklarheitenregel* according to which ambiguous clauses should be interpreted in favor of the debtor, is also recognized by both literature and case law.[602] As explained above, this latter principle is consistent with the *contra stipulatorem* principle, which is the Roman basis of the *Unklarheitenregel*[603] and Article 1190 (former Article 1162) of the CC. Fr.[604]

[C] Turkish Law

[1] Interpretation in Contracts in Mecelle-i Ahkâm-ı Adliyye

Historically, more importance was attributed in Turkish law to the interpretation of contracts than it is today. The Mecelle-i Ahkâm-ı Adliyye (Mecelle), which was drafted between 1868 and 1876 and which served as a civil code in the Ottoman Empire, included many provisions relating to the interpretation of contracts among its introductory provisions. The Ottoman legislators did not merely put these provisions into the introduction to the Mecelle, but they also ranked them as first among the introductory provisions. Nevertheless, these provisions were not systematically listed.

The reasons underlying the importance attributed to the interpretation of contracts in the Mecelle must be understood in the context of the historical conditions that influenced the codification of the Ottoman civil law. Although the Divân-ı Âhkam-ı Adliyye (Ministry of Justice in the Ottoman Empire) drafted the Mecelle by taking the principles of the Hanafi sect of Islam into consideration,[605] the CC. Fr. had a considerable influence on this code due to the political conditions of that period.[606] One of the most striking examples of this influence is the parallelism between the provisions of these codes relating to the interpretation of contracts.

The Mecelle's provisions on this subject begin with Article 2, according to which "[a] matter is determined according to intention; that is to say, the effect to be given to

600. BGE 115 II 269; 107 II 230; 109 II 219; 110 II 146; 99 II 292, www.bger.ch (accessed December 7, 2018); BGer 4C 215/2002; 4C 351/2002, www.servat.unibe.ch (accessed December 7, 2018); Gauch, Aepli, Casanova, *supra* n. 533, at 33; Aepli, *supra* n. 490, at n. 10.
601. BGer 4C.37 /2003, www.servat.unibe.ch (accessed December 7, 2018).
602. BGE 113 II 441, www.bger.ch (accessed December 7, 2018); Wiegand, *supra* n. 491, at n. 40.
603. *See*, section §2.01[B][2][b], The Emergence of Principles of Objective Interpretation in the Classical Period, *supra*.
604. *See*, section §3.02[A][4][c] Article 1190 (Former Article 1162) of the CC. Fr., *supra*.
605. Cengiz İlhan, *Günümüz Türkçesiyle Mecelle*, 42 (2nd ed., Yetkin, 2014).
606. A. Refik Gür, *Hukuk Tarihi ve Tefekkürü Bakımından Mecelle*, 13-14 (3rd ed., Sebil, 1993); Ahmet Cemil Yıldırım, *Ottoman Mecelle as a Secular Uniform Law Instrument*, 10 International Journal of Turcologia 19, 33-36 (2015).

any particular transaction must conform to the object of such transaction."[607] Although this article appears to address not only contracts but also legal transactions in general, it is inspired from former Article 1158 of the CC. Fr.,[608] which provides for the interpretation of contracts in accordance with their subject matter. This former article of the CC. Fr. was based on Iulianus' text in *Dig.* 50, 17, 67.[609]

Article 3 of the Mecelle that follows is almost a literal translation of Article 1188(1) (former Article 1156) of the CC. Fr., which sets forth the most basic principle of subjective interpretation, and which is based on Papinianus' text in *Dig.* 50, 16, 219.[610] This article particularly addresses the interpretation of contracts providing that "[i]n contracts, effect is given to intention and meaning and not to words and phrases. Consequently, a contract for sale subject to a right of redemption has the force of a pledge."[611]

Article 43 of the Mecelle was also inspired by former Article 1160 of the CC. Fr.[612] and provided that "[a] matter recognized by custom is regarded as though it were a contractual obligation."[613]

The Mecelle included further provisions on the interpretation of legal transactions, and contracts in particular, in Articles 60-65.[614] Article 63 is a particularly interesting provision, which provides that "[a] reference to part of an indivisible thing is regarded as a reference to the whole."[615] Although Pothier ranked this principle in

607. "*Bir işten maksat neyse, hüküm ona göredir. Yani, bir iş üzerine terettüb edecek hüküm, ol işten maksad ne ise ona göre olur.*" İlhan, *supra* n. 605, at 46-47, translation taken from http://www.iium.edu.my/deed/lawbase/al_majalle/al_majalleintro.html (accessed December 7, 2018).

608. Former Art. 1158 of the CC. Fr. reads as follows:

> Words susceptible of two meanings must be taken in the meaning that best suits the subject matter of the contract.

supra n. 130.

609. *See*, section §2.01[B][2][b], The Emergence of Principles of Objective Interpretation in the Classical Period, *supra*.

610. *See*, section §2.01[B][2][a], The Emergence of Principles of Subjective Interpretation in the Classical Period, *supra*.

611. "*Ukûd'da itibar, makaasıd ve maânîyedir, elfâz ve mebanîye değildir. Binaen-alâ-zâlik 'bey' bi'l-vefâ'da' rehin hükmü cereyan eder.*" İlhan, *supra* n. 605, at 46-47, translation taken from http://www.iium.edu.my/deed/lawbase/al_majalle/al_majalleintro.html (accessed December 7, 2018).

612. Article 1160:

> Clauses which are commonly used in a contract shall be filled in, even though they have not been inserted.

supra n. 130.

613. "*Örfen ma'ruf olan şey, şart kılınmış gibidir.*" İlhan, *supra* n. 605, at 50-51, translation taken from http://www.iium.edu.my/deed/lawbase/al_majalle/al_majalleintro.html (accessed December 7, 2018).

614. *See* http://www.iium.edu.my/deed/lawbase/al_majalle/al_majalleintro.html (accessed December 7, 2018).

615. "*Mütecezzî olmayan bir şeyin bazını zikretmek, küllünü zikr gibidir.*" İlhan, *supra* n. 605, at 52-53, translation taken from http://www.iium.edu.my/deed/lawbase/al_majalle/al_majalleintro.html (accessed December 7, 2018).

the ninth place in his *Traité des obligations*,[616] the French legislators did not include it in the CC. Fr. Ottoman legislators however, included this principle in the Mecelle, which demonstrates that they considered not only the black letter rules of the CC. Fr. but also the sources on which they are based.

Another basic principle of the interpretation of contracts can be found in Article 65 of the Mecelle. According to this article, "[a] description with reference to a thing present is of no effect, but the contrary is the case if such thing is not present. Example: When a vendor who is about to sell a grey horse, such grey horse being present at the meeting where the sale took place, states that he is selling a brown horse for so many thousand piastres, his offer is held to be good and the word brown is of no effect. But if he sells a grey horse which is not present and he describes it as brown, the description is held to be good but the sale is not concluded."[617] This provision is a clear expression of the principle of *falsa demonstratio non nocet*, according to which false description does not vitiate.

[2] Interpretation of Contracts in Modern Turkish Law

[a] Article 19(1) of the TBK

In modern Turkish legislation, the general provisions on the interpretation of contracts are very limited and unsystematic. This is because in 1926 Turkey adopted the Swiss OR together with the Swiss *Zivilgesetzbuch*. The Code of Obligations (*Borçlar Kanunu*, BK) of 1926 follows the OR in addressing the interpretation of contracts with only one provision, which is Article 18(1) of both codes.[618]

In 2012, the BK of 1926 was replaced with the Turkish Code of Obligations (*Türk Borçlar Kanunu*, TBK), and the provision on the interpretation of contracts was preserved under Article 19(1) of the TBK. Article 19 of the TBK reads as follows:

> D. Interpretation of contracts, simulation
>
> In deciding the type or terms of a contract, the true intention and mutual assent of the parties should be taken into consideration, disregarding any expression which may have been used either by mistake or so as to disguise true intention of the parties.

616. Pothier, *supra* n. 37, at n. 92.
617. "*Hâzırdaki vasıf lağv ve gâibdeki vasıf muteberdir. Meselâ, bâyi' meclis-i bey'de hâzır olan bir kır atı, satacak olduğu halde 'şu yağız atı şu kadar bin kuruşa sattım' dese icabı muteber olup, yağız ta'biri lağv olur, amma meydanda olmayan bir kır atı yağız diye satsa, vasıf muteber olmakla bey' mün'akid olmaz.*"; İlhan, *supra* n. 605, at 52-53, translation taken from http://www.iium.edu.my/deed/lawbase/al_majalle/al_majalleintro.html (accessed December 7, 2018).
618. *See*, section §3.03[B][1] Generally, *supra*.

> A person who is bound by the terms and conditions of a contract and obligations stated therein, cannot assert simulation as a defense against a third party who relies his claim on such an acknowledgement.[619]

The second paragraph of this article addresses simulation, and it is not related with the interpretation of contracts. The phrase "so as to disguise true intention of the parties" in the first paragraph also refers to simulation and not to interpretation. As explained above, the reason for which the Swiss and Turkish legislators addressed both interpretation and simulation in the same article is that they consider these concepts inseparable. In the former, the parties unconsciously give a different appearance to their contract, whereas in the latter, they do so deliberately.[620]

As for the first paragraph of this article, it is an expression of the most basic rule of interpretation, which is based on Papinianus' text in *Dig.* 50, 16, 219 and which provides that the true intent of the parties must be sought without limitation to an examination of the meaning of the words they used.[621] By adopting the Swiss OR in 1926, the Turkish legislators appear to have also adopted the "will theory" (*Willenstheorie*), which bases the interpretation of contracts on the will of the parties.[622]

Nevertheless, according to Kocayusufpaşaoğlu/Hatemi/Serozan/Arpacı, Article 19(1) of the TBK cannot be regarded as a genuine provision of contractual interpretation. This is because this provision does not address how to determine the true intent of the parties.[623] These authors, however, accurately acknowledge that Article 19(1) of the TBK is an expression of the principle of *falsa demonstratio non nocet*. Since the true intent of the parties prevails over the wording of their contract, erroneous statements of the parties should not vitiate the legal consequences that the parties intended.[624]

In Turkish law, there are no separate provisions for the interpretation of contracts and the interpretation of statements, as there is in German law.[625] According to Eren, and Oğuzman/Öz, Article 19(1) of the TBK does not apply to the interpretation of statements, as it can apply only to contracts concluded pursuant to Article 1 of the TBK.[626] According to this article:

---

619. "*D. Sözleşmelerin yorumu, muvazaalı işlemler MADDE 19- Bir sözleşmenin türünün ve içeriğinin belirlenmesinde ve yorumlanmasında, tarafların yanlışlıkla veya gerçek amaçlarını gizlemek için kullandıkları sözcüklere bakılmaksızın, gerçek ve ortak iradeleri esas alınır. Borçlu, yazılı bir borç tanımasına güvenerek alacağı kazanmış olan üçüncü kişiye karşı, bu işlemin muvazaalı olduğu savunmasında bulunamaz.*" *Türk Borçlar Kanunu*, S. 6098 (Official Gazette 2.4.2011/27836), 10759-10760, http://www.mevzuat.gov.tr/MevzuatMetin/1.5.6098.pdf (accessed December 7, 2018), translation taken from Çağlar Özel, *Türk Borçlar Kanunu / Turkish Code of Obligations*, 89 (3rd ed., Ankara, 2016).
620. *See*, section §3.03[B][4] Article 18/1 of the OR, *infra*; Kramer, Schmidlin, *supra* n. 38, at n. 10.
621. *See*, section §2.01[B][2][a], The Emergence of Principles of Subjective Interpretation in the Classical Period, *supra*; Selahattin Sulhi Tekinay, Sermet Akman, Haluk Burcuoğlu, Atilla Altop, *Tekinay Borçlar Hukuku Genel Hükümler*, 149-150 (7th ed., Filiz, 1993).
622. Wiegand, *supra* n. 491, at n. 1.
623. Kocayusufpaşaoğlu, Hatemi, Serozan, Arpacı, *supra* n. 588, at 332.
624. *Ibid.*; Gökhan Antalya, *Borçlar Hukuku Genel Hükümler*, Vol. 1, 492 (Legal, 2015); *see also* Wiegand, *supra* n. 491, at n. 16.
625. *See*, section §3.03[A][3] Provisions of the BGB Relating to the Interpretation of Contracts (§ 133 and § 157 of the BGB), *supra*.
626. Fikret Eren, *Borçlar Hukuku Genel Hükümler*, 488 (23rd ed., Yetkin, 2018); Kemal Oğuzman, Turgut Öz, *Borçlar Hukuku Genel Hükümler*, Vol. 1, 191 (16th ed., Vedat, 2018).

The contract is concluded by mutual and consentaneous expression of intent of the parties.

The expression of intent may be expressed or implied.[627]

According to Oğuzman/Öz, judges seek to determine the common meaning of respective statements of the parties when there are disputes on interpretation. If a judge finds that their respective statements are not compatible with each other, then he determines that no contract has been formed. This is done through the interpretation of the statements of the parties.[628]

This distinction is indeed the one between disputes regarding a meeting of the minds and "pure interpretation disputes" (*reiner Auslegungsstreit*), examined above in Swiss law.[629] In the former, the judge seeks to determine whether there has ever been a meeting of the minds and therefore whether or not the contract exists. In the latter, the existence of the contract is not disputed and its meaning is sought through interpretation.[630]

There is no doubt that Article 18/1 of the OR and Article 19(1) of the TBK apply to pure interpretation disputes. What is controversial is whether these articles can also apply to the interpretation of statements for the determination of whether or not a contract has been formed. In Swiss law, the dominant view holds that they can, since contracts are formed by mutual statements.[631] Additionally, Swiss courts apply Article 18/1 of the OR to the interpretation of statements and unilateral transactions by analogy.[632] Therefore, it would seem reasonable to also adopt the same view in Turkish law. A sharp distinction between the interpretation of contracts and statements is neither possible, nor meaningful, nor even compatible with general tendencies in comparative law.

Another issue of conflict is whether a judge may interpret a contract brought before him ex officio. According to Eren, he cannot. The parties must have requested that the judge interpret their contract in order for him to be able to interpret it.[633] Akyol argues, however, that judges may not only make both explanatory and complementary interpretation ex officio but also are bound to do so.[634]

The *Yargıtay* (the Turkish high court) appears to have adopted the second view. It reverses decisions in which lower courts have not interpreted contracts brought before them, holding that they are bound to interpret contracts according to Article

627. "*Sözleşme, tarafların iradelerini karşılıklı ve birbirine uygun olarak açıklamalarıyla kurulur. İrade açıklaması, açık veya örtülü olabilir.*" TBK, *supra* n. 619, at 10757, translation taken from Özel, *supra* n. 619, at 77.
628. Oğuzman, Öz, *supra* n. 626, at 191.
629. *See*, section §3.03[B][2] The Use of the Principle of Trust in Disputes Regarding the Meeting of the Minds and "Pure Interpretation Disputes", *supra*.
630. Pierre Tercier, Pascal Pichonnaz, H. Murat Develioğlu, *Borçlar Hukuku—Genel Hükümler*, 297 (On İki Levha, 2016); Antalya, *supra* n. 624, at 489; Ceren Damar, *Sözleşmenin Yorumu*, Çankaya Üniversitesi Hukuk Fakültesi Dergisi, C. 1 S. 2, 89, 95-96 (2016).
631. Jäggi, Gauch, *supra* n. 502, at n. 80; Aepli, *supra* n. 490, at n. 2; Gauch, Aepli, Casanova, *supra* n. 533, at 31. For the opposing view, *see*, Wiegand, *supra* n. 491, at nn. 2 and 8-9.
632. BGer 4C.16/2000 (24.1.01) E. 2a, *supra* n. 512; BGE 115 II 323, *supra* n. 533.
633. Eren, *supra* n. 626, at 488.
634. Şener Akyol, *Sözlemenin Yorumu*, 144 (Vedat, 2010).

19(1) of the TBK (former Article 18(1) of the BK) even when the parties have not requested the court to interpret it.[635]

As regards the qualification of contracts, both the literature[636] and case law[637] agree that lower courts are not bound to the qualification given by the parties, but that they must qualify contracts ex officio.

As these examples indicate, the *Yargıtay* considers decisions relating to the interpretation of contracts to be reviewable on appeal. The general tendency in comparative law is to recognize that the interpretation of contracts is a question of facts, not law.[638] However, the *Yargıtay* appears to have considered this question to be a question of law. In many cases, the *Yargıtay* has reversed decisions of lower courts where they appointed experts for the interpretation of contracts. The *Yargıtay* ruled in these decisions that "the interpretation of contracts forms part of the judges' profession, as it requires general legal knowledge."[639]

Akyol, and Tercier/Pichonnaz/Develioğlu argue, however, that the determination of the true meaning of a contract is a question of fact.[640] Nevertheless, these authors do not criticize the *Yargıtay*'s review of decisions relating to the interpretation of contracts. Akyol holds that the *Yargıtay* can also reverse decisions when lower courts failed to comply with procedural rules while establishing the facts of a case.[641] Akyol goes further to state that in these situations, the *Yargıtay* can even modify decisions of lower courts instead of reversing them. According to him, this method would reduce the workload of the courts and avoid further delays in court procedures.[642]

635. 11. HD., E. 1978/1019, K. 1978/1601, T. 30.3.1978; 7. HD., E. 1982/10108, K. 1982/11889, T. 15.10.1982; 14. HD., E. 1985/1106, K. 1985/4243, T. 11.6.1985; HGK., E. 1984/11-502, K. 1986/220, T. 12.3.1986; HGK., E. 1996/2-925, K. 1997/192, T. 12.3.1997; 19. HD., E. 2000/8538, K. 2001/3634, T. 11.5.2001; 13. HD., E. 2011/348, K. 2011/14630, T. 18.10.2011, www.kazanci.com (accessed December 7, 2018).
636. Kocayusufpaşaoğlu, Hatemi, Serozan, Arpacı, *supra* n. 588, at 338.
637. 11. HD., E. 1978/1019, K. 1978/1601, T. 30.3.1978; HGK., E. 1993/6-94, K. 1993/450, T. 16.6.1993; 22. HD., E. 2013/8240, K. 2014/8158, T. 15.4.2014; HGK., E. 2000/19-839, K. 2000/879, T. 10.5.2000; 13. HD., E. 2005/6577, K. 2005/11498, T. 5.7.2005; 7. HD., E. 1982/10108, K. 1982/11889, T. 15.10.1982; HGK., E. 1997/2-10, K. 1997/275, T. 2.4.1997, www.kazanci.com (accessed December 7, 2018).
638. *See*, sections §3.02[A][3] Review of Decisions Relating to the Interpretation of Contracts (French Law); §3.02[B][3] Review of Decisions Relating to the Interpretation of Contracts (Italian Law); §3.03[A][1] Generally (German Law); §3.03[B][3] The Significance of the Distinction Between Subjective and Objective Interpretation for Reviewability of Decisions (Swiss Law); §3.04[B][1], Generally (US Law), *infra*.
639. 15. HD., E. 1990/5347, K. 1990/5455, T. 12.12.1990; 15. HD., E. 1990/4450, K. 1991/1798, T. 8.4.1991; 15. HD., E. 1991/1695, K. 1991/5031, T. 24.10.1991; HGK., E. 1993/15-164, K. 1993/501, T. 30.6.1993; 15. HD., E. 1993/441, K. 1994/176, T. 20.1.1994; 15. HD., E. 1995/6686, K. 1995/7439, T. 13.12.1995; 15. HD., E. 1997/4847, K. 1997/5342, T. 11.12.1997; 15. HD., E. 1999/5061, K. 2000/1432, T. 29.3.2000; 19. HD., E. 2004/8054, K. 2005/4169, T. 18.4.2005, www.kazanci.com (accessed December 7, 2018).
640. Akyol, *supra* n. 634, at 146; Tercier, Pichonnaz, Develioğlu, *supra* n. 630, at 298.
641. Akyol, *supra* n. 634, at 146.
642. *Ibid.*, at 145.

However, the debate on this issue may have been resolved with the establishment of the Regional Courts of Appeal in Turkey in 2016.[643] The Regional Courts of Appeal have the authority to review the decisions of the courts of first instance regarding not only legal issues but also de novo review of case facts. Therefore, the Yargıtay can reasonably be expected to limit its review to legal issues only and leave the review of decisions that apply to the determination of the meaning of a contract to the Regional Courts of Appeal.

[b] *The Will Theory, the Theory of Declaration, and the Trust Theory*

Although Article 19(1) of the TBK reflects the will theory, neither the subjective will theory nor the objective theory of declaration has been adopted in Turkish law in an absolute manner.[644] Nevertheless, as explained above, it can be observed that the subjective theory prevails in Swiss literature and case law.[645] Both Swiss literature and courts agree that the subjective method of interpretation precedes the objective method[646] and that the objective theories (such as the trust theory, *Vertrauenstheorie*) only apply when the true intent of the parties cannot be determined through subjective interpretation.[647]

Due to the influence of German law, however, Turkish literature regards the will theory with suspicion, and it is more resistant to the subjective approach.[648] Eren distinguishes between the interpretation of contracts and the interpretation of statements and addresses this issue under the latter heading. According to him, the will theory only considers the subjective intent and interests of the party who makes the declaration and not those of the addressee. For this reason, this theory is also incompatible with the principle of legal security. In support of his argument, Eren also points out that Article 1(1) of the TBK rejects the will theory since it bases the formation of contracts on the declarations of intention of the parties and not on their intent.[649]

Although some authors identify the will theory with the "subjective theory of declaration,"[650] Eren distinguishes these two theories and states that in the former, only the will or intent of the party who makes the declaration is taken as a basis, whereas in the latter, the subjective meaning as understood by the addressee prevails.

---

643. Regional Courts of Appeal were established and started to function as of 20.07.2016, on the basis of the Law on Establishment, Duties and Jurisdiction of First Instance Courts and Regional Courts of Appeal No 5235, dated 26.9.2004.
644. Safa Reisoğlu, *Borçlar Hukuku Genel Hükümler*, 100 (25th ed., Beta, 2014); Akyol, *supra* n. 634, at 54-55.
645. *See*, section §3.03[B][1] Generally, *supra*.
646. BGE 92 II 347; 99 II 285; 101 II 331; 111 II 287, *supra* n. 502; Gauch, Schluep, *supra* n. 502, at 1,201 and 1,225; Jäggi, Gauch, *supra* n. 502, at nn. 306 et seq.; Aepli, *supra* n. 490, at nn. 3, 7-9; *see also*, Oğuzman, Öz, *supra* n. 626, at 193.
647. Wiegand, *supra* n. 491, at n. 1 and 3; Aepli, *supra* n. 490, at n. 9.
648. In accordance with the prevailing view in Swiss law, Kaplan argues that objective interpretation does not apply if the intent of the parties can be determined. İbrahim Kaplan, *Hakimin Sözleşmeye Müdahalesi*, 41 (3rd ed., Yetkin, 2013).
649. Eren, *supra* n. 626, at 150.
650. Altan Fahri Gülerci, Ayşe Kılınç, *6098 Sayılı Yeni TBK ile Karşılaştırmalı Borçlar Hukuku Genel Hükümler*, 89 (Yetkin 2011).

He further states that the common weakness of both theories is that they only consider the position of one of the parties and do not protect the other party.[651]

Furthermore, Eren also criticizes the theory of declaration for being based on only the objective understanding of a reasonable third person,[652] disregarding the will of both the party making the declaration and the addressee.[653]

As a result, Turkish law makes use of the trust theory in order to objectivize the subjective approach, as is the case with Swiss law.[654] However, owing to the influence of Eren's views in the literature, the trust theory is recognized in a more efficient manner in Turkish law than in Swiss law. Although Swiss law regards this theory as a subsidiary theory that applies only when the real intent of the parties cannot be determined,[655] Turkish literature attributes priority to this theory.[656] In the words of Oktay-Özdemir, "it is an unanimously accepted fact that the true intent of the parties must be determined through the trust theory."[657]

The trust theory is based on the principle of good faith and fair dealing set forth in Article 2(1) of the TMK.[658] Some authors further subdivide the trust theory into the classical trust theory (which is identical with the theory of declaration)[659] and the new trust theory.[660]

The distinctive feature of the new trust theory is that it provides for taking into account the subjective circumstances in which the parties found themselves when the declaration was made. These subjective circumstances make the interpretation even more subjective. In this theory, the understanding of both an abstract third person and the subjective circumstances of the actual addressee are taken into consideration, including his cultural background and level of education.[661] The purpose of this theory is to provide a balanced protection of the interests of both parties and to maintain legal security.[662]

651. Eren, *supra* n. 626, at 149-150.
652. Gülerci, Kılınç, *supra* n. 650, at 89.
653. Eren, *supra* n. 626, at 151.
654. *Ibid.*, at 152.
655. Wiegand, *supra* n. 491, at n. 1 and 3; Aepli, *supra* n. 490, at n. 9.
656. Saibe Oktay (Özdemir), *İsimsiz Sözleşmelerin Geçerliliği, Yorumu ve Boşluklarının Tamamlanması*, İstanbul Üniversitesi Hukuk Fakültesi Dergisi, C. LV, S. 1-2, 263, 279 (1996); Eren, *supra* n. 626, at 154; Gülerci, Kılınç, *supra* n. 650, at 89. On this point Kaplan and Tercier/Pichonnaz /Develioğlu disagree with the prevailing opinion in Turkish literature, Kaplan, *supra* n. 648, at 38; Tercier, Pichonnaz, Develioğlu, *supra* n. 630, at 299-300. Antalya also acknowledges that the objective method of interpretation is a subsidiary method. However, he holds that the interpretation of contracts is based on the trust theory, Antalya, *supra* n. 624, at 490 and 493.
657. Oktay-Özdemir, *supra* n. 656, at 154.
658. Eren, *supra* n. 626, at 152; Kocayusufpaşaoğlu, Hatemi, Serozan, Arpacı, *supra* n. 588, at 335; Oktay-Özdemir, *supra* n. 656, at 279.
659. Eren, *supra* n. 626, at 153; Gülerci, Kılınç, *supra* n. 650, at 89.
660. Eren, *supra* n. 626, at 152-153, Gülerci, Kılınç, *supra* n. 650, at 89.
661. Eren, *supra* n. 626, at 154-155, Gülerci, Kılınç, *supra* n. 650, at 89; Reisoğlu, *supra* n. 644, at 100.
662. Eren, *supra* n. 626, at 154.

[c] Principles of Literal Interpretation

Although the only general provision in Turkish and Swiss legislation regarding the interpretation of contracts is a provision for subjective interpretation based on the intent of the parties, this does not imply that the text of a contract is not important. To the contrary, the literature acknowledges that the words used by the parties are the primary tools for a determination of their true intent.[663] The *Yargıtay* also confirmed the priority of the literal interpretation in a decision where it held that "contracts are to be primarily interpreted according to the rules of logic and grammar."[664]

In another decision, the *Yargıtay* referred to a dictionary for determining the meaning of an expression in a contract.[665] In this decision, the *Yargıtay* interpreted the phrase "*rüsum içinde*" in the contract of a usufructuary lease, which is an unusual expression meaning "taxes included" and ruled that the value-added tax should be borne by the lessee.

The Turkish literature also recognizes the principles of literal interpretation according to which the words used by the parties must be understood in their natural sense, and not in their special or technical sense,[666] and technical or commercial terms are to be understood in their specific sense when the parties to the contract are from the same field of business.[667]

The true intent of the parties constitutes the limits of the literal interpretation. Judges cannot strictly adhere to the wording of a contract so as to disregard the true intent of the parties, even if the wording of a contract appears to be "clear" to them. Therefore, the *in claris non fit interpretatio* rule, which has not been generally adopted in comparative law, has not been adopted in Turkish law either. Swiss and Turkish literatures recognize that this rule is in contradiction with Articles 18(1) of the OR and 19(1) of the TBK, which acknowledges that the true intent of the parties may differ from the wording of a contract, no matter how clear the latter is.[668]

Swiss law considers the *in claris non fit interpretatio* rule as outdated and overly formalistic, giving absolute priority to the literal meaning. Both Swiss literature and[669]

663. Tekinay, Akman, Burcuoğlu, Altop, *supra* n. 621, at 148; Eren, *supra* n. 626, at 491; Oğuzman, Öz, *supra* n. 626, at 192; Oktay-Özdemir, *supra* n. 656, at 280; Kaplan, *supra* n. 648, at 42; İbrahim Kaplan, *Banka Sözleşmelerinin Yorumu ve Tamamlanması*, Banka ve Ticaret Hukuku Dergisi, C. XIV, S. 2, 17 (1987); Antalya, *supra* n. 624, at 491.

664. *"sözleşmenin yorumu(nun) öncelikle mantık ve gramer kurallarına göre yapılaca(ğını)"*, 11. HD., E. 1997/10396, K. 1998/1278, T. 2.3.1998, www.kazanci.com (accessed December 7, 2018), author's translation.

665. 14. HD., E. 2007/426, K. 2007/1574, T. 21.2.2007, www.kazanci.com (accessed December 7, 2018).

666. Oğuzman, Öz, *supra* n. 626, at 192-193; Eren, *supra* n. 626, at 491; Oktay-Özdemir, *supra* n. 656, at 280; Kaplan, *supra* n. 648, at 42-43; Tercier, Pichonnaz, Develioğlu, *supra* n. 630, at 298; Antalya, *supra* n. 624, at 492.

667. Kaplan, *supra* n. 648, at 43; Eren, *supra* n. 626, at 491; Tercier, Pichonnaz, Develioğlu, *supra* n. 630, at 298; Antalya, *supra* n. 624, at 492.

668. Kramer, Schmidlin, *supra* n. 38, at n. 47; Kocayusufpaşaoğlu, Hatemi, Serozan, Arpacı, *supra* n. 588, at 333; Eren, *supra* n. 626, at 491; Tercier, Pichonnaz, Develioğlu, *supra* n. 630, at 299; Antalya, *supra* n. 624, at 491; Damar, *supra* n. 630, at 99-100.

669. Gauch, Schluep, *supra* n. 502, at 1,221; Jäggi, Gauch, *supra* n. 502, at n. 368.

the *Bundesgericht*[670] reject this rule. German literature and case law also unanimously accept that *in claris non fit interpretatio* cannot be considered as a legal principle because the determination of whether a statement is "clear" or not can be made only through a process of interpretation.[671]

This being the case, in a decision of the *Yargıtay Hukuk Genel Kurulu* (General Assembly of the Civil Chambers of the Court of Cassation), the *Yargıtay* reversed a domestic arbitral award because, among other reasons, "this clause of the contract is so clear as to not require interpretation; it is not possible to interpret the contract in the light of its addendums and to reach a different conclusion."[672] However, this decision remains an exception in Turkish case law. Therefore, although this decision is binding on lower courts and the opinion contains language that recalls the *in claris non fit interpretatio* rule, it should not be considered as an implied recognition of that rule.

[d] Relevance of Usages

Another provision of interpretation in Turkish legislation is found in Article 2(1) of the Turkish Commercial Code (*Türk Ticaret Kanunu*, TTK), entitled "Commercial Usages." According to this paragraph:

> In the absences of any clause to the contrary in the Law, practice may not be taken as a basis for judgment as long as it is not admitted as commercial usage. However, practices are also to be taken into consideration for the interpretation of declarations of intention.[673]

This paragraph sets forth a hierarchy between commercial usages and practices in favor of the former. The second sentence states an exception to the rule that practices may not be taken as a basis for judgment, according to which practices do not need to have reached the level of usage before being considered in the interpretation of statements. In German law, however, practices must have reached the level of usage in order to be taken into consideration for the purposes of interpretation.[674]

In both German and Turkish law, there is no doubt that usages can be taken into account in interpreting statements and contracts. Article 2(1) of the TTK is an indirect expression of this principle, which is based on Ulpianus' text in *Dig.* 50, 17, 34.[675]

670. BGE ZBJV 1995, 131, S. 241.
671. BGHZ 86, 41, 46 mwN = NJW 1983, 672; BGH NJW 2002, 1260, 1261; NJW-RR 1996, 1458; BAG NJW 2005, 1144, 1144 f.; DB 1975, 1368; RGZ 163, 324, 328 f.; 158, 119, 124; Busche, *supra* n. 399, at nn. 53-55; Singer, *supra* n. 398, at n. 9; Looschelders, *supra* n. 393, at, n. 27.
672. HGK., E. 1995/15-1114, K. 1996/302, T. 24.4.1996, www.kazanci.com (accessed December 7, 2018).
673. "*Kanunda aksine bir hüküm yoksa, ticari örf ve âdet olarak kabul edildiği belirlenmedikçe, teamül, mahkemenin yargısına esas olamaz. Ancak, irade açıklamalarının yorumunda teamüller de dikkate alınır.*" *Türk Ticaret Kanunu*, S. 6102 (Official Gazette 14.2.2011/27846), 10975, http://www.mevzuat.gov.tr/MevzuatMetin/1.5.6102.pdf (accessed December 7, 2018), author's translation.
674. *See*, section §3.03[A][3][b] § 133 of the BGB, *supra*; Looschelders, *supra* n. 393, at nn. 59 et seq.
675. *See*, section §2.01[B][2][b], The Emergence of Principles of Objective Interpretation in the Classical Period, *supra*.

The second sentence of this article addresses the "interpretation of declarations of intention," a broad expression which also includes the statements of offer and acceptance. Accordingly, Turkish literature acknowledges the importance of commercial usages and practices in the interpretation of both contracts and statements. According to Oktay-Özdemir, usages are especially relevant in the interpretation of *contractus innominati*.[676] Likewise, Kaplan points out the importance of usages in the interpretation of banking contracts and states that the Uniform Customs and Practice (UCP) 600 rules of the International Chamber of Commerce (ICC) often acquire binding force in these types of contracts.[677] He further states that the common meanings of INCOTERMS must be taken into consideration in the interpretation of international sales contracts.[678]

Furthermore, a decision of the *Yargıtay* confirmed that a banking contract must be interpreted by taking into account the usages in the banking sector.[679]

[e] *Article 23 of the TBK and the Contra Stipulatorem Rule*

The *contra stipulatorem* rule, providing that ambiguous clauses must be interpreted against the party who drafted them, became more important in Turkish law with the promulgation of Article 23 of the new TBK, which sets forth this rule in the context of standard terms as follows:

> Where the provisions in standardized terms are not perspicuous or comprehensible and have more than one meaning, it is interpreted against the interests of the draftsman and in favor of other party.[680]

This provision is not the only provision in Turkish legislation on the principle of *contra stipulatorem*. Article 5(4) of the Consumer Protection Law (*Tüketicinin Korunması Hakkında Kanun*, TKK) also contains a similar provision for consumer contracts. According to this paragraph:

> In cases where all terms offered to the consumer are in written form, these terms must always be drafted in plain, intelligible language. Where there is doubt about the meaning of a term, the most favorable interpretation to the consumer shall prevail.[681]

676. Oktay-Özdemir, *supra* n. 656, at 282.
677. Kaplan, *supra* n. 663, at 5-6.
678. Kramer, Schmidlin, *supra* n. 38, at n. 32; Kaplan, *supra* n. 648, at 58 and 61.
679. 11. HD., E. 1978/1019, K. 1978/1601, T. 30.3.1978, www.kazanci.com (accessed December 7, 2018).
680. "*Genel işlem koşullarında yer alan bir hüküm, açık ve anlaşılır değilse veya birden çok anlama geliyorsa, düzenleyenin aleyhine ve karşı tarafın lehine yorumlanır.*"; TBK, *supra* n. 619 at 10760, translation taken from Özel, *supra* n. 619, at 91.
681. "*Sözleşme şartlarının yazılı olması hâlinde, tüketicinin anlayabileceği açık ve anlaşılır bir dilin kullanılmış olması gerekir. Sözleşmede yer alan bir hükmün açık ve anlaşılır olmaması veya birden çok anlama gelmesi hâlinde; bu hüküm, tüketicinin lehine yorumlanır.*" *Tüketicinin Korunması Hakkında Kanun*, S. 6502 (Official Gazette 28.11.2013/28835), 12153 http://www.mevzuat.gov.tr/MevzuatMetin/1.5.6502.pdf (accessed December 7, 2018), translation taken

The Turkish legislators did not include the *contra stipulatorem* or *contra proferentem* rule among the general provisions but addressed this principle only within the provisions relating to standard terms and consumer protection. Does this choice of the legislators imply that this principle only applies in these two contexts? Does Turkish law refuse to recognize that the *contra stipulatorem* rule applies to an individually negotiated, ambiguous contract term? The present author is of the opinion that drawing such a conclusion would be excessive.

It is true that the *contra stipulatorem* rule is narrowly interpreted in the Romano-Germanic legal tradition.[682] Accordingly, some Turkish authors also argue that this rule should only apply to standard terms and consumer contracts.[683]

According to them, Article 23 of the TBK is a subsidiary rule of interpretation and all the methods of interpretation must be exhausted for applying this rule.[684]

In addition to that, the Banks Association of Turkey has criticized Article 23 of the TBK for being inconsistent with the freedom of contract and equality of the parties, and they proposed its removal from the draft TBK in a report prepared before the TBK was passed.[685] The proposal of the Banks Association of Turkey was not surprising, since banking contracts are usually formed through standard terms and are an important field of application of Article 23 of the TBK.[686] Nevertheless, Article 23 remained in the TBK, against the interests of the banks.

However, the opposing view holds that interpretation of ambiguous terms against the parties who supplied them[687] and in favor of the parties who undertake an obligation by these terms[688] is a general principle of law. According to this view, this principle emanates from the general principle of good faith and fair dealing, expressed in Article 2(1) of the TMK.[689]

---

from Hakan Tokbaş, Özlem Tüzüner, *Milli Şerh (National Commentary) 6502 Sayılı Tüketicinin Korunması Hakkında Kanun Şerhi (Commentary on the Consumer Protection Law No. 6502)*, 122 (Aristo, 2016).

682. *See*, sections §3.03[A][3][c] § 157 of the BGB; §3.03[B][5] Principles of Interpretation Developed Through Case Law, *supra*.
683. Kocayusufpaşaoğlu, Hatemi, Serozan, Arpacı, *supra* n. 588, at 239; Akyol, *supra* n. 634, at 72; Tekinay, Akman, Burcuoğlu, Altop, and Kaplan point out that this rule is "more important" for the interpretation of standard clauses. Tekinay, Akman, Burcuoğlu, Altop, *supra* n. 621, at 151-152; Kaplan, *supra* n. 648, at 74. These authors also uphold the principle of *favor debitoris*, Tekinay, Akman, Burcuoğlu, Altop, *supra* n. 621, at 152; Kaplan, *supra* n. 648, at 72-73; Eren, *supra* n. 626, at 494.
684. Kocayusufpaşaoğlu, Hatemi, Serozan, Arpacı, *supra* n. 588, at 239; Umut Yeniocak, *Türk Borçlar Kanunu'nun Getirdiği Yenilikler ve Değişiklikler*, 60 (2nd ed., Seçkin, 2013).
685. Yeniocak, *supra* n. 684, at 59-60.
686. İbrahim Kaplan, *supra* n. 663, at 18.
687. Tercier, Pichonnaz, Develioğlu, *supra* n. 630, at 301; Antalya, *supra* n. 624, at 497; Oğuzman, Öz, *supra* n. 626, at 193-194 (these authors refer to 13. HD., E. 1981/6416, K. 1981/7369, T. 18.11.1981). Kocayusufpaşaoğlu, Hatemi, Serozan, Arpacı also acknowledge that the *contra proferentem* rule is a general principle of law. Kocayusufpaşaoğlu, Hatemi, Serozan, Arpacı, *supra* n. 588, at 336.
688. Oktay-Özdemir, *supra* n. 656, at 281; Oğuzman, Öz, *supra* n. 626, at 194 (these authors refer to 4. HD., E. 1957/206, K. 1957/4566, T. 16.7.1957).
689. Akyol, *supra* n. 634, at 135-136.

The present author adheres to the view that this principle, which is based on Celsus' text in *Dig.* 34, 5, 26[690] and Ulpianus' text in *Dig.* 45, 1, 38, 18 (Ulp. 49 ad Sab.),[691] is a general principle of law,[692] and the fact that the Turkish legislators did not set it forth in the TBK as such cannot prevent it from being so. This principle constitutes a limit to the freedom of contract drawn by the principle of good faith and fair dealing. As long as this latter principle survives, the *contra stipulatorem* rule will survive as well.

Turkish legislators merely provided special aspects of this rule in Article 23 of the TBK and Article 5(4) of the TKK. A general principle of law cannot be limited or abrogated by special provisions for standard terms and consumer contracts. For this reason, the *contra stipulatorem* rule should apply not only to standard terms and consumer contracts but also to any ambiguous term, including individually negotiated ones. The general tendency in uniform law is also to recognize this rule as a general principle.[693]

[f] Principles of Interpretation Developed Through Case Law or Recognized in the Literature

Although the general provisions relating to the interpretation of contracts are very limited in Turkish law, general principles of the interpretation of contracts are widely recognized in the literature and applied in practice, as is the case with the Swiss and German legal systems.

The most important basis of the application of the non-codified principles of contractual interpretation is Article 2(1) of the TMK, which addresses the principle of good faith and fair dealing. According to the opinion maintaining that Article 19(1) of the TBK is not a genuine provision of interpretation, Article 2(1) of the TMK is the only general provision relating to the interpretation of contracts in Turkish legislation.[694] Kocayusufpaşaoğlu/Hatemi/Serozan/Arpacı concur with this poisition, stating that "when the real intent of contracting parties is to be sought, it must be sought in the light of Article 2(1) of the TMK, taking all the relevant circumstances into account."[695]

690. *Dig.* 34, 5, 26, *supra* n. 52.
691. *Dig.* 45, 1, 38, 18, *supra* n. 53.
692. *See*, section §2.01[B][2][b], The Emergence of Principles of Objective Interpretation in the Classical Period, *supra*.
693. *See*, sections §4.03[B][6] Article 4.6 of the UPICC; §4.04[A][2][c] Article 5:103 of the PECL; §4.04[B][2][c] Article II—8:103 of the DCFR; §4.04[C][2][h] Article 65 of the CESL; §4.05[B][4] Trans-Lex Principle No. IV.5.4, *infra*.
694. Kocayusufpaşaoğlu, Hatemi, Serozan, Arpacı, *supra* n. 588, at 332.
695. *Ibid.*, at 333. These authors hold that the principle of good faith and fair dealing (Art. 2(1) of the TMK) also applies to gap-filling, Kocayusufpaşaoğlu, Hatemi, Serozan, Arpacı, *supra* n. 588, at 339.

The Turkish literature recognizes the principle of good faith and fair dealing as a principle of contractual interpretation.[696] The *Yargıtay* has also confirmed this understanding, recognizing this principle as a principle of interpretation of contracts.[697] However, Turkish legislation does not include a specific provision on the principle of interpretation according to good faith and fair dealing, like § 157 of the BGB or Article 1366 of the CC. It. Nevertheless, this does not prevent this principle from being applied in practice. This principle applies on the basis of Article 2(1) of the TMK, as is the case with Swiss law, where it applies on the basis of Article 2(1) of the ZGB.[698]

Another principle frequently applied in practice despite not being expressed in the legislation is the principle of interpretation according to the purpose of the contract.[699] In many decisions, the *Yargıtay* has held that contracts must be interpreted according to the real purpose of the contracting parties.[700]

Additionally, the principle of *ut res magis valeat quam pereat*, according to which an interpretation giving effect to the terms of a contract must prevail, is recognized both by Turkish literature[701] and case law.[702]

Another principle recognized by both the literature[703] and case law[704] is the principle of systematic interpretation. As in Swiss law,[705] Turkish law also interprets this principle broadly, as to signify not only the interpretation of a contract as a whole but also interpretation by taking into account all of the circumstances that affected the contract. These include any circumstances that can shed a light on the intent of the parties, such as the time and place of the conclusion of the contract, statements made

696. Eren, *supra* n. 626, at 493; Kaplan, *supra* n. 648, at 65 et seq.; Kocayusufpaşaoğlu, Hatemi, Serozan, Arpacı, *supra* n. 588, at 333; Tercier, Pichonnaz, Develioğlu, *supra* n. 630, at 301; Antalya, *supra* n. 624, at 494.
697. HGK, E. 1995/15-745, K. 1995/965, T. 15.11.1995, www.kazanci.com (accessed December 7, 2018).
698. BGE 95 II 437; 96 II 141; 99 II 285; 107 II 163; 110 II 146; 111 II 293, *supra* n. 504; Gauch, Schluep, *supra* n. 502, at 1,224.
699. Kaplan, *supra* n. 648, at 49 et seq.; Antalya, *supra* n. 624, at 492.
700. 9. HD., E. 1975/29973, K. 1975/52852, T. 24.12.1975; 11. HD., E. 1978/1019, K. 1978/1601, T. 30.3.1978; HGK., E. 1978/6-261, K. 1978/567, T. 9.6.1978; 7. HD., E. 1982/10108, K. 1982/11889, T. 15.10.1982; 14. HD., E. 1985/1106, K. 1985/4243, T. 11.6.1985; 14. HD., E. 1989/8074, K. 1990/7581, T. 28.9.1990; 19. HD., E. 1992/9844, K. 1993/2621, T. 8.4.1993; HGK., E. 1993/13-801, K. 1994/58, T. 16.2.1994; HGK., E. 1996/2-925, K. 1997/192, T. 12.3.1997; HGK., E. 2000/1-744, K. 2000/755, T. 12.4.2000; 15. HD., E. 2002/38, K. 2002/1749, T. 11.4.2002; 2. HD., E. 2006/20180, K. 2006/17687, T. 14.12.2006; 15. HD., E. 1995/6686, K. 1995/7439, T. 13.12.1995, www.kazanci.com (accessed December 7, 2018).
701. Tekinay, Akman, Burcuoğlu, Altop, *supra* n. 621, at 151; Eren, *supra* n. 626, at 495; Oğuzman, Öz, *supra* n. 626, at 194; Kocayusufpaşaoğlu, Hatemi, Serozan, Arpacı, *supra* n. 588, at 336; Kaplan, *supra* n. 648, at 71-72; Oktay-Özdemir, *supra* n. 656, at 281; Kaplan, *supra* n. 663, at 18.
702. 4. HD., E: 13113/1977 K:12134/1978, T. 26.10.1978; HGK E. 1983/14-79 K. 1985/182 T. 8.3.1985; 14. HD. E. 1990/216, K. 1990/8009, T. 9.10.1990; 14. HD., E. 1989/8074, K. 1990/7581, T. 28.9.1990, www.kazanci.com (accessed December 7, 2018).
703. Eren, *supra* n. 626, at 494; Kocayusufpaşaoğlu, Hatemi, Serozan, Arpacı, *supra* n. 588, at 333; Oktay-Özdemir, *supra* n. 656, at 280; Oğuzman, Öz, *supra* n. 626, at 193; Tekinay, Akman, Burcuoğlu, Altop, *supra* n. 621, at 151; Kaplan, *supra* n. 648, at 67 et seq.; Tercier, Pichonnaz, Develioğlu, *supra* n. 630, at 298 and 301; Antalya, *supra* n. 624, at 492.
704. 4. HD., E: 13113/1977, K:12134/1978, www.kazanci.com (accessed December 7, 2018).
705. Kramer, Schmidlin, *supra* n. 38, at n. 16, n. 44; Gauch, Aepli, Casanova, *supra* n. 533, at 31; Wiegand, *supra* n. 491, at nn. 12-13 and 18.

during the negotiations, other documents exchanged between the parties, prior or subsequent conduct of the parties, their purpose, their manner of performance, relevant usages and practices in the place of performance, etc.[706]

The *Yargıtay* also recognizes and applies the principle of systematic interpretation in its broader sense. In a decision relating to a cottonseed production contract, the *Yargıtay* held that this particular contract must be interpreted according to the types of seeds suggested by the relevant Regional (cotton) Research Institute, even though the contract did not refer to such criterion.[707] In an older decision, the *Yargıtay* held that "when interpreting contracts, the manner of performance of the parties must be taken into consideration."[708] Furthermore, the *Yargıtay* confirmed this point in another decision when interpreting a concession agreement that provided for a tax exemption for the year 1998; the *Yargıtay* considered that the parties also applied the tax exemption for the two subsequent years and ruled that they were bound by this practice.[709]

In a more striking decision, the *Yargıtay* interpreted a phrase on a bond in light of the subjective conditions in which the parties were in when they signed it. In that decision, the *Yargıtay* interpreted the phrase "paid" on the bond by taking into consideration the level of education of the party who wrote it and held that he did not mean that the amount on the bond was actually paid but that he received another bond instead of the first.[710]

According to another rule of interpretation, statements of waiver must be interpreted narrowly.[711] Likewise, the *Yargıtay* has also held that penal clauses must be interpreted narrowly.[712] This decision is in accordance with the rule of Swiss law, which provides a narrow interpretation of clauses deviating from dispositive rules.[713]

---

706. Kocayusufpaşaoğlu, Hatemi, Serozan, Arpacı, *supra* n. 588, at 333-334; Akyol, *supra* n. 634, at 84; Oktay-Özdemir, *supra* n. 656, at 280; Kaplan, *supra* n. 648, at 45 et seq.; Tercier, Pichonnaz, Develioğlu, *supra* n. 630, at 298-299; Antalya, *supra* n. 624, at 493-494.
707. 11. HD., E. 2012/4327, K. 2012/7609, T. 11.5.2012, www.kazanci.com (accessed December 7, 2018).
708. HGK., E. 1978/6-261, K. 1978/567, T. 9.6.1978; Tekinay, Akman, Burcuoğlu, Altop, *supra* n. 621, at 153.
709. 19. HD., E. 2000/8538, K. 2001/3634, T. 11.5.2001, www.kazanci.com (accessed December 7, 2018).
710. HGK., E. 1984/11-502, K. 1986/220, T. 12.3.1986, www.kazanci.com (accessed December 7, 2018).
711. Kocayusufpaşaoğlu, Hatemi, Serozan, Arpacı, *supra* n. 588, at 336; Tekinay, Akman, Burcuoğlu, Altop, *supra* n. 621, at 152; Kaplan, *supra* n. 648, at 69 et seq.; Oktay-Özdemir, *supra* n. 656, at 281; Antalya, *supra* n. 624, at 497.
712. HGK. E. 1958/3, K. 1959/1, T. 7.1.1959, www.kazanci.com (accessed December 7, 2018).
713. BGE 115 II 268, BGE 122 III 121; 119 II 372; 117 II 621; 115 II 479; 113 II 51, www.bger.ch (accessed December 7, 2018); BGer 5C.87/2002; 5C.36/2001, www.servat.unibe.ch (accessed December 7, 2018); Wiegand, *supra* n. 491, at n. 39; Aepli, *supra* n. 490, at n. 9; Gauch, Schluep, *supra* n. 502, at 1,230; Gauch, Aepli, Casanova, *supra* n. 533, at 33; *see also*, Kaplan, *supra* n. 648, at 74; Eren, *supra* n. 626, at 495; Tercier, Pichonnaz, Develioğlu, *supra* n. 630, at 301; Antalya, *supra* n. 624, at 495.

Turkish legal literature also recognizes the principle that contracts must be interpreted based on the time of their conclusion.[714] Kocayusufpaşaoğlu/Hatemi/Serozan/Arpacı state that the intent of the parties that must be sought is their intent at the time of the conclusion of the contract. Subsequent statements of the parties can be taken into consideration only to the extent that they shed light on their intent at that time.[715]

Another point that should be kept in mind is the practice of the *Yargıtay* toward filling the gaps of contracts under the pretext of interpreting them.[716] In disputes arising out of construction contracts, where contractors register independent sections about which the contracts are silent on their own name, the *Yargıtay* has developed a principle according to which these sections belong to all the parties to the contract in proportion to their shares. In many cases, the *Yargıtay* filled the gaps of construction contracts with this principle.[717] In these decisions, the *Yargıtay* avoided stating that it filled contractual gaps, even though it actually did. Conversely, it has held that it merely "interpreted" them, with the likely purpose of avoiding the impression that it actively interferes in contractual relationships.

§3.04 COMMON LAW

[A] English Law

[1] Generally

English law, differing from U.S. law,[718] does not distinguish between ascertainment of the meaning of a contract and determination of its legal consequences. A practical result of this is that the terms "interpretation" and "construction" are used interchangeably and to cover both functions,[719] although one may observe that the use of the latter term is more common in English law. Accordingly, Chitty on Contracts defines construction as "the process by which a court determines the meaning and legal effect of a contract."[720]

714. Oğuzman, Öz, *supra* n. 626, at 194; Eren, *supra* n. 626, at 493; Kocayusufpaşaoğlu, Hatemi, Serozan, Arpacı, *supra* n. 588, at 335; Akyol, *supra* n. 634, at 58; Tercier, Pichonnaz, Develioğlu, *supra* n. 630, at 297 and 300; Antalya, *supra* n. 624, at 494; Damar, *supra* n. 630, at 101-102.
715. Kocayusufpaşaoğlu, Hatemi, Serozan, Arpacı, *supra* n. 588, at 335.
716. Kaplan, *supra* n. 648, at 40.
717. 15. HD., E. 1990/5347, K. 1990/5455, T. 12.12.1990; 15. HD., E. 1995/2958, K. 1995/5641, T. 18.10.1995; 15. HD., E. 1995/6686, K. 1995/7439, T. 13.12.1995; 15. HD., E. 2009/1005, K. 2010/779, T. 15.2.2010, www.kazanci.com (accessed December 7, 2018).
718. *See*, section §3.04[B][1] Generally, *infra*.
719. Ewan McKendrick, *Construction of Terms*, in Joseph Chitty, Hugh Beale (eds.), *Chitty on Contracts*, Vol 1, *General Principles*, 1037 (32nd ed., Sweet & Maxwell, 2015) (McKendrick, Chitty on Contracts), p.; Vogenauer, *supra* n. 131, at 973; Williams, *supra* n. 12, at 224-225.
720. McKendrick, *supra* n. 719, at 1037.

Some continental lawyers are of the opinion that English law has a formalist character, which is also reflected in its approach to the interpretation of contracts.[721] The fact underlying this opinion is the absolute dominance of the objective approach to the interpretation of contracts in English law.[722] Zimmermann compares English law's formalism with that of Roman law, stating that it stems from the concern for avoiding any risk of misunderstanding. According to this author, formalism of English law causes legal documents to be written in a casuistic manner to avoid abstraction and prevents judges from drawing principles from legislation or "develop[ing] the law as an integral whole."[723] Accordingly, English judges only interpret contracts from a concrete perspective in the cases before them without developing general principles, as Roman lawyers used to do.[724]

Nonetheless, the continental perception about formalism of English law is so strong that it reaches the level of prejudice and causes the concepts of English law to be misunderstood by continental lawyers. As a result of this prejudice, and by conflating English law with U.S. law, some continental lawyers believe that the "plain meaning rule" as understood in U.S. law applies to the interpretation of contracts in English law.[725] Vogenauer identifies this rule with *in claris non fit interpretatio* and defines it to mean that "[t]he interpreter may not deviate from the clear and unambiguous meaning of a contract term, even if other criteria of interpretation point in another direction."[726] Zimmermann refers to a text by Paulus in *Dig.* 32, 25, 1 as the basis of this rule and identifies it as the reason for the objective approach of English courts to the interpretation of contracts based on declarations.[727]

It is true that the plain meaning rule exists in English law, but only in the context of the interpretation of norms and not in the interpretation of contracts. As regards its scope, this rule requires the cessation of the activity of interpretation when a satisfactory meaning for a norm has been reached.[728] The underlying reason that continental lawyers misperceive this rule is likely their perception of the plain meaning rule in the suggested sense,[729] or in a further conflation of common law principles, as a synonym for the "parol evidence rule"[730] in U.S. law.

721. Zimmermann, *supra* n. 11, at 623; Vogenauer, *supra* n. 131, at 975.
722. *See*, section §3.04[A][2] Objective Approach, *infra*.
723. Zimmermann, *supra* n. 11, at 623.
724. Williams, *supra* n. 12, at 224.
725. Vogenauer, *supra* n. 131, at 975; Zimmermann, *supra* n. 11, at 622; Fontaine, de Ly, *supra* n. 5, at 127-128.
726. Vogenauer, *supra* n. 131, at 975.
727. *Dig.* 32, 25, 1, *supra* n. 37; Zimmermann, *supra* n. 11, at 622.
728. James Fagan, *The Legal Phoenix: The Plain Meaning Rule Is Dead, Long Live the Rule*, 29 (2) California Western Law Review 373 (1993); Neil Duxbury, *Elements of Legislation*, 154 (Cambridge University Press, 2013). There is an opinion in Italian literature which interprets the *in claris non fit interpretatio* rule in the same sense. *See*, section §3.02[B][2] The Discussion on the *In Claris Non Fit Interpretatio* Rule, *supra*.
729. *See*, section §3.04[B][4][a] (Non)interpretation Rules: The Parol Evidence Rule, the Plain Meaning Rule, and the Four Corners Rule, *infra*.
730. Peter Linzer, *The Comfort of Certainty: Plain Meaning and the Parol Evidence Rule*, 71 (3) Fordham Law Review 801 (2002); Richard Hyland (Rapporteur), *CISG Advisory Council*

The scope of the interpretation of contracts is narrow in English law when compared with civil law. The absolute dominance of the objective interpretation leaves no room for subjective interpretation. Likewise, "complementary interpretation," which certain civil jurisdictions regard as a type of interpretation, does not have a proper equivalent in English law.[731]

It is possible, however, to state that a functional equivalent[732] of complementary interpretation in English law exists in the doctrine of "implied terms."[733] This doctrine is based on the presumed will of the parties, rather than their true will. Implied terms are those arising from the presumed intent of the parties based upon the customary or default rules from which parties did not expressly deviate.[734]

In the 1881 decision of *Dahl v. Nelson, Donkin, & Co.*,[735] Lord Watson defined implied terms as follows:

> When the parties to a ... contract ... have not expressed their intentions in a particular event, but have left these to implication, a Court of Law, in order to ascertain the implied meaning of the contract, must assume that the parties intended to stipulate for that which is fair and reasonable, having regard to their mutual interests and to the main objects of the contract.[736]

According to Calnan, the doctrine of implied terms may apply only if "the parties must objectively have intended them."[737] A determination of this intent can be made when these terms are either so obvious that the parties did not need to express them or when they are indispensable to make the contract work.[738] For this reason the application of implied terms is exceptional.[739]

Opinion No. 3, Parol Evidence Rule, Plain Meaning Rule, Contractual Merger Clause and the CISG, October 23, 2004, n. 1.3, https://www.trans-lex.org/500153 (accessed December 7, 2018).

731. Vogenauer, *supra* n. 131, at 973.
732. Zweigert, Kötz, *supra* n. 4, at 34 et seq.; Oğuz, *supra* n. 275, at 68 et seq.; Kornet, *supra* n. 420, at 157.
733. *Liverpool City Council v. Irwin* [1977] A.C. 239; Zweigert, Kötz, *supra* n. 4, at 407-408; Vogenauer, *supra* n. 131, at 973; Sir Kim Lewison, *The Interpretation of Contracts*, 191 et seq. (4th ed., Sweet & Maxwell, 2007); Fontaine, de Ly, *supra* n. 5, at 127; McKendrick, *supra* n. 719, at 985 et seq.; Patrick S. Atiyah, Stephen A. Smith, *Atiyah's Introduction to the Law of Contract*, 155 et seq. (6th ed., Clarendon, 2005); Michael Furmston, *Cheshire, Fifoot & Furmston's Law of Contract*, 183 et seq. (17th ed., Oxford University Press, 2017); Kornet, *supra* n. 420, at 157.
734. Hadžimanović, *supra* n. 507, at 141; Lewison, *supra* n. 733, at 191 et seq., *Luxor (Eastbourne) Ltd. v. Cooper*, [1941] A.C. 108, [1941] 1 All E.R. 33 (H.L.); *see* http://swarb.co.uk/luxor-eastbourne-v-cooper-hl-1941/ (accessed December 7, 2018).
735. *Dahl v. Nelson, Donkin, & Co.*, 6 App. Cas. 38, 59 (1881), http://www.lawandsea.net/List_of_Cases/D/Dahl_v_Nelson_1881_6_AppCas38.html (accessed December 7, 2018).
736. *Dahl v. Nelson, Donkin, & Co.*, *supra* n. 735, at 59-60.
737. Richard Calnan, *Principles of Contractual Interpretation*, 153 (2nd ed., Oxford University Press, Croydon, 2017).
738. *Ibid.*
739. The decision of Lord Hoffmann in *Attorney General of Belize v. Belize com* [2009] 1 WLR 1988 is one of these exceptions.

[2] Objective Approach

The subjective approach finds its roots in Roman law and remains dominant in most continental legal systems. This approach is based on the ascertainment of the intent of the parties (*voluntas*).[740] The approach of English law, however, is based on literal interpretation and focuses on a determination of the meaning of the words used by parties.[741] Lord Denman defined this approach in his 1833 decision of *Rickman v. Carstairs*, "[t]he question in this and other cases of construction of written documents is not what was the intention of the parties, but what is the meaning of the words they have used."[742]

Literal interpretation prevails over the real intent of the parties in English law. For this reason, objective theory characterizes the English approach to the interpretation of contracts.[743] The real or subjective intent of the parties is not relevant, and only their extrinsic expressions are the proper subject of interpretation.[744] In other words, the subject of interpretation is not the real intent of the parties, what they meant, or what they understood. Rather, it is what a reasonable third person in the same position with the parties would have understood from the statements and conduct of the parties.[745]

According to Lewison, a reason for the adoption of the objective theory is that contracts are written to be read by a third person in situations not predicted by the parties.[746] Because of this, "[f]or the purpose of the interpretation of contracts, the intention of the parties is the meaning of the contract. There is no intention independent of that meaning."[747]

Likewise, Furmston points out that "the courts, like all human tribunals, cannot peer into the minds of the parties and must be content with external phenomena."[748]

Calnan, however, links the adoption of the objective approach in the interpretation of contracts to the objective theory of the common law of contract.[749] According to him, there are three main reasons for the adoption of the objective approach: the first reason is the difficulty in establishing the subjective intent of parties, especially in complex contracts.[750] The second reason is that objective interpretation promotes legal certainty, saving time and cost.[751] The third reason is that the objective approach protects third parties, such as assignees.[752]

740. *See*, section §2.01[B][1] Generally, *supra*.
741. Williams, *supra* n. 12, at 224-225; Calnan, *supra* n. 737, at 14; Kornet, *supra* n. 420, at 158.
742. *Rickman v. Carstairs* 5 B. & Ad. 663 (1833); Williams, *supra* n. 12, at 225.
743. Calnan, *supra* n. 737, at 14; McKendrick, *supra* n. 719, at 1038; Lewison, *supra* n. 733, at 6-7 and 24; Kornet, *supra* n. 420, at 157.
744. Atiyah, Smith, *supra* n. 733, at 134; Calnan, *supra* n. 737, at 14; McKendrick, *supra* n. 719, at 1038; Lewison, *supra* n. 733, at 6; Kornet, *supra* n. 420, at 158-159.
745. McKendrick, *supra* n. 719, at 1038; Calnan, *supra* n. 737, at 11.
746. Lewison, *supra* n. 733, at 7.
747. *Ibid.*, at 31.
748. Furmston, *supra* n. 733, at 84.
749. Calnan, *supra* n. 737, at 16.
750. *Ibid.*, at 17; *see also*, Kornet, *supra* n. 420, at 160.
751. Calnan, *supra* n. 737, at 18; *see also*, Kornet, *supra* n. 420, at 160-161.
752. Calnan, *supra* n. 737, at 18.

On this point, Atiyah and Smith state that it is certain that the parties to a dispute would almost always interpret the terms of their contract in different ways, otherwise there would be no dispute, and for this reason, the courts are almost never interested in the inherent intent of the parties.[753]

The objective character of the process of the interpretation of contracts has an important procedural consequence. Since the subjective intent of the parties is irrelevant, subjective declarations of intent and statements by the parties in negotiations cannot be relied upon as facts or circumstances underlying a contract. Contrary to continental legal systems, they are not regarded as subjects of interpretation in English law.[754] Lord Wright stated this point in a decision of 1935,[755] and Lord Hoffman confirmed it in his 1997 decision of *Investors Compensation Scheme v. West Bromwich Building Society*,[756] which will be explored in greater depth below. The position of English courts has not changed thereafter.[757]

The fact that subjective declarations of intent cannot be used for the interpretation of contracts does not mean that they cannot be used for a determination of the intent of the parties either. If the common inherent intent of the parties is different than the wording of the contract, the parties are allowed to rectify their contract by establishing their real intent (rectification for common mistake) and to rely on precontractual negotiations and subjective declarations of intent for this purpose.[758] Therefore, the remedy of rectification for a common mistake can be considered as a functional equivalent of the principle of *falsa demonstratio non nocet*. As will be shown below, the practical approach of English law is not as distant from that of continental legal systems as it appears to be at first sight.

Even though the objective approach dominates English law, this does not mean that the intent of the parties is irrelevant. On the contrary, the purpose of interpretation is to establish the intent of the parties to the contract.[759] The process of interpretation is therefore based on the objective manifestation of intent. In this process, the background facts at the time of the conclusion of the contract are also taken into

753. Atiyah, Smith, *supra* n. 733, at 134-135; *see also*, Kornet, *supra* n. 420, at 160.
754. Calnan, *supra* n. 737, at 63.
755. *IRC v. Raphael* [1935] AC 96; Lewison, *supra* n. 733, at 24 et seq.
756. *Investors Compensation Scheme v. West Bromwich Building Society* [1997] UKHL 28; [1998] 1 All ER 98; [1998] 1 WLR 896 (June 19, 1997), http://www.bailii.org/uk/cases/UKHL/1997/28.html (accessed December 7, 2018); *see*, section §3.04[A][5] Lord Hoffman's Five Principles of the Interpretation of Contracts, *infra*.
757. *See also* Lord Hoffman's decision in *Mannai Investments Co. Ltd. v. Eagle Star Life Assurance Co. Ltd.* [1997] 2 WLR 945, http://www.bailii.org/uk/cases/UKHL/1997/19.html (accessed December 7, 2018); Lord Steyn's decision in *Sirius International Insurance Co. v. FAI General Insurance Ltd* [2004] UKHL 54, http://www.bailii.org/uk/cases/UKHL/2004/54.html (accessed December 7, 2018); *See also*, *Weston v. Dayman* [2006] EWCA Civ 1165, http://www.bailii.org/ew/cases/EWCA/Civ/2006/1165.html (accessed December 7, 2018); *Chartbrook Ltd v. Persimmon Homes Ltd* [2009] UKHL 38, http://www.bailii.org/uk/cases/UKHL/2009/38.html (accessed December 7, 2018).
758. Calnan, *supra* n. 737, at 63; *Investors Compensation Scheme v. West Bromwich*, *supra* n. 756; *see*, section §3.04[A][5] Lord Hoffman's Five Principles of the Interpretation of Contracts, *infra*.
759. Calnan, *supra* n. 737, at 11; Kornet, *supra* n. 420, at 158.

consideration.[760] A certain parallelism can be observed between the efforts of continental systems toward objectivizing their subjective approaches[761] and the objective approach of English law.

[3] The Parol Evidence Rule and Merger Clauses

An important divergence between English law and continental legal systems lies in the so-called parol evidence rule, which is perceived by continental lawyers to be an indication of the rigidity of English law. Studies on the interpretation of contracts are usually found in books on the law of evidence, because of the importance traditionally attributed to this rule.[762] Even though the parol evidence rule is an old principle widely debated in the literature, its application in practice is very limited. According to Calnan, it is a "dead letter rule."[763] Yet this rule is still applied, albeit rarely.[764]

In an 1833 decision, Lord Denman defined the parol evidence rule as follows:

> [I]f there be a contract which has been reduced into writing, verbal evidence is not allowed to be given of what passed between the parties, either before the written instrument was made, or during the time it was in a state of preparation, so as to add to or subtract from, or in any manner vary or qualify the written contract.[765]

Likewise, P.O. Lawrence J. stated in a 1924 decision that "[i]t is firmly established as a rule of law that parol evidence cannot be admitted to add to, to vary or contradict a deed or other written instrument."[766]

The sphere of application of the parol evidence rule has not remained limited to oral evidence but has been expanded to also exclude extrinsic evidence in writing, such as drafts, preliminary agreements, and letters of negotiation.[767]

The parol evidence rule is based on an essentially legitimate concern. Chitty on Contracts explains that this rule "upholds the value of written proof, effectuates the finality intended by the parties in recording their contract in written form, and eliminates great inconvenience and troublesome litigation in many instances."[768] Similarly, according to Vogenauer, the intended purpose of the parol evidence rule is to prevent the parties from using their conduct in the negotiations or after the execution of a contract from adding to the contract or changing its terms. In other words, the main purpose of this principle is to guarantee legal security.[769]

760. *Ibid.*, at 15; Kornet, *supra* n. 420, at 166-171.
761. *See*, sections §3.02[B][4] Views Pertaining to the Objectivity of the Subjective Interpretation (Italian Law); §3.03[B][4][b] Objective Interpretation (Swiss Law); §3.03[C][2][b] The Will Theory, the Theory of Declaration, and the Trust Theory (Turkish Law), *supra*.
762. Williams, *supra* n. 12, at 225.
763. Calnan, *supra* n. 737, at 31.
764. *Shogun Finance v. Hudson* [2004] 1 AC 919; Calnan, *supra* n. 737, at 30.
765. *Gross v. Lord Nugent* (1833) 5 B. & Ad. 58, 64; McKendrick, *supra* n. 719, at 1070.
766. *Jacobs v. Batavia & General Plantations Trust Ltd* [1924] 1 Ch. 287; Lewison, *supra* n. 733, at 85 et seq.; Calnan, *supra* n. 737, at 30; Canaris, Grigoleit, *supra* n. 5, at 458-459; Guenter Treitel, *The Law of Contract*, 192 (Sweet & Maxwell, 2011).
767. McKendrick, *supra* n. 719, at 1070.
768. *Ibid.*
769. Vogenauer, *supra* n. 131, at 975.

Calnan agrees that the reason for which most commercial contracts are made in writing is the concern of the parties to ensure legal security in their business relations. When parties negotiate and write down their agreement, they do so with the expectation that their written agreement will be given effect. [770] The parol evidence rule, according to Calnan, is a means of giving effect to the written agreement of the parties.[771]

Even though the parol evidence rule is based on a legitimate concern, an interpretation that disregards evidence extrinsic to the text of a contract is practically impossible.[772] Therefore, as early as the late nineteenth century, English courts have reduced the effect of this rule by recognizing many exceptions to it and begun to regard this rule as a rebuttable presumption.[773] Indeed, the scope of application of this rule is much more limited than it appears to be at first sight.[774]

The exceptions to the parol evidence rule are almost as old as the rule itself. For instance, the *Smith v. Chadwick* decision of 1884 explains that if there is a document that has been produced simultaneously with, shortly before or shortly after the text of the main contract, and if that document is related to the subject matter of the contract, it must be taken into consideration in the interpretation of the contract of the parties.[775]

In 1891, a court ruled that it was possible to refute the presumption that the intent of the parties is only composed of their written agreement.[776] In a subsequent decision in 1896, Lord Russell confirmed this point as follows:

> [A]lthough when the parties arrive at a definite written contract the implication or presumption is very strong that such contract is intended to contain all the terms of their bargain, it is a presumption only, and it is open to either of the parties to allege that there was, in addition to what appears in the written agreement, an antecedent express stipulation not intended by the parties to be excluded, but intended to continue in force with the express written agreement.[777]

Since a "presumption" is at stake, the burden of proof lies upon the party who seeks to rebut the presumption.[778]

In 1986, the Law Commission discussed the parol evidence rule and decided that "there is no rule of law that evidence is rendered inadmissible or is to be ignored solely because a document exists which looks like a complete contract."[779]

770. Calnan, *supra* n. 737, at 27.
771. *Ibid.*, at 30.
772. Canaris, Grigoleit, *supra* n. 5, at 459.
773. *Ibid*; Vogenauer, *supra* n. 131, at 975; Zweigert, Kötz, *supra* n. 4, at 407.
774. McKendrick, *supra* n. 719, at 1071.
775. *Smith v. Chadwick* (1884) 9 App Cas 187, http://swarb.co.uk/smith-v-chadwick-hl-1884/ (accessed December 7, 2018); *Manks v. Whiteley* [1914] A.C. 132; McKendrick, *supra* n. 719, at 1055.
776. *Mercantile Bank of Sydney v. Taylor* (1891) 12 LR (NSW) 252; McKendrick, *supra* n. 719, at 1070.
777. *Gillespie Bros. & Co v. Cheney*, Eggar & *Co* (1896) 2 Q.B. 59; McKendrick, *supra* n. 719, at 1071.
778. Canaris, Grigoleit, *supra* n. 5, at 459.
779. Law Com. 154, 1986, Cmnd. 9700; McKendrick, *supra* n. 719, at 1072; Canaris, Grigoleit, *supra* n. 5, at 459.

In the light of these developments, Calnan proposes a new, more modest definition for the parol evidence rule. According to him, this rule means that "[w]here the contract is in writing, it is the writing which is the primary source of the parties' objective intention."[780] In this sense, by continental standards, the parol evidence rule becomes an unobjectionable rule, also found in continental legal systems.[781]

As the traditional application of the parol evidence rule has evolved, parties have started to use the so-called merger clause or entire agreement clause for ensuring legal security in practice.[782] Through these clauses, parties seek to avoid the use of extrinsic evidence as a basis for contractual liability by affirmatively stating that the agreement between the parties is only composed of their written contract. The aim of merger clauses, albeit in a roundabout way, is to ensure that any prior written or oral statements of the parties will not give rise to any liability.[783]

Whether these clauses prevent the parties from relying on extrinsic evidence in the interpretation of their contracts is a controversial issue. In 1989, a court stated that the presence of this kind of clause in a contract is an "insuperable hurdle" for the parties to rely on their extrinsic statements.[784] In a more recent decision, however, the court held that entire agreement clauses do not necessarily operate in the way in which its terms would suggest, and the particular circumstances of the case are also to be taken into consideration. [785] Therefore, these clauses do not prevent the parties from introducing extrinsic evidence with the aim of shedding a light on the circumstances that the parties were in at the time of the conclusion of the contract. The prevailing opinion in the literature[786] and the dominant tendency in uniform law[787] are to narrowly interpret the effect of these clauses for the exclusion of extrinsic evidence in the interpretation of contracts.

[4] Other Principles of Interpretation

From an unprejudiced perspective, it is possible to observe that the principles and practice of the interpretation of contracts in English law are not really as distant from continental legal systems as they appear to be at first sight.[788]

The functional equivalent of some of the most basic principles of the interpretation of contracts in continental legal systems also exist and are being applied in English law. The abovementioned doctrine of "rectification for common mistake" is one of them. This doctrine provides that if both parties shared the same intent but made a

780. Calnan, *supra* n. 737, at 27.
781. *See*, sections §3.02[B][6][a] Article 1362 of the CC. It.; §3.03[A][2] Types or Methods of Interpretation in German Law; §3.03[B][4][a] Subjective Interpretation; §3.03[C][2][c] Principles of Literal Interpretation, *supra*.
782. Vogenauer, *supra* n. 131, at 975; Calnan, *supra* n. 737, at 32.
783. McKendrick, *supra* n. 719, at 1076; Calnan, *supra* n. 737, at 32.
784. *McGrath v. Shah* [1989] 57 PCR 452.
785. *Ravennavi SpA v. New Century Shipbuilding Co Ltd* [2006] EWHC 733; Lewison, *supra* n. 733, at 100.
786. Vogenauer, *supra* n. 131, at 975; Canaris, Grigoleit, *supra* n. 5, at 459.
787. Hyland, *supra* n. 730, at n. 3.
788. Hadžimanović, *supra* n. 507, at 274-275.

mistake while expressing it, the common intent of the parties prevails.[789] In words of Calnan, "[i]f a written contract does not record the parties' common intention at the time it was entered into, it will be amended to reflect that intention."[790] The function of this doctrine is the same with the principle of *falsa demonstratio non nocet*, according to which the common, real intent of the parties will prevail over the wording of their contract.[791]

The principle[792] or the method[793] of systematic interpretation found in continental legal systems is also present in English law. A contract must be interpreted in its entirety[794] because the obligations of the parties in one part of a contract cannot be understood without regard to the context of the contract as a whole.[795] In a decision of 1900, the court held that "[t]he deed must be read as a whole in order to ascertain the true meaning of its several clauses, and that the words of each clause should be interpreted as to bring them into harmony with the other provisions of the deed if that interpretation does no violence to the meaning of which they are naturally susceptible."[796]

As regards the subjective aspect of systematic interpretation, Chitty on Contracts states that even though the meaning of the contract must be sought within the text, the circumstances surrounding the making of the contract and which the parties were aware of must also be taken into consideration.[797] Not only the literal meaning of the words but also their context is relevant in the interpretation of contracts.[798] The practice of the courts further confirms this point.[799]

According to Calnan, the interpretation of a contract as a whole also requires courts to give effect to each part of the contract.[800] In this way, Calnan establishes a link between the principle of systematic interpretation and the *ut res magis magis valeat quam pereat* principle in continental legal systems. In Chitty on Contracts, this latter principle is explained in a very similar way to the provisions of Article 1191 (former Article 1157) of the CC. Fr. and Article 1367 of the CC. It.: "If the words used in an

789. Vogenauer, *supra* n. 131, at 975.
790. Calnan, *supra* n. 737, at 171; *see also Chartbrook Ltd v. Persimmon Homes Ltd* [2009] UKHL 38, *supra* n. 757.
791. Zweigert, Kötz, *supra* n. 4, at 404.
792. *See*, sections §3.02[A][4][b] Article 1189 (Former Article 1161) of the CC. Fr.; §3.02[B][6][b] Article 1363 of the CC. It., *supra*.
793. *See*, sections §3.03[A][2] Types or Methods of Interpretation in German Law; §3.03[B][4][a] Subjective Interpretation, *supra*.
794. McKendrick, *supra* n. 719, at 1052; Kornet, *supra* n. 420, at 164.
795. Calnan, *supra* n. 737, at 35.
796. *N.E. Ry. v. Hastings*, [1900] A. C. 260; McKendrick, *supra* n. 719, at 1052.
797. McKendrick, *supra* n. 719, at 1038-1039; Kornet, *supra* n. 420, at 169.
798. Calnan, *supra* n. 737, at 81 et seq.
799. *William Hare v. Shepherd Construction* [2010] All ER (D) 168 (Mar); *Enviroco v. Farstad Supply* [2011] 1 WLR 921; *Prenn v. Simmonds* [1971] 1 WLR 1381, [1971] 3 All ER 237; *Reardon Smith Line Ltd. v. Yngvar Tangen-Hansen* [1976] 1 WLR 989, [1976] 2 Lloyd's Rep 621, [1976] 3 All ER 570; Kornet, *supra* n. 420, at 169-170.
800. Calnan, *supra* n. 737, at 44.

agreement are susceptible of two meanings, one of which would validate the instrument or the particular clause, and the other render it void, ineffective or meaningless, the former sense is to be adopted."[801]

Chitty on Contracts also states that the principles that govern the interpretation of contracts are the same at law and in equity, and equity also requires an objective interpretation.[802] An important consequence of equity has been the adoption of the rule of objective interpretation according to which ambiguous terms must be interpreted against the parties who supplied them. This rule emerged in court decisions as early as the seventeenth century,[803] and it is not interpreted narrowly, as is the case with the Italian,[804] German,[805] and Swiss[806] legal systems.

Nevertheless, the *contra stipulatorem* or *contra proferentem* rule is rarely applied in practice, even though it is discussed in the literature. This is because most large-scale commercial contracts typically emerge as a result of negotiations, and it would be impossible to determine who supplied which clause. Calnan also points out that the interpretation of single clauses according to their authors is inconsistent with the principle of analyzing the contract as a whole.[807]

Another principle of objective interpretation found in most continental legal systems is the interpretation of contracts in accordance with local customs. This principle was first adopted in English law in the *Studdy v. Sanders* decision of 1826.[808] In this case, a contract for the sale of "cider" was involved. The buyer used the word "cider" in the sense of "apple wine," whereas the seller understood it as "apple juice." The court ruled that the subject of the contract was apple juice because the meaning of the word "cider" was apple juice at the place of the conclusion of the contract.

[5] Lord Hoffman's Five Principles of the Interpretation of Contracts

English legislators have not codified the rules and principles of the interpretation of contracts. Therefore, they are not as systematic as in continental legal systems. Nevertheless, there have been some efforts to construct a list of these principles.

The most cited list is, without doubt, the five principles stated by Lord Hoffmann in the 1997 decision of *Investors Compensation Scheme v. West Bromwich Building Society* by the House of Lords.[809] Following this decision, the importance of the interpretation of contracts has increased, and more decisions have been made on this issue. The same Lord Hoffmann has issued some of these decisions. The five principles listed in *Investors Compensation Scheme v. West Bromwich Building Society* have also

801. McKendrick, *supra* n. 719, at 1062.
802. *Ibid.*, at 1038.
803. *Ibid.*, at 1063-64, this author refers to *Manchester College v. Trafford* (1679) 2 Show 31 and *Dairy Containers Ltd v. Tasman Orient Line CV*—[2004] All ER (D) 289.
804. *See*, section §3.02[B][6][h] Article 1370 of the CC. It., *supra*.
805. *See*, section §3.03[A][3][c] § 157 of the BGB, *supra*.
806. *See*, section §3.03[B][5] Principles of Interpretation Developed Through Case Law, *supra*.
807. Calnan, *supra* n. 737, at 110.
808. *Studdy v. Sanders* (1826) 5 B. & C. 628, http://swarb.co.uk/studdy-v-sanders-and-others-1823/ (accessed December 7, 2018); McKendrick, *supra* n. 719, at 1050.
809. *Investors Compensation Scheme v. West Bromwich Building Society*, *supra* n. 756.

been quoted in subsequent decisions and have become the primary source of contract interpretation.[810]

The first principle cited in this decision is fairly broad and defines the interpretation of contracts to include background knowledge:

> Interpretation is the ascertainment of the meaning which the document would convey to a reasonable person having all the background knowledge which would reasonably have been available to the parties in the situation in which they were at the time of the contract.[811]

This definition was also referred to in the *Zeus Tradition Marine Ltd v. Bell* decision.[812]

According to the second principle, the reasonable person standard applies:

> Subject to the requirement that it should have been reasonably available to the parties and to the exception to be mentioned next, it [the admissible background] includes absolutely anything which would have affected the way in which the language of the document would have been understood by a reasonable man.[813]

This principle is an expression of the principle of systematic interpretation in continental law. According to this principle, contracts must be interpreted in light of the underlying circumstances. The circumstances that are known by the parties and that are relevant to determine the intent of the parties at the time of the contract must be taken into consideration.[814] Kornet accurately criticizes the expression "absolutely anything," and in that it leaves uncertain the scope of the background information to be considered for the purposes of interpretation.[815]

The third principle, however, states that there are limits to the application if not the scope:

> The law excludes from the admissible background the previous negotiations of the parties and their declarations of subjective intent. They are admissible only in an action for rectification.[816]

Lord Hoffman also repeated the same principle in the *Chartbrook Ltd v. Persimmon Homes Ltd*[817] decision of 2009, by reference to the *Investors Compensation Scheme v. West Bromwich Building Society* decision.

According to the fourth principle, there are limits to literal interpretation:

> The meaning which a document (or any other utterance) would convey to a reasonable man is not the same thing as the meaning of its words. The meaning of

810. Atiyah, Smith, *supra* n. 733, at 148; Calnan, *supra* n. 737, at 6; Lewison, *supra* n. 733, at 1; Kornet, *supra* n. 420, at 164-165.
811. *Investors Compensation Scheme v. West Bromwich Building Society*, *supra* n. 756.
812. *Zeus Tradition Marine Ltd v. Bell* (The Zeus V) [2000] 2 Lloyd's Rep 587, www.i-law.com (accessed December 7, 2018).
813. *Investors Compensation Scheme v. West Bromwich Building Society*, *supra* n. 756.
814. Calnan, *supra* n. 737, at 49; Kornet, *supra* n. 420, at 166-167.
815. Kornet, *supra* n. 420, at 167.
816. *Investors Compensation Scheme v. West Bromwich Building Society*, *supra* n. 756.
817. *Chartbrook Ltd v. Persimmon Homes Ltd* [2009] UKHL 38, *supra* n. 757.

> words is a matter of dictionaries and grammars; the meaning of the document is what the parties using those words against the relevant background would reasonably have been understood to mean. The background may not merely enable the reasonable man to choose between the possible meanings of the words which are ambiguous but even (as occasionaly happens in ordinary life) to conclude that the parties must, for whatever reason, have used the wrong words or syntax.[818]

The first part of the fourth principle states that the meaning understood by a reasonable third person with the relevant background prevails over the literal meaning of the words. This principle is parallel to the prohibition of purely literal interpretation found in continental legal systems.[819]

In the second part of the fourth principle, Lord Hoffman almost quotes the *falsa demonstratio non nocet* principle, also referring to his previous opinion on *Mannai Investments Co. Ltd. v. Eagle Star Life Assurance Co. Ltd.* in 1997.[820] The *Jumbo King Ltd v. Faithful Properties Ltd.* [821] decision of 1999 also cites the same principle.

Lord Hoffman's fifth and the final principle goes a step further toward subjective intent:

> The "rule" that words should be given their "natural and ordinary meaning" reflects the common sense proposition that we do not easily accept that people have made linguistic mistakes, particularly in formal documents. On the other hand, if one would nevertheless conclude from the background that something must have gone wrong with the language, the law does not require judges to attribute to the parties an intention which they plainly could not have had.[822]

Lord Hoffman referred to Lord Diplock's decision in *The Antaios Compania Neviera S.A. v. Salen Rederierna A.B.* when explaining the rule in this paragraph.[823]

This principle also has two aspects. First, it states that the words must be interpreted according to their "natural and ordinary meaning."[824] However, if the terms have a special meaning (scientific, commercial, technical, and so on) and if the terms have been used in that special meaning, that meaning prevails.[825] This principle, first

818. *Investors Compensation Scheme v. West Bromwich Building Society, supra* n. 756.
819. *See*, sections §3.02[A][4][a] Article 1188 (Former Article 1156) of the CC. Fr.; §3.02[B][6][a] Article 1362 of the CC. It.; §3.03[A][3][b] § 133 of the BGB; §3.03[B][5] Principles of Interpretation Developed Through Case Law, *supra*.
820. *Mannai Investments Co. Ltd. v. Eagle Star Life Assurance Co. Ltd., supra* n. 757.
821. *Jumbo King Ltd v. Faithful Properties Ltd* [1999] 3 HKLRD 757.
822. *Investors Compensation Scheme v. West Bromwich Building Society, supra* n. 756.
823. *The Antaios Compania Neviera S.A. v. Salen Rederierna* A.B. 19851 A.C. 191.
824. McKendrick, *supra* n. 719, at 1041; Lewison, *supra* n. 733, at 148 et seq.; Kornet, *supra* n. 420, at 177.
825. *Schuler v. Wickman Machine Tool Sales* [1974] AC 235; McKendrick, *supra* n. 719, at 1050-1051 and 1086; Lewison, *supra* n. 733, at 164 et seq.; Calnan, *supra* n. 737, at 89-90; Kornet, *supra* n. 420, at 163.

expressed by Hugo Grotius,[826]is also found in Romano-Germanic legal systems,[827] as well as in the U.S. law.[828]

The second aspect of this principle is that a meaning not intended by the parties cannot be attributed to their contract through interpretation. This principle is also found in the former Article 1163 of the CC. Fr and Article 1364 of the CC. It.

Sir Anthony Clarke M.R. first stated the same principle in a decision of 2008,[829] referring to Lord Hoffman's decision, and then in another decision in 2009.[830] Lord Dyson repeated this principle in his opinion on the *Chipsaway International Ltd v. Kerr* decision of 2009.[831]

[B] U.S. Law

[1] Generally

The development of the interpretation of contracts in U.S. law has been radically different than in English law. A distinction between ascertainment of the meaning of the contract and determination of its legal consequences is made in U.S. law, differing from English law,[832] and this distinction has some important consequences. A terminological consequence of this distinction is that the terms "interpretation" and "construction" are not used interchangeably. Interpretation aims at the ascertainment of the meaning of the words and expressions used by the parties, whereas construction aims at the determination of their legal effects and consequences.[833]

On the basis of this distinction, Corbin points out that interpretation is a linguistic activity, whereas construction is a legal one.[834] As a consequence, gap-filling cannot be considered to be an activity of interpretation, but it is more appropriate to classify gap-filling as a sort of construction.[835] Likewise, supplementation of contracts with customary rules cannot be considered to be interpretation, because this is a matter of gap-filling, and therefore, construction.[836]

826. Grotius, *supra* n. 107, at n. III.
827. *See*, sections §3.03[B][4][a] Subjective Interpretation; §3.03[C][2][c] Principles of Literal Interpretation, *infra*.
828. *See*, section §3.04[B][3] Subjectivization of the Interpretation of Contracts: the UCC and the Restatement (Second) of Contracts, *supra*.
829. *Cosmos Holidays Plc v. Dhanjal Investments Ltd.* [2009] EWCA Civ 316.
830. *Pratt v. Aigaion Insurance Company SA* [2009] 1 Lloyd's Rep. 225; *see* http://www.bailii.org/ew/cases/EWCA/Civ/2008/1314.html (accessed December 7, 2018).
831. *Chipsaway International Ltd. v. Kerr* [2009] EWCA Civ 320, http://www.bailii.org/ew/cases/EWCA/Civ/2009/320.html (accessed December 7, 2018).
832. *See*, section §3.04[A][1] Generally, *supra*.
833. Samuel Williston, *Williston on Sales*, Vol. 1, 360 (Alphonse M. Squillante, John R. Fonseca (eds.), 4th ed., LCP-BW, 1973, hereinafter "Williston on Sales"); Samuel Williston, Walter H.E. Jaeger, *A Treatise on the Law of Contracts*, Vol. 4, 320 (3rd ed., Mount Kisco—Baker Voorhis & Co., 1961, hereinafter "Williston on Contracts").
834. Corbin, *supra* n. 69, at 8-9.
835. *Ibid.*, at 10-11.
836. *Ibid.*, at 240 et seq., especially at 244.

Another essential consequence of this distinction is that while ascertainment of the meaning of the contract terms is considered to be a question of fact, determination of their legal consequences is a question of law, as is the case in the German[837] and Swiss[838] legal systems. As the interpretation of contract is a question of fact in the U.S. legal system, it has to be considered by juries, or for a bench trial, the judge acting for this purpose strictly in the capacity of a fact finder in place of a jury.[839] Construction, however, may only be considered by judges, because it is a legal question. For the same reason, construction is reviewable on appeal.[840]

In the history of U.S. law, the approaches to the interpretation of contracts have been far from consistent and have gone through a significant evolution. In other words, the search for a balance between subjective and objective theories led to considerable shifts between extreme approaches. This is because the objective and subjective theories that have influenced the law of contracts in general have also influenced the issue of the interpretation of contracts.[841]

The objective approach dominated from the nineteenth to the mid-twentieth century, which occasionally led to rigid and formalistic consequences. The objective approach was reflected in court decisions and the Restatement (First) of Contracts.[842] However, this approach experienced a radical change after the mid-twentieth century when a new and relatively subjective approach found its expression in the Uniform Commercial Code (UCC) and especially in the Restatement (Second) of Contracts.[843]

In this way, U.S. law succeeded in squeezing the phases of evolution that continental legal systems experienced over two thousand years into only two centuries. However, the downside to this rapid evolution has been the simultaneous presence of the extreme points of the two approaches in U.S. positive law, and therefore, a decrease in legal certainty, predictability, and uniformity of the rules to be applied in the interpretation of contracts.

At the end of the day, one could even say that the subjective approach prevails today in the U.S. law because of the UCC's approach, which is based on the intent of the parties. This approach clearly distinguishes U.S. law from the common law tradition based on the objective approach.[844]

---

837. *See*, section §3.03[A][1] Generally, *supra*.
838. *See*, section §3.03[B][3] The Significance of the Distinction Between Subjective and Objective Interpretation for Reviewability of Decisions, *supra*.
839. Corbin, *supra* n. 69, at 218-219; Joseph M. Perillo, *Calamari and Perillo on Contracts*, 164 (5th ed., Thomson West, 2003).
840. Corbin, *supra* n. 69, at 220 et seq.; Vogenauer, *supra* n. 69, n. 9.
841. E. Allan Farnsworth, William F. Young~~ Jr., Carol Sanger, Neil B. Cohen, Richard Brooks,~~ *Contracts, Cases, and Materials*~~,~~ 459 (8th ed., Foundation Press—Thomson West, 2013).
842. *See*~~, section §3.04[B][2]~~ The Objective Approach and The Restatement (First) of Contracts, *infra*.
843. *See*~~, section §3.04[B][3] Subjectivization of the Interpretation of Contracts: The UCC and the Restatement (Second) of Contracts,~~ *infra*~~.~~
844. Antje Baumann, *Regeln der Auslegung internationaler Handelsgeschäfte, Eine vergleichende Untersuchung der UNIDROIT Principles, der Principles of European Contract Law, des Uniform Commercial Code und des deutschen Rechts*, 58 (V&R Unipress, 2004), http://www.trans-lex.org/100150 (accessed December 7, 2018).

Nonetheless, the subjective approach also found its expression in the early period, when the interpretation of contracts was relatively formalistic in the U.S. Williston defined the purpose of the interpretation as the "ascertainment of the intention of the parties."[845] Many court decisions referred to the intent of the parties as the basis of the interpretation of contracts in this period.[846] It should also be mentioned that the approach of this period was never so "formalistic" as to adopt the *in claris non fit interpretatio* rule prohibiting the interpretation of "clear" terms and expressions.[847]

Likewise, even though the subjective approach may prevail overall in U.S. law today, Farnsworth states that if the parties attach different meanings to the contract, it is without doubt that the meaning will be determined through objective criteria.[848] Moreover, the plain meaning rule, which represents the rigid and formalistic approach to the issue, still survives and is being applied by the courts despite the shift to the subjective approach.[849]

[2] The Objective Approach and the Restatement (First) of Contracts

The rigid and formalistic approach in the early period of the U.S. law was not limited to a reasonable objective approach, as was the case with English law, but totally denied the intent of the parties. In a 1911 decision, the Federal Court for the Southern District of New York court ruled that:

> A contract has, strictly speaking, nothing to do with the personal, or individual, intent of the parties. A contract is an obligation attached by the mere force of law to certain acts of the parties, usually words, which ordinarily accompany and represent a known intent.[850]

The Supreme Court of Virginia repeated the same formalistic approach in its decision in *Lucy v. Zehmer*,[851] where the court refused to interpret the acknowledgment of a deed of sale written on the back of a restaurant receipt by a drunk person according to the intent of the parties (a drunken joke according to the seller) and thus held it to

845. Williston, *supra* n. 833 (Williston on Contracts), at 304.
846. *See*, for instance, *Beneficial Fire & Casualty Ins. Co. v. Kurt Hitke & Co.* (1956) 46 Cal.2d 517; *Liberty National Bank & Trust Co. v. Bank of America National Trust & Savings Association*, 218 F2d 831 (CA) (1955); *Republic Pictures Corp. v. Rogers*, 213 F. 2d 662 (CA 9) (1954), http://openjurist.org/213/f2d/662/republic-pictures-corp-v-rogers (accessed December 7, 2018).
847. Williston, *supra* n. 833 (Williston on Sales), at 366.
848. "There may be little disagreement over the proposition that, where the parties have in fact attached different meanings to their language, an objective standard should determine which meaning will prevail." Farnsworth, Young, Sanger, Cohen, Brooks, *supra* n. 841, at 459.
849. *See*, section §3.04[B][4][a] (Non)interpretation Rules: The Parol Evidence Rule, the Plain Meaning Rule, and the Four Corners Rule, *infra*.
850. *Hotchkiss v. Nat'l City Bank of N.Y.*, 200 F. 287, 293 (S.D.N.Y. 1911).
851. *Lucy v. Zehmer*, 196 Va. 493; 84 S.E.2d 516 (1954).

be a valid contract. This decision became a symbol of the rigid and formalistic approach of U.S. law in that period.[852]

Williston, the defender of the rigid and formalistic approach to the interpretation of contracts, defines the purpose of interpretation with reference to "intention," as "ascertainment of the intention of the parties."[853] However, he also stated in the same work, as regards contracts made in writing that "[i]t is not the intention of the parties that is material, but the meaning that the court gives to their manifestations."[854] Therefore, according to Williston, if a contract is made in writing, then even the common intent of the parties will have no effect unless it is also made in writing.[855]

Accordingly, Williston focused on the literal interpretation of contracts and determined four rules that he qualifies as "primary rules."[856] These are as follows:

(1) The common and normal meaning of language will be given to the words of a contract unless the circumstances show that in a particular case a special meaning should be attached to it.[857]
(2) Technical terms or words of art will be given their technical meaning unless the context or local usage shows a contrary intention, and under this principle mercantile terms in mercantile contracts will be given the meaning which merchants ordinarily give them.[858]
(3) The writing will be read as a whole, and every part will be interpreted with reference to the whole, and if possible it will be so interpreted as to give effect to its general purpose.[859]
(4) The circumstances under which a writing was made may always be shown. The question the court is seeking to answer was the meaning of the writing at the time and place when the contract was made, and all the surrounding circumstances at that time necessarily throw light upon the meaning of the contract.[860]

852. Barak D. Richman, Dennis Schmelzer, *When Money Grew on Trees: The Untold Story of Lucy v. Zehmer*, 61 Duke Law Journal 1511-1562 (2012), https://scholarship.law.duke.edu/cgi/viewcontent.cgi?article=2979&context=faculty_scholarship (accessed December 7, 2018).
853. Williston, *supra* n. 833 (Williston on Contracts), at 304.
854. *Ibid.*, at 338-339.
855. *Ibid.*, at 499 et seq.
856. *Ibid.*, at 705 et seq.
857. *Ibid.*, at 705; *Matsuo Yoshida v. Liberty Mutual Insurance* 240 F2d 824 (CA 9) (1957), http://openjurist.org/240/f2d/824/matsuo-yoshida-v-liberty-mutual-insurance-company (accessed December 7, 2018).
858. Williston, *supra* n. 833 (Williston on Contracts), at 707-709; *Greenberg v. Continental Casualty Co.* 24 Cal. App. 2d 506. [1938.], http://law.justia.com/cases/california/court-of-appeal/2d/24/506.html (accessed December 7, 2018).
859. Williston, *supra* n. 833 (Williston on Contracts), at 710-711; *Boardman v. Lessees of Reed and Ford*, 31 US 328 (1832) https://supreme.justia.com/cases/federal/us/31/328/case.html (accessed December 7, 2018).
860. Williston, *supra* n. 833 (Williston on Contracts), at 716; *Deerhurst Estates v. Meadow Homes*, Inc. 64 N.J. Super. 134 (1960). *See* http://law.justia.com/cases/new-jersey/appellate-division-published/1960/64-n-j-super-134-0.html (accessed December 7, 2018).

These are all indeed generally accepted principles that also exist in continental jurisdictions. The first two are the most basic principles of literal interpretation,[861] whereas the last two principles refer to the principle of systematic interpretation[862] and the principle of *ut res magis magis valeat quam pereat.*[863] Mentioning these principles without reference to the intent of the parties, however, reflects an absolute objective approach.

This objective approach also found its expression in the Restatement (First) of Contracts, published in 1932 by the American Law Institute (ALI). Unsurprisingly, the rapporteur of this work was Samuel Williston. Interpretation is defined in § 226 (entitled "[w]hat is interpretation?") of this text as follows:

> Interpretation of words and of other manifestations of intention forming an agreement, or having reference to the formation of an agreement, is the ascertainment of the meaning to be given to such words and manifestations.[864]

This definition manifestly reflects an objective approach as it is based only on the words and other manifestations by the parties, and not on their intent. In "comment b" to the same paragraph, the exclusion of the subjective theory was stated in more express terms:

> Comment b—The meaning that shall be given to manifestations of intention is not necessarily that which the party from whom the manifestation proceeds, expects or understands.[865]

[3] Subjectivization of the Interpretation of Contracts: The UCC and the Restatement (Second) of Contracts

In 1940, a few years after the publication of the Restatement (First) of Contracts, the ALI and the National Conference of Commissioners on Uniform State Laws (NCCUSL) began drafting the UCC.[866] This text was first published in 1951 and contributed considerably to the unification of commercial law in the U.S. Various chapters of the UCC have been revised thereafter over the years.

861. *See*, sections §3.03[A][2] Types or Methods of Interpretation in German Law; §3.03[B][4][a] Subjective Interpretation; §3.03[C][2][c] Principles of Literal Interpretation; §3.04[A][5] Lord Hoffman's Five Principles of the Interpretation of Contracts, *supra*.
862. *See*, sections §3.02[A][4][b] Article 1189 (Former Article 1161) of the CC. Fr.; §3.02[B][6][b] Article 1363 of the CC. It.; §3.03[A][2] Types or Methods of Interpretation in German Law; §3.03[B][4][a] Subjective Interpretation; §3.03[C][2][f] Principles of Interpretation Developed Through Case Law or Recognized in the Literature, *supra*.
863. *See*, sections §3.02[A][4][d] Article 1191 (Former Article 1157) of the CC. Fr.; §3.02[B][6][e] Article 1367 of the CC. It.; §3.03[A][3][c] § 157 of the BGB; §3.03[B][5] Principles of Interpretation Developed Through Case Law; §3.03[C][2][f] Principles of Interpretation Developed Through Case Law or Recognized in the Literature; §3.04[A][4] Other Principles of Interpretation, *supra*.
864. American Law Institute, *Restatement of the Law of Contracts*, Vol. 1, 305 (American Law Institute Publishers, 1932) (*Restatement (First) of Contracts*), at 305.
865. ALI, *supra* n. 864, at 305.
866. *UCC*, http://www.law.cornell.edu/ucc (accessed December 7, 2018).

The UCC does not offer a definition for the interpretation of contracts, differing from the Restatement (First) of Contracts. However, UCC § 1 Article 2, entitled "General Definitions and Principles of Interpretation," contains detailed provisions of a casuistic nature regarding how to understand the expressions used in contracts. For instance, forty-three definitions are provided in § 1-201 for various expressions in the contractual language.[867]

The 1951 version of the UCC § 1-205, entitled "Course of Dealing and Usage of Trade," sets forth that negotiations between the parties and usages must be taken as a basis for the interpretation of the expressions and that all the provisions of the contract must be interpreted in a coherent way.[868]

Following the 2001 revision of the UCC, the provisions of this paragraph with small changes were placed under § 1-303 entitled "Course of Performance, Course of Dealing, and Usage of Trade."[869] The definition of the "course of dealing" in subsection (b) of this paragraph acknowledges that these might be taken into consideration in the interpretation of the expressions and conduct of the parties. According to this comment:

> (b) A "course of dealing" is a sequence of conduct concerning previous transactions between the parties to a particular transaction that is fairly to be regarded as establishing a common basis of understanding for interpreting their expressions and other conduct.[870]

Subsection (d) of the same paragraph states more expressly that the course of performance, course of dealing, and usages can be taken into consideration in the interpretation of the contract:

> (d) A course of performance or course of dealing between the parties or usage of trade in the vocation or trade in which they are engaged or of which they are or should be aware is relevant in ascertaining the meaning of the parties' agreement, may give particular meaning to specific terms of the agreement, and may supplement or qualify the terms of the agreement. A usage of trade applicable in the place in which part of the performance under the agreement is to occur may be so utilized as to that part of the performance.[871]

Subsection (e) of this paragraph sets forth the principle of systematic interpretation, by saying that the listed tools of interpretation must be interpreted as consistent with each other. This subsection also provides a hierarchy between the listed tools of interpretation. According to this provision:

867. ALI & NCCUSL, *Uniform Commercial Code—Official Texts and Comments*, 14 et seq. (Thomson West, 2008); James J. White, Robert S. Summers, Robert A. Hillman, *Uniform Commercial Code*, Vol. 1, 12 et seq. (6th ed., West, 2012); *see* http://www.law.cornell.edu/ucc/1/1-201 (accessed December 7, 2018).
868. *See*, the 1951 version of the UCC, http://www.mindserpent.com/ucc/ucc1.html (accessed March 22, 2019).
869. ALI & NCCUSL, UCC, *supra* n. 867, at 30 et seq.; White, Summers, Hillman, *supra* n. 867, at 46 et seq.; *see* http://www.law.cornell.edu/ucc/1/1-303 (accessed December 7, 2018).
870. ALI & NCCUSL, UCC, *supra* n. 867, at 30; White, Summers, Hillman, *supra* n. 867, at 46.
871. *Ibid.*

(e) Except as otherwise provided in subsection (f), the express terms of an agreement and any applicable course of performance, course of dealing, or usage of trade must be construed whenever reasonable as consistent with each other. If such a construction is unreasonable: (1) express terms prevail over course of performance, course of dealing, and usage of trade; (2) course of performance prevails over course of dealing and usage of trade; and (3) course of dealing prevails over usage of trade.[872]

Subsection (f) of this paragraph lays down the principle known as *protestatio facto contraria non valet* in continental jurisdictions.[873] According to this subsection:

(f) Subject to Section 2-209, a course of performance is relevant to show a waiver or modification of any term inconsistent with the course of performance.[874]

Besides the abovementioned rules, Official Comment no. 1 to § 1-205 of the 1951 version and § 1-303 of the 2001 version defines the general approach to the interpretation of contracts more precisely. This comment reads as follows:

1. This Act rejects both the "lay-dictionary" and the "conveyancer's" reading of a commercial agreement. Instead the meaning of the agreement of the parties is to be determined by the language used by them and by their action, read and interpreted in the light of commercial practices and other surrounding circumstances. The measure and background for interpretation are set by the commercial context, which may explain and supplement even the language of a formal or final writing.[875]

The shift of the focus from the manifestation of intent in the Restatement of Contracts into the understanding of the parties in the UCC represents a clear subjectivization of the approach to the interpretation of contracts. With these words, the authors of the UCC emphasize that they reject the objective meaning of a commercial agreement as abstracted from its concrete commercial context and surrounding circumstances and that these must be taken into consideration in the interpretation of any commercial agreement.

In 1962, only eleven years after the publication of the UCC, the ALI started to undertake studies for the revision of the Restatement of Contracts. Farnsworth, the rapporteur of these studies, criticizes the objective approach to the interpretation of contracts. Therefore, the Restatement (Second) of Contracts, which was published in 1981, adopted an approach that was even more subjective than that of the UCC. Even though the approach of this text does not focus on the "intent" of the parties, it focuses on their "purpose." The Restatement (Second) of Contracts includes detailed provisions on the interpretation of contracts and the statements of the parties beginning with § 200, which offers a simple and neutral definition of interpretation:

§ 200. Interpretation of Promise or Agreement

872. *Ibid.*
873. *See*, section §3.03[A][3][b] § 133 of the BGB, *supra*.
874. ALI & NCCUSL, UCC, *supra* n. 867, at 30; White, Summers, Hillman, *supra* n. 867, at 46.
875. ALI & NCCUSL, UCC, *supra* n. 867, at 31; for the 1951 version of the UCC, *see*, *supra* n. 868.

> Interpretation of a promise or agreement or a term thereof is the ascertainment of its meaning.[876]

Contrary to the neutral language of § 200, however, § 201 reads almost like a manifesto of the subjective approach to the interpretation of contracts. This paragraph lays down the principle of *falsa demonstratio non nocet*, which is also laid down in continental codes in jurisdictions where the subjective approach is dominant.[877] It goes even further, stating that if a common intent cannot be determined, then contracts must be interpreted according to the intent of one of the parties. It does so without offering one word about objective interpretation as a second possibility. This paragraph reads as follows:

> § 201. Whose Meaning Prevails
> (1) Where the parties have attached the same meaning to a promise or agreement or a term thereof, it is interpreted in accordance with that meaning.
> (2) Where the parties have attached different meanings to a promise or agreement or a term thereof, it is interpreted in accordance with the meaning attached by one of them if at the time the agreement was made
> (a) that party did not know of any different meaning attached by the other, and the other knew the meaning attached by the first party; or
> (b) that party had no reason to know of any different meaning attached by the other, and the other had reason to know the meaning attached by the first party.
> (3) Except as stated in this Section, neither party is bound by the meaning attached by the other, even though the result may be a failure of mutual assent.[878]

The Restatement (Second) of Contracts § 202 lists some of the basic rules of interpretation under the title "*Rules In Aid of Interpretation.*" These are as follows:

> § 202. Rules In Aid Of Interpretation
> (1) Words and other conduct are interpreted in the light of all the circumstances, and if the principal purpose of the parties is ascertainable it is given great weight.
> (2) A writing is interpreted as a whole, and all writings that are part of the same transaction are interpreted together.
> (3) Unless a different intention is manifested,
> (a) where language has a generally prevailing meaning, it is interpreted in accordance with that meaning;
> (b) technical terms and words of art are given their technical meaning when used in a transaction within their technical field.
> (4) Where an agreement involves repeated occasions for performance by either party with knowledge of the nature of the performance and opportunity for objection to it by the other, any course of performance accepted or acquiesced

---

876. American Law Institute, *Restatement of the Law (Second), Contracts*, Vol 2, 82 (American Law Institute Publishers, 1981).
877. *See*, sections §3.02[A][4][a] Article 1188 (Former Article 1156) of the CC. Fr. (French Law); §3.02[B][6][a] Article 1362 of the CC. It. (Italian Law); §3.03[A][3][b] § 133 of the BGB (German Law); §3.03[B][4] Article 18/1 of the OR (Swiss Law); §3.03[C][2][a] Article 19(1) of the TBK (Turkish Law), *supra*.
878. ALI, *supra* n. 876, at 83.

in without objection is given great weight in the interpretation of the agreement.

(5) Wherever reasonable, the manifestations of intention of the parties to a promise or agreement are interpreted as consistent with each other and with any relevant course of performance, course of dealing, or usage of trade.[879]

The first subsection of this paragraph does not expressly refer to the intent of the parties but still adopts a subjective criterion by basing the interpretation on "the principal purpose of the parties."

This paragraph lays down some important elements of the systematic interpretation, in accordance with UCC § 1-303. These are the interpretation of contracts "in the light of all the circumstances" (subsection 1), the interpretation of contracts and all the documents that make part of a transaction as a whole (subsection 2), and the interpretation of manifestations of intent as consistent with each other (subsection 5).

The third subsection expressly refers to the intention of the parties and sets forth some principles of literal interpretation, which are found also in continental legal systems. According to this subsection, the intent of the parties must be given more weight than the generally prevailing meaning of the words they used. This provision is in accordance with the general rule in § 201.

Another general provision of the Restatement (Second) of Contracts on the interpretation of contracts is § 203. Subsection (a) of this paragraph lays down the *ut res magis magis valeat quam pereat* principle. Subsection (b) reiterates the content of § 1-303 UCC with the same expressions. In other subsections, the rules of literal interpretation found in continental legal systems are listed. Although the authors of the Restatement (Second) of Contracts did not provide for any hierarchy between the provisions of this paragraph and the other rules of interpretation, the provisions of this paragraph can be assumed to be subsidiary rules. This is because the common feature of the rules listed in this paragraph is that they apply only in case of doubt between different possible meanings. This paragraph reads as follows:

§ 203 Standards of Preference In Interpretation

In the interpretation of a promise or agreement or a term thereof, the following standards of preference are generally applicable:

(a) an interpretation which gives a reasonable, lawful, and effective meaning to all the terms is preferred to an interpretation which leaves a part unreasonable, unlawful, or of no effect;
(b) express terms are given greater weight than course of performance, course of dealing, and usage of trade, course of performance is given greater weight than course of dealing or usage of trade, and course of dealing is given greater weight than usage of trade;
(c) specific terms and exact terms are given greater weight than general language;
(d) separately negotiated or added terms are given greater weight than standardized terms or other terms not separately negotiated.[880]

879. *Ibid.*, at 86 et seq.
880. *Ibid.*, at 92-93.

Even though the Restatement (Second) of Contracts is a nonbinding, soft-law text, it is relevant in representing the general approach to contract law in the U.S. legal literature and especially the significant change in the approach to the interpretation of contracts. Nevertheless, the nonbinding nature of this text has prevented the subjective approach from being adequately reflected in practice. In consequence, important divergences between the approach of the Restatement (Second) of Contracts and the principles applied in practice occasionally arise.

[4] Principles Developed Through Case Law and Literature

[a] (Non)interpretation Rules: The Parol Evidence Rule, the Plain Meaning Rule, and the Four Corners Rule

[i] The Parol Evidence Rule

Formalistic rules of interpretation that limit the interpretation of contracts still survive despite the adoption of the subjective approach by the UCC and the Restatement (Second) of Contracts.

One of these formalistic rules is the parol evidence rule. As this rule does not have a precise definition, it is the most suitable one to be interpreted in a moderate manner. Perillo points out that "few things are darker than this rule"[881] because of the diversity of opinions on it and the lack of unanimity on its definition and therefore on its scope and nature. Nevertheless, just after this observation, Perillo proposes the most moderate possible definition for this rule. According to him "[a] rule of substantive law states that whenever contractual intent is sought to be ascertained from among several expressions of agreement by the parties, an earlier tentative agreement will be rejected in favor of a latter expression that is final."[882]

This formulation of the parol evidence rule seems unobjectionable from the point of view of comparative law. However, this rule is generally conceived in a stricter sense. Williston defines the parol evidence rule by stating that "this rule requires, in the absence of fraud, duress, mutual mistake, or something of that kind, the exclusion of extrinsic evidence, oral or written, where the parties have reduced their agreement to an integrated writing."[883]

Indeed, this rule has had certain limitations from the outset. Its most important limitation is that it precludes only the use of oral or written evidence of the facts until the time of the conclusion of the contract. This rule does not apply to the evidence of

881. Perillo refers to J. Thayer, *A Preliminary Treatise on Evidence at Common Law* 390 (Boston, 1898); Perillo, *supra* n. 839, at 122.
882. Perillo, *supra* n. 839, at 124.
883. Williston, *supra* n. 833 (Williston on Contracts), at 948-949. Also Eric A. Posner defines this rule with similar words: "A court will refuse to use evidence of the parties' prior negotiations in order to interpret a written contract unless the writing is (1) incomplete, (2) ambiguous, or (3) the product of fraud, mistake, or a similar bargaining defect." Eric A. Posner, *The Parol Evidence Rule, the Plain Meaning Rule, and the Principles of Contractual Interpretation*, 46 University of Pennsylvania Law Review 533, 534 (1998).

the facts after the contract is made.[884] Accordingly, the parol evidence rule applies only when the final agreement of the parties is written and binding upon them.[885] In this situation, the language of the contract is the starting point of the interpretative activity.[886]

Nonetheless, it should also be mentioned that the term "parol" evidence is misleading, because this rule excludes not only oral but also written evidence such as emails or letters that predate the final agreement.[887] For this reason, Perillo points out that the expression of "extrinsic evidence" used in the UCC is more appropriate.[888]

Posner observes that there are two different positions in the application of this rule. Some courts exclude extrinsic evidence and rely only on the final written agreement of the parties (the "hard-PER" approach).[889] The decision in the *Martin v. Berens* case of 1871 best illustrates this approach. In this decision the court held that:

> ~~Where parties, without any fraud or mistake, have deliberately put their engagements in writing, the law declares the writing to be not only the best, but the only evidence of their agreement.~~[890]

However, some courts have taken both the final written agreement and extrinsic evidence into consideration (the "soft-PER" approach).[891] As early as 1912, the Supreme Court held in *Porto Rico Sugar Co. v. Lorenzo decision* that no matter how express the wording of a contract is, parol evidence may be necessary to shed a light on its meaning.[892]

Likewise, in its *Pacific Gas & Electric Co. v. G.W. Thomas Drayage & Rigging Co.* decision of 1968, the Supreme Court of California ruled in an opinion authored by Chief Justice Roger J. Traynor that:

> Although extrinsic evidence is not admissible to add to, detract from, or vary the terms of a written contract, these terms must first be determined before it can be decided whether or not extrinsic evidence is being offered for a prohibited purpose. The fact that the terms of an instrument appear clear to a judge does not preclude the possibility that the parties chose the language of the instrument to express different terms ... Accordingly, rational interpretation requires at least a preliminary consideration of all credible evidence offered to prove the intention of the parties.[893]

884. Williston, *supra* n. 833 (Williston on Contracts), at 951; Perillo, *supra* n. 839, at 125; Vogenauer, *supra* n. 131, at 976.
885. Perillo, *supra* n. 839, at 124.
886. Farnsworth, Young, Sanger, Cohen, Brooks, *supra* n. 841, at 405.
887. *Ibid.*, at 407; Perillo, *supra* n. 839, at 125.
888. Perillo, *supra* n. 839, at 125.
889. Posner, *supra* n. 883, at 534.
890. *Martin v. Berens*~~, 67 Pa. 459, 463 (1871);~~ Farnsworth, Young, Sanger, Cohen, Brooks, *supra* n. 841, at 408.
891. Posner, *supra* n. 883, at 534.
892. *Porto Rico Sugar Co. v. Lorenzo*~~, 222 U.S. 481 (1912)~~ https://supreme.justia.com/cases/federal/us/222/481/case.html (accessed December 7, 2018); Corbin, *supra* n. 69, at 418~~.~~
893. *Pacific Gas & Electric Co. v. G.W. Thomas Drayage & Rigging Co.*, 69 Cal.2d 33 (1968), http://www.west.net/~smith/PGE_v_Drayage.htm (accessed December 7, 2018).

Posner also points out that the approach of single jurisdictions to the parol evidence rule may vary considerably over time, and "[i]n virtually every jurisdiction, one finds irreconcilable cases, frequent changes in doctrine, confusion, and cries of despair."[894]

In U.S. law, unlike in English law,[895] the parol evidence rule is not a procedural rule as the name suggests; it is a substantial rule.[896] According to Corbin, this rule is related to what the contract covers and what it does not.[897] Therefore, Corbin does not regard this rule as a rule of interpretation either.[898] Corbin adheres to the soft-PER approach, and his views have generally been influential in U.S. law.[899]

Although not always regarded as a procedural rule, the parol evidence rule has some important procedural consequences. An important function of the parol evidence rule in U.S. law is to limit the evidence available to juries regarding the interpretation of a contract, which is a legal issue. Accordingly, only judges can apply the parol evidence rule and not juries.[900] Another consequence of the substantial nature of this rule is that any objection to its application or rejection of its application can be raised on appeal, even if it was not raised at trial.[901]

[ii] Legislative Texts on the Parol Evidence Rule

§ 237 to § 244 of the Restatement (First) of Contracts of 1932 contain detailed provisions under the title "Parol Evidence Rule."[902] With the influence of Williston, the rapporteur of the Restatement (First) of Contracts, these provisions focus on the notion of "integration" of the contract and exceptions to it.

§ 237 entitled "Parol Evidence Rule; Effect of Integration on Prior or Contemporaneous Agreements" sets forth that the integration of an agreement, in principle, makes all the prior oral and written agreements as well as contemporaneous oral agreements inoperative. This paragraph reads as follows:

> § 237 Parol Evidence Rule; Effect of Integration on Prior or Contemporaneous Agreements.
>
> Except as stated in §§ 240, 241 the integration of an agreement makes inoperative to add or to vary the agreement all contemporaneous oral agreements relating to the same subject-matter; and also, unless the integration is void, or voidable and avoided, all prior oral or written agreements relating thereto. If either void or

894. Posner, *supra* n. 883, at 539-540.
895. *See*, section §3.04[A][3] The Parol Evidence Rule and Merger Clauses, *supra*.
896. Corbin, *supra* n. 69, at 357; Perillo, *supra* n. 839, at 124 and 129.
897. Corbin, *supra* n. 69, at 357.
898. *Ibid.*, at 412-413.
899. Posner, *supra* n. 883, at 568-569.
900. Honnold, *supra* n. 496, at § 110; Perillo, *supra* n. 839, at 126.
901. *Tahoe National Bank v. Phillips*, 4 Cal.3d 11. [Sac. No. 7857. In Bank Feb. 5, 1971.], http://scocal.stanford.edu/opinion/tahoe-national-bank-v-phillips-32918 (accessed December 7, 2018); Perillo, *supra* n. 839, at 126.
902. ALI, *supra* n. 864, at 331 et seq.

voidable and avoided, the integration leaves the operation of prior agreements unaffected.[903]

§§ 238-244 that follow this paragraph list the exceptions to this rule and the situations in which the agreements prior to or contemporaneous with the integration, and even the negotiations between the parties (§ 242)[904] are operative or relevant.

§ 2-202 of the UCC of 1951 is a more clear provision relating to the parol evidence rule. This paragraph expressly states that this rule does not prevent the course of dealing, course of performance, and trade usages from being used for the purpose of explanation or supplementation of the final agreement of the parties. This approach of the UCC is in accordance with Corbin's observation that the parol evidence rule is indeed not a rule of interpretation.[905]

This paragraph was subjected to fundamental changes in the 2003 reform. The title and the structure of the paragraph have been amended. Moreover, although the 1951 version of the UCC referred to a "writing" as a final expression of the agreement of the parties,[906] the authors of the 2003 version chose the expression "in a record." § 2-202 of the UCC after the 2003 reform reads as follows:

> UCC § 2-202: Final Expression in a Record: Parol or Extrinsic Evidence
> (1) Terms with respect to which the confirmatory records of the parties agree or which are otherwise set forth in a record intended by the parties as a final expression of their agreement with respect to such terms as are included therein may not be contradicted by evidence of any prior agreement or of a contemporaneous oral agreement but may be supplemented by evidence of:
>   (a) by course of performance, course of dealing, or usage of trade (Section 1-303); and
>   (b) consistent additional terms unless the court finds the record to have been intended also as a complete and exclusive statement of the terms of the agreement.
> (2) Terms in a record may be explained by evidence of course of performance, course of dealing, or usage of trade without a preliminary determination by the court that the language used is ambiguous.[907]

§ 213 of the Restatement (Second) of Contracts of 1981, however, focused more on the exceptions to the parol evidence rule than the rule itself, in conformity with the provisions of §§ 237 ff. of the Restatement (First) of Contracts. § 213 of the Restatement (Second) of Contracts reads as follows:

> § 213. Effect of Integrated Agreement on Prior Agreements (Parol Evidence Rule)
> (1) A binging integrated agreement discharges prior agreements to the extent that it is inconsistent with them.
> (2) A binding completely integrated agreement discharges prior agreements to the extent that they are within its scope.
> (3) An integrated agreement that is not binding or that is voidable and avoided does not discharge a prior agreement. But an integrated agreement, even

903. *Ibid.*, at 331-332.
904. *Ibid.* at 341.
905. Corbin, *supra* n. 69, at 412-413.
906. For the 1951 version of the UCC, *see*, *supra* n. 868.
907. ALI & NCCUSL, UCC, *supra* n. 867, at 68; White, Summers, Hillman, *supra* n. 867, at 12 et seq.

> though not binding, may be effective to render inoperative a term which would have been part of the agreement if it had not been integrated.[908]

[iii] The Plain Meaning Rule

Taking into account all of the abovementioned developments, it is possible to conclude that the parol evidence rule did not have a significant and long-lasting restrictive effect on the interpretation of contracts. However, the situation is not the same with the plain meaning rule.

According to the plain meaning rule, a judge cannot take any extrinsic evidence into account if he finds that the meaning of the term or provision of the agreement, which is the subject matter of the dispute, is clear. In other words, the parties are not allowed to rely on extrinsic evidence for alleging that their intention was different than the unambiguous wording of their agreement.[909]

Farnsworth explains the function of this rule in two stages. The judge first examines whether the contract language is unambiguous. If he finds it to be so, he excludes all extrinsic evidence. If he finds in the first phase that the meaning of the contract language is ambiguous, he determines the meaning of the contract by admitting extrinsic evidence as to its meaning.[910] In terms of its meaning, this rule is nothing less than the *in claris non fit interpretatio* rule, which is generally rejected by comparative law and uniform law.[911]

This rule was also expressly rejected in comment b to § 212 of the Restatement (Second) of Contracts with the following words: "It is sometimes said that extrinsic evidence cannot change the plain meaning of a writing, but meaning can almost never be plain except in a context."[912]

Nonetheless, the rejection of the plain meaning rule by this soft-law document did not have any significant effect in practice, and this rule of noninterpretation is still being applied in U.S. law.[913] In the *Nicholson Air Services v. Allegany County* decision of 1998, the court applied the plain meaning rule by stating that:

> When the language of the contract is clear, the court will presume that the parties intended what they expressed, even if the expression differs from the parties' [actual] intentions at the time they created the contract.[914]

908. ALI, *supra* n. 876, at 129.
909. Farnsworth, Young, Sanger, Cohen, Brooks, *supra* n. 841, at 421; Perillo, *supra* n. 839, at 151.
910. Farnsworth, Young, Sanger, Cohen, Brooks, *supra* n. 841, at 421; *Pacific Gas & Electric Co. v. G.W. Thomas Drayage & Rigging Co.*, 69 Cal.2d 33, 69 Cal.Rptr. 561, 442 P.2d 641 (1968), http://www.west.net/~smith/PGE_v_Drayage.htm (accessed December 7, 2018).
911. Fontaine, de Ly, *supra* n. 5, at 125.
912. ALI, *supra* n. 876, at 126.
913. *Heritage Res., Inc. v. NationsBank*, 939 S.W.2d 118, 121 (Tex. 1996); *Lyons v. Montgomery*, 701 S.W.2d 641, 643 (Tex.1985). *McLean House v. Maichak*, 231 Va. 347, 349, 344 S.E.2d 889, 890 (1986); *Gordonsville Energy v. Virginia Elec. & Power Co.*, 257 Va. 344, 354, 512 S.E.2d 811, 817 (1999); *Nicholson Air Services v. Allegany County*, 120 Md. App. 47, 706 A.2d 124 (1998).
914. *Nicholson Air Services v. Allegany County*, 120 Md. App. 47, 706 A.2d 124 (1998); Perillo, *supra* n. 839, at 151; James M. Underwood, *Supplemental Serendipity: Congress' Accidental Improvement of Supplemental Jurisdiction*, 37 Akron Law Review 653, 696-697 (2004).

In this decision, the court expressly favored the plain meaning rule and rejected the principle of *falsa demonstratio non nocet*, which is one of the most fundamental principles of the interpretation of contracts in both comparative law and uniform law.

[iv] The Four Corners Rule

Another rule that restricts the interpretation of contracts in U.S. law is the four corners rule. According to this rule, the meaning of a contract must be determined within the limits of the four corners of the contract.[915]

Corbin notes that courts have not always been very willing to apply this rule and defines this rule in the following words "words must have one, and only one, true and correct meaning, that this meaning must be sought only by poring over the words within the four corners of the paper, that extrinsic evidence of intention will not be heard, or that evidence of surrounding circumstances will be admissible only in cases of latent ambiguity."[916]

The common feature of the parol evidence rule and four corners rule is that they both prevent the use of extrinsic evidence in the interpretation of contracts. The parol evidence rule precludes the use of prior agreements and the course of dealing in the interpretation of a contract but not the use of the course of performance. The four corners rule, however, prohibits the use of extrinsic evidence about the phases both prior to and after the conclusion of the contract.[917]

Perillo criticizes this rule for being unreasonable and bearing heavy consequences. He states that it is not possible to determine that an agreement is complete only by looking at the text of a contract.[918] Nevertheless, this is a restrictive rule that bears heavy consequences and continues to be applied today.[919]

[b] Other Rules of Interpretation Recognized in the Literature

The parol evidence rule, the plain meaning rule, and the four corners rule mentioned above appear to be incompatible with the principle of systematic interpretation in its broader sense, which is generally recognized in comparative law. [920] Still, the principle

915. Richard Posner, *The Law and Economics of Contract Interpretation*, 83 Texas Law Review 1581, 1596 (2005); *Federal Deposit Ins. Corp. v. W.R. Grace &Co.*, 877 F.2d 614, 621 (7th Cir. 1989).
916. Corbin, *supra* n. 69, at 26; Corbin refers to *American Sumatra Tobacco Corp. v. Willis*~~, 5 Cir., 170 F.2d 215 (C.A. 5th, 1948)~~ http://tx.findacase.com/research/wfrmDocViewer.aspx/xq/fac.19481021_0040112.C05.htm/qx (accessed December 7, 2018) as an exception to this rule.
917. Vogenauer, *supra* n. 131, at 976.
918. Perillo, *supra* n. 839, at 132.
919. *Independent Energy Corp. v. Trigen Energy Corp.*, 944 F. Supp. 1184 (S.D.N.Y 1996), http://law.justia.com/cases/federal/district-courts/FSupp/944/1184/1485585/ (accessed December 7, 2018); *Air Safety, Inc. v. Teachers Realty Corp.*, 185 Ill. 2d 457, 706 N.E.2d 882 (1999), http://caselaw.findlaw.com/il-supreme-court/1258870.html (accessed December 7, 2018).
920. *See*, sections §3.02[A][4][b] Article 1189 (Former Article 1161) of the CC. Fr.; §3.02[B][6][b] Article 1363 of the CC. It.; §3.03[A][2] Types or Methods of Interpretation in German Law; §3.03[B][4][a] Subjective Interpretation; §3.03[C][2][f] Principles of Interpretation Developed

of systematic interpretation has been expressed in § 303 of the UCC after the 2001 reform and in § 202 (1) and (5) of the Restatement (Second) of Contracts.

The principle of systematic interpretation is also recognized by most authors, including Williston, the representative of the strictest approach to the interpretation of contracts. Williston states that a contract should be interpreted in its entirety, and the intent of the parties must be ascertained from the consideration of their contract as a whole. Individual words and expressions must be considered together with the other parts of the contract.[921] Corbin also confirms that contracts must be interpreted as a whole and adds that the legal effect of a contract can only be determined in its entirety.[922]

Williston also points out that the surrounding circumstances at the time of the conclusion of the contract have to be taken into consideration and includes this principle among his four primary rules of interpretation.[923] Corbin goes one step further from Williston and states that the statements of the parties regarding the interpretation of their contract, the course of dealing, and the course of performance, which are mentioned as tools of interpretation in § 303 of the UCC and § 202 (5) of the Restatement (Second) of Contracts, must also be taken into consideration. He refers to this rule as "practical interpretation."[924] Posner also refers to this rule with the same words as § 303 of the UCC.[925]

Both Williston and Corbin also mention the principle according to which the meaning that would render the contract valid should be applied,[926] which is generally recognized in comparative law.[927] Corbin also uses the "Latin maxim" of *ut res magis valeat quam pereat*, albeit without reference to Iulianus *Dig.* 34, 5, 12 (13).[928]

Williston also states the *contra stipulatorem* or *contra proferentem* rule, albeit without mentioning its name. According to him, doubts arising from the ambiguity of language should be interpreted against the author of the writing, because it is possible to avoid them while writing the contract.[929] In addition to that, Williston points out that the expressions, acts, or declarations of the parties relating to the interpretation of their

Through Case Law or Recognized in the Literature; §3.04[A][5] Lord Hoffman's Five Principles of the Interpretation of Contracts, *supra*.

921. Williston, *supra* n. 833 (Williston on Contracts), at 305-306.
922. Corbin, *supra* n. 69, at 183.
923. Williston, *supra* n. 833 (Williston on Contracts), at 716; *see also*, section §3.04[B][2] The Objective Approach and The Restatement (First) of Contracts, *supra*.
924. Corbin, *supra* n. 69, at 249.
925. Posner, *supra* n. 883, at 558-559.
926. Williston, *supra* n. 833 (Williston on Contracts), at 747; Corbin, *supra* n. 69, at 4, especially at 167 et seq.
927. *See*, sections §3.02[A][4][d] Article 1191 (Former Article 1157) of the CC. Fr.; §3.02[B][6][e] Article 1367 of the CC. It.; §3.03[A][3][c] § 157 of the BGB; §3.03[B][5] Principles of Interpretation Developed Through Case Law; §3.03[C][2][f] Principles of Interpretation Developed Through Case Law or Recognized in the Literature; §3.04[A][4] Other Principles of Interpretation, *supra*.
928. Corbin, *supra* n. 69, at 4. For Iulianus' text in *Dig.* 34, 5, 12 (13) (Iul. 50 *Dig.*); *see*, section §2.01[B][2][b], The Emergence of Principles of Objective Interpretation in the Classical Period, *supra*.
929. Williston, *supra* n. 833 (Williston on Contracts), at 760 et seq. Also Posner adheres to this view. Posner, *supra* n. 883, at 558.

contract should be given weight.[930] He also states that contractual clauses must only be interpreted narrowly in some exceptional cases, especially in public interest contracts, non-liability clauses, forfeitures, and penalties.[931]

Corbin, however, also mentions the *contra proferentem* rule and defines it more clearly than Williston. Corbin states that according to this principle, the meaning that is less favorable to the party who chose the words should be adopted. He also adds that this rule is a subsidiary rule that should only be applied when the meaning of the words in a contract cannot be ascertained through literal interpretation,[932] as is the case in some continental legal systems.[933]

Finally, the doctrine of *implied terms*, which is related to complementary interpretation, has also found its expression in U.S. law through the influence of English law.[934] Corbin refers to this doctrine and states that there can be implied terms regarding both the facts and the law.[935]

Also § 226 of the Restatement (Second) of Contracts recognizes the doctrine of implied terms. This paragraph reads as follows:

> § 226. How an Event May Be Made a Condition
>
> An event may be made a condition either by the agreement of the parties or by a term supplied by the court.[936]

930. Williston, *supra* n. 833 (Williston on Contracts), at 789-790.
931. *Ibid.*, at 326-327.
932. Corbin, *supra* n. 69, at 262.
933. *See*, sections §3.02[B][6][h] Article 1370 of the CC. It.; §3.03[A][3][c] § 157 of the BGB; §3.03[B][5] Principles of Interpretation Developed Through Case Law; §3.03[C][2][e] Article 23 of the TBK and the *Contra Stipulatorem* Rule, *supra*.
934. *The Estate of Angeline v. Bachmeier*, No. 25344-5-II., June 26, 2001—WA Court of Appeals, http://caselaw.findlaw.com/wa-court-of-appeals/1364291.html (accessed December 7, 2018); in this decision, the court applied the doctrine of implied terms by referring to Lord Watson's decision in *Dahl v. Nelson, Donkin, & Co.*, 6 App. Cas. 38, 59 (1881).
935. Corbin, *supra* n. 69, at 276-277.
936. ALI, *supra* n. 876, at 170.

CHAPTER 4
Interpretation of Contracts in Uniform Law

§4.01 GENERALLY

An examination of the developments of the late twentieth century in international law reveals that the path chosen by the drafters of uniform law has been to provide detailed provisions on the interpretation of contracts, as is the case with the Latin legal systems. Conversely, the Romano-Germanic approach, which limits the legislation on this issue to a few provisions, has not been adopted in uniform law.

Nevertheless, the provisions in uniform law on the interpretation of contracts do not reflect the approach or method of codification found in any particular legal family. One may observe that uniform law texts have developed their own method and developed this method over the course of time.[937] According to this method, a subjective rule is set forth first, according to which the common intent of the parties should be sought, and prevail over the wording of the contract. Then, an objective rule follows, according to which, if the common intent of the parties cannot be determined, then the contract should be interpreted in accordance with the understanding of a reasonable third person in the same circumstances as the parties.

A list of the circumstances that must (or should) be taken into consideration follows these first two rules. This list usually includes factors for consideration such as the circumstances which the parties were in at the time of the conclusion of the contract, the nature and purpose of the contract, the usages, statements, and conduct of the parties; and the principle of good faith and fair dealing.

The order of the rules that follow these first three steps varies in different uniform law instruments, except for the CISG, where these provisions are limited to one article that includes only the abovementioned steps. However, the method and order of the first three steps adopted by the CISG also inspired other uniform law texts that

937. However, Vogenauer argues that the drafters of uniform law instruments followed the French model. Vogenauer, *supra* n. 131, at 974.

followed. The *contra proferentem* rule is placed just after the first three steps in the PECL and Draft Common Frame of Reference (DCFR), whereas this rule is found in the last provisions on the issue in the UNIDROIT Principles and Common European Sales Law (CESL), the latter of which have given priority to the principle of systematic interpretation over the *contra proferentem* rule.

Even though there are some differences between the provisions on the interpretation of contracts in different uniform law texts, they all adopt the same methodology and their differences are not very significant. This is due to several factors: they have been written in close periods in time, they target the same communities, they respond to the same needs, and the same experts have been involved in their drafting processes.

However, the most important reason for the similarity of the provisions of different uniform law texts on the interpretation of contracts and their autonomy from any particular legal family is that they are also based on the principles that emanated from arbitral case law, along with comparative studies. The application of the provisions of particular legal systems relating to the interpretation of contracts by arbitral tribunals led to the development of the principles of interpretation within the frame of the *lex mercatoria*.[938] The principles of *lex mercatoria* relating to the interpretation of contracts, on the one hand, confirmed some of the principles generally recognized by the domestic laws, and on the other hand, paved the way for their recognition by uniform law instruments.

Arbitral case law adopted the abovementioned method, according to which, the common intent of the parties should be sought first,[939] and if the common intent of the parties cannot be determined, then the contract should be interpreted objectively.[940] The prohibition of purely literal interpretation, a fundamental rule of subjective

938. Filali Osman, *Les principes généraux de la lex mercatoria—contribution à l'étude d'un ordre juridique anational*, 208 et seq. (LGDJ, 1992).

939. Osman, *supra* n. 938, at 210 et seq.; ICC Award No. 1434, Clunet 1976, 978 et seq., at 982 https://www.trans-lex.org/201434 (accessed December 7, 2018); ARAMCO-Award, ILR 1963, 117 et seq., at 172 https://www.trans-lex.org/260800 (accessed December 7, 2018); CRCICA Award no. 64/1995, in: Mohie Eldin I. Alam Eldin, Arbitral Awards of the Cairo Regional Centre of International Commercial Arbitration, The Hague 2000, 175 et seq., at 715 https://www.trans-lex.org/250613 (accessed December 7, 2018); ICC Award No. 12290, Collection of ICC Arbitral Awards 2008-2011, 831 et seq., at 833 https://www.trans-lex.org/212290 (accessed December 7, 2018); ICC Award No. 13129, Collection of ICC Arbitral Awards 2008-2011, 329 et seq., at 337 https://www.trans-lex.org/213129 (accessed December 7, 2018); ICC Award No. 3460, Clunet 1981, 939 et seq., at 940 https://www.trans-lex.org/203460 (accessed December 7, 2018); ICC Award No. 4145 (Second Interim Award), YCA 1987, 97 et seq. (also published in: Clunet 1985, at 985 et seq.), at 101-102 https://www.trans-lex.org/204145 (accessed December 7, 2018); ICC Award No. 8694, Clunet 1997, 1056 et seq., at 1057 https://www.trans-lex.org/208694 (accessed December 7, 2018); ICSID Award, *AMCO Asia Corp. et al. v. The Republic of Indonesia et al.*, YCA 1985, 61 et seq., at 62, https://www.trans-lex.org/240100 (accessed December 7, 2018); ICC Award No. 13278, YCA 2008, 118 et seq., at 125, https://www.trans-lex.org/213278 (accessed December 7, 2018).

940. ICC Award No. 10671, Clunet 2005, 1268 et seq., at 1272 https://www.trans-lex.org/210672 (accessed December 7, 2018); ICC Award No. 14581, YCA 2012, 62 et seq., at 72 https://www.trans-lex.org/214581 (accessed December 7, 2018); ICC Award No. 7331, Clunet 1995, 1001 et seq., at 1003 https://www.trans-lex.org/207331 (accessed December 7, 2018); ICC Award No. 8908, ICC Bull. 10/No. 2 (1999), 83 et seq., at 86 https://www.trans-lex.org/208908 (accessed December 7, 2018).

interpretation, is also recognized by arbitral case law.[941] However, arbitral tribunals also acknowledge that the starting point of interpretation is the wording of the agreement.[942]

Another principle adopted by arbitral case law is the principle of systematic interpretation.[943] Arbitral tribunals apply this principle broadly, not only to include the interpretation of a contract as a whole but also taking account of all the relevant circumstances that affected the deal.[944]

Arbitral case law also recognizes and attributes significant importance to the principle of *ut res magis valeat quam pereat*, or *l'effet utile*, according to which an interpretation that renders a contract valid should be preferred.[945]

One of the most important principles of interpretation of the *lex mercatoria* is, not surprisingly, the principle of interpretation according to good faith and fair dealing.[946] However, Osman correctly observes that the downside of this principle is the vagueness of its character.[947]

The *contra stipulatorem* or *contra proferentem* rule is also a general principle of interpretation recognized and applied by arbitral tribunals.[948]

941. Osman, *supra* n. 938, at 216; ICC Award No. 1434, *supra* n. 939, at 982; ICC Award No. 4145, *supra* n. 939, at 102.
942. ICC Award No. 5961, Clunet 1997, 1051 et seq., at 1052 https://www.trans-lex.org/205961 (accessed December 7, 2018); ICC Award No. 1434, *supra* n. 939 at 982.
943. Osman, *supra* n. 938, at 218-219; CRCICA Award no. 64/1995, *supra* n. 939, at 715; ICC Award No. 8694, *supra* n. 939, at 1057; ICC Award No. 12290, *supra* n. 939, at 833.
944. Osman, *supra* n. 938, at 211-212; ICC Award No. 1434, *supra* n. 939, at 982; Iran-US Claims Tribunal, *First Travel Corp. v. Iran*, 9 IRAN-U.S. C.T.R., 360 et seq., at 367-368 https://www.trans-lex.org/231600 (accessed December 7, 2018); ICC Award No. 5961, *supra* n. 942, at 1052-1053; ICC Award No. 4145, *supra* n. 939, at 102.
945. Osman, *supra* n. 938, at 210 et seq., especially at 220-228; ICC Award No. 1434, *supra* n. 939, at 982; ICC Award No. 4145, *supra* n. 939, at 102; Ad Hoc Award of May 27, 1991, YCA 1992, 11 et seq., at 16 https://www.trans-lex.org/260400 (accessed December 7, 2018); ICC Award No. 3380, YCA 1982, 116 et seq. (also published in: Clunet 1981, at 928 et seq.) at 118, https://www.trans-lex.org/203380 (accessed December 7, 2018); ICC Award No. 7920, YCA 1998, 80 et seq., at 81-81 https://www.trans-lex.org/207920 (accessed December 7, 2018); ICC Award No. 8365, Clunet 1997, 1078 et seq., at 1080 https://www.trans-lex.org/208365 (accessed December 7, 2018); ICSID Award, *Asian Agricultural Products Ltd. v. The Republic of Sri Lanka*, YCA 1991, 106 et seq., at 113-114 https://www.trans-lex.org/240500 (accessed December 7, 2018).
946. Osman, *supra* n. 938, at 247; ICC Award No. 5065, Clunet 1987, 1039 et seq., at 1043 https://www.trans-lex.org/205065 (accessed December 7, 2018); ICC Award No. 1434, *supra* n. 939 at 982; ICSID Award, *AMCO Asia Corp. et al. v. The Republic of Indonesia et al.*, *supra* n. 939 at 63.
947. Osman, *supra* n. 938, at 255.
948. China January 7, 2000 CIETAC Arbitration proceeding (Cysteine case) http:/cisgw3.law.pace.edu/cases/00107cl.html (accessed December 7, 2018); ICC Award No. 3460, *supra* n. 939, at 939; ICC Award No. 7110, 10 ICC Bull. No. 2, 1999, 1029 et seq., at 44 https://www.trans-lex.org/207110 (accessed December 7, 2018); ICC Award No. 7710, Clunet 2001, 1147 et seq., at 1152 https://www.trans-lex.org/207710; Society of Maritime Arbitrators, Inc., New York, Award No. 2972, *Nordic American Shipping A/S v. Bayoil Inc.*, YCA 1995, 126 et seq., at 131 https://www.trans-lex.org/250300 (accessed December 7, 2018). However, the arbitral tribunal in Iran-US Claims Tribunal Case No. 34 pointed out the subsidiary nature of this principle, *see*, Iran-US Claims Tribunal, Award in Case No. 34, YCA 1987, 257, at 259 https://www.trans-lex.org/232400 (accessed December 7, 2018).

§4.02 ARTICLE 8 OF THE CISG

[A] Generally

Article 8 of the CISG deals with the interpretation of the statements and conduct of the parties to a contract for the international sale of goods. This article reads as follows:

> Article 8
> (1) For the purposes of this Convention statements made by and other conduct of a party are to be interpreted according to his intent where the other party knew or could not have been unaware what that intent was.
> (2) If the preceding paragraph is not applicable, statements made by and other conduct of a party are to be interpreted according to the understanding that a reasonable person of the same kind as the other party would have had in the same circumstances.
> (3) In determining the intent of a party or the understanding a reasonable person would have had, due consideration is to be given to all relevant circumstances of the case including the negotiations, any practices which the parties have established between themselves, usages and any subsequent conduct of the parties.[949]

The fact that this article focuses on the interpretation of statements and conduct, and not the interpretation of contracts is an unusual choice, is also found only in German law (§ 133 of the BGB). For this reason, some authors suggest that the Romano-Germanic legal tradition[950] and especially the German BGB,[951] has influenced this article of the CISG. However, one may say that this article is closer to the position of Latin legal systems considering that it is more comprehensive than the provisions found in Romano-Germanic legal systems that it combines subjective and objective methods of interpretation and that it provides for a hierarchy of these methods of interpretation. Moreover, an arbitral tribunal observed that Article 8 of the CISG states rules that correspond to the principles generally accepted in international commerce.[952]

Although Article 8 of the CISG is more comprehensive than the provisions of the Romano-Germanic legal systems on the issue, according to Lookofsky, one cannot reasonably expect this article to replace the case law on this broad and important subject. Therefore, courts may need to apply more special rules of interpretation than those provided in Article 8 of the CISG. Lookofsky suggests that the courts should refer

949. United Nations Convention on Contracts for the International Sale of Goods adopted on April 11, 1980 (CISG) http://www.uncitral.org/uncitral/en/uncitral_texts/sale_goods/1980CISG.html (accessed December 7, 2018).
950. Bruno Zeller, *Determining the Contractual Intent of Parties under the CISG and Common Law—A Comparative Analysis*, 4 (4) European Journal of Law Reform 629, 635 (2002).
951. Vogenauer, *supra* n. 131, at 974; Peter Schlechtriem, *Uniform Sales Law—The UN-Convention on Contracts for the International Sale of Goods*, 39 (Manz, 1986).
952. UNCITRAL, *Digest of Article 8 case law*, in *2016 UNCITRAL Digest of case law on the United Nations Convention on the International Sale of Goods*, § 1 http://www.uncitral.org/pdf/english/clout/CISG_Digest_2016.pdf (accessed December 7, 2018); CLOUT case No. 303, ICC Award No. 7331, *supra* n. 940.

to the general principles laid down in the CISG while applying more specific rules and to base these rules on sources other than the CISG, such as *lex mercatoria*.[953]

The origin of Article 8 of the CISG is the UNIDROIT Draft Law for the Unification of Certain Rules Relating to Validity of Contracts of International Sale of Goods (ULVC).[954] The first paragraph of Article 8 of the CISG corresponds to paragraphs 1 and 2 of Article 3 of the ULVC, whereas, the second paragraph of Article 8 of the CISG corresponds to paragraph 3 of Article 3.[955]

The most important distinction between Article 3 of the ULVC and Article 8 of the CISG lies in the position of the provision of paragraph 3 of Article 8 of the CISG that seems more related to the interpretation of contracts than the interpretation of statements, which corresponds to paragraph 1 of Article 4 of the ULVC.[956] The reason for this difference is that even though the Working Group on Article 8 of the CISG had decided that this article should only deal with the interpretation of statements, the Commission later decided to add provisions on the interpretation of contracts into this article as well.[957]

Another difference between the two articles is that the ULVC refers to the statements and conduct of the "parties," whereas the CISG speaks of the statements by or conduct of "a party." The Working Group made this change in 1978.[958]

953. Joseph Lookofsky, *Understanding the CISG, A Compact Guide to the 1980 United Nations Convention on Contracts for the International Sale of Goods*, 43 (Kluwer Law International-DJØF, 2008).
954. E. Allan Farnsworth, *Article 8*, in *Bianca-Bonell Commentary on the International Sales Law*, 94-95 (Giuffrè, 1987); Alberto Zuppi, *Article 8*, in Stefan Kröll, Loukas Mistelis, Pilar Perales Viscasillas (eds.), *United Nations Convention on Contracts for the International Sale of Goods (CISG) Commentary*, 142 et seq., § 6 (C.H. Beck/Hart/Nomos, 2011).
955. Article 3 ULVC reads as follows:

> Statements by and acts of the parties shall be interpreted according to their actual common intent, where such an intent can be established.
>
> If the actual common intent of the parties cannot be established, statements by and acts of the parties shall be interpreted according to the intent of one of the parties, where such an intent can be established and the other knew or ought to have known what that intent was.
>
> If neither of the preceding paragraphs is applicable, the statements by and the acts of the parties shall be interpreted according to the intent that reasonable persons would have had in the same situation as the parties.

Farnsworth, *supra* n. 954, at 95-96.

956. Article 4(1) of the ULVC reads as follows:

> In applying the preceding Article due consideration shall be given to all relevant circumstances, including any negotiations between the parties, any practices which they have established between themselves, any usages which reasonable persons in the same situations as the parties usually consider to be applicable, the meaning usually given in any trade concerned to any expressions, provisions or contractual forms which are commonly used, and any conduct of the parties subsequent to the conclusion of the contract.

Farnsworth, *supra* n. 954, at 96.

957. Farnsworth, *supra* n. 954, at 94-95, the author refers to Yearbook, IX (1978), 62.
958. Farnsworth, *supra* n. 954, at 95, the author refers to Yearbook, IX (1978), 63.

The third remarkable difference between the two articles is the replacement of the expression of "where ... the other knew or ought to have known what that intent was" in Article 3(2) of the ULVC with the expression "where the other party knew or could not have been unaware what that intent was" in Article 8(1) of the CISG. The reason for this change is that the Working Group found the ULVC text to be too subjective and aimed at objectivizing it.[959]

In addition, the position of Article 8 of the CISG was also changed in the drafting process. This original intent was to place this article in Part II. It was later moved to Part I, laying down the general principles and expanding the sphere of application of this article to cover both Part II on the formation of the contract and Part III on the sale of goods.[960]

This article sets forth the subjective method of interpretation in the first paragraph and the objective method of interpretation in the second paragraph and provides for a hierarchy of them accordingly. The courts must try to determine the intent of a party making the statement first, and when this is not possible, it will then interpret the statement according to the understanding of a reasonable person.[961]

Transition of the subjective method of interpretation to the objective method represents a successful solution in the search for a balance between the two approaches. According to Honnold, a purely subjective approach on the basis of the will of the parties is outdated. In his words, "current references to 'will' as the basis for contract resemble the echoes of distant thunder from a storm that has passed."[962]

The CISG is silent as to whether the interpretation of statements and contracts is a question of fact or a question of law. As shown above, this classification has significant consequences in particular legal systems, especially in U.S. law, where this classification is relevant to determine whether juries or judges will consider the issue.[963] Moreover, this classification determines whether or not decisions on the interpretation of contracts are reviewable on appeal in jurisdictions where the appeal is limited to the questions of law.[964]

959. *Ibid.*, 34.

960. Joseph Lookofsky, *1980 United Nations Convention on Contracts for the International Sale of Goods, Article 8 Interpretation of Statements by Parties*, in J. Herbots (ed.), R. Blanpain (general ed.), *International Encyclopaedia of Laws—Contracts*, Suppl. 29, § 82 (Kluwer Law International, 2000).

961. Farnsworth, *supra* n. 954, at 98; Lookofsky, *supra* n. 960, at § 84; Lookofsky, *supra* n. 953, at 43; Wiegand, *supra* n. 491, at nn. 12-13; Peter Huber, Alastair Mullis, *The CISG: A New Textbook for Students and Practitioners*, 12 (Sellier European Law Publishers, 2007); Zuppi, *supra* n. 954, at § 3; UNCITRAL Digest 2016, *supra* n. 952, at § 6; [SWITZERLAND Handelsgericht Aargau 26 November 2008]; [SWITZERLAND Appellationsgericht Basel-Stadt 26 September 2008]; [SWITZERLAND Zivilgericht Basel-Stadt 8 November 2006].

962. Honnold, *supra* n. 496, at § 106.

963. *See*, section §3.04[B][1] Generally, *supra*.

964. Martin Schmidt-Kessel, *Article 8*, in Peter Schlechtriem, Ingeborg Schwenzer (eds.), *Commentary on the UN Convention on the International Sale of Goods (CISG)*, n. 60 (2nd (English) ed., C.H. Beck, 2005).

According to one opinion,[965] which was also adopted by an arbitral tribunal,[966] the subjective interpretation found under Article 8(1) of the CISG is a question of fact, because it aims at determining the intent of the parties, whereas the objective interpretation under Article 8(2) of the CISG is a question of law, since it will be made according to the principle of good faith and fair dealing.

According to Zuppi, another issue left unresolved by Article 8 of the CISG is whether the real intent or the expressed intent of a party making the statement will be considered.[967] In addition, this article is silent about situations where the meaning of a statement cannot be determined, even though all the tools of interpretation mentioned in the article have been exhausted.[968] Moreover, according to the same author, it is not clear whether the methods described in this article can also be used for complementary interpretation.[969] As will be demonstrated below,[970] there are other important questions left untouched by Article 8 of the CISG.

[B] The Scope of Application of Article 8 of the CISG and Interpretation Based on the Intent of Only One of the Parties

Article 8 of the CISG refers to the interpretation of "statements made by and other conduct of a party" and not to the interpretation of contracts, as is the case with § 133 of the BGB.[971] The fact that this article bases the interpretation of a statement on the intent of only one party does not pose a problem as long as the interpretation of a statement of offer or acceptance or a notice relating to the performance or avoidance is in question. This article was placed in Part I on the general principles, instead of Part II on the formation of the contract where it was originally intended to appear. Therefore, its scope of application has been expanded to cover also Part III dealing primarily with performance.[972] For this reason, there is no doubt that this article applies to all unilateral statements and conduct, related with either the formation or performance of a contract.[973]

What about a situation where the interpretation of a bilateral sales contract and not a unilateral statement is in question? The provisions of Article 8 are the most relevant provisions of the CISG to the interpretation of contracts; however, they do not expressly deal with this issue. Will they apply to the interpretation of contracts

965. Zuppi, *supra* n. 954, at § 3.
966. ICC Award No. 9187, http://cisgw3.law.pace.edu/cisg/wais/db/cases2/999187i1.html (accessed December 7, 2018), http://www.unilex.info/case.cfm?pid = 1&do = case&id = 466&step = FullText (accessed December 7, 2018).
967. Zuppi, *supra* n. 954, at § 4.
968. *Ibid.*
969. *Ibid.*
970. *See*, sections §4.02[B] The Scope of Application of Article 8 of the CISG, and Interpretation Based on the Intent of Only One of the Parties; §4.02[C] Failure of Mutual Assent and Error, *infra*.
971. *See*, section 3.03[A][3] Provisions of the BGB Relating to the Interpretation of Contracts (§ 133 and § 157 of the BGB), *infra*.
972. Lookofsky, *supra* n. 960, at § 82.
973. Farnsworth, *supra* n. 954, at 100.

anyway? How and on which basis? There are various approaches to these questions. The common feature of all of them is that they reach the conclusion that Article 8 of the CISG also applies to the interpretation of contracts.

According to Sacco, the expression "statements made by and other conduct of a party are to be interpreted according to his intent" in Article 8(1) of the CISG should be understood to mean "interpreted according to the intent of a reasonable person" and not the intent of a party, because a contract is, by definition, the meeting of the wills of the parties.[974]

The majority opinion, also adopted by the United Nations Commission on International Trade Law (UNCITRAL) Secretariat Commentary, does not interpret the text of Article 8 of the CISG but only holds that this article also covers the interpretation of contracts because it applies to offer and acceptance, which give rise to a contract.[975] According to the UNCITRAL Secretariat Commentary, the CISG treats a sales contract to be the product of two unilateral acts. Therefore, Article 8 of the CISG applies not only to the interpretation of any statement or conduct but also to the interpretation of offer and acceptance for the purposes of determining whether a contract has been formed and for determining the content of a contract.[976] Schmidt-Kessel, who adheres to this opinion, states that there is no doubt that this article also applies to the interpretation of contracts.[977]

The present author, however, is of the opinion that it is not possible to reach this conclusion so directly. While it is beyond doubt that the conclusion reached by the Secretariat is unavoidable from a functional standpoint, it does not seem possible to draw this conclusion only from the text of Article 8 of the CISG.

As this article is inspired by § 133 of the BGB and only addresses the interpretation of statements and conduct but not of contracts, it differs from the general tendency in comparative law. Therefore, it would have been more appropriate to consider the purpose of the legislators of the BGB of 1900 in writing § 133 of the BGB in a manner to only address the interpretation of the statements, together with § 157 of the BGB addressing the interpretation of contracts. The German legislators at that time aimed to distinguish between the interpretation of statements and contracts in order to make the latter subject to objective criteria. The application of BGB in the decades that followed its enactment, however, has shown that this distinction was not practicable.[978]

---

974. Sacco, *supra* n. 7, at 232.
975. UNCITRAL Secretariat, *Guide to CISG Article 8, Secretariat Commentary (closest counterpart to an Official Commentary)*, nn. 1-2 http://cisgw3.law.pace.edu/cisg/text/secomm/secomm-08.html (accessed December 7, 2018); Honnold, *supra* n. 496, at § 105; Farnsworth, *supra* n. 954, at 96-97; Schmidt-Kessel, *supra* n. 964, at n. 3; Zuppi, *supra* n. 954, at § 2; Franco Ferrari, *Article 8*, in Franco Ferrari, Harry Flechtner, Ronald A. Brand (eds.), *The Draft UNCITRAL Digest and Beyond: Cases, Analysis and Unresolved Issues in the U.N. Sales Convention*, 172 et seq., 175-176 (Sellier European Law Publishers, 2004); Peter Huber, *Some Introductory Remarks on the CISG*, Internationales Handelsrecht (6/2006) 228-238, at 234 (2006), http://www.cisg.law.pace.edu/cisg/biblio/huber-08.html (accessed December 7, 2018).
976. UNCITRAL Secretariat, *supra* n. 975, at nn. 1-2.
977. Schmidt-Kessel, *supra* n. 964, at n. 3.
978. *See*, section §3.03[A][3][a] Relationship Between the Two Paragraphs, *supra*.

Turning to the text of the CISG, there is no other provision expressly treating the interpretation of contracts, as is the case with § 157 of the BGB. It is unfortunate that the authors of Article 8 of the CISG, though inspired by § 133 of the BGB, ignored this fact and the eighty years of experience of German courts.

Farnsworth and Lookofsky correctly point out that taking a position on Article 8 of the CISG that it can also apply to the interpretation of contracts does not expressly stem from the text of the article and therefore that this article is not well drafted.[979]

Lookofsky goes a step further than Farnsworth and also proposes a solution to this problematic situation: the interpretation of contracts is a matter governed by the CISG, as contracts are common statements of the parties. Article 7(2) indicates what should be done concerning matters governed by the CISG but not expressly settled in it. Such matters must be settled in conformity with the general principles on which the CISG is based. Lookofsky correctly suggests that Article 8 of the CISG can apply to the interpretation of contracts through the application of Article 7(2) of the CISG.[980]

However, both arbitral tribunals[981] and domestic courts[982] directly apply Article 8 of the CISG to the interpretation of contracts. It should also be mentioned that the application of Article 8 of the CISG to the interpretation of statements of offer and acceptance[983] and to the conduct of the parties regarding the performance of a contract[984] are more common than its application to the interpretation of contracts.

Some court decisions have held that the rules of interpretation in domestic laws do not apply in cases where the CISG applies because Article 8 of the CISG covers the entire issue of the interpretation of contracts.[985] Nevertheless, a Belgian court has held that the contract of the parties precedes the CISG in the hierarchy of the rules applicable to the dispute, and therefore Article 8 of the CISG only applies when the text of a contract is not "clear." [986] With this unfortunate decision in a CISG case, the court has applied the *in claris non fit interpretatio* rule, which has generally been rejected in comparative and uniform law.

979. Farnsworth, *supra* n. 954, at 100; Lookofsky, *supra* n. 960, at § 83.
980. Lookofsky, *supra* n. 960, at § 83.
981. UNCITRAL Digest 2016, *supra* n. 952, at § 3, CLOUT case No. 303, ICC Award No. 7331, *supra* n. 940.
982. UNCITRAL Digest 2016, *supra* n. 952, at § 3, [FINLAND Appellate Court Helsinki 31 May 2004]; CLOUT case No. 877 [SWITZERLAND Bundesgericht 22 December 2000].
983. UNCITRAL Digest 2016, *supra* n. 952, at § 1, CLOUT case No. 429 [GERMANY Oberlandesgericht Frankfurt 30 August 2000]; CLOUT case No. 424 [AUSTRIA Oberster Gerichtshof 9 March 2000]; [GERMANY Landgericht Zwickau 19 March 1999]; CLOUT case No. 189 [AUSTRIA Oberster Gerichtshof 20 March 1997]; CLOUT case No. 176 [AUSTRIA Oberster Gerichtshof 6 February 1996]; CLOUT case No. 334 [SWITZERLAND Obergericht des Kantons Thurgau 19 December 1995]; CLOUT case No. 330 [SWITZERLAND Handelsgericht des Kantons St. Gallen 5 December 1995]; CLOUT case No. 106 [AUSTRIA Oberster Gerichtshof 10 November 1994].
984. UNCITRAL Digest 2016, *supra* n. 952, at § 1, CLOUT case No. 270 [GERMANY Bundesgerichtshof 25 November 1998]; CLOUT case No. 282 [GERMANY Oberlandesgericht Koblenz 31 January 1997].
985. UNCITRAL Digest 2016, *supra* n. 952, at § 2, CLOUT case No. 932 [SWITZERLAND Obergericht des Kantons Thurgau 12 December 2006]; [FINLAND Appellate Court Helsinki 31 May 2004]; CLOUT case No. 5 [GERMANY Landgericht Hamburg 26 September 1990].
986. UNCITRAL Digest 2016, *supra* n. 952, at § 5, [BELGIUM Hof van Beroep Antwerpen 24 April 2006].

[C] Failure of Mutual Assent and Error

There is no doubt that Article 8 of the CISG applies to the interpretation of offer and acceptance giving rise to a contract. According to the view adopted by the UNCITRAL Secretariat and favored by Farnsworth, this function of Article 8 of the CISG is intended for use in the determination of whether a contract has actually been formed, and if so, for the determination of its content.[987]

However, a problem arises however when the statements taken as offer and acceptance are not found to constitute a contract. Article 8 of the CISG is silent on the situation of a lack of agreement (failure of mutual assent). Therefore, there is no unanimity in the literature as to how to solve such situations.

Farnsworth and Schlechtriem point out the fact that a troublesome feature of Article 8 of the CISG is that it is silent on this point.[988] Article 8 of the CISG says nothing about what should be done if one party makes an offer with a different intent than what a reasonable person would understand from that offer, and the other party accepts the offer with a different intent than that of the first party.[989] What can be drawn from the first two paragraphs of Article 8 of the CISG is that the courts are not allowed to rely on the subjective, internal intent of only one of the parties.[990]

One may consider that in such a situation no contract has been formed.[991] It is also possible to consider this situation as a divergence between the real intent and the declared intent, otherwise known as an "error."[992] The prevailing opinion is that either way, this situation is a matter of validity and that it has to be solved according to the domestic law applicable by virtue of the rules of private international law because Article 4(a) of the CISG expressly excludes the question of validity from the scope of the CISG.[993]

However, a closer look at Article 4 of the CISG reveals that questions of validity are not exclusively left to domestic laws. According to this article, "*except as otherwise expressly provided in this Convention,* it is not concerned with: (a) the validity of the contract."[994] (emphasis added)

According to the minority opinion[995] to which the present author also adheres, the interpretation of the statements of offer and acceptance pursuant to Article 8 of the CISG for the purpose of the determination of whether a contract has been formed

987. Farnsworth, *supra* n. 954, at 96-97; UNCITRAL Secretariat, *supra* n. 975, at nn. 1-2.
988. Farnsworth, *supra* n. 954, at 100; Schlechtriem, *supra* n. 951, at 39.
989. Farnsworth, *supra* n. 954, at 100.
990. Schlechtriem, *supra* n. 951, at 39.
991. Farnsworth, *supra* n. 954, at 100; Zuppi, *supra* n. 954, at § 7; Zeller, *supra* n. 950, at 633-634.
992. Farnsworth, *supra* n. 954, at 101; Schmidt-Kessel, *supra* n. 964, at n. 6; Lookofsky, *supra* n. 953, at 43; Karl H. Neumayer, Catherine Ming, in François Dessemontet (ed.), *Convention de Vienne sur les contrats de vente internationale de marchandises—Commentaire*, 114 (CEDIAC, 1993).
993. Farnsworth, *supra* n. 954, at 101; Lookofsky, *supra* n. 953, at 43; Zuppi, *supra* n. 954, at § 7; Zeller, *supra* n. 950, at 633-634.
994. Article 4 of the CISG, *supra* n. 949.
995. Milena Djordjevic, *Article 4*, in Stefan Kröll, Loukas Mistelis, Pilar Perales Viscasillas (eds.), *United Nations Convention on Contracts for the International Sale of Goods (CISG) Commentary*, 62 et seq., § 6 (C.H. Beck/Hart/Nomos, 2011); Schmidt-Kessel, *supra* n. 964, at nn. 4-5.

constitutes an exception to Article 4 of the CISG. This is due to two reasons: first, it would be inconsistent to argue that Article 8 of the CISG applies to the interpretation of statements of offer and acceptance, but a domestic law must apply to the determination whether these statements form a contract, and second, such a method appears to be contrary to the purpose of taking into account the international character of the CISG and promoting its uniform application as expressed in Article 7(1) of the CISG.[996] For these reasons, it should be acknowledged that Article 8 of the CISG also applies to the issue of the validity of contracts or single clauses, such as the retention of title clauses, as previously mentioned by the present author.[997]

[D] Provisions of Article 8 of the CISG

[1] Article 8(1) of the CISG—Subjective Interpretation

The first paragraph of Article 8 of the CISG lays down a rule of subjective interpretation because it is based on the intent of a party in the interpretation of a statement or conduct of that party.[998] The subject of this paragraph is not the common intent of the parties, unlike the general tendency in continental legal systems,[999] but the intent of only one of the parties, as is the case with § 133 of the BGB.[1000] Nonetheless, undeclared or unexpressed intent is not the subject matter of interpretation according to this provision.[1001]

Farnsworth states that the meaning of a statement or conduct has to be taken into consideration according to the time when it had its effect and not at the time of the dispute. For instance, according to him, a statement of offer or acceptance should be interpreted by reference to the time of the conclusion of a contract.[1002] Schmidt-Kessel, however, objects to Farnsworth and states that the time to which reference must be made in the sense of Article 8(1) of the CISG is not the time when a statement or conduct had its effect, but at the time when it was made.[1003] Although there is no case law on the issue, Schmidt-Kessel's suggestion sounds more appropriate as Article 8(1) of the CISG takes the intent of the party making the statement (or conduct) as a basis.

996. Article 7(1) of the CISG reads as follows: "In the interpretation of this Convention, regard is to be had to its international character and to the need to promote uniformity in its application and the observance of good faith in international trade." *Supra* n. 949.
997. Schmidt-Kessel, *supra* n. 964, at nn. 4-5; Ahmet Cemil Yıldırım, *Lack of Uniform Application Regarding Transfer of Property in International Sales Contracts with Particular Regard to Retention of Title Clauses*, in Şükran Şıpka, Ahmet Cemil Yıldırım (eds.), *Yeni Türk Borçlar Kanunu ve CISG'e Göre Satış Sözleşmeleri (Sales Contracts under the New Turkish Code of Obligations and the CISG)*, 209 (On İki Levha, 2012).
998. Honnold, *supra* n. 496, at § 107; Farnsworth, *supra* n. 954, at 97.
999. UNCITRAL Secretariat, *supra* n. 975, at nn. 3-4; Canaris, Grigoleit, *supra* n. 5, at 448.
1000. *See*, section 3.03[A][3] Provisions of the BGB Relating to the Interpretation of Contracts (§ 133 and § 157 of the BGB), *infra*.
1001. UNCITRAL Digest 2016, *supra* n. 952, at § 8, [SWITZERLAND Zivilgericht Basel-Stadt 8 November 2006]; CLOUT case No. 911 [SWITZERLAND Cour de justice de Genève 12 May 2006]; CLOUT case No. 5 [GERMANY Landgericht Hamburg 26 September 1990].
1002. Farnsworth, *supra* n. 954, at 97.
1003. Schmidt-Kessel, *supra* n. 964, at n. 18.

In a situation where a statement (or conduct) has its effect after it has been made, and its meaning changes in the meantime, the meaning at the time when it was made should prevail.

In principle, Article 8(1) of the CISG lays down a rule of subjective interpretation as it is based on the intent of the party making the statement (or conduct). This provision, however, is not a purely subjective rule of interpretation because it also bears two elements of objective interpretation. First, the intent of the party making the statement must be determined in an objective context, by taking all relevant circumstances of the particular case into consideration pursuant to Article 8(3) of the CISG.[1004] On this basis, one author even suggests that the CISG adopted the trust principle of Romano-Germanic legal systems.[1005]

The other factor that objectivizes the approach of Article 8(1) of the CISG is the condition that "the other party knew or could not have been unaware what that intent was."[1006] If the addressee does not know or cannot reasonably be expected to be aware of the intent of the party making the declaration, Article 8(1) cannot apply. In this situation, the statement (or conduct) is to be interpreted according to Article 8(2) of the CISG.[1007]

Article 8(1) of the CISG sets forth two conditions for the intent to be taken as a basis of interpretation of a statement or conduct. The first is that the addressee knows the real intent of the party making the statement despite the wording of that statement. In this situation, there will be a subjective consensus. The common intent of the parties will prevail in the interpretation of the meaning of the statement, even if the objective meaning of the wording of the statement is different from that meaning. This is, indeed, an expression of the rule of *falsa demonstratio non nocet.*[1008]

The second condition is the negative condition that the addressee cannot be unaware of the real intent of the party making the statement. This is an objective criterion aiming at protecting the party making the statement from future claims by the addressee. Some authors argue that the responsibility of the addressee under this provision is the equivalent of liability for gross negligence.[1009]

These conditions are especially relevant when representatives, agencies, or brokers are involved in the transaction.[1010] For instance, French courts have held in two cases that the sellers could not be unaware of the intention of the buyers to market the goods in France and therefore, the contracts had to be interpreted according to the standards in that country.[1011]

1004. *Ibid.*, at n. 12.
1005. Neumayer, Ming, *supra* n. 992, at 111-112.
1006. UNCITRAL Secretariat, *supra* n. 975, at nn. 3-4; Honnold, *supra* n. 496, at § 107; Farnsworth, *supra* n. 954, at 97.
1007. UNCITRAL Secretariat, *supra* n. 975, at n. 4.
1008. UNCITRAL Digest 2016, *supra* n. 952, at § 9; [GERMANY Oberlandesgericht Hamm 12 November 2001]; Farnsworth, *supra* n. 954, at 97; Huber, Mullis, *supra* n. 961, at 12; Ferrari, *supra* n. 975, at 177; Huber, *supra* n. 975, at 235.
1009. Huber, Mullis, *supra* n. 961, at 12; Ferrari, *supra* n. 975, at 177.
1010. Schmidt-Kessel, *supra* n. 964, at n. 14.
1011. *SARL Bri. "Bonaventure" v. SPAE*, Cour d'appel de Grenoble, RG/3275, February 22, 1995, http://www.cisg.law.pace.edu/cisg/wais/db/cases2/950222f1.html (accessed December 7,

Schmidt-Kessel argues that the conditions set forth in Article 8(1) of the CISG will only come into play if the declared intent of the party making the statement is different from the objective meaning that a reasonable person of the same kind as the other party would have understood in the same circumstances according to Article 8(2) of the CISG. According to him, if the declared intent can be clearly understood by a reasonable person in the same circumstances with the addressee, this intent cannot be interpreted according to the *in claris non fit interpretatio* rule.[1012] A Spanish court has also held that if the terms of a contract are clear, the parties could not allege that their undeclared intent should prevail.[1013] This decision has been quoted in the UNCITRAL Digest without any comment as if there was no problem regarding this decision.[1014]

The opinion of the present author is that it is not appropriate to include this most controversial rule into the application of the CISG through an erroneous interpretation. The interpretation of the Spanish court, to which UNCITRAL did not object, is erroneous for two reasons. First, according to the methodology adopted by the court, a statement must first be interpreted objectively in order to determine whether it is clear or not. It can only be interpreted according to the subjective method if it is found to be unclear as a result of the objective test. This methodology clearly contradicts the hierarchy between the subjective and objective methods set forth in paragraph 8(1) and 8(2), respectively. Second, the *in claris non fit interpretatio* rule adopted by the court is incompatible with the principle of *falsa demonstratio non nocet* expressed in Article 8(1) of the CISG.

Nevertheless, Article 8(1) is rarely applied in practice because of the difficulty in establishing that the addressee knew or could not have been unaware of a particular meaning of a statement or conduct.[1015] As a result, Article 8(2) of the CISG is applied more frequently than Article 8(1) of the CISG.[1016]

[2] Article 8(2) of the CISG—Objective Interpretation

There is a hierarchy between Article 8(1) and 8(2) of the CISG, and the latter paragraph only applies when the intent of a party making the statement (or conduct) cannot be determined according to the former paragraph. In this situation, statements or conduct

---

2018); *M. Caiato Roger v. La Société française de factoring international factor France "S.S.F." (SA)*, Cour d'appel de Grenoble, 93/4126, September 13, 1995, http://cisgw3.law.pace.edu/cases/950913f1.html (accessed December 7, 2018); Honnold, *supra* n. 496, at § 107; Zeller, *supra* n. 950, at 641.

1012. Schmidt-Kessel, *supra* n. 964, at n. 17.

1013. "[A]rticle 8(1) of the CISG, in recognizing subjective criteria for interpretation, invites an inquiry as to the true intent of the parties, but excludes the use of in-depth psychological investigations. Therefore, if the terms of the contract are clear, they are to be given their literal meaning, so parties cannot later claim that their undeclared intentions should prevail." [SPAIN Audiencia Provincial de Navarra, sección 3ª 27 December 2007].

1014. UNCITRAL Digest 2016, *supra* n. 952, at § 6.

1015. Farnsworth, *supra* n. 954, at 98.

1016. Huber, Mullis, *supra* n. 961, at 13; Ferrari, *supra* n. 975, at 181; UNCITRAL Digest 2016, *supra* n. 952, at § 10; Huber, *supra* n. 975, at 235; CLOUT case No. 222 [UNITED STATES Court of Appeals (11th Circuit) 29 June 1998]; CLOUT case No. 932 [SWITZERLAND Obergericht des Kantons Thurgau 12 December 2006].

"are to be interpreted according to the understanding that a reasonable person of the same kind as the other party would have had in the same circumstances" pursuant to Article 8(2) of the CISG.

The objective method of interpretation described in this paragraph is referred to as "reasonable interpretation" both in the literature[1017] and in case law,[1018] as it is based on the understanding of a reasonable person.

Although the 1978 draft of the CISG only dealt with the understanding of a "reasonable person," this expression has been changed to a "reasonable person of the same kind as the other party" in the Vienna Convention of 1980. The aim of this change was to clarify that the understanding of the addressee has to be taken into consideration and not that of the party making the statement.[1019] The UNCITRAL Secretariat Commentary states that in a determination of the intent of a party or the understanding of a reasonable person, the words actually used must be examined first but that the examination should not be limited to the words even if they appear to be "clear."[1020] In this way, the Secretariat adopted the *falsa demonstratio non nocet* rule, and rejected the *in claris non fit interpretatio* rule, albeit without using the terms.

Honnold points out that this provision puts the party who writes a contract under an obligation to write it so clearly as to be understood by a reasonable person of the same kind as the other party, and therefore, the basis of this provision is the *contra proferentem* rule.[1021] A decision of a German court has also expressed the same opinion.[1022] It is true that the *contra proferentem* rule has a special sphere of application in international sales transactions. Parties with different languages and different legal backgrounds are involved, and the same terms may have different meanings in different languages or different legal cultures.[1023] For this reason, statements must be interpreted according to the understanding of a reasonable third person of the same kind as the addressee and not the understanding of either the party making the statement or the addressee.

Contrary to Honnold, Farnsworth states that this provision functions both ways. In situations where Article 8(1) of the CISG does not apply, statements or conduct must be interpreted according to the understanding of a reasonable person of the same kind and in the same circumstances as the other party. Either party may rely on this objective meaning of statements or conduct, and whoever alleges that meaning has the burden to prove it.[1024] If the party making the declaration relies on the objective

1017. Lookofsky, *supra* n. 953, at 43-44.
1018. UNCITRAL Digest 2016, *supra* n. 952, at § 11, [UNITED STATES District Court, Colorado 6 July 2010]; CLOUT case No. 273 [GERMANY Oberlandesgericht München 9 July 1997]; [NETHERLANDS Rechtbank Arnhem 11 February 2009].
1019. UNCITRAL Secretariat, *supra* n. 975, at n. 5; Farnsworth, *supra* n. 954, at 96, the author refers to *Official Records*, II, 423.
1020. UNCITRAL Secretariat, *supra* n. 975, at n. 5.
1021. Honnold, *supra* n. 496, at § 107.1.
1022. UNCITRAL Digest 2016, *supra* n. 952, at § 20, [GERMANY Oberlandesgericht Stuttgart 31 March 2008].
1023. Honnold illustrates this point with the terms "warranty," "condition," "disclaimer," and "trust." Honnold, *supra* n. 496, at § 107.1.
1024. Farnsworth, *supra* n. 954, at 98.

meaning of his own declaration, he has to prove that a reasonable person of the same kind and in the same circumstances as the addressee would have understood his intent in the way alleged. Likewise, if the addressee relies on the objective meaning of a statement or conduct, he has to prove that a reasonable person of the same kind as and in the same circumstances with him would have understood the objective meaning in the same way he did.[1025]

The understanding of a "reasonable person" that is to be taken as a basis for interpretation according to Article 8(2) of the CISG is not an abstract person but a reasonable person of the same kind as the other party with respect to linguistic background and technical skills.[1026] This paragraph requires the judge to put himself in the position of the addressee in the same circumstances. Therefore, this provision sets forth an objective criterion, and what the addressee actually understood from the statement or conduct is not relevant.[1027]

According to Zuppi, the criterion of "the understanding of a reasonable person" in this paragraph also includes the degree of duty of care and due diligence owed by a reasonable person in the same circumstances.[1028]

In practice, Article 8(2) of the CISG applies for various purposes, such as the interpretation of statements relating to the qualities of the goods sold,[1029] the determination of whether a party had implicitly waived its right to argue that a notice of lack of conformity in the goods was not timely,[1030] and the determination of how the parties allocated risk.[1031]

[3] Article 8(3) of the CISG—Relevant Circumstances of the Case

Article 8(3) of the CISG states that all relevant circumstances of a case are to be taken into consideration in both the subjective and objective interpretation of statements or conduct, without limit to a literal interpretation of the words. This paragraph also provides a non-exhaustive list of the relevant circumstances to be considered.[1032] Honnold points out that this paragraph covers the interpretation of contracts in a more expressive manner than the first two paragraphs because the relevant circumstances listed here relate more to contracts than unilateral statements or conduct.[1033]

1025. *Ibid.*, at 99-100.
1026. *Ibid.*, at 98.
1027. Huber, Mullis, *supra* n. 961, at 13; Ferrari, *supra* n. 975, at 179-180, Neumayer, Ming, *supra* n. 992, at 112.
1028. Zuppi, *supra* n. 954, at § 21.
1029. UNCITRAL Digest 2016, *supra* n. 952, at § 14, CLOUT case No. 877 [SWITZERLAND Bundesgericht 22 December 2000].
1030. UNCITRAL Digest 2016, *supra* n. 952, at § 16, CLOUT case No. 270 [GERMANY Bundesgerichtshof 25 November 1998].
1031. UNCITRAL Digest 2016, *supra* n. 952, at § 17, CLOUT case No. 317 [GERMANY Oberlandesgericht Karlsruhe 20 November 1992].
1032. UNCITRAL Digest 2016, *supra* n. 952, at § 21; UNCITRAL Secretariat, *supra* n. 975, at n. 6; Zuppi, *supra* n. 954, at § 25.
1033. Honnold, *supra* n. 496, at § 109.

This paragraph requires the objective circumstances that affected a contract to be taken into consideration for a determination of the intent of a party or the understanding of a reasonable person. Therefore, this paragraph implicitly acknowledges the possibility that the same statement of offer may have different meanings for different addressees in different countries and different circumstances, leading to different legal consequences.[1034]

This paragraph objectivizes the interpretation under Article 8 of the CISG as a whole, considering that the circumstances listed in this paragraph are to be taken into consideration not only in the objective interpretation pursuant to Article 8(2) of the CISG but also in the subjective interpretation according to Article 8(1) of the CISG.[1035] For this reason, this paragraph is welcomed by authors from common law jurisdictions, which generally adopt an objective approach to the interpretation of contracts.[1036]

Usages, which are one of the circumstances listed in this paragraph, are to be understood in the broad sense, so as to cover not only local but also international trade usages and usages of particular trades and industries, as is the case with Article 9(2) of the CISG.[1037] Article 9(2) of the CISG deals with usages as a gap-filling instrument, differing from Article 8(3) of the CISG, where usages are only one of the circumstances to be taken into consideration in the interpretation of statements or conduct.[1038]

Another element mentioned in Article 8(3) of the CISG is the "subsequent conduct of the parties." According to an Austrian court decision, this expression includes "acceptance of the goods, payment of the purchase price, sending of an invoice or its signing by the buyer."[1039] Ferrari, however, points out that this expression must be interpreted narrowly, in the sense that subsequent conduct of the parties can only be used with the aim of a determination of the intent of the parties at the time when statement was made or contract was concluded.[1040] The reason underlying this narrow interpretation is the concern that the use of subsequent conduct for the purposes of the interpretation of contracts might lead to alteration of the terms of contracts through unilateral subsequent conduct.[1041]

Nonetheless, Ferrari states that in the event of a divergence between subsequent conduct of a party and his statements at the time of the conclusion of the contract, his conduct should prevail according to the *protestatio facto contraria non valet* principle,

1034. Neumayer, Ming, *supra* n. 992, at 113-114.
1035. Schmidt-Kessel, *supra* n. 964, at n. 12.
1036. Zeller, *supra* n. 950, at 637; Honnold, *supra* n. 496, at § 111.
1037. Article 9(2) of the CISG reads as follows: "The parties are considered, unless otherwise agreed, to have impliedly made applicable to their contract or its formation a usage of which the parties knew or ought to have known and which in international trade is widely known to, and regularly observed by, parties to contracts of the type involved in the particular trade concerned." *Supra* n. 949.
1038. Schlechtriem, *supra* n. 951, at 39.
1039. UNCITRAL Digest 2016, *supra* n. 952, at § 24, [AUSTRIA Oberlandesgericht Linz 23 March 2005].
1040. Ferrari, *supra* n. 975, at 187, the author refers to CLOUT case No. 215 [SWITZERLAND Bezirksgericht St. Gallen 3 July 1997], CLOUT case No. 5 [GERMANY Landgericht Hamburg 26 September 1990].
1041. Huber, Mullis, *supra* n. 961, at 14; Huber, *supra* n. 975, at 235.

which has also been adopted in German law.[1042] If subsequent conduct of both parties conflicts with their original common intent, the parties may be regarded to have modified their contract according to Article 29 of the CISG.[1043]

The present author, however, is of the opinion that the principle of good faith and fair dealing constitutes a limit to the principle of *protestatio facto contraria non valet*, and for this reason, subsequent conduct of a party making a statement can only be interpreted in favor of the other party. Interpretation of subsequent conduct of a party in his favor would lead to unilateral alteration of the terms of a contract, which is incompatible with the *pacta sunt servanda* principle.

Both literature and case law agree that Article 8 also applies to the interpretation of standard contract terms and general conditions since the list in Article 8(3) of the CISG is not exhaustive.[1044] Therefore, courts in CISG countries cannot interpret them according to their domestic laws. Moreover, Schmidt-Kessel rightly points out that Article 8 of the CISG also applies to a determination of the validity of standard contract terms and general conditions, as an exception to Article 4(a) of the CISG.[1045]

Likewise, the question of whether the parties are bound by standard contract terms, statements, or notices written in a language other than the contract language is also to be answered according to Article 8 of the CISG.[1046]

[E] Rules of Interpretation Not Covered by the CISG

Article 8 of the CISG is a very limited text, composed of only three paragraphs. Thus, one cannot expect it to cover all of the rules of interpretation of contracts and statements.[1047] The courts cannot apply their domestic laws either, as this article of the CISG expressly settles the matter of interpretation. For this reason, there is controversy

---

1042. *See*, section §3.03[A][3][b] § 133 of the BGB, *supra*.
1043. Ferrari, *supra* n. 975, at 188.
1044. Schmidt-Kessel, *supra* n. 964, at n. 59; Ferrari, *supra* n. 975, at 189; UNCITRAL Digest 2016, *supra* n. 952, at § 31; [GERMANY Bundesgerichtshof 31 December 2001] (Internationales Handelsrecht 14 ff. 2002); [UNITED STATES District Court, Maryland 8 February 2011]; [GERMANY Oberlandesgericht Celle 24 July 2009]; [NETHERLANDS Rechtbank Utrecht 21 January 2009]; [GERMANY Oberlandesgericht München 14 January 2009]; [GERMANY Landgericht Landshut 12 June 2008]; [ITALY Tribunale di Rovereto 21 November 2007]; CLOUT case No. 827 [NETHERLANDS Hof 's-Hertogenbosch 29 May 2007]; CLOUT case No. 828 [NETHERLANDS Hof 's-Hertogenbosch 2 January 2007]; [GERMANY Landgericht Coburg 12 December 2006]; [ITALY Tribunale di Rovereto 24 August 2006]; CLOUT case No. 750 [AUSTRIA Oberster Gerichtshof 31 August 2005]; [AUSTRIA Oberlandesgericht Linz 8 August 2005]; [AUSTRIA Oberlandesgericht Linz 23 March 2005]; CLOUT case No. 831 [NETHERLANDS Hoge Raad 28 January 2005]; CLOUT case No. 821 [GERMANY Oberlandesgericht Karlsruhe 20 July 2004]; [GERMANY Oberlandesgericht Düsseldorf 21 April 2004]; CLOUT case No. 592 [GERMANY Oberlandesgericht Düsseldorf 30 January 2004]; CLOUT case No. 819 [GERMANY Landgericht Trier 8 January 2004]; CLOUT case No. 534 [AUSTRIA Oberster Gerichtshof 17 December 2003]; [GERMANY Oberlandesgericht Düsseldorf 25 July 2003]; CLOUT case 445 [GERMANY Bundesgerichtshof 31 October 2001].
1045. Schmidt-Kessel, *supra* n. 964, at n. 59.
1046. UNCITRAL Digest 2016, *supra* n. 952, at §§ 33-35; CLOUT case No. 132 [GERMANY Oberlandesgericht Hamm 8 February 1995]. [ITALY Tribunale di Rovereto 21 November 2007]; CLOUT case No. 409 [GERMANY Landgericht Kassel 15 February 1996].
1047. Lookofsky, *supra* n. 953, at 43.

surrounding whether the rules of interpretation not covered by this article can be used in cases where the CISG applies.

Schmidt-Kessel purports that two basic principles of interpretation of contracts must apply in the context of the application of this article. The first is to give priority to the text of a contract over all other elements of interpretation set out in Article 8(3) of the CISG.[1048] This principle has generally been adopted in comparative law.[1049] The second is the principle of systematic interpretation, according to which a contract must be interpreted as a whole.[1050] This principle has also found its expression in legislation or case law in most legal systems.[1051]

Nevertheless, according to Schmidt-Kessel, good faith and fair dealing was not adopted as a principle of interpretation by the CISG. The authors of Article 8 have deliberately avoided any reference to this principle. Instead, they have expressly defined the objective criteria that they have adopted. For this reason, Article 8 of the CISG cannot be used for the purpose of avoiding unfair contract terms.[1052]

UNCITRAL and the case law, however, have approached this issue in a different way. A German court decision has derived a general duty from Article 8 of the CISG to take into account the interests of the opposing party while performing one's own obligation.[1053] This duty is indeed a special aspect of the principle of good faith and fair dealing adopted as a rule of interpretation under § 157 of the BGB. UNCITRAL has referred to this decision in its *Digest* without criticizing or making any comment on it.[1054]

Moreover, explicit references to the principle of good faith and fair dealing made by Swiss and German courts in the context of Article 8(3) of the CISG have also been referred to in the UNCITRAL Digest, by stating that the principle of good faith must also be taken into account in interpreting statements or other conduct of parties.[1055] In this way, the principle of good faith and fair dealing, which is not recognized in common law jurisdictions, has been inserted into their law as a rule of interpretation, along with its general expression in Article 7(1) of the CISG.

1048. Schmidt-Kessel, *supra* n. 964, at n. 20.
1049. *See*, sections §3.02[B][6][a] Article 1362 of the CC. It. (Italian Law); §3.03[A][2] Types or Methods of Interpretation in German Law (German Law); §3.03[B][4][a] Subjective Interpretation (Swiss Law); §3.03[C][2][c] Principles of Literal Interpretation (Turkish Law); §3.04[A][3] The Parol Evidence Rule and Merger Clauses (English Law), *supra*.
1050. Schmidt-Kessel, *supra* n. 964, at n. 29.
1051. *See*, sections §3.02[A][4][b] Article 1189 (Former Article 1161) of the CC. Fr. (French Law); §3.02[B][6][b] Article 1363 of the CC. It. (Italian Law); §3.03[A][2] Types or Methods of Interpretation in German Law (German Law); §3.03[B][4][a] Subjective Interpretation (Swiss Law); §3.03[C][2][f] Principles of Interpretation Developed Through Case Law or Recognized in the Literature (Turkish Law); §3.04[A][5] Lord Hoffman's Five Principles of the Interpretation of Contracts (English Law); §3.04[B][4][b] Other Rules of Interpretation Recognized in the Literature (US Law) *supra*.
1052. Schmidt-Kessel, *supra* n. 964, at n. 30.
1053. UNCITRAL Digest 2016, *supra* n. 952, at § 4, [GERMANY Oberlandesgericht Köln 2 July 2007].
1054. UNCITRAL Digest 2016, *supra* n. 952, at § 4.
1055. *Ibid.*, at § 29, CLOUT case No. 251 [SWITZERLAND Handelsgericht des Kantons Zürich 30 November 1998]; CLOUT case No. 166 [GERMANY Schiedsgericht der Handelskammer Hamburg, 21 June 1996]. *See, also* Neumayer, Ming, *supra* n. 992, at 113.

Another rule of interpretation that was not covered by the CISG, but whose application is discussed in the literature, is the *contra proferentem* rule, according to which ambiguous expressions are to be interpreted against the party who wrote them. Zuppi,[1056] and Neumayer/Ming[1057] are of the opinion that this rule can apply within the context of Article 8 of the CISG. As mentioned above, Honnold also argues that this rule constitutes the basis of Article 8(2),[1058] and this view was adopted in a German court decision.[1059] According to the opposing view, however, this rule does not explicitly derive from the text of the CISG.[1060]

This being the situation, there is no unanimity in the literature as to the applicability of this rule in the context of the CISG. Huber/Mullis state that if the intent of the party making the statement cannot be ascertained, the statement has to be interpreted according to its objective meaning to be determined pursuant to Article 8(2) of the CISG. According to these authors, this objective interpretation prevails over the *contra proferentem* rule, which is not referred to in the CISG. Nevertheless, they admit that in most cases it would not be permissible to interpret ambiguous terms in favor of the party making the statement.[1061]

Schmidt-Kessel and Lookofsky, for their part, suggest that the courts can apply the *contra proferentem* rule through Article 7(2) of the CISG,[1062] by stating that this rule is in conformity with the general principles upon which the CISG is based, or by referring to other sources than the CISG, such as *lex mercatoria.*[1063] The present author is of the opinion that the *contra proferentem* rule can apply in the context of Article 8 of the CISG through Article 7(2) of the CISG and by reference to Article 4.6 of the UNIDROIT Principles.[1064]

[F] Parol Evidence Rule, Merger Clauses, and Article 8(3) of the CISG

As set out above, Article 8(3) of the CISG requires all relevant circumstances, including negotiations between the parties, to be taken into consideration in the interpretation of statements or contracts. For this reason, this paragraph prevents the application of the parol evidence rule, which precludes the parties from relying on extrinsic evidence

1056. Zuppi, *supra* n. 954, at § 24.
1057. Neumayer, Ming, *supra* n. 992, at 115.
1058. Honnold, *supra* n. 496, at § 107.1.
1059. UNCITRAL Digest 2016, *supra* n. 952, at § 20, [GERMANY Oberlandesgericht Stuttgart 31 March 2008].
1060. Schmidt-Kessel, *supra* n. 964, at n. 59; Huber, Mullis, *supra* n. 961, at 15; Lookofsky, *supra* n. 953, at 43; Huber, *supra* n. 975, at 236.
1061. Huber, Mullis, *supra* n. 961, at 15; Huber, *supra* n. 975, at 236.
1062. Schmidt-Kessel, *supra* n. 964, at nn. 47-48.
1063. Lookofsky, *supra* n. 953, at 43.
1064. *See*, section §4.03[B][6] Article 4.6 of the UPICC, *infra*. *See also*, Joseph M. Perillo, *Editorial Remarks on the Manner in Which the UNIDROIT Principles May Be used to Interpret or Supplement CISG Article 8*, i http://www.cisg.law.pace.edu/cisg/principles/uni8.html (accessed December 7, 2018).

when they have reduced their agreement to a final writing.[1065] The authors of the CISG have made an explicit choice in this regard and deliberately left the "outdated" parol evidence rule outside the scope of the CISG.[1066] This choice is also in conformity with Article 11 of the CISG, according to which a contract of sale may be proved by any means.[1067]

Even though the literature unanimously confirms that Article 8(3) of the CISG precludes the application of the parol evidence rule in domestic legal systems, a U.S. court applied this rule in a 1993 case where the CISG applied; however, this decision was criticized by UNCITRAL.[1068] In 2004, the CISG Advisory Council issued an opinion, according to which the CISG excludes the parol evidence and plain meaning rules, and stating that the effect of merger clauses is limited.

In this way, UNCITRAL successfully prevented an erroneous practice in U.S. courts. Some U.S. courts expressly confirmed in subsequent decisions that Article 8(3) of the CISG precludes the application of the parol evidence rule.[1069]

The situation of the effect of merger clauses, however, is not as clear as the situation with the parol evidence rule. These clauses state that the writing contains the entire contract and aim to prevent the use of extrinsic evidence for establishing liability. Farnsworth[1070] and Lookofsky[1071] point out that the text of Article 8 of the CISG is not clear as to whether a merger clause can limit or preclude the application of Article 8(3) of the CISG. According to Lookofsky, this may lead to problems regarding, for instance, the description of the goods pursuant to Article 35 of the CISG.[1072]

Farnsworth states that courts must examine the effects of merger clauses on the application of Article 8(3) of the CISG on a case-by-case basis. He adds, however, that courts must evaluate the validity of merger clauses according to applicable domestic law since the issue of validity is excluded from the scope of the CISG pursuant to Article 4(a) of the CISG.[1073] Therefore, a uniform application on this point seems difficult to reach.

For his part, Zuppi maintains that Article 8(3) of the CISG does not only preclude the application of the parol evidence rule, but it also allows courts to look beyond the four corners of a contract, even if it includes a merger clause.[1074] The CISG Advisory

1065. Hyland, *supra* n. 730, at n. 1.3; Honnold, *supra* n. 496, at § 110; Huber, Mullis, *supra* n. 961, at 13; Ferrari, *supra* n. 975, at 186; Lookofsky, *supra* n. 960, at § 86; Lookofsky, *supra* n. 953, at 42-43; Schmidt-Kessel, *supra* n. 964, at nn. 32 et seq.; Huber, *supra* n. 975, at 235.
1066. Honnold, *supra* n. 496, at § 110.
1067. Schmidt-Kessel, *supra* n. 964, at n. 32; Huber, *supra* n. 975, at 235.
1068. UNCITRAL Digest 2016, *supra* n. 952, at § 25, CLOUT case No. 24 [UNITED STATES Court of Appeals (5th Circuit) 15 June 1993].
1069. UNCITRAL Digest 2016, *supra* n. 952, at § 25, [UNITED STATES District Court, Eastern District of Pennsylvania 29 January 2010]; CLOUT case No. 222 [UNITED STATES Court of Appeals (11th Circuit) 29 June 1998]; CLOUT case No. 578 [UNITED STATES District Court, Western District of Michigan 17 December 2001]; CLOUT case No. 434 [UNITED STATES District Court, Northern District of Illinois 28 August 2001]; CLOUT case No. 419 [UNITED STATES District Court, Northern District of Illinois 27 October 1998].
1070. Farnsworth, *supra* n. 954, at 101.
1071. Lookofsky, *supra* n. 960, at § 86.
1072. *Ibid.*
1073. Farnsworth, *supra* n. 954, at 101.
1074. Zuppi, *supra* n. 954, at § 26, 8(3).

Council also expressed its opinion in 2004, stating that "[t]he effect [of a merger clause] may be to prevent a party from relying on evidence of statements or agreements not contained in the writing. Moreover, if the parties so intend, a Merger Clause may bar evidence of trade usages. However, in determining the effect of such a Merger Clause, the parties' statements and negotiations, as well as all other relevant circumstances shall be taken into account."[1075] Therefore, the CISG Advisory Council also acknowledges in a roundabout way that a merger clause is not an "insuperable hurdle" to the application of Article 8(3) of the CISG.

In accordance with the opinion of the CISG Advisory Council, a U.S. court held in 2006 that a merger clause could not preclude the application of Article 8(3) of the CISG, that the merger clause must reflect the intent of the parties, and that if it does not, it would have no effect.[1076]

§4.03 CHAPTER 4 OF THE UPICC

[A] Generally

In 1971, UNIDROIT began work on "The Progressive Codification of International Trade Law," which is the predecessor of the UPICC. Following the Working Group on the formation of contracts, the Working Group for the provisions on the interpretation of contracts was the second one to be established, and this subject has been the most studied one.[1077] This is because the interpretation of contracts is of significant importance in international commercial contracts. According to Bonell, there are three reasons for this: first, the parties to an international commercial transaction are usually from different countries and have to communicate with each other by using terms and expressions which are not always familiar to them; second, each trade sector has its own usages and practices, which have to be taken into consideration in the determination of the meaning of the words used by the parties; and third, because of the spread of the use of general conditions or standard forms of contract in international commercial transactions, there is a special need for the interpretation of these conditions. For these reasons, UNIDROIT focused on these three aspects of the interpretation of contracts.[1078]

In 1994, the results of the work on The Progressive Codification of International Trade Law were published as the UPICC. The draft texts were more comprehensive than the final text of the fourth chapter of the UPICC on the interpretation of contracts, which is composed only of eight articles, whereas the 1977 draft included eleven

1075. CISG Advisory Council Opinion No. 3, n. 4, https://www.cisg.law.pace.edu/cisg/CISG-AC-op3.html (accessed December 7, 2018).

1076. UNCITRAL Digest 2016, *supra* n. 952, at § 26, [UNITED STATES District Court, Southern District of New York 23 August 2006].

1077. For the list of the preparatory work and documents of the 2016 edition of the UPICC, *see* https://unidroit.org/unidroit-principles-2016/preparatory-work (accessed December 7, 2018).

1078. Michael Joachim Bonell, *The UNIDROIT Initiative For the Progressive Codification of International Trade Law*, 27 International and Comparative Law Quarterly 413, 427 (1978).

articles.[1079] One of the reasons for this difference is that the provisions relating to general conditions and standard forms of contracts, which today are placed in another chapter, were placed in this chapter in previous drafts. Articles 8-10 of the draft correspond to Article 2.1.19-2.1.22 of the UPICC relating to standard terms.[1080] Because of the exclusion of these provisions from the scope of the fourth chapter, the Official Comments to the fourth chapter refer to Article 2.1.19 for the interpretation of standard terms.[1081]

Another important difference between the 1977 draft text and the text of the UPICC as published in 1994 is that although a special aspect of the principle of good faith and fair dealing as a rule of interpretation was ranked in the first place in the 1977 draft,[1082] it was excluded from the 1983 draft[1083] and did not appear in the final version. The reason for this radical change is the influence of the CISG, which was adopted in 1980 and which did not include the principle of good faith and fair dealing as a rule of interpretation.

Nevertheless, some authors argue that the provisions of the UPICC on the interpretation of contracts are based on the principle of good faith and fair dealing.[1084] Bonell even argues that the principle of good faith and fair dealing may be regarded as the underlying purpose of all the rules of interpretation set forth in Chapter 4.[1085] The absence of a provision on the principle of interpretation in accordance with good faith and fair dealing in Chapter 4 does not pose any problem in practice, and arbitral tribunals make explicit reference to this principle when interpreting contracts according to Chapter 4 of the UPICC.[1086]

Other differences between the draft texts and the final text of Chapter 4 of the UPICC relate, to a large extent, to the outline of the provisions and not to their content.[1087] One of these differences is to be found in Article 4.8 of the UPICC entitled

1079. UNIDROIT 1977, Study L—Doc. 12.

1080. *Ibid.*, at 13 et seq.; Bonell, *supra* n. 1078, Art. 8, at 434 *at seq.*, Art. 9, at 436, Art., at 437.

1081. Article 4.1 of the UPICC, Official Comment n. 4, 138 https://unidroit.org/instruments/commercial-contracts/unidroit-principles-2016 (accessed December 7, 2018). However, Vogenauer holds that the provisions of the Chapter 4 apply also to the interpretation of standard terms, Vogenauer, *supra* n. 69, nn. 3-4.

1082. This provision reads as follows: "*The interpretation of contracts shall be in accordance with good faith and the principles of fair dealing*", UNIDROIT 1977, Study L—Doc. 12, at 3; Bonell, *supra* n. 1078, at 428.

1083. UNIDROIT 1983, Study L—Doc. 25, at 12.

1084. Michael Joachim Bonell, *An International Restatement of Contract Law—The UNIDROIT Principles of International Commercial Contracts*, 84 (Transnational Juris Publications Inc., 1994); Gabriël A. Moens, Lisa Cohn, Darren Peacock, *Australia*, in Michael Joachim Bonell (ed.), *A New Approach to International Commercial Contracts—The UNIDROIT Principles of International Commercial Contracts*, 37 (Kluwer Law International, 1999).

1085. Bonell, *supra* n. 1084, at 84; Le Net, *Rules of Interpretation of Contracts under the UNIDROIT Principles and Their Possible Adoption in Vietnamese Law*, 7 *Uniform Law Review* 1017, 1029 (2002).

1086. ICC Award No. 8908 http://www.unilex.info/case.cfm?id=663 (accessed December 7, 20 18); ICC Award No. 11295 http://www.unilex.info/case.cfm?id=1070 (accessed December 7,
2018).

1087. Articles 2, 3, 4, 5, 6, and 11 of the 1977 draft correspond to Arts 4.5, 4.4, 4.3(d), 4.1, 4.3, and 4.6 of the UPICC. Articles 1 and 7 of the 1977 draft were excluded from the final version.

"[s]upplying an omitted term," which did not appear in previous drafts. This article is included in Chapter 4, even though it is not related to the interpretation of contracts in the strict sense. The authors of the UPICC intended to clarify the distinction between the explanatory interpretation and complementary interpretation by regulating them in different articles. However, the UPICC also includes provisions on implied terms under a different chapter, and the difference between the scope of these provisions and Article 4.8 remains unclear, as will be explained below.[1088]

Even though previous drafts of the UPICC were based on comparative studies of the provisions and doctrines on the interpretation of contracts in individual legal systems, the drafts that date after 1983 and therefore the final text were influenced to a great extent by Article 8 of the CISG.[1089] Considering that the origin of Article 8 of the CISG is the ULVC,[1090] one may say that the final text of the UPICC is still based on a work by the UNIDROIT Institute. Nevertheless, the most significant difference between Article 8 of the CISG and Chapter 4 of the UPICC is that the UPICC explicitly regulates the interpretation of contracts, whereas the CISG only deals with the interpretation of statements and conduct.[1091] For this reason, as Perillo observes, the UPICC fills an important gap in the CISG.[1092]

The final text of Chapter 4 of the UPICC includes eight articles, of which seven are related to the interpretation of contracts in the strict sense. For this reason, it can be stated that the authors of this text adopted the approach of the Latin legal systems, which include detailed provisions on the interpretation of contracts and not that of the Romano-Germanic legal systems, which limit them to a few. Basedow criticizes the UPICC for providing such detailed provisions on this subject. According to him, although the provisions of Chapter 4 can be approved by everyone, their use in the interpretation of particular contracts has to be discussed, and they should only apply on a case-by-case basis.[1093]

As regards their content, the rules in Chapter 4 of the UPICC do not reflect the approach of any particular jurisdiction, and they successfully establish a balance between the subjective and objective theories.[1094] Article 4.1 of the UPICC provides that the common intent of the parties prevails if it can be established. If it cannot be established, the contract will be interpreted objectively, according to the criterion of

---

Articles 8, 9, and 10 of the 1977 draft correspond Arts 2.1.19-2.1.22 of the UPICC. UNIDROIT 1977, Study L—Doc. 12; Bonell, *supra* n. 1078, at 429 et seq.

1088. Article 5.1.1 and 5.1.2 of the UPICC cover implied terms, UPICC, *supra* n. 1081, at 151-152. For the discussion on this overlap, *see*, section §4.03[B][8] Article 4.8 of the UPICC, *infra*.
1089. Vogenauer, *supra* n. 69, n. 6; Eckart J. Brödermann, *UNIDROIT Principles of International Commercial Contracts—An Article-by-Article Commentary*, 110 (Nomos, 2018).
1090. *See*, section §4.02[A] Generally, *supra*.
1091. Vogenauer, *supra* n. 69, n. 6; Michael Joachim Bonell, *The UNIDROIT Principles and CISG—Sources of Inspiration for English Courts?*, 11 *Uniform Law Review* 305, 313 (2006).
1092. Perillo, *supra* n. 1064, at i.
1093. Jürgen Basedow, *Germany*, in Michael Joachim Bonell (ed.), *A New Approach to International Commercial Contracts—The UNIDROIT Principles of International Commercial Contracts*, 133 (Kluwer Law International, 1999).
1094. Bonell, *supra* n. 1091, at 313; Franz Werro, Eva Maria Besler, Switzerland, in Michael Joachim Bonell (ed.), *A New Approach to International Commercial Contracts—The UNIDROIT Principles of International Commercial Contracts*, 346 (Kluwer Law International, 1999).

reasonableness.[1095] According to Article 4.3 of the UPICC, the preliminary negotiations between the parties and the conduct of the parties subsequent to the conclusion of the contract are among the circumstances that have to be taken into consideration for a determination of either the common intent of the parties or the understanding of a reasonable third person.[1096]

According to Vogenauer, some of the articles of Chapter 4 of the UPICC successfully reflect "universal hermeneutic truths."[1097] Despite the extensive and detailed appearance of the provisions of Chapter 4, it is true that they are indeed the expression of the minimum common ground on which a consensus could be built. In particular, the UPICC did not include the *in claris non fit interpretatio* rule,[1098] which is most debated in various jurisdictions and to which different meanings are attached, especially in Italian law.[1099]

A controversial issue in comparative law that remained unresolved in the UPICC is whether the interpretation of contracts is a question of fact or law. The Working Group only addressed this issue in their 1987 report, where they concluded that the interpretation is a "legal problem and not only one of grammar or logic."[1100] Although Vogenauer derives from this expression the conclusion that the interpretation of contracts is a question of law,[1101] it might be more appropriate to state that the authors of the UPICC deliberately refrained from providing a clear answer to this issue. This observation is also confirmed by the fact that the Official Comments to the UPICC do not address this issue.

There can be two reasons for which the UPICC does not address this issue in any manner. The first reason is that the question whether the interpretation of contracts is a question of fact or law has different legal consequences in different legal systems. In most continental legal systems, this distinction determines whether or not decisions on the interpretation of contracts are reviewable on appeal,[1102] whereas, in common law jurisdictions that have jury systems, such as the U.S.,[1103] it also determines whether the interpretation of contracts will be considered by juries (and judges functioning as fact finders) or by judges (ruling only on matters of law). The authors of the UPICC may have preferred not to address a question that would lead to such different procedural consequences in different jurisdictions. The second reason is that as a soft-law text, the UPICC is intended for use in international arbitration more than in domestic courts.

1095. Werro, Besler, *supra* n. 1094, at 346.
1096. Bonell, *supra* n. 1091, at 313.
1097. Vogenauer, *supra* n. 69, n. 8.
1098. Alpa, *supra* n. 250, at 342.
1099. *See*, section §3.02[B][2] The Discussion on the *In Claris Non Fit Interpretatio* Rule, *supra*.
1100. UNIDROIT 1987 Study L—Doc. 14, at 4.
1101. Vogenauer, *supra* n. 69, nn. 8-9.
1102. *See*, sections §3.02[A][3] Review of Decisions Relating to the Interpretation of Contracts (French Law); §3.02[B][3] Review of Decisions Relating to the Interpretation of Contracts (Italian Law); §3.03[A][1] Generally (German Law); §3.03[B][3] The Significance of the Distinction Between Subjective and Objective Interpretation for Reviewability of Decisions (Swiss Law), *supra*.
1103. *See*, section §3.04[B][1] Generally, *supra*.

Because of the absence of juries and appeal proceedings in international arbitration, the authors of the UPICC may have also found it unnecessary to address this question.

[B] Provisions of Chapter 4 of the UPICC

[1] Article 4.1 of the UPICC

Article 4.1 (Intention of the parties)
(1) A contract shall be interpreted according to the common intention of the parties.
(2) If such an intention cannot be established, the contract shall be interpreted according to the meaning that reasonable persons of the same kind as the parties would give to it in the same circumstances.[1104]

The rule of interpretation expressed in this article has become the most basic rule of interpretation of the UNIDROIT Principles, after the exclusion of the rule of interpretation according to good faith and fair dealing from previous drafts.[1105]

This article includes both the subjective method of interpretation based on the intent of the parties and the objective method based on the understanding of reasonable persons. The second paragraph of this article sets forth a hierarchy between these two methods in favor of the former, in conformity with French, Italian, Swiss, and Turkish legal systems, as well as the CISG.[1106]

Baumann argues, on the basis of the priority of the subjective method, that the subjective approach dominates the provisions on the interpretation of contracts of the UPICC.[1107] Vogenauer, and Moens/Cohn/Peacock, however, are of the opinion that Article 4.1 successfully combines and establishes a balance between the objective and subjective approaches.[1108] Both Article 4.3 and the Official Comments to Article 4.1 state that in order to establish the common intention of the parties pursuant to the first paragraph, all the relevant circumstances of the case, some of which are listed in Article 4.3, must be taken into consideration.[1109] This approach also makes the first paragraph subject to objective criteria. Therefore, the observation that the subjective approach dominates in the UPICC does not seem accurate.

The second paragraph sets forth the objective criterion of reasonableness. As Baumann rightly observes, this criterion adopted by the UPICC reflects the objective approach of the common law tradition and not the objective approach of the continental jurisdictions, especially that of the German law.[1110]

1104. UPICC, *supra* n. 1081, at 137.
1105. Vogenauer, *supra* n. 69, Art. 4.1, n. 1.
1106. *Ibid.*, Art. 4.1, n. 2; Calnan, *supra* n. 737, at 14; Werro, Besler, Switzerland, *supra* n. 1094, at 347.
1107. Baumann, *supra* n. 844, at 59.
1108. Vogenauer, *supra* n. 69, Art. 4.1, n. 16; Moens, Cohn, Peacock, *supra* n. 1084, at 37.
1109. Official Comments, 4.1, n. 3; UPICC, *supra* n. 1081, at 138; Vogenauer, *supra* n. 69, Art. 4.1, n. 4; Brödermann, *supra* n. 1089, at 110-111.
1110. Baumann, *supra* n. 844, at 58-59.

According to the black letter text of Article 4.1 of the UNIDROIT Principles, Article 4.1 (1) is the rule and Article 4.1 (2) is an exception thereof.[1111] However, the first Official Comment to this article states that the "practical importance of the principle should not be over-estimated." This is because of two reasons: first, parties to international commercial contracts are unlikely to use technical or commercial terms in different meanings from their usual meanings and second, it is extremely difficult to establish that a particular meaning has been the common intent of the parties at the time of the conclusion of a contract.[1112]

For these reasons, contrary to the wording of the article, in practice, Article 4.1 (2) functions as the rule and Article 4.1 (1) as the exception.[1113] Indeed, the rule–exception relationship had been established in the opposite way in the 1978 draft on the basis of the above considerations.[1114] Subsequently, the current version of the article prevailed because of the importance attached to the principle of party autonomy.[1115] In arbitral practice, Article 4.1 is usually referred to in its entirety for supplementing domestic laws and Article 4.2 and 4.3 are often mentioned together with Article 4.1.[1116]

The Official Comments state that the expression "reasonable persons of the same kind as the parties" in the second paragraph should be understood as "persons with, for example, the same linguistic knowledge, technical skill, or business experience as the parties."[1117] These criteria are applied by arbitral tribunals in practice, as will be shown below.

An arbitral tribunal in Switzerland interpreted an arbitration clause by supplementing Article 18/1 of the OR with Article 4.1 and 4.2 of the UNIDROIT Principles and based its decision on the understanding of "reasonable persons."[1118] In the arbitration clause, the parties referred to the "international trade arbitration organization in Zurich." The respondent alleged an invalidity of the arbitration clause and challenged the jurisdiction of the arbitral tribunal on the basis of the nonexistence of such an organization. However, the arbitral tribunal held the arbitration clause valid by stating

1111. Vogenauer, *supra* n. 69, Art. 4.1, n. 8.
1112. Official Comments, Art. 4.1, n. 1 UPICC, *supra* n. 1081, at 137; Vogenauer, *supra* n. 69, Art. 4.1, nn. 11-12; Alpa, *supra* n. 250, at 342.
1113. Vogenauer, *supra* n. 69, Art. 4.1, nn. 11-12.
1114. "The contract and its individual terms shall be interpreted in such a way as they would be understood by reasonable persons in the situation of the parties. However, the actual common intent of the parties shall prevail when such an intent can be established." UNIDROIT 1978 Study L-Doc 13, at 9.
1115. Vogenauer, *supra* n. 69, Art. 4.1, n. 13.
1116. *See*, for instance, ICC Award No. 10335 http://www.unilex.info/case.cfm?id=699 (accessed December 7, 2018); International Court of Arbitration of the Chamber of Industry and Commerce of the Russian Federation Award No. 83/2008 http://www.unilex.info/case.cfm?id=1477 (accessed December 7, 2018); International Court of Arbitration of the Chamber of Industry and Commerce of the Russian Federation Award No. 11/2002 http://www.unilex.info/case.cfm?id=857 (accessed December 7, 2018); ICC Award No. 9651 http://www.unilex.info/case.cfm?id=692 (accessed December 7, 2018).
1117. Official Comments, 4.1, n. 2 UPICC, *supra* n. 1081, at 138; Vogenauer, *supra* n. 69, Art. 4.1, n. 5.
1118. Zurich Chamber of Commerce Award No. 16, November 25, 1994, http://www.unilex.info/case.cfm?id=642 (accessed December 7, 2018); Vogenauer, *supra* n. 69, Art. 4.1, n. 6; Zeller, *supra* n. 950, at 636.

that the parties could only have meant the "Zurich Chamber of Commerce." The tribunal based its decision on the understanding of an "average/diligent businessman," by referring to Article 4.1 and 4.2 of the UNIDROIT Principles.

In an ICC case between the members of a group of accounting and auditing consultancy companies, an arbitral tribunal applied the provisions of Chapter 4 of the UPICC as the "general principles of law ... commonly accepted by the legal systems of most countries."[1119] In this case, the dispute arose from an ambiguity in the contract between the parties as to whether a party was allowed to access the information and technology developed by the other, without paying for or participating in the development of that technology. The arbitral tribunal ruled that it was not entitled to use that technology without paying for it and based its decision on the criterion of the understanding of "reasonable persons of the same kind as the parties" set forth in Article 4.2 of the UNIDROIT Principles.

Another ICC case discussed the scope of the applicable law clause in a contract.[1120] The arbitral tribunal in this case held that the applicable law clause not only applies to issues relating to the contract after its conclusion but also to issues relating to the formation thereof. In reaching this conclusion, the arbitral tribunal applied Article 4.2 of the UPICC and expressly referred to the criterion of "reasonable persons of the same kind as the parties."

[2] Article 4.2 of the UPICC

Article 4.2 (Interpretation of statements and other conduct)
(1) The statements and other conduct of a party shall be interpreted according to that party's intention if the other party knew or could not have been unaware of that intention.
(2) If the preceding paragraph is not applicable, such statements and other conduct shall be interpreted according to the meaning that a reasonable person of the same kind as the other party would give to it in the same circumstances.[1121]

This article "corresponds almost literally to Article 8(1) and (2) CISG," as stated in the Official Comments.[1122] The principal field of application of this article is the interpretation of the statements made in the process of the formation of the contract. However, it can also be used for the interpretation of unilateral statements, such as notices of defective goods or notices of avoidance.[1123] In an arbitral award, this article has been used for the interpretation of a notice of termination.[1124]

1119. ICC Award No. 9797 http://www.unilex.info/case.cfm?id=668 (accessed December 7, 2018).
1120. ICC Award No. 9651 http://www.unilex.info/case.cfm?id=692 (accessed December 7, 2018).
1121. UPICC, *supra* n. 1081, at 138-139.
1122. Official Comments, 4.2, n. 1, UPICC, *supra* n. 1081, at 139.
1123. *Ibid.*
1124. Camera Arbitrale Nazionale ed Internazionale di Milano Award No. A-1795/51, December 1, 1996 http://www.unilex.info/case.cfm?id=622 (accessed December 7, 2018).

According to this article, a statement or other conduct must first be interpreted according to the intent of the party making the statement (or conduct), and where it is not possible to determine his intent, according to the understanding of a reasonable person of the same kind as the other party. This article sets forth a hierarchy between the subjective and objective methods of interpretation, as is the case with Article 8(1) and 8(2) of the CISG and Article 4.1 of the UPICC.[1125] As mentioned above, the criterion of "reasonableness" originated from the common law tradition.[1126]

Relevant circumstances, some of which are listed in Article 4.3 of the UNIDROIT Principles, must be taken into consideration in the interpretation of statements or conduct pursuant to this article.[1127]

Even though the rule-exception relationship set forth in the two paragraphs of Article 4.1 of the UPICC is also reiterated in this article, Vogenauer correctly points out that this relationship works in the opposite direction in practice, and Article 4.2(2) is the rule, while Article 4.2(1) is the exception.[1128] He also observes that the practical relevance of Article 4.2(1) is even more limited compared to that of Article 4.1(1), because of the difficulty in establishing that "the other party knew or could not have been unaware of" the intent of the party making the declaration.[1129]

[3] Article 4.3 of the UPICC

Article 4.3 (Relevant circumstances)

In applying Articles 4.1 and 4.2, regard shall be had to all the circumstances, including

(a) preliminary negotiations between the parties;
(b) practices which the parties have established between themselves;
(c) the conduct of the parties subsequent to the conclusion of the contract;
(d) the nature and purpose of the contract;
(e) the meaning commonly given to terms and expressions in the trade concerned;
(f) usages.[1130]

This article lists the relevant circumstances to be taken into consideration in the interpretation of contracts, statements, and conduct of the parties according to Article 4.1 and 4.2 of the UPICC on an exemplary basis.[1131] Although Article 8(3) of the CISG appears to have been a source of inspiration for this article, Article 4.3 of the UPICC is more comprehensive. In particular, it differs from its predecessor by including "the

1125. Alpa, *supra* n. 250, at 342-343.
1126. *Ibid.*, at 342.
1127. Official Comments, 4.2, n. 2, UPICC, *supra* n. 1081, at 139; Vogenauer, *supra* n. 69, Art. 4.2, nn. 5 et seq.; Brödermann, *supra* n. 1089, at 112.
1128. Vogenauer, *supra* n. 69, Art. 4.2, n. 8.
1129. *Ibid.*
1130. UPICC, *supra* n. 1081, at 140.
1131. Official Comments, 4.3, n. 1, UPICC, *supra* n. 1081, at 140; Alpa, *supra* n. 250, at 343; Vogenauer, *supra* n. 69, Art. 4.3, nn. 1-2; Brödermann, *supra* n. 1089, at 112-113.

nature and purpose of the contract" in subparagraph (d).[1132] The influence of the Latin legal tradition on the inclusion of this element in the list is evident.[1133]

The inclusion of "the nature and purpose of the contract" in this article is also a consequence of some general policies underlying the UNIDROIT Principles. Vogenauer lists the policy issues that must be taken into account as economic and legal consequences, rationality and fairness, and equity of a particular interpretation.[1134]

Baumann states that the practical significance of "the conduct of the parties subsequent to the conclusion of the contract" is very limited in comparative law, especially as regards the German legal system.[1135] However, this tool of interpretation is recognized not only in Romano-Germanic legal systems[1136] but also in Latin[1137] and common law legal systems.[1138] It also appears in Article 1362 of the CC. It., § 1-303 of the UCC, § 202 (5) of the Restatement (Second) of Contracts, and Article 8(3) of the CISG.

Moreover, in an ad hoc arbitration, the arbitral tribunal used the subsequent conduct of the parties for the interpretation of their contract by referring to Article 4.3 of the UPICC, because of a lack of clarity on this point in the applicable New Zealand law.[1139] Subsequent conduct of the parties is especially relevant for the interpretation of long-term contracts, as also illustrated by the 2016 edition of the Official Comments.[1140]

Article 4.3 of the UPICC and the parol evidence rule recognized in common law jurisdictions appear to be incompatible with each other. This is because the relevant circumstances listed in Article 4.3 as exemplary suggest that any extrinsic evidence can be used for the purpose of the interpretation of a contract.[1141] Moens/Cohn/Peacock criticize that aspect of this article and argue that the parol evidence rule reduces contractual disputes and gives effect to the agreement of the parties.[1142]

However, Furmston counters that most jurisdictions (including common law jurisdictions) recognize the use of all kinds of extrinsic evidence in the interpretation of

1132. Net, *supra* n. 1085, at 1025.
1133. Former Art. 1158 of the CC. Fr., *supra* n. 130; section §3.02[B][6][g] Article 1369 of the CC. It., *supra*. Alpa argues that the inclusion of this element in Art. 4.3 of the UPICC is due to the influence of the principle of interpretation according to good faith and fair dealing, Alpa, *supra* n. 250, at 343.
1134. Bonell, *supra* n. 1084, at 84; Vogenauer, *supra* n. 69, Art. 4.3, nn. 20 et seq.
1135. Baumann, *supra* n. 844, at 59-60.
1136. *See*, sections §3.03[A][3][b] § 133 of the BGB (German Law); §3.03[B][4][b] Objective Interpretation (Swiss Law); §3.03[C][2][f] Principles of Interpretation Developed Through Case Law or Recognized in the Literature (Turkish Law), *supra*.
1137. *See*, sections §3.02[A][4][a] Article 1188 (Former Article 1156) of the CC. Fr. (French Law); §3.02[B][6][a] Article 1362 of the CC. It. (Italian Law), *supra*.
1138. *See*, sections §3.04[A][2] Objective Approach (English Law); §3.04[B][3] Subjectivization of the Interpretation of Contracts: The UCC and the Restatement (Second) of Contracts (US Law), *supra*.
1139. Ad Hoc Award of 1995, Auckland, http://www.unilex.info/case.cfm?id=628 (accessed December 7, 2018).
1140. Official Comments, 4.3, n. 3 UPICC, *supra* n. 1081, at 142; Brödermann, *supra* n. 1089, at 114.
1141. Vogenauer, *supra* n. 69, Art. 4.3, n. 27; Moens, Cohn, Peacock, *supra* n. 1084, at 38.
1142. Moens, Cohn, Peacock, *supra* n. 1084, at 38.

contracts, even though it appears to be contrary to the traditional English approach.[1143] Moens/Cohn/Peacock also agree that the use of "practices which the parties have established between themselves," "the meaning commonly given to terms and expressions in the trade concerned," and "usages" listed as the relevant circumstances in Article 4.3 of the UPICC for the interpretation of contracts are in conformity with the common law tradition.[1144]

Following the example of Article 8(3) of the CISG, Article 4.3 of the UPICC does not list the circumstances to be taken into consideration exhaustively. Accordingly, Vogenauer states that the words used by the parties must also be taken into consideration that they are the most important factor in the interpretation of a contract, and therefore they should prevail over other factors.[1145] His idea was put into practice in an International Centre for Settlement of Investment Disputes (ICSID) arbitration, where the arbitral tribunal evaluated the effect of a merger clause in a contract on the applicability of Article 4.1 of the UPICC. In this case, the arbitral tribunal held that the merger clause, in principle, could not impede the application of Article 4.1 of the UPICC; however, the language of the contract prevailed over other factors for the determination of the common intent of the parties, and therefore a party was not entitled to argue an obligation which was not recorded in the agreement.[1146]

Canaris/Grigoleit argue that a list of the circumstances to be taken into consideration in the interpretation of contracts, such as the one in Article 4.3 of the UPICC, is not functional. According to them, if specific factors are listed, it will never be possible to list them all, whereas, if general factors are listed, that would be a statement of the obvious.[1147] However, Article 4.3 of the UPICC appears to have found a middle path.

[4] Article 4.4 of the UPICC

> Article 4.4 (Reference to contract or statement as a whole)
>
> Terms and expressions shall be interpreted in the light of the whole contract or statement in which they appear.[1148]

This provision is an expression of the principle of systematic interpretation, which is recognized in most legal systems.[1149] This principle also requires the evaluation of the transaction between the parties as a whole. Therefore, other documents and

1143. Michael Furmston, *United Kingdom*, in Michael Joachim Bonell (ed.), *A New Approach to International Commercial Contracts—The UNIDROIT Principles of International Commercial Contracts*, 384-385 (Kluwer Law International, 1999).
1144. Moens, Cohn, Peacock, *supra* n. 1084, at 39.
1145. Vogenauer, *supra* n. 69, Art. 4.3, n. 3; Brödermann, *supra* n. 1089, at 113-114.
1146. ICSID Award in *Joseph Charles Lemire v. Ukraine*, ARB/06/18; IIC 424 (2010), http://www.unilex.info/case.cfm?id=1533 (accessed December 7, 2018).
1147. Canaris, Grigoleit, *supra* n. 5, at 456.
1148. UPICC, *supra* n. 1081, at 144.
1149. *See*, sections §3.02[A][4][b] Article 1189 (Former Article 1161) of the CC. Fr. (French Law); §3.02[B][6][b] Article 1363 of the CC. It. (Italian Law); §3.03[A][2] Types or Methods of Interpretation in German Law (German Law); §3.03[B][4][a] Subjective Interpretation (Swiss Law); §3.03[C][2][f] Principles of Interpretation Developed Through Case Law or Recognized

contracts between the parties must also be taken into consideration in the interpretation of single clauses or expressions.[1150] Accordingly, Vogenauer points out that a contract must be interpreted in a consistent manner and that inconsistencies have to be remedied by way of interpretation.[1151]

Even though Article 4.4 of the UPICC requires the interpretation of a contract as a whole, it does not provide for a hierarchy between the terms or parts of a contract. However, the Official Comments state that the preamble may be relevant for the interpretation of the operative parts,[1152] specific provisions prevail over general rules, and the provisions to which the parties gave priority prevail over other provisions.[1153]

[5] Article 4.5 of the UPICC

> Article 4.5 (All terms to be given effect)
>
> Contract terms shall be interpreted so as to give effect to all the terms rather than to deprive some of them of effect.[1154]

The origin of this article is Ulpianus' text in *Dig.* 45, 1, 80, where he stated the *ut res magis valeat quam pereat* principle.[1155] This article is based on the presumption that the parties would not use words to no purpose.[1156] However, the emphasis made to give effect to "all the terms" appears to be unfortunate in that it neglects the possibility that some contractual provisions cannot be given effect in any way. Accordingly, in an ICC arbitration, an arbitral tribunal used Article 4.5 of the UPICC for supplementing the law chosen by the parties and rightfully interpreted this article as a rule according to which "contract terms should be interpreted as to give effect to as many of them as possible."[1157]

The policy that underlies this article is preservation of contract.[1158] Accordingly, in an ICC award, the arbitral tribunal referred to Article 4.5 of the UPICC together with the *in favorem validitatis* principle.[1159]

---

in the Literature (Turkish Law); §3.04[A][5] Lord Hoffman's Five Principles of the Interpretation of Contracts (English Law); §3.04[B][4][b] Other Rules of Interpretation Recognized in the Literature (US Law) *supra*.

1150. Vogenauer, *supra* n. 69, Art. 4.4, n. 4.
1151. *Ibid.*, n. 5.
1152. This expression of the Official Comments has been referred to in the Arbitration Court of the Lausanne Chamber of Commerce and Industry Award of January 25, 2002, http://www.unilex.info/case.cfm?id=863 (accessed December 7, 2018).
1153. Official Comments, 4.4, n. 2, UPICC, *supra* n. 1081, at 145; Vogenauer, *supra* n. 69, Art. 4.4, n. 5; Brödermann, *supra* n. 1089, at 115.
1154. UPICC, *supra* n. 1081, at 145.
1155. Vogenauer, *supra* n. 69, Article 4.5, n. 1. These words actually belong to Iulianus, *Dig.* 34, 5, 12 (13) (Iul. 50 *Dig.*), *see*, section §2.01[B][2][b], The Emergence of Principles of Objective Interpretation in the Classical Period, *supra*.
1156. Official Comments, Art. 4.5, UPICC, *supra* n. 1081, at 146.
1157. ICC Award No. 8547 http://www.unilex.info/case.cfm?id=688 (accessed December 7, 2018).
1158. Vogenauer, *supra* n. 69, Art. 4.5, n. 2.
1159. ICC Award No. 11869 http://www.unilex.info/case.cfm?id=1659 (accessed December 7, 2018).

The UPICC does not provide for a hierarchy between the articles of Chapter 4. However, the Official Comments state that Article 4.5 only applies when the meaning of the terms remained unclear notwithstanding the application of Article 4.1-4.3 of the UPICC, expressly recognizing the hierarchy between Article 4.5 and the preceding articles.[1160]

[6] Article 4.6 of the UPICC

> Article 4.6 (Contra proferentem rule)
>
> If contract terms supplied by one party are unclear, an interpretation against that party is preferred.[1161]

The rationale of this rule is to place the risk of ambiguity in a contract upon the party who drafted the terms of the contract, or who provided the standard terms.[1162] For this reason, a contract term must have at least two possible meanings for this article to apply.[1163]

Official Comments expressly state that the *contra proferentem* rule applies not only to individually negotiated terms but also to standard terms,[1164] differing from some continental legal systems where this rule is interpreted narrowly.[1165] This is also in conformity with the approach of common law jurisdictions, where this rule applies to every kind of commercial transaction.[1166]

The language adopted in this article according to which "an interpretation ... is preferred," appears to be in contrast with the more rigid language of the preceding articles where contracts "shall be interpreted." According to Vogenauer, this is because of two reasons: first, the authors of the UPICC did not want to limit the application of this article with standard terms and second, they did not aim at penalizing the party supplying the term.[1167] Indeed, it is possible to observe that in practice, Article 4.6 of the UPICC applies to individually negotiated terms more frequently than to standard terms.[1168]

1160. Official Comments, 4.5 UPICC, *supra* n. 1081, at 146; Vogenauer, *supra* n. 69, Art. 4.5, n. 4; Brödermann, *supra* n. 1089, at 116.
1161. UPICC, *supra* n. 1081, at 146.
1162. Official Comments, 4.6, UPICC, *supra* n. 1081, at 146; Vogenauer, *supra* n. 69, Art. 4.6, n. 2; Brödermann, *supra* n. 1089, at 117.
1163. Vogenauer, *supra* n. 69, Article 4.6, n. 4; Brödermann, *supra* n. 1089, at 117.
1164. Official Comments, 4.6, UPICC, *supra* n. 1081, at 146.
1165. *See*, sections §3.02[B][6][h] Article 1370 of the CC. It. (Italian Law); §3.03[A][3][c] § 157 of the BGB (German Law); §3.03[B][5] Principles of Interpretation Developed Through Case Law (Swiss Law); §3.03[C][2][e] Article 23 of the TBK and the *Contra Stipulatorem* Rule (Turkish Law), *supra*.
1166. Moens, Cohn, Peacock, *supra* n. 1084, at 40. *See*, section §3.04[A][4] Other Principles of Interpretation, *supra*.
1167. Vogenauer, *supra* n. 69, Art. 4.6, n. 9.
1168. Ad Hoc Award of December 10, 1997, Buenos Aires http://www.unilex.info/case.cfm?id=646 (accessed December 7, 2018); ICC Award No. 8261 http://www.unilex.info/case.cfm?id=624 (accessed December 7, 2018); ICC Award No. 11869 http://www.unilex.info/case.cfm?id=1659 (accessed December 7, 2018); International Court of Arbitration of the Chamber of Industry and Commerce of the Russian Federation Award No. 108/2011 http://www.unilex.info/case.cfm?id=1730 (accessed December 7, 2018).

Nonetheless, Vogenauer also observes that this article has a "quasi-penal" character and that it is not concerned with the true intent of the parties.[1169] He holds that this article shall apply only when an ambiguity persists after the application of the basic rules of interpretation set forth in Article 4.1-4.5 of the UPICC, even though this condition is not expressly spelled out in Chapter 4.[1170] He adds that this was also the view of the Working Group, as expressed in a Working Paper.[1171]

However, neither black letter rules nor the Official Comments to Article 4.6 of the UPICC refer to a hierarchy between Article 4.6 and other articles of Chapter 4. The fact that the Official Comments to Article 4.5 of the UPICC expressly provide for a hierarchy between this article and the preceding articles suggest that the ultimate decision of the authors of the UPICC has not been to adopt a hierarchy between Article 4.6 and the other rules of interpretation.

[7] Article 4.7 of the UPICC

> Article 4.7 (Linguistic discrepancies)
>
> Where a contract is drawn up in two or more language versions which are equally authoritative there is, in case of discrepancy between the versions, a preference for the interpretation according to a version in which the contract was originally drawn up.[1172]

This article only applies when all language versions of a contract are equally authoritative.[1173] If the parties have given priority to a specific version of their contract, there is no doubt regarding the version that will prevail. The application of this article is not very common in practice because in contracts written in more than one language, parties usually indicate which version should prevail. Nevertheless, this article has already been applied in two cases, where the parties did not indicate which version of their contract was to be given priority.[1174]

The authors of the UPICC also preferred to use softer language ("there is ... a preference for the interpretation") in this article than the one in the other articles, as is the case with Article 4.6. This is because the authors of the UPICC intended to leave some room for exceptions. If the parties have prepared their contract on the basis of an international instrument, such as the INCOTERMS or the UCP, an interpretation on the basis of that instrument may be preferable.[1175]

1169. Vogenauer, *supra* n. 69, Art. 4.6, n. 2.
1170. Vogenauer refers to UNIDROIT 1991, PC—Misc 15, at 38-41.
1171. Vogenauer, *supra* n. 69, Art. 4.6, n. 5.
1172. UPICC, *supra* n. 1081, at 147.
1173. Official Comments, 4.7, UPICC, *supra* n. 1081, at 147; Vogenauer, *supra* n. 69, Art. 4.7, n. 3.
1174. International Court of Arbitration of the Chamber of Industry and Commerce of the Russian Federation Award No. 217/2001 http://www.unilex.info/case.cfm?id=856 (accessed December 7, 2018); *TOV Oba-Trans v. TOV DSF Logistics Ukraine*, Kyiv Commercial Court of Appeal, 910/21449/13, January 13, 2014, http://www.unilex.info/case.cfm?id=1763 (accessed December 7, 2018).
1175. Official Comments, 4.7 UPICC, *supra* n. 1081, at 148; Vogenauer, *supra* n. 69, Art. 4.7, n. 5; Brödermann, *supra* n. 1089, at 118.

This article is generally welcomed as an innovative article aiming at responding to the needs of international practice.[1176] However, Canaris/Grigoleit criticize this article for ignoring the fact that the parties translate their contracts in order to have a better understanding and therefore, according to them, the assumption that the original version better reflects the intent of the parties is speculative.[1177]

[8] Article 4.8 of the UPICC

Article 4.8 (Supplying an omitted term)

(1) Where the parties to a contract have not agreed with respect to a term which is important for a determination of their rights and duties, a term which is appropriate in the circumstances shall be supplied.

(2) In determining what is an appropriate term regard shall be had, among other factors, to
  (a) the intention of the parties;
  (b) the nature and purpose of the contract;
  (c) good faith and fair dealing;
  (d) reasonableness.[1178]

This article does not relate to the interpretation of contracts in the strict sense, but to gap-filling, or complementary interpretation, which is excluded from the scope of this study. The distinction between the explanatory interpretation, under Article 4.1-4.7 of the UPICC, and complementary interpretation is also emphasized in the Official Comments.[1179]

The essential problem with Article 4.8 of the UPICC is that it deals with the same subject matter and overlaps with Article 5.1.2 of the UPICC entitled "implied obligations."[1180] Although Article 5.1.2 was drafted at an early stage in 1986, Article 4.8 was inserted into the text in 1991, when the drafting process of Chapter 4 was almost finished.[1181]

According to the Official Comments, as amended in 2016, Article 4.8 applies "without prejudice to the application of Article 5.1.2, where appropriate," because the former applies on a more individual basis, whereas the latter is a general gap-filling

1176. Vogenauer, *supra* n. 131, at 977.
1177. Canaris, Grigoleit, *supra* n. 5, at 462-463.
1178. UPICC, *supra* n. 1081, at 148.
1179. Official Comments, 4.8, n. 1 UPICC, *supra* n. 1081, at 149; Vogenauer, *supra* n. 69, Art. 4.8, n. 1; Brödermann, *supra* n. 1089, at 118-119.
1180. This article reads as follows:

  (Implied obligations)
  Implied obligations stem from
  (a) the nature and purpose of the contract;
  (b) practices established between the parties and usages;
  (c) good faith and fair dealing;
  (d) reasonableness.

1181. UPICC, *supra* n. 1081, at 151.
  Vogenauer, *supra* n. 69, Art. 4.8, n. 8.

solution. However, the illustrations provided for these articles in the Official Comments do not appear to explain the difference between the two articles.[1182]

Subsection (2)(c) refers to the principle of good faith and fair dealing. Although the early drafts of Chapter 4 had ranked this principle in the first place, it was excluded from the drafts after 1983 and did not appear in the final version of the UPICC.[1183] However, the principle of good faith and fair dealing is a core principle in both explanatory and complementary interpretation of contracts.[1184] An ICC arbitral tribunal also referred to subsection (2)(c) of this article together with the general principle of good faith and fair dealing in Article 1.7 of the UPICC for the interpretation of the scope of a settlement agreement.[1185]

This article also refers to the criterion of "reasonableness," which was inspired by common law systems. This reference crystallizes the distinction between this criterion and the principle of good faith and fair dealing.[1186] The influence of § 204 Restatement (Second) of Contracts examined above is felt not only in the criterion of reasonableness but throughout the text of Article 4.8 of the UPICC, including its title.[1187]

1182. "A distribution franchise agreement provides that the franchisee may not engage in any similar business for a year after the termination of the agreement. Although the agreement is silent on the territorial scope of this prohibition, it is, in view of the particular nature and purpose of the franchise agreement, appropriate that the prohibition be restricted to the territory where the franchisee had exploited the franchise." Illustration II, Official Comments, 4.8, n. 3, UPICC, *supra* n. 1081, at 150.

"A rents a full computer network to B and installs it. The contract says nothing as to A's possible obligation to give B at least some basic information concerning the operation of the system. This may however be considered to be an implied obligation since it is obvious, and necessary for the accomplishment of the purpose of such a contract, that the provider of sophisticated goods should supply the other party with a minimum of information." Illustration I, Official Comments, 5.1.2, UPICC, *supra* n. 1081, at 152.

1183. *See*, section §4.03[A] Generally, *supra*.

1184. Alpa, *supra* n. 250, at 343.

1185. ICC Award No. 8908 http://www.unilex.info/case.cfm?id=663 (accessed December 7, 2018).

1186. Alpa, *supra* n. 250, at 343.

1187. This paragraph reads as follows:

> §204. SUPPLYING AN OMITTED ESSENTIAL TERM
>
> When the parties to a bargain sufficiently defined to be a contract have not agreed with respect to a term which is essential to a determination of their rights and duties, a term which is reasonable in the circumstances is supplied by the court.

ALI, *supra* n. 876, at 96; *see*, section §3.04[B][3] Subjectivization of the Interpretation of Contracts: The UCC and the Restatement (Second) of Contracts, *supra*; Brödermann, *supra* n. 1089, at 118.

§4.04 RELEVANT PROVISIONS OF THE UNIFORM LAW INSTRUMENTS OF THE EU

[A] Principles of European Contract Law (PECL)

[1] Generally

The Principles of European Contract Law (PECL) is a soft-law instrument prepared by the Commission on European Contract Law, headed by Prof. Ole Lando. For this reason, they are also known as the "Lando Principles." The application of these principles is not common because of their nonbinding nature and the opt-in method they adopt.[1188] Nevertheless, these principles aim at harmonizing the law of obligations of EU countries, and they are intended to constitute the seed of a European Civil Code.[1189] The PECL is an important instrument of uniform law for two reasons: first, because it has been adopted by the EU, the leading reference for economic, commercial, and legal integration; and second, because it harmonizes the law of Latin, Romano-Germanic, common law, and Scandinavian legal systems.

The PECL drafting process began in 1982 and has been conducted to a considerable extent by the same experts who authored the UPICC during the same time period. For this reason, both of these instruments are in harmony with each other in many respects.[1190] The first part of the PECL was published in 1995, and the second and third parts followed in 1999 and 2002. The PECL also constituted the main point of reference for subsequent uniform law instruments of the EU.

The provisions regarding the interpretation of contracts are provided in Chapter 7 of the original version and Chapter 5 of the subsequent versions of the PECL.

[2] Chapter 5 of the PECL

[a] Article 5:101 of the PECL

Article 5:101 (Ex Article 7.101/ 101A)—General Rules of Interpretation

(1) A contract is to be interpreted according to the common intention of the parties even if this differs from the literal meaning of the words.

(2) If it is established that one party intended the contract to have a particular meaning, and at the time of the conclusion of the contract the other party could not have been unaware of the first party's intention, the contract is to be interpreted in the way intended by the first party.

1188. Article 1:101 of the PECL "(2) These Principles will apply when the parties have agreed to incorporate them into their contract or that their contract is to be governed by them." PECL, *supra* n. 192, at 95.

1189. The Commission on European Contract Law, *Introduction to the Principles of European Contract Law* https://www.cisg.law.pace.edu/cisg/text/peclcomments.html (accessed December 7, 2018).

1190. Michael Joachim Bonell, *The UNIDROIT Principles of International Commercial Contracts and the Principles of European Contract Law—Similar Rules for the Same Purposes*, 26 *Uniform Law Review* 229, 234 et seq. (1996).

(3) If an intention cannot be established according to (1) or (2), the contract is to be interpreted according to the meaning that reasonable persons of the same kind as the parties would give to it in the same circumstances.[1191]

This article sets forth the most basic rules of contractual interpretation under the PECL. Differing from the UPICC, the PECL only addresses the interpretation of contracts and not the interpretation of statements and other conduct. The first subsection expressly provides the principle of priority of the common intent of the parties to the literal meaning of the words, in conformity with continental jurisdictions but unlike Article 4.1 of the UPICC.[1192]

Another difference between this article and Article 4.1 of the UPICC is that according to subsection (2) of Article 5:101 of the PECL, it is possible to interpret a contract in a way intended by one of the parties. In order to do this, however, it must be established that the other party could not have been unaware of the intent of the first party at the time of the conclusion of the contract.

This subsection suggests that a contract has to be interpreted according to its meaning at the time when it was concluded and in accordance with good faith and fair dealing. A similar provision can also be found in Article 4.2.1 of the UPICC, albeit in the context of the interpretation of statements and other conduct, and not the interpretation of contracts.

The third subsection of this article sets forth a hierarchy between subjective and objective methods of interpretation and lays down the criteria for the latter, in almost the same words as Article 4.1 and 4.2 of the UPICC. According to these criteria, if an ambiguity cannot be overcome through subjective interpretation, the contract has to be interpreted "according to the meaning that reasonable persons of the same kind as the parties would give to it in the same circumstances."

The PECL also provides a definition of reasonableness in Article 1:302, according to which "[u]nder these Principles reasonableness is to be judged by what persons acting in good faith and in the same situation as the parties would consider to be reasonable. In particular, in assessing what is reasonable the nature and purpose of the contract, the circumstances of the case, and the usages and practices of the trades or professions involved should be taken into account."[1193]

The Commentary to Article 5:101 of the PECL rejects the rule of *in claris non fit interpretatio* by stating that "any kind of contract may need interpretation," even when "clauses seem clear enough."[1194] However, the Commentary also states that "the judge must not, under the guise of interpretation, modify the clear and precise meaning of the

1191. PECL, *supra* n. 192, at 287.

1192. Wissink, *supra* n. 192, at 244; S. Ferreri, *Interpretation*, in Luisa Antoniolli, Anna Veneziano (eds.), *Principles of European Contract Law and Italian Law*, Vol. 2, 251 (Kluwer Law International, 2005); Vakhtang Bachiashvili, *Contract Interpretations According to the Principles of European Contract Law and Expediency of Implementation of These Principles in Georgian Legislation*, Ivane Javakhishvili Tbilisi State University Faculty of Law Journal of Law 1, 8 (2013).

1193. PECL, *supra* n. 192, at p. 126.

1194. *Ibid.*, at 287; Wissink, *supra* n. 192, at 249; Ferreri, *supra* n. 1192, at 251.

contract."[1195] Even though this comment is based on a justifiable reason, the use of the expression "clear and precise meaning of the contract" seems inappropriate as it suggests that the meaning of a contract could be clear even before the interpretation, and it is reminiscent of the *in claris non fit interpretatio* rule.

Another difference between the provisions of the UPICC and the PECL is that the PECL does not include a provision corresponding to Article 4.8 of the UPICC entitled "Supplying an omitted term." As regards complementary interpretation, Comments to Article 5:101 of the PECL refer to Article 6:102 of the PECL on implied obligations, which is the only provision in the PECL on this issue.[1196] However, Article 4.8 of the UPICC overlaps with Article 5.1.2 of the UPICC on implied obligations.[1197]

Interestingly, the Working Group for Chapter 4 of the UPICC and the PECL were both chaired by Prof. Ole Lando. This suggests that the overlap in the UPICC was not intentional.

[b] Article 5:102 of the PECL

Article 5:102 (ex Article 7.102)—Relevant Circumstances

In interpreting the contract, regard shall be had, in particular, to:

(a) the circumstances in which it was concluded, including the preliminary negotiations;
(b) the conduct of the parties, even subsequent to the conclusion of the contract;
(c) the nature and purpose of the contract;
(d) the interpretation which has already been given to similar clauses by the parties and the practices they have established between themselves;
(e) the meaning commonly given to terms and expressions in the branch of activity concerned and the interpretation similar clauses may already have received;
(f) usages; and
(g) good faith and fair dealing.[1198]

This article provides a non-exhaustive list of the factors to be taken into consideration in the interpretation of contracts.[1199] Although this article corresponds to Article 4.3 of the UPICC, it includes important differences. Primarily, the first sentence of Article 4.3 of the UPICC states that in the interpretation of a contract "regard shall be had to all the circumstances," whereas the same is provided in subsection (a) of Article 5:102 of the PECL, referring to both the circumstances in which the contract was concluded and the circumstances of the preliminary negotiations.

Another difference is that subsection (b) of this article emphasizes that the conduct of the parties must be taken into consideration "even subsequent to the conclusion of the contract." From a common law perspective, the absence of the word

1195. PECL, *supra* n. 192, at 288.
1196. *Ibid.*, at 287; Wissink, *supra* n. 192, at 241.
1197. *See*, section §4.03[B][8] Article 4.8 of the UPICC, *supra*.
1198. PECL, *supra* n. 192, at 291.
1199. *Ibid.*; Wissink, *supra* n. 192, at 247; Ferreri, *supra* n. 1192, at 257; Bachiashvili, *supra* n. 1192, at 11.

"even" in Article 4.3 of the UPICC may also suggest that only the conduct of the parties subsequent to the conclusion of the contract is to be taken into consideration and not their conduct prior to the conclusion of the contract. The PECL, however, makes it clear that the conduct of the parties prior to the conclusion of the contract is also a tool of interpretation, in conformity with the continental tradition.[1200]

Will the statements of the parties prior to the conclusion of the contract also be taken into consideration? Article 5:102 of the PECL only mentions the conduct of the parties and not their statements. What will be the effect of a merger clause to the use of statements that were made during the negotiations phase in the interpretation of a contract? The answers to these questions are provided under a different chapter of the PECL. According to Article 2:105(3) of the PECL "[t]he parties' prior statements may be used to interpret the contract. This rule may not be excluded or restricted except by an individually negotiated clause."[1201] With this provision, the authors of the PECL codified the idea that the effect of merger clauses should be limited with respect to the interpretation of contracts, developed through the application of Article 8 of the CISG.[1202]

There is a terminological difference between subsection (e) of this article and Article 4.3 of the UPICC: although the UPICC states that the meaning commonly given to terms and expressions "in the trade concerned" is a factor to be considered, the PECL speaks of the meaning given "in the branch of activity concerned." The reason for this difference can be found in the difference between the scopes of application of these texts. Although the UPICC only applies to international commercial contracts, the PECL has a broader scope that covers not only commercial but also non-commercial transactions. This broad expression has also been preserved in subsequent uniform law instruments of the EU, because of the increase in the importance of consumer contracts.

Another sign of the continental tradition in the PECL, and another important difference with Article 4.3 of the UPICC, is subsection (g) of Article 5:102, which lays down the principle of good faith and fair dealing as a principle of interpretation. Even though this principle was ranked in the first place in early drafts of the UPICC, it has been excluded from the text because of the influence of the CISG.[1203] However, the PECL includes this concept, not as a general principle for the interpretation of contracts but as one of the elements to be taken into consideration in the interpretation of contracts.

1200. Wissink, *supra* n. 192, at 247; Ferreri, *supra* n. 1192, at 257.
1201. PECL, *supra* n. 192, at 152.
1202. *See*, section §4.02[F] Parol Evidence Rule, Merger Clauses, and Article 8(3) of the CISG, *supra*; Bachiashvili, *supra* n. 1192, at 11-12.
1203. *See*, section §4.03[A] Generally, *supra*.

[c] *Article 5:103 of the PECL*

Article 5:103 (ex Article 7.103)—Contra Proferentem Rule

Where there is doubt about the meaning of a contract term not individually negotiated, an interpretation of the term against the party who supplied it is to be preferred.[1204]

This article expressly lays down the principle of *contra proferentem*, referring to it by name, as does Article 4.6 of the UPICC. This rule is placed just after the elements or circumstances to be taken into consideration in the interpretation of contracts, differing from the UPICC, where it is placed among the last provisions of Chapter 4. The authors of the PECL also used softer language in this article by stating that "an interpretation ... is to be preferred," as is the case with Article 4.6 of the UPICC. This manner of expression suggests that this rule is not of the same weight as the other rules of interpretation. The Comments to the PECL also expressly state that this rule is not an absolute principle, and exceptions to it are always possible.[1205]

Another difference between this article and Article 4.6 of the UPICC is that the PECL requires a contract term to have not been individually negotiated in order for this rule to apply.[1206] The Official Comments to Article 4.6 of the UPICC expressly state that the *contra proferentem* rule applies not only to standard terms but also to individually negotiated terms. The difference between these two texts is another consequence of the dominance of the continental influence on the PECL, in contrast to the balance sought by the authors of the UPICC between the continental and common law approaches.

The manner of expression of Article 5:103 of the UPICC is also preserved in the provisions of other uniform law instruments of the EU that correspond to this article.[1207]

[d] *Article 5:104 of the PECL*

Article 5:104 (ex Article 7.104)—Preference to Negotiated Terms

Terms which have been individually negotiated take preference over those which are not.[1208]

This rule provides a hierarchy between individually negotiated terms and standard terms and can be considered to be an expression of a rule of logic. The rationale underlying this rule is the priority already given to the common intent of the parties.[1209]

The UPICC includes a similar rule in Article 2.1.21, among the provisions relating to standard terms, a chapter other than Chapter 4 on the interpretation of contracts.[1210]

1204. PECL, *supra* n. 192, at 294.
1205. *Ibid.*; Wissink, *supra* n. 192, at 250.
1206. Ferreri, *supra* n. 1192, at 260; Bachiashvili, *supra* n. 1192, at 15.
1207. *See*, sections §4.04[B][2][c] Article II—8:103 of the DCFR; §4.04[C][2][h] Article 65 of the CESL, *infra*.
1208. PECL, *supra* n. 192, at 295.
1209. *Ibid.*; Wissink, *supra* n. 192, at 253.
1210. This article reads as follows:

The authors of the PECL could have also placed this provision after Article 2:104 entitled "Terms Not Individually Negotiated."[1211] However, they appear to have considered this rule to be more of a rule of interpretation rather than a rule relating to standard terms.

For this article to apply, there must be a conflict between a standard term and an individually negotiated term. The Comments to the PECL state that this rule even applies to oral modifications of a contract,[1212] but this comment appears to be pushing the limits of the binding force of contracts.

[e] *Article 5:105 of the PECL*

> **Article 5:105 (ex Article 7.105)—Reference to Contract as a Whole**
>
> Terms are interpreted in the light of the whole contract in which they appear.[1213]

This provision is an expression of the principle of systematic interpretation, which is recognized in most legal systems.[1214] This article corresponds to Article 4.4 of the UPICC. The provision of the UPICC on this topic is more comprehensive, however, in the sense that it deals not only with the interpretation of terms but also of expressions.[1215]

Nevertheless, the Comments to Article 5:105 of the PECL state that this rule also applies to transactions composed of a group of contracts, and that in this situation, the expression "whole contract" must be understood to be "whole group of contracts."[1216]

Canaris/Grigoleit hold that the rule laid down in Article 5:105 of the PECL is not a genuine rule of interpretation but only a statement of the obvious. Accordingly, they state that this rule could also be placed under Article 5:102 of the PECL, among the other elements to be taken into consideration in the interpretation of contracts.[1217] However, this rule is one of the most fundamental rules of interpretation, and it has its

---

> (Conflict Between Standard Terms and Non-standard Terms) In case of conflict between a standard term and a term which is not a standard term the latter prevails.

UPICC, *supra* n. 1081, at 71.

1211. This article reads as follows:

> "Article 2:104: Terms Not Individually Negotiated
> (1) Contract terms which have not been individually negotiated may be invoked against a party who did not know of them only if the party invoking them took reasonable steps to bring them to the other party's attention before or when the contract was concluded.
> (2) Terms are not brought appropriately to a party's attention by a mere reference to them in a contract document, even if that party signs the document." PECL, *supra* n. 192, at 149.

1212. PECL, *supra* n. 192, at 295.
1213. *Ibid.*, at 296.
1214. Bachiashvili, *supra* n. 1192, at 16.
1215. *See*, section §4.03[B][4] Article 4.4 of the UPICC, *supra*.
1216. PECL, *supra* n. 192, at 296; Wissink, *supra* n. 192, at 254.
1217. Canaris, Grigoleit, *supra* n. 5, at 463.

historical basis in a text by Celsus in *Dig.* 1, 3, 24.[1218] Therefore, it appears appropriate to provide this rule in a separate article.

[f] Article 5:106 of the PECL

Article 5:106 (ex Article 7.106)—Terms to Be Given (Full) Effect

An interpretation which renders the terms of the contract lawful, or effective, is to be preferred to one which would not.[1219]

This article is an expression of the principle of *ut res magis valeat quam pereat*, stated by Iulianus, in *Dig.* 34, 5, 12 (13),[1220] and the principle of *favor negotii*.[1221] This provision differs from Article 4.5 of the UPICC, to which it corresponds, in that it is not concerned with giving effect to "all the terms" of a contract, but with giving effect to "terms." This formulation appears to be more realistic than that of the UPICC, since it may not always be possible or reasonable to give effect to all the terms of a contract.

[g] Article 5:107 of the PECL

Article 5:107 (ex Article 7.107)—Linguistic Discrepancies

Where a contract is drawn up in two or more language versions none of which is stated to be authoritative, there is, in case of discrepancy between the versions, a preference for the interpretation according to the version in which the contract was originally drawn up.[1222]

This article corresponds to Article 4.7 of the UPICC. The Comment to this article correctly points out that "it is important to read this provision with the contra proferentem rule of Article 5:103 if the original version was drafted by one of the parties."[1223]

Differing from the related provision of the UPICC, Article 5:107 of the PECL speaks of versions of a contract in different languages "none of which is stated to be authoritative." This expression is narrower than the expression of Article 4.7 of the UPICC, which requires different versions to be "equally authoritative," because it appears to be ignoring situations in which parties provide in their contracts that different language versions are equally authoritative.[1224] However, the expression of

1218. *See*, section §2.01[B][2][b], The Emergence of Principles of Objective Interpretation in the Classical Period, *supra*.
1219. PECL, *supra* n. 192, at 297.
1220. *See*, section §2.01[B][2][b], The Emergence of Principles of Objective Interpretation in the Classical Period, *supra*.
1221. PECL, *supra* n. 192, at 297; Ferreri, *supra* n. 1192, at 266.
1222. PECL, *supra* n. 192, at 298.
1223. *Ibid.*
1224. Christiane Wendehorst, *Interpretation*, in Reiner Schulze (ed.), *Common European Sales Law (CESL) Commentary*, 314 (C.H. Beck/Hart/Nomos, 2012).

Article 5:107 of the PECL has also been reiterated in subsequent uniform law instruments of the EU.[1225]

The reason for this divergence between the provisions of the UPICC and PECL is indeed not an omission but a choice.[1226] The authors of the PECL expressly stated in the Commentary that if different versions of the contract are declared to be equally authoritative, Article 5:107 of the PECL does not apply, and the ambiguity arising out of the divergence between different versions has to be overcome through the general principles of interpretation. The Commentary further states that "it is not possible simply to give precedence to one version," in contrast to the provision of Article 4.7 of the UPICC.[1227]

[B] Draft Common Frame of Reference

[1] Generally

The Study Group on a European Civil Code and the Research Group on Existing European Commission (EC) Private Law jointly published the Draft Common Frame of Reference—Principles, Definitions and Model Rules of European Private Law (DCFR) in 2008. This text was further revised in 2009. The provisions of the DCFR on contract law are based on the PECL, and as the name suggests, the DCFR is intended to become the Common Frame of Reference (CFR) for European private law.

The purpose of this draft is to serve as a model for the CFR, to promote the legal science, and to inspire legislators within the EU regarding private law issues.[1228] The DCFR is more comprehensive than the PECL. It is composed of ten books, and it includes model rules on specific contracts, noncontractual obligations (especially torts and unjust enrichment), and certain matters of moveable property, which are not covered under the PECL.[1229]

The DCFR was prepared by the Study Group on a European Civil Code, which is the successor of the Commission on European Contract Law that prepared the PECL, and it is based on the provisions of the PECL. However, its scope of application is broader than that of the PECL, as it also covers matters of consumer protection.[1230]

The provisions on the interpretation of contracts are provided under Chapter 8 entitled "Interpretation" of Book II entitled "Contracts and Other Juridical Acts" of the

1225. *See*, sections §4.04[B][2][g] Article II—8:107 of the DCFR; §4.04[C][2][d] Article 61 of the CESL, *infra*.
1226. Wissink, *supra* n. 192, at 257.
1227. PECL, *supra* n. 192, at 298; Wissink, *supra* n. 192, at 256.
1228. Christian von Bar, Eric Clive and Hans Schulte-Nölke and Hugh Beale, Johnny Herre, Jérôme Huet, Matthias Storme, Stephen Swann, Paul Varul, Anna Veneziano, Fryderyk Zoll (eds.), *Draft Common Frame of Reference (DCFR) Prepared by the Study Group on a European Civil Code and the Research Group on EC Private Law (Acquis Group) Based in Part on a Revised Version of the Principles of European Contract Law*, 7-8 (Sellier European Law Publishers, 2009).
1229. DCFR, *supra* n. 1228, at 23-24.
1230. *Ibid*, at 30.

DCFR. This chapter is composed of two sections, which deal with the "Interpretation of Contracts" and the "Interpretation of Other Juridical Acts," respectively.

[2] Chapter II—8 of the DCFR

[a] Article II—8:101 of the DCFR

> II.—8:101: General rules
> (1) A contract is to be interpreted according to the common intention of the parties even if this differs from the literal meaning of the words.
> (2) If one party intended the contract, or a term or expression used in it, to have a particular meaning, and at the time of the conclusion of the contract the other party was aware, or could reasonably be expected to have been aware, of the first party's intention, the contract is to be interpreted in the way intended by the first party.
> (3) The contract is, however, to be interpreted according to the meaning which a reasonable person would give to it:
> (a) if an intention cannot be established under the preceding paragraphs; or
> (b) if the question arises with a person, not being a party to the contract or a person who by law has no better rights than such a party, who has reasonably and in good faith relied on the contract's apparent meaning.[1231]

The DCFR only addressed the interpretation of contracts under this article, and not the interpretation of statements or other conduct, in conformity with the PECL. However, the interpretation of other judicial acts is dealt with under the following section.

This article provides a hierarchy between the subjective and objective methods of interpretation. According to subparagraph (3)(a), the objective method is applied if the ambiguity still persists despite the application of the subjective method. This being the case, Schulze/Zoll argue that "[t]his rule reflects the Germanic tradition of the interpretation of juridical acts."[1232] Nevertheless, German law does not provide a hierarchy between the subjective and objective methods of interpretation.[1233]

One may observe radical differences between this article of the DCFR and Article 4.1 of the UPICC. Even though the criterion for subjective interpretation laid down in the first subsection is identical with the one in the PECL, as regards the objective interpretation, the criterion of the understanding of "a reasonable person" is not followed by the expression "of the same kind as the parties would give it in the same circumstances." According to Wendehorst, this is remedied by the objective criteria in the second subsection.[1234] However, the second subsection is more specific, and its scope is narrower than the basic criterion of objective interpretation.

1231. *Ibid*, at 216.
1232. Reiner Schulze, Frydeyk Zoll, *European Contract Law*, 104 (C.H. Beck/Hart/Nomos, 2016).
1233. Looschelders, *supra* n. 393, at, n. 3; Singer, *supra* n. 398, at n. 3; Busche, *supra* n. 399, at n. 18; *see*, section §3.03[A][3][a] Relationship Between the Two Paragraphs, *supra*.
1234. Wendehorst, *supra* n. 1224, at 304.

The second subsection rephrases the second subsection of Article 5:101 of the PECL, which does not have an equivalent in the UPICC. Although for a contract to be interpreted in a way intended by one of the parties, Article 5:101(2) of the PECL requires that "the other party could not have been unaware of the first party's intention,"[1235] but Article II—8:101(2) of the DCFR requires that "the other party was aware, or could reasonably be expected to have been aware, of the first party's intention." The DCFR text added a subjective dimension to the PECL's provision and therefore lightened the burden of proof for the party relying on his own intent.

Subparagraph (2)(b) of Article II—8:101 deals with situations where third persons have relied in good faith on the "contract's apparent meaning." This subsection provides that contracts must be interpreted according to the understanding of a reasonable person, not only when an intent cannot be established under the first two paragraphs but also in cases involving such third parties. Schulze/Zoll point out that such situations may occur in the event of an assignment of rights arising from a contract.[1236]

The expression of a "contract's apparent meaning" in subparagraph (2)(b) suggests that this provision can only apply when it is established that the intent of the parties was different than the literal meaning of the contract, which is already difficult enough. Moreover, third persons also have to prove that they relied on this apparent meaning "reasonably and in good faith." Therefore, this subsection is unlikely to have wide application in practice.

[b] Article II—8:102 of the DCFR

II.—8:102: Relevant matters

(1) In interpreting the contract, regard may be had, in particular, to:
  (a) the circumstances in which it was concluded, including the preliminary negotiations;
  (b) the conduct of the parties, even subsequent to the conclusion of the contract;
  (c) the interpretation which has already been given by the parties to terms or expressions which are the same as, or similar to, those used in the contract and the practices they have established between themselves;
  (d) the meaning commonly given to such terms or expressions in the branch of activity concerned and the interpretation such terms or expressions may already have received;
  (e) the nature and purpose of the contract;
  (f) usages; and
  (g) good faith and fair dealing.

(2) In a question with a person, not being a party to the contract or a person such as an assignee who by law has no better rights than such a party, who has reasonably and in good faith relied on the contract's apparent meaning, regard may be had to the circumstances mentioned in sub-paragraphs (a) to (c) above

1235. *See*, section §4.04[A][2][a] Article 5:101 of the PECL, *supra*.
1236. Schulze, Zoll, *supra* n. 1232, at 104.

> only to the extent that those circumstances were known to, or could reasonably be expected to have been known to, that person.[1237]

This article corresponds to and is based to a large extent on Article 5:102 of the PECL. Nevertheless, according to this article, "regard may be had" to the listed matters, whereas Article 5:102 of the PECL provides that "regard shall be had" to them. This expression suggests that the authors of the DCFR aimed at emphasizing the nonbinding nature of this provision.

Another difference between these provisions is found in the order of the listed matters. The "nature and purpose of the contract" is ranked the fifth in Article II—8:102 of the DCFR, whereas it was ranked the third in Article 5:102 of the PECL. It is possible to observe that the reason for this difference between the two texts is that the authors of the DCFR considered the nature and purpose of the contract less important, since subsections (c) and (d) of Article II—8:102 of the DCFR reiterate subsections (d) and (e) of Article 5:102 of the PECL in almost the same words.

Subsection (2) of this article deals with third persons relying in good faith on the apparent meaning of a contract, as does subparagraph (3)(b) of Article II—8:101. Matters listed between subparagraph (1)(a) and (1)(c) will be taken into consideration to the extent that third persons know or can reasonably be expected to know them. According to Zuppi, this provision is based on the principle of good faith and fair dealing, and in questions related with third persons, contracts must be interpreted in light of the circumstances that were known or ought to have been known by them and in accordance with good faith and fair dealing.[1238]

[c] Article II—8:103 of the DCFR

> II.—8:103: Interpretation against supplier of term or dominant party
> (1) Where there is doubt about the meaning of a term not individually negotiated, an interpretation of the term against the party who supplied it is to be preferred.
> (2) Where there is doubt about the meaning of any other term, and that term has been established under the dominant influence of one party, an interpretation of the term against that party is to be preferred.[1239]

This article corresponds to Article 4.6 of the UPICC and Article 5:103 of the PECL and lays down the *contra proferentem* rule without mentioning its name, unlike its predecessors. Schulze/Zoll argue that this rule is not a general principle of interpretation and hold that it should only apply to consumer contracts.[1240] Although they base their view on the Unfair Terms Directive of the EU, this opinion appears to neglect the role of this principle in legal history, comparative law, and uniform law.

For the first subsection of this article to apply, the disputed term must not have been individually negotiated, as is the case with Article 5:103 of the PECL. However,

1237. DCFR, *supra* n. 1228, at 216.
1238. Zuppi, *supra* n. 954, at § 30.
1239. DCFR, *supra* n. 1228, at 217.
1240. Schulze, Zoll, *supra* n. 1232, at 105.

according to subsection (2), this article applies not only to standard terms but also to individually negotiated terms that have been established under the dominant influence of one party. It is worthy to mention that this provision does not have an equivalent in the PECL, the UPICC, or in the CESL.[1241]

The party under whose influence the disputed term was established will almost always be the one that supplies that term. Therefore, the scope of application of subsection (2) of Article II—8:103 of the DCFR is very limited. For this reason, this subsection should be understood in the context that nothing in the rules of interpretation allows the abuse of dominant influence.

[d] Article II—8:104 of the DCFR

> II.—8:104: Preference for negotiated terms
>
> Terms which have been individually negotiated take preference over those which have not.[1242]

This article repeats the same words as Article 5:104 of the PECL.[1243] This provision is based on the idea that priority will be given to the common intent of the parties, and it provides a hierarchy between the terms that have been individually negotiated and the ones that have not. For this provision to apply, there must be a conflict between an individually negotiated term and a standard term.

Schulze/Zoll correctly observe that this rule primarily concerns the process of contract formation, since it "expresses the principle that non-negotiated terms do not become a part of the contract if the corresponding negotiated terms are contradictory."[1244]

[e] Article II—8:105 of the DCFR

> II.—8:105: Reference to contract as a whole
>
> Terms and expressions are to be interpreted in the light of the whole contract in which they appear.[1245]

This article lays down the principle of systematic interpretation and reiterates the content of Article 5:105 of the PECL with a minor difference.[1246] Although Article 5:105 of the PECL only deals with the interpretation of terms, Article II—8:105 of the DCFR also deals with the interpretation of expressions, as does Article 4.4 of the UPICC which corresponds to this article.[1247] Unlike the UPICC, however, this article does not provide

---

1241. Zuppi, *supra* n. 954, at § 33; Michael Joachim Bonell, Roberta Peleggi, UNIDROIT Principles of International Commercial Contracts and Draft Common Frame of Reference: A Synoptical Table, 14 *Uniform Law Review* 437, 453 (2009).
1242. DCFR, *supra* n. 1228, at 217.
1243. *See*, section §4.04[A][2][d] Article 5:104 of the PECL, *supra*.
1244. Schulze, Zoll, *supra* n. 1232, at 106.
1245. DCFR, *supra* n. 1228, at 217.
1246. *See*, section §4.04[A][2][e] Article 5:105 of the PECL, *supra*.
1247. *See*, section §4.03[B][4] Article 4.4 of the UPICC, *supra*.

for the interpretation of expressions "in the light of the whole ... statement." Therefore, it is not clear from the text or the title of this article whether it also applies to the interpretation of statements. Considering that this article is based on the principle of systematic interpretation, it must be acknowledged that it does.

[f] Article II—8:106 of the DCFR

> II.—8:106: Preference for interpretation which gives terms effect
>
> An interpretation which renders the terms of the contract lawful, or effective, is to be preferred to one which would not.[1248]

This article corresponds to Article 4.5 of the UPICC and Article 5:106 of the PECL and lays down the principles of *ut res magis valeat quam pereat* and *favor negotii* in the same words as the corresponding provision of the PECL.[1249] Therefore, this article states that an interpretation that renders the "terms" of a contract lawful or effective should be preferred, but it is not concerned with giving effect to "all the terms" of a contract, unlike Article 4.5 of the UPICC. The expression adopted by the European texts appears to be more reasonable than the expression of the UPICC since the aim of the interpretation is not to give effect to all the terms of a contract.

According to Schulze/Zoll, the rule expressed in this article is in conflict with the *contra proferentem* or *contra stipulatorem* rule laid down in Article II—8:103 of the DCFR, because in the interpretation of nonnegotiated terms, the purpose cannot be to give effect to them. They suggest that the application of Article II—8:106 of the DCFR must be combined with the fairness test.[1250]

[g] Article II—8:107 of the DCFR

> II.—8:107: Linguistic discrepancies
>
> Where a contract document is in two or more language versions none of which is stated to be authoritative, there is, in case of discrepancy between the versions, a preference for the interpretation according to the version in which the contract was originally drawn up.[1251]

This article reiterates the text of Article 5:107 of the PECL.[1252] Consequently, it differs from Article 4.7 of the UPICC in excluding situations where there is a discrepancy between different language versions that were declared equally authoritative. In these situations, the DCFR does not give priority to any version, following the example of the PECL, and the ambiguity must be overcome through the general principles of interpretation.

1248. DCFR, *supra* n. 1228, at 217.
1249. Gerard McMeel, Hans Christoph Grigoleit, *Interpretation of Contracts*, in Gerhard Dannemann, Stefan Vogenauer (eds.), *The Common European Sales Law in Context*, 362 (Oxford University Press, 2013).
1250. Schulze, Zoll, *supra* n. 1232, at 106.
1251. DCFR, *supra* n. 1228, at 218.
1252. *See*, section §4.04[A][2][g] Article 5:107 of the PECL, *supra*.

Schulze/Zoll point out that the relationship of this article to the *contra proferentem* (or *contra stipulatorem*) rule should have been further clarified, and they hold that the *contra proferentem* rule should prevail, at least in consumer law cases.[1253]

[C] Proposal for a Common European Sales Law

[1] Generally

The CESL was published as a proposal to the EC in 2011.[1254] This instrument was based on the provisions of the DCFR relating to sales contracts and was intended to harmonize sales law in EU countries. The CESL originally covered both business-to-business and business-to-consumer transactions, with a view to harmonize the rules on these areas. The CESL was intended to constitute an alternative regime to domestic sales laws of EU Member States.

In 2013, the Legal Affairs Committee adopted a report backing the proposal but suggesting however to change the legal form of the CESL from an optional code to a directive. In 2014, the European Parliament adopted a legislative resolution supporting the legal form of an optional instrument but proposing to limit its scope to cross-border business-to-consumer transactions only.[1255] This legislative resolution also brought some changes to the provisions of the CESL relating to the interpretation of contracts.

Nevertheless, the Commission placed the proposal for the CESL on the list of proposals to be modified or withdrawn in December 2014, indicating that the proposal was to be modified in order to unleash the potential of e-commerce in the digital single market.[1256]

The Commission adopted a modified proposal for a directive "on certain aspects concerning contracts for the online and other distance sales of goods" in 2015.[1257] This text was intended to replace the Consumer Sales Directive of 1999. It was narrower in scope than the preceding texts and did not include the provisions on the interpretation of contracts. The Commission amended this proposal in October 2017.[1258]

1253. Schulze, Zoll, *supra* n. 1232, at 107.
1254. European Commission, *Proposal for a Regulation of the European Parliament and of the Council on a Common European Sales Law*, COM (2011) 635 final, 2011/0284 (COD), Brussels, October 11, 2011, 2-6 (CESL, first version).
1255. European Parliament, *European Parliament legislative resolution of 26 February 2014 on the proposal for a regulation of the European Parliament and of the Council on a Common European Sales Law* http://www.europarl.europa.eu/sides/getDoc.do?type=TA&language=EN&reference=P7-TA-2014-0159 (accessed December 7, 2018) (CESL, second version).
1256. European Commission, *Work Program 2015*, COM(2014) 910.
1257. European Commission, *Proposal for a Directive of the European Parliament and of the Council on certain aspects concerning contracts for the online and other distance sales of goods*, COM (2015) 635 final, 2011/0288 (COD), Brussels, December 09, 2015 https://eur-lex.europa.eu/legal-content/EN/TXT/?uri=COM%3A2015%3A635%3AFIN (accessed December 7, 2018).
1258. European Commission, *Amended proposal for a DIRECTIVE OF THE EUROPEAN PARLIAMENT AND OF THE COUNCIL on certain aspects concerning contracts for the online and other distance sales of goods, amending Regulation (EC) No 2006/2004 of the European Parliament and of the Council and Directive 2009/22/EC of the European Parliament and of the Council and repealing Directive 1999/44/EC of the European Parliament and of the Council*, COM

The first and second versions of the CESL include rules on the interpretation of contracts in Articles 58-65 and Articles 58-62, respectively, under Chapter 6 entitled "Interpretation," in Part III entitled "Assessing What Is in the Contract." The provisions of this chapter only deal with the interpretation of contracts, and the rules of interpretation of unilateral statements and conduct are provided in Article 12. Additionally, the rules for contractual gap-filling are provided in Article 68 entitled "Contract terms which may be implied."[1259]

Even though these provisions have been subsequently excluded from the proposal, they are relevant to demonstrate the evolution of the provisions on the interpretation of contracts from PECL and DCFR, into the CFR.

[2] Part III, Chapter 6 of the CESL

[a] Article 58 of the CESL

Article 58 of the first version of the CESL reads as follows:

> Article 58
>
> General rules on interpretation of contracts
> 1. A contract is to be interpreted according to the common intention of the parties even if this differs from the normal meaning of the expressions used in it.
> 2. Where one party intended an expression used in the contract to have a particular meaning, and at the time of the conclusion of the contract the other party was aware, or could be expected to have been aware, of that intention, the expression is to be interpreted in the way intended by the first party.
> 3. Unless otherwise provided in paragraphs 1 and 2, the contract is to be interpreted according to the meaning which a reasonable person would give to it.[1260]

This article has been amended in the second version of the CESL as follows:

> Article 58
>
> General rules on interpretation of contracts
> 1. A contract is to be interpreted according to the common intention of the parties even if this differs from the normal meaning of the expressions used in it.
> 2. Where one party intended an expression used in the contract **or equivalent conduct** to have a particular meaning, and at the time of the conclusion of the contract the other party was aware, or could be expected to have been aware, of that intention, the expression **or equivalent conduct** is to be interpreted in the way intended by the first party. **[Am. 122]**
> 3. Unless otherwise provided in paragraphs 1 and 2, the contract is to be interpreted according to the meaning which a reasonable person would give to it.

(2017) 637 final, 2015/0288 (COD), Brussels, October 31, 2017 https://eur-lex.europa.eu/legal-content/EN/TXT/?uri=COM%3A2017%3A637%3AFIN (accessed December 7, 2018).

1259. CESL, first version, *supra* n. 1254, at 37 and 62; Wendehorst, *supra* n. 1224, at 304.

1260. CESL, first version, *supra* n. 1254, at 60.

3a. **Expressions used in a contract shall be interpreted in the light of the contract as a whole. [Am. 123]**
3b. **The rules in this Chapter shall apply to the interpretation of an offer, acceptance or other unilateral statement indicating intention, or equivalent conduct, with appropriate adaptations. [Am. 124].**[1261]

The wording of the first subsection is based on Article 5:101 of the PECL and lays down the most basic principle of the subjective interpretation, according to which common intent of the parties prevail over the literal meaning of the contract. This subsection is also an expression of the *falsa demonstratio non nocet* principle.[1262]

The second subsection deals with the interpretation of a contract in accordance with the understanding of one of the parties, as Article 5:101(2) of the PECL and Article II—8:101(2) of the DCFR. Wendehorst criticizes the criterion that "the other party ... could be expected to have been aware" in this subsection in being difficult to establish. According to her, this condition should be assumed to have been met only in situations in which it is evident that the addressee understood the expression by the other party.[1263]

Although the first version of the CESL did not address the interpretation of the conduct of the parties,[1264] the authors of the CESL added the phrase "expression ... or equivalent conduct" into subsection 2 of Article 58 of the second version of the CESL. The change made it clear that this subsection also applies to the interpretation of conduct, bringing it closer to Article 4.1 and 4.2 of the UPICC.

Subsection 3 of this article lays down the objective method of interpretation. This subsection adopts the criterion of the understanding of a "reasonable person," which was also adopted by the PECL and the UPICC. Unlike these two instruments, but as is the case with the DCFR, the CESL does not complete this criterion with the criteria of "same kind as the parties" and "in the same circumstances." This difference of Article 58 of the CESL from Article 4.1 of the UPICC and Article 5:101 of the PECL makes this article more ambiguous than its predecessors.[1265] The reason for this difference is that the authors of the CESL took Article 8:101 of the DCFR as a basis for Article 58 of the CESL. They did not intend to exclude or to limit these criteria.[1266]

An important difference between the first and second versions of the CESL is that the principle of systematic interpretation, which was expressed in Article 60 of the CESL in the first version, has been placed under Article 58 in subsection 3a. This article will be examined below.

Another difference between the two versions is that subsection 3b was added to the second version in order to make it clear that this article also applies to the interpretation of statements and conduct, with appropriate adaptations.

1261. CESL, second version, *supra* n. 1255, at 135-136.
1262. Wendehorst, *supra* n. 1224, at 305.
1263. *Ibid.*
1264. Wendehorst was of the opinion that this article applies also to the interpretation of conduct of the parties, in the absence of any more specific provision on this issue in the CESL. Wendehorst, *supra* n. 1224, at 305-306.
1265. Wendehorst, *supra* n. 1224, at 306.
1266. *Ibid.*

[b] Article 59 of the CESL

Article 59 of the first version of the CESL reads as follows:

> Article 59
>
> Relevant matters
>
> In interpreting a contract, regard may be had, in particular, to:
>
> (a) the circumstances in which it was concluded, including the preliminary negotiations;
> (b) the conduct of the parties, even subsequent to the conclusion of the contract;
> (c) the interpretation which has already been given by the parties to expressions which are identical to or similar to those used in the contract;
> (d) usages which would be considered generally applicable by parties in the same situation;
> (e) practices which the parties have established between themselves;
> (f) the meaning commonly given to expressions in the branch of activity concerned;
> (g) the nature and purpose of the contract; and
> (h) good faith and fair dealing.[1267]

This article has been amended in the second version of the CESL as follows:

> Article 59
>
> Relevant matters
>
> In interpreting a contract, regard may be had, in particular, to:
>
> (a) the circumstances in which it was concluded, ~~including the preliminary negotiations~~;
> [Am. 125]
> (b) the conduct of the parties, ~~even~~ **prior, during and** subsequent to the conclusion of the contract; **[Am. 126]**
> (c) the interpretation which ~~has already been given by the parties~~ **the parties have previously given** to expressions which are identical to or similar to those used in the contract; **[Am. 127]**
> (d) usages which would be considered generally applicable by parties in the same situation;
> (e) practices which the parties have established between themselves;
> (f) the meaning commonly given to expressions in the branch of activity concerned;
> (g) the nature and purpose of the contract; and
> (h) good faith and fair dealing.[1268]

This article provides a non-exhaustive list of the matters to which regard "may be had" in the interpretation of contracts, following the example of Article II—8:102 of the DCFR, although softening the language compared with Article 4.3 of the UPICC and Article 5:102 of the PECL, which both state that regard "shall be had" to the listed

---

1267. CESL, first version, *supra* n. 1254, at 60.
1268. CESL, second version, *supra* n. 1255, at 136-137.

elements. The most important difference between this article and Article II—8:102 of the DCFR is that the latter deals with the protection of the rights of third persons in subsection (2), whereas Article 59 of the CESL is silent on this issue. McMeel and Grigoleit find this change appropriate, as the reference to third-party rights in the DCFR was not well founded, and it is unlikely that the rights of third parties are affected by sales contracts.[1269]

Although the first subsection included preliminary negotiations as a matter to be taken into consideration, this expression was deleted from the second version. The change brought this provision into conformity with Article 72 of the CESL, which deals with merger clauses. According to Article 72(2), parties may agree in a contract that their prior statements cannot be used to interpret their contract.[1270] This provision has also been preserved in the second version of the CESL.[1271] Moreover, according to subsections (3) and (4) of Article 72 of the CESL, in contracts between a trader and a consumer, the consumer is not bound by a merger clause, and the parties may not exclude the application of this article to the detriment of the consumer.[1272]

The subsection (a) mentions "the circumstances in which [a contract] was concluded" as a matter to which regard may be had in the interpretation of a contract. According to Wendehorst, this broad expression includes the time and place of the conclusion of the contract and the means of communication used by the parties.[1273] Wendehorst also states that "the meaning commonly given to expressions in the branch of activity concerned" listed in subsection (f) is indeed the starting point of the interpretation. However, the reason this matter was placed in this article is that the authors of the CESL intended to emphasize the importance of "the branch of activity concerned."[1274]

Although it did not appear among the provisions on the interpretation of contracts of the UPICC, the principle of good faith and fair dealing, which has appeared in all uniform law instruments of the EU, was placed in subparagraph (h) of Article 59 of the CESL. However, this principle is not provided as a general principle of interpretation but only as one of the matters to which regard may be paid. Therefore, according to Wendehorst, courts cannot use this reference to the principle of good faith and fair dealing for rendering decisions according to equity.[1275]

[c] Article 60 of the CESL

Article 60

Reference to contract as a whole

1269. McMeel, Grigoleit, *supra* n. 1249, at 354.
1270. Article 72(2) of the CESL reads as follows: "Unless the contract otherwise provides, a merger clause does not prevent the parties' prior statements from being used to interpret the contract."CESL, first version, *supra* n. 1254, at 64.
1271. CESL, second version, *supra* n. 1255, at 148.
1272. CESL, first version, *supra* n. 1254, at 64; CESL, second version, *supra* n. 1255, at 148; Wendehorst, *supra* n. 1224, at 308.
1273. Wendehorst, *supra* n. 1224, at 310.
1274. *Ibid.*, at 311.
1275. *Ibid.*

Expressions used in a contract are to be interpreted in the light of the contract as a whole.[1276]

This provision, which appeared in Article 60 of the first version of the CESL, was moved to subsection 3(a) of Article 58 of the second version. This article is an expression of the principle of systematic interpretation and reflects a gradual change in the wording of the corresponding provisions of uniform law instruments of the EU. Article 5:105 of the PECL deals only with the interpretation of "terms," whereas the scope of Article II—8:105 of the DCFR was expanded to include both "terms and expressions." The CESL, however, narrowed the scope of this article down to the interpretation of "expressions" only.

It is evident that the authors of uniform law instruments of the EU may not have intended these changes to result in different consequences. For this reason, it is reasonable and in conformity with the principle of systematic interpretation that all three provisions apply to the interpretation of both terms and expressions. In addition, as Wendehorst correctly states, these provisions should apply not only to single contracts but also to groups of contracts between the parties, as is the case with Article 5:105 of the PECL.[1277]

The principle of systematic interpretation must apply along with the matters listed in Article 59 of the CESL. When interpreting a contract, for instance, its nature and purpose should be drawn from the whole contract.[1278] Wendehorst even argues that the rule set forth in Article 60 does not need to be expressed in a separate article and that it would have been sufficient to place it among the matters to be taken into consideration under Article 59.[1279] Indeed, the authors of the CESL placed this rule under Article 58 in the second version of the text. The present author, however, is of the opinion that this basic and well-established principle of interpretation deserves to be expressed under a separate article and that its position in the first version of the CESL was more appropriate.

[d] Article 61 of the CESL

Article 61

Language discrepancies

Where a contract document is in two or more language versions none of which is stated to be authoritative and where there is a discrepancy between the versions, the version in which the contract was originally drawn up is to be treated as the authoritative one.[1280]

Article 61, 61a, and 61b of the second version of the CESL read as follows:

Article 61

1276. CESL, first version, *supra* n. 1254, at 60.
1277. Wendehorst, *supra* n. 1224, at 313.
1278. *Ibid.*, at 312.
1279. *Ibid.*, at 313.
1280. CESL, first version, *supra* n. 1254, at 61.

Language discrepancies

Where a contract document is in two or more language versions none of which is stated to be authoritative and where there is a discrepancy between the versions, the version in which the contract was originally drawn up is to be treated as the authoritative one.

Where a contract document in the consumer's national language has been used, that version shall be considered as the authoritative one. The parties may not, to the detriment of the consumer, exclude the application of this paragraph or derogate from or vary its effects. [Am. 129]

Article 61a

Preference for interpretation which gives effect to contract terms

An interpretation which gives effect to contract terms shall prevail over one which does not.

[Am. 130]

Article 61b

Interpretation in favour of consumers

1. **Where there exists any doubt about the meaning of a contract term in a contract between a trader and a consumer, the interpretation most favourable to the consumer shall prevail unless the term in question was supplied by the consumer.**
2. **The parties may not, to the detriment of the consumer, exclude the application of this Article or derogate from, or vary, its effects. [Am. 131].**[1281]

This article deals with different language versions of a contract "none of which is stated to be authoritative," like its predecessors Article 5:107 of the PECL and Article II—8:107 of the DCFR. Therefore, this provision excludes situations in which different language versions are declared to be "equally authoritative," unlike Article 4.7 of the UPICC. Even though such a situation is very common in practice, the authors of uniform law texts of the EU preferred to leave this issue to the general principles of interpretation.[1282]

Article 61 (1) of the CESL is a rebuttable presumption. If the common intent of the parties can be established and it would lead to a conclusion that is different than the one that would result from this article, the contract must be interpreted according to the common intent of the parties, pursuant to Article 58(1) of the CESL.[1283]

Likewise, in the event of a conflict between the meaning obtained through the application of Article 61 (1) of the CESL and the meaning obtained through other rules of interpretation, the latter meanings would prevail. For instance, an interpretation that gives effect to contract terms (Article 63, first version and Article 61a, second version of the CESL), or in favor of consumers (Article 64, first version and Article 61b, second version of the CESL) should be preferred.[1284] The authors of the CESL have made the

1281. CESL, second version, *supra* n. 1255, at 138-139.
1282. Wendehorst, *supra* n. 1224, at 314.
1283. *Ibid.*, at 315.
1284. *Ibid.*

relationship between these rules clearer by placing Article 61a and 61b just after Article 61 of the second version of the CESL, which correspond to Articles 63 and 64 of the first version, respectively.

[e] *Article 62 of the CESL*

Article 62

Preference for individually negotiated contract terms

To the extent that there is an inconsistency, contract terms which have been individually negotiated prevail over those which have not been individually negotiated within the meaning of Article 7.[1285]

This article was modified in the second version of the CESL as follows:

Article 62

~~Preference for~~ **Contract terms which are not** individually negotiated ~~contract terms~~

[Am. 132]

1. To the extent that there is an inconsistency, contract terms which have been individually negotiated prevail over those which have not been individually negotiated within the meaning of Article 7.

1a. **Where, despite Article 61b, there exists doubt about the meaning of a contract term which has not been individually negotiated within the meaning of Article 7, an interpretation of the term against the party who supplied it shall prevail. [Am. 133]**[1286]

This article of the CESL refers to Article 7 of the CESL entitled "[n]ot individually negotiated contract terms," unlike its predecessors. Even though this article expresses a self-evident rule, it is relevant for situations in which contract terms that were individually negotiated and that were not individually negotiated are in conflict with each other.[1287]

This rule has two principal fields of application. The first is when changes have been made to standard contract terms, which convert standard terms into individually negotiated terms in the sense of this article. The second is when there are oral amendments to standard terms. As a rule, if there is a merger clause in the contract in the sense of Article 72 of the CESL, these oral amendments will be ineffective. Nonetheless, oral amendments will be effective in consumer contracts, since consumers are not bound by merger clauses according to Article 72(3).[1288]

The authors of the CESL added subsection 1a to Article 62, according to which, contract terms that were not individually negotiated and remain ambiguous despite the application of Article 61b (Article 64 in the first version of the CESL) must be interpreted against the party who supplied them. This subsection corresponds to Article 65 of the first version of the CESL. However, it is doubtful whether this

1285. CESL, first version, *supra* n. 1254, at 61.
1286. CESL, second version, *supra* n. 1255, at 139-140.
1287. Wendehorst, *supra* n. 1224, at 317.
1288. *Ibid.*, at 316-317.

provision was really necessary since Article 61b provides that these clauses must be interpreted in favor of consumers, and it is almost always the trader and not the consumer who supplies such terms.

[f] Article 63 of the CESL

Article 63

Preference for interpretation which gives contract terms effect

An interpretation which renders the contract terms effective prevails over one which does not.[1289]

This article has been renumbered Article 61a in the second version of the CESL; it is an expression of the principles of *favor negotii* and *magis ut res valeat quam pereat*,[1290] and it is based on the presumption that the parties would not use words to no purpose.[1291] For this reason, an interpretation that gives effect to contract terms must be applied over one that makes the terms ineffective or absurd. Likewise, an interpretation that renders a term more functional should be applied over one that renders it nonfunctional or unnecessary.[1292]

This article also functions as a rebuttable presumption. Wendehorst points out that the parties may copy and paste standard clauses into their contract in order to feel more secure. In such situations, it would be contrary to the purpose of this article to attribute a meaning that was not meant by the parties to a contract. [1293]

[g] Article 64 of the CESL

Article 64

Interpretation in favour of consumers

1. Where there is doubt about the meaning of a contract term in a contract between a trader and a consumer, the interpretation most favourable to the consumer shall prevail unless the term was supplied by the consumer.
2. The parties may not, to the detriment of the consumer, exclude the application of this Article or derogate from or vary its effects.[1294]

Article 64 of the first version of the CESL was renumbered Article 61b in the second version. This article only covers consumer contracts for the purpose of consumer protection. [1295] Therefore, it does not correspond to any provision in the

1289. CESL, first version, *supra* n. 1254, at 61.
1290. Wendehorst, *supra* n. 1224, at 317; McMeel, Grigoleit, *supra* n. 1249, at 362.
1291. Wendehorst, *supra* n. 1224, at 318.
1292. *Ibid.*
1293. *Ibid.*
1294. CESL, first version, *supra* n. 1254, at 61.
1295. Wendehorst, *supra* n. 1224, at 320.

preceding EU uniform law texts, which are of wider scope.[1296] The scope of application of this article is very limited because standard terms are usually used in consumer contracts, the trader parties usually supply these terms, and the general principle of *contra proferentem* laid down in Article 65 (Article 62(1a) in the second version) already covers this situation. Accordingly, Schulze/Zoll suggest that this article should be placed among the rules on unfair terms.[1297]

The second subsection of this article emphasizes the mandatory nature of the first subsection, in conformity with the consumer protection policy. This subsection, however, should not be interpreted to mean than it is possible to exclude the application of other rules of interpretation in consumer transactions.[1298]

[h] Article 65 of the CESL

> Article 65
>
> Interpretation against supplier of a contract term
>
> Where, in a contract which does not fall under Article 64, there is doubt about the meaning of a contract term which has not been individually negotiated within the meaning of Article 7, an interpretation of the term against the party who supplied it shall prevail.[1299]

This article is an expression of the *contra stipulatorem* or *contra proferentem* rule, even though it does not mention it by name. It corresponds to Articles 5:103 of the PECL and II—8:103 of the DCFR, and it has been renumbered Article 62(1a) in the second version of the CESL. The wording of this article is closer to the wording of the corresponding article in the PECL than the provisions of the DCFR, as is also the case with Article 58 of the CESL. In particular, Article 65 of the CESL does not contain a provision on the interpretation against a dominant party, corresponding to subsection (2) of Article II—8:103 of the DCFR.[1300]

An important difference between the CESL and its predecessors, the PECL and the DCFR, is the position of this article among the provisions relating to the interpretation of contracts. Although the *contra stipulatorem* or *contra proferentem* rule is placed just after the matters to be taken into consideration in both preceding texts, it is ranked last among the rules of interpretation in the CESL.

The phrase "in a contract which does not fall under Article 64" suggests that this article only applies to business-to-business transactions.[1301] The authors of the CESL did not declare this provision to be of a mandatory nature, unlike Article 64 of the

1296. However, the Council Directive 93/13/EEC of April 5, 1993, on unfair terms in consumer contracts contains a similar provision as Art. 5., https://eur-lex.europa.eu/legal-content/EN/TXT/?uri=celex%3A31993L0013 (accessed December 7, 2018); Wendehorst, *supra* n. 1224, at 320.
1297. Schulze, Zoll, *supra* n. 1232, at 109.
1298. Wendehorst, *supra* n. 1224, at 323.
1299. CESL, first version, *supra* n. 1254, at 61.
1300. McMeel and Grigoleit find the aspect of "one-sided dominance" vague and nonfunctional. McMeel, Grigoleit, *supra* n. 1249, at 360.
1301. Wendehorst, *supra* n. 1224, at 324.

CESL. However, this does not mean that the parties may exclude the application of this article since such an interpretation would be contrary to its nature and purpose.[1302]

§4.05 TRANS-LEX PRINCIPLES

[A] Generally

The Trans-Lex Principles form part of the trans-lex knowledge and codification web-platform for transnational commercial law (www.trans-lex.org) prepared by the Center for Transnational Law (CENTRAL) of the University of Cologne. These principles provide a non-exhaustive list of the principles of the new *lex mercatoria* on the basis of comprehensive comparative references. International arbitral awards are one of the most important sources of these principles, and as a result, the Trans-Lex Principles accurately describe the *lex mercatoria* rules and principles as they emanate from international arbitral practice.

These principles function as a guide to the electronic sources available on the trans-lex database in the form of references to each principle. The CENTRAL director Prof. Klaus Peter Berger and his team regularly update these principles and the references to them.

CENTRAL began a Commentary to the Trans-Lex Principles in 2012 and has revised it four times since then, the most recent being in 2016.

Chapter IV ("Contract") section 5 ("Interpretation") of the Trans-Lex Principles is dedicated to the rules on the interpretation of contracts and is composed of six articles.

[B] Chapter IV, Section 5 of the Trans-Lex Principles

[1] Trans-Lex Principle No. IV.5.1

No—IV.5.1—Intentions of the parties

> The construction of a contract has to determine the common intention of the parties or, if no such intention can be determined, the meaning that reasonable parties of the same kind as the parties would give to it in the same circumstances, taking into account, in particular, the nature and purpose of the contract, the conduct of the parties and the meaning commonly given to contract terms and expressions in the trade concerned.[1303]

A terminological remark is in order at this point. Although section 5 of Chapter IV is entitled "Interpretation," the term "construction" is used interchangeably with the term interpretation in this article, in accordance with British terminology. However, in U.S. law these terms are not used interchangeably. Interpretation signifies the ascertainment of the meaning of the words and expressions in a contract, whereas construction means the determination of the legal effects and consequences of

1302. *Ibid.*, at 326.
1303. *See* http://www.trans-lex.org/924000 (accessed December 7, 2018).

them.[1304] The Trans-Lex Principles do not explain the reason for this preference in favor of the British terminology.

This article begins with the principle of subjective interpretation adopted by most jurisdictions and uniform law texts, according to which the primary purpose of the interpretation is to determine the common intent of the parties. The title of the article also refers to this principle.

The article continues with objective interpretation as a secondary method of interpretation, in accordance with Latin jurisdictions and other uniform law texts. It lays down the criterion that "the meaning that reasonable parties of the same kind as the parties would give to it in the same circumstances," which ensures an objective interpretation tailored to the specific circumstances of each case. Finally, the article offers a non-exhaustive list of some of the matters to be taken into consideration in objective interpretation.

This article combines rules that are expressed in two or three articles in most other uniform law instruments in one sentence. The cost of unifying the objective and subjective methods of interpretation and the matters to be taken into consideration in one single sentence is the apparent ambiguity in the application of the matters to the methods. This article can be read as if the listed matters that must be taken into consideration only apply to objective interpretation and not to subjective interpretation, unlike other uniform law texts. However, the philosophy underlying the Trans-Lex Principles suggests that it was not the intent of the authors to embark on a radical deviation from the general tendencies in uniform law. Therefore, the listed matters should also be taken into account in subjective interpretation.

The Commentary to the Trans-Lex Principles refers to the principle of good faith as the basis of this article, adding one more basic principle of interpretation into its context.[1305] The Commentary further refers to the "presumption of professional competence," "reasonable distribution of contractual rights and duties," and "common commercial objective" of the parties.[1306] In addition, the Commentary includes "the conduct of a party subsequent to the conclusion of the contract" and "previous contracts of the same kind concluded between the parties" as other matters to be taken into consideration in the interpretation of contracts.[1307]

Unlike other uniform law texts, Article No. IV.5.5 of the Trans-Lex Principles includes a special provision for the principle of *falsa demonstratio non nocet*. Therefore, this principle is not mentioned in Article IV.5.1.

1304. Williston, *supra* n. 833 (Williston on Sales), at 360; Williston, *supra* n. 833 (Williston on Contracts), at 320.
1305. Commentary to Trans-Lex Principle No. IV.5.1, Comment 1 http://www.trans-lex.org/924000 (accessed December 7, 2018).
1306. Commentary to Trans-Lex Principle No. IV.5.1, Comment 2 http://www.trans-lex.org/924000 (accessed December 7, 2018).
1307. Commentary to Trans-Lex Principle No. IV.5.1, Comment 3 http://www.trans-lex.org/924000 (accessed December 7, 2018).

[2] Trans-Lex Principle No. IV.5.2

No—IV.5.2—Context-oriented interpretation

Contractual stipulations shall be interpreted taking into account the whole contract in which they appear.[1308]

As in most other uniform law texts, this article sets forth the principle of systematic interpretation. However, this provision differs from other texts in that it addresses the interpretation of "contractual stipulations," which is a more comprehensive category than the interpretation of "terms" and/or "expressions."

The wording of this article suggests that the text of the contract is the only thing that can be taken into account in the interpretation of contractual stipulations. However, the title of the article, which refers to "context-oriented interpretation," implies that extrinsic evidence could also be taken into consideration. Accordingly, the Commentary states that "a letter of intent concluded prior to the contract" may also be used in the interpretation of clauses of a contract.[1309]

[3] Trans-Lex Principle No. IV.5.3

No—IV.5.3—Interpretation in favour of effectiveness of contract

Where there is doubt about the meaning of a contract term, an interpretation should be preferred that makes the contract lawful or effective ("ut res magis valeat quam pereat"; "effet utile").[1310]

For the first time in uniform law, this article lays down the principle of interpretation in favor of the effectiveness of contract with an explicit reference to the words of Iulianus in *Dig.* 34, 5, 12 (13) (Iul. 50 Dig.).[1311]

The Commentary states that this principle is a consequence of subjective interpretation, which is based on the common intent of the parties, set forth in Principle IV.5.1.[1312]

[4] Trans-Lex Principle No. IV.5.4

No—IV.5.4—Interpretation against the party that supplied the term

Where, after the interpretation of a contract term that has been supplied by one party, doubts remain as to the meaning of that term, an interpretation against that party is to be preferred ("contra proferentem").[1313]

1308. *See* http://www.trans-lex.org/927000 (accessed December 7, 2018).
1309. Commentary to Trans-Lex Principle No. IV.5.2, Comment 2 http://www.trans-lex.org/927000 (accessed December 7, 2018).
1310. *See* http://www.trans-lex.org/925000 (accessed December 7, 2018).
1311. *See*, section §2.01[B][2][b], The Emergence of Principles of Objective Interpretation in the Classical Period, *supra*.
1312. Commentary to Trans-Lex Principle No. IV.5.3, Comment 1 http://www.trans-lex.org/925000 (accessed December 7, 2018).
1313. *See* http://www.trans-lex.org/926000 (accessed December 7, 2018).

This article lays down the *contra proferentem* rule, referring to it by name. For this rule to apply, there must remain doubts about the meaning of a term supplied by one party after the application of the other rules of interpretation. This article demonstrates that the authors of the Trans-Lex Principles consider the *contra proferentem* rule to be a subsidiary rule.

The Comment to this article states that this rule applies not only to standard terms but also when supplied by one party, to terms that do not have the quality of standard terms.[1314]

[5] Trans-Lex Principle No. IV.5.5

No—IV.5.5 - Falsa demonstratio rule

In case the parties have used the wrong term but mean the same thing, their common intention prevails ("falsa demonstratio non nocet").[1315]

The authors of the Trans-Lex Principles set forth the principle of *falsa demonstratio non nocet* in this article, even referring to it by name. A separate article on this principle is a feature intrinsic to the Trans-Lex Principles. Even though this principle is the logical consequence of the principle of the priority of the common intent of the parties as provided in Article IV.5.1, the authors of the Trans-Lex Principles preferred to provide these principles in separate provisions. Their decision appears to be an expression of the importance of these principles individually and their independence from each other. The Comment to this article points out the relationship between these principles, providing that the *falsa demonstratio non nocet* principle is a "specific example of Principle IV.5.1."[1316]

[6] Trans-Lex Principle No. IV.5.6

No—IV.5.6—Rights and duties of the parties under "FOB" and "CIF"

If the parties have agreed on a sale "FOB" or "CIF," the respective rights and duties of the parties under the contract are to be determined according to the latest version of the International Commercial Terms (INCOTERMS®) issued by the International Chamber of Commerce (ICC) unless the parties have indicated that a different meaning is to be attributed to the term used.[1317]

This provision is another distinctive feature of the Trans-Lex Principles, and it is an expression of a rule that stems from the court decisions and arbitral awards that can be found in the Trans-Lex web-platform. Nevertheless, this provision also makes it clear that this rule is not an absolute principle and that the parties may attribute different meanings to Free on Board (FOB) or Cost, Insurance, and Freight (CIF) terms.

1314. Commentary to Trans-Lex Principle No. IV.5.4, http://www.trans-lex.org/926000 (accessed December 7, 2018).
1315. *See* http://www.trans-lex.org/928000 (accessed December 7, 2018).
1316. Commentary to Trans-Lex Principle No. IV.5.5 http://www.trans-lex.org/928000 (accessed December 7, 2018).
1317. *See* http://www.trans-lex.org/928500 (accessed December 7, 2018).

Considering that the common intent of the parties prevails over the rule expressed in this article, one may say that the exception stated in this article, indeed, leads to the rule expressed in Principle IV.5.1.

The Comment to this article also correctly points out that "[w]hile not all of the INCOTERMS® have assumed the quality of transnational law, the FOB and CIF terms can be qualified as such due to their worldwide use and recognition in international trade and transport."[1318]

[7] Trans-Lex Principle No. IV.5.7

No—IV.5.7—Merger Clauses

(a) Where a contract in writing includes a term stating that the document contains all contract terms ("merger clause," "entire agreement clause"), any prior statements, undertakings or agreements which are not contained in the document do not form part of the contract.

(b) Unless the contract otherwise provides, a merger clause does not prevent the parties' prior statements from being used to interpret the contract.[1319]

This article addresses merger clauses that originate from common law tradition but provides a rule that reflects international practice. Even though the intent to limit the effects of merger clauses underlying this rule has been adopted by most international legislators, a black letter rule of interpretation expressing this idea is another distinctive feature of the Trans-Lex Principles.[1320]

The first paragraph provides a definition of a merger or entire agreement clause and spells out its legal consequences. This paragraph is not per se a rule of interpretation. However, Trans-Lex Principles do not contain any other provision where these clauses are defined or need to be defined. Therefore, the first paragraph appears to have been provided for explanatory purposes only. Further explanations relating to merger or entire agreement clauses have been provided in the Commentary.[1321]

The second paragraph expresses a rule that emerged as a result of the debates on the relationship between Article 8 of the CISG and merger clauses,[1322] according to which the latter do not prevent the prior statements of the parties from being used in the interpretation of contracts. Moreover, the Commentary states that an interpretation in the light of the prior statements of the parties "may [even] result in the modification of the written text of the contract or in the assumption of an implied term."[1323]

1318. Commentary to Trans-Lex Principle No. IV.5.6, Comment 1 http://www.trans-lex.org/928500 (accessed December 7, 2018).
1319. *See* http://www.trans-lex.org/928550 (accessed December 7, 2018).
1320. PECL contains a similar provision in Art. 2:105(3), PECL, *supra* n. 192, at 152; *see also*, section §4.04[A][2][b] Article 5:102 of the PECL, *supra*.
1321. Commentary to Trans-Lex Principle No. IV.5.7, Comments 1 and 2 http://www.trans-lex.org/928550 (accessed December 7, 2018).
1322. *See*, section §4.02[F] Parol Evidence Rule, Merger Clauses, and Article 8(3) of the CISG, *supra*.
1323. Commentary to Trans-Lex Principle No. IV.5.7, Comment 3 http://www.trans-lex.org/928550 (accessed December 7, 2018).

CHAPTER 5

Final Remarks on General Tendencies in Comparative and Uniform Law on the Interpretation of Contracts

§5.01 BASIC DISCUSSIONS

[A] Scope of the Regulations on the Interpretation of Contracts

The principles of the interpretation of contracts in modern codifications reflect, to varying degrees, those that have developed since the classical period of Roman law. Although Latin legal systems provide comprehensive regulations on this issue, Romano-Germanic legal systems limit their codification to a few broad provisions. The principle of leaving a great deal of space for judicial discretion, which was found in the Historical School of Jurisprudence, underlies the Romano-Germanic tendency to limit the provisions on the interpretation of contracts.[1324] The emergence and development of the principles of contractual interpretation in common law jurisdictions is even more recent and limited.[1325]

Nevertheless, one may observe that the lack of detailed provisions on this subject does not create any problems, and it is also possible to find all of the principles of contractual interpretation that have been codified in Latin jurisdictions in case law and literature in Romano-Germanic[1326] and common law jurisdictions.[1327]

1324. *See*, section §3.03[A][1] Generally, *supra*.
1325. *See*, sections §3.04[A][1] Generally (English Law); §3.04[B][1] Generally (US Law), *infra*.
1326. *See*, sections §3.03[A][2] Types or Methods of Interpretation in German Law (German Law); §3.03[B][5] Principles of Interpretation Developed Through Case Law (Swiss Law); §3.03[C][2][f] Principles of Interpretation Developed Through Case Law or Recognized in the Literature (Turkish Law), *supra*.
1327. Sections §3.04[A][4] Other Principles of Interpretation (English Law); §3.04[B][4][b] Other Rules of Interpretation Recognized in the Literature (US Law), *supra*.

The authors and legislators of the uniform law texts appear to have preferred the Latin approach, which provides detailed provisions on the interpretation of contracts. This was a reasonable choice because leaving a great deal of space for judicial discretion, as did Romano-Germanic legislators, would have been contrary to the purpose of establishing laws to apply uniformly among different legal systems based upon different traditions. However, the rules provided in uniform law texts differ from those of Latin jurisdictions in that they do not only codify the principles of Roman law but also include innovative provisions to respond to the needs of today's international business practice.[1328]

[B] Review of Decisions Relating to the Interpretation of Contracts

Jurists and legal scholars in many jurisdictions have debated whether or not decisions relating to the interpretation of contracts are reviewable on appeal. The main issue underlying these discussions is whether the interpretation of contracts is a question of fact or law.[1329] Furthermore, the answer to this question determines whether judges or juries will decide on the interpretation of contracts in common law jurisdictions where there is a jury system.[1330]

Although some legal systems consider this issue to be a question of fact, and in principle should, therefore, exclude it from review on appeal, the general tendency in comparative law, even within jurisdictions that consider it to be a question of fact, has been to acknowledge that decisions relating to the interpretation of contracts are reviewable on appeal. To facilitate this principle in jurisdictions where the interpretation of contracts is considered to be a question of fact, high courts have developed various and efficient tools to review these decisions.[1331]

The 1987 Report of the UNIDROIT Working Group, according to which interpretation is a "legal problem and not only one of grammar or logic," best expresses the approach adopted in uniform law on this point.[1332]

1328. *See*, for instance, sections §4.03[B][7] Article 4.7 of the UPICC; §4.05[B][7] Trans-Lex Principle No. IV.5.7, *supra*.

1329. *See*, sections §3.02[A][3] Review of Decisions Relating to the Interpretation of Contracts (French Law); §3.02[B][3] Review of Decisions Relating to the Interpretation of Contracts (Italian Law); §3.03[A][1] Generally (German Law); §3.03[B][3] The Significance of the Distinction Between Subjective and Objective Interpretation for Reviewability of Decisions (Swiss Law), *supra*.

1330. Section §3.04[B][1], Generally (US Law), *supra*.

1331. *See*, sections §3.02[A][3] Review of Decisions Relating to the Interpretation of Contracts (French Law); §3.02[B][3] Review of Decisions Relating to the Interpretation of Contracts (Italian Law), *supra*.

1332. *See*, section §4.03[A] Generally, *supra*.

[C] Scope of the Rules on the Interpretation of Contracts

In comparative and uniform law, there are three approaches regarding the scope of the rules on interpretation. Domestic and international legislators have addressed the interpretation of statements,[1333] the interpretation of contracts,[1334] or both together.[1335]

In jurisdictions where one of the first two approaches has been adopted, the application of the rules of interpretation of statements to the interpretation of contracts or vice versa is a controversial issue. This issue is most debated in German law, which includes two general provisions in the BGB, one on the interpretation of statements and the other on the interpretation of contracts. The discussions in German law center on whether a distinction between the rules on the interpretation of statements and the rules on the interpretation of contracts is necessary or practicable. The answer reached by German case law and literature is that it was not. Since contracts are the product of two corresponding statements, it is neither practical nor even possible to create sharp distinctions between the interpretation of statements and the interpretation of contracts.[1336]

The general tendency in comparative and uniform law has also been to apply the rules that appear to address only the interpretation of statements to the interpretation of contracts and vice versa.

[D] The Principle of Good Faith and Fair Dealing as a Principle of Interpretation

Another issue that is frequently discussed in individual legal systems and uniform law is the special aspect of the principle of good faith and fair dealing as it applies to contractual interpretation. This rule, first expressed by Hugo Donellus,[1337] is generally recognized in both Latin and Romano-Germanic legal families,[1338] as well as in uniform law.[1339] However, in certain common law jurisdictions that do not recognize the general principle of good faith and fair dealing, a special aspect of this principle as it would apply to the interpretation of contracts is also not recognized.

The role of good faith and fair dealing as a rule of interpretation are perceived differently in the Romano-Germanic and Latin legal systems. The Romano-Germanic

1333. *See*, section §4.02[B] The Scope of Application of Article 8 of the CISG, and Interpretation Based on the Intent of Only One of the Parties, *supra*.
1334. Sections §3.03[B][4] Article 18/1 of the OR (Swiss Law); §3.03[C][2][a] Article 19(1) of the TBK (Turkish Law), *supra*.
1335. *See*, section §3.03[A][3] Provisions of the BGB Relating to the Interpretation of Contracts (§ 133 and § 157 of the BGB), *supra*.
1336. *See*, section §3.03[A][3][a] Relationship Between the Two Paragraphs, *supra*.
1337. *See*, section §2.02 Humanist and Naturalist Schools of Law and the Divergence of Approaches among Continental Legal Systems, *supra*.
1338. *See*, sections §3.02[B][6][d] Article 1366 of the CC. It.; §3.03[A][3][c] § 157 of the BGB; §3.03[B][4][b] Objective Interpretation; §3.03[C][2][f] Principles of Interpretation Developed Through Case Law or Recognized in the Literature, *supra*.
1339. *See*, sections §4.02[E] Rules of Interpretation not Covered by the CISG; §4.03[A] Generally; §4.04[A][2][b] Article 5:102 of the PECL; §4.04[B][2][b] Article II—8:102 of the DCFR; §4.04[C][2][b] Article 59 of the CESL; §4.05[B][1] Trans-Lex Principle No. IV.5.1, *supra*.

system attributes significant importance is to this principle because of its limited codification of the rules of interpretation. The BGB contains only two paragraphs on interpretation, and one (§157 of the BGB) addresses the principle of good faith and fair dealing in interpretation. It is not surprising that this general principle takes on greater significance in the absence of detailed provisions on the interpretation of contracts.

In Latin jurisdictions, which contain detailed provisions on the interpretation of contracts, it is unclear whether or not good faith and fair dealing as a rule of interpretation is necessary. In Italian law, which references this principle in Article 1366 of the CC. It., the location of this article within the rules of interpretation is debatable. One opinion adopts the supremacy of good faith and fair dealing as a rule of interpretation against other rules of interpretation, while the other view, to which the *Corte di Cassazione* also adheres, holds that this principle is a rule that should only be applied as a last resort after exhausting the other rules of interpretation.[1340]

As regards uniform law, it can be observed that uniform law texts refrain from referring to the principle of good faith and fair dealing in the interpretation of contracts. This is due to the influence of the CISG, which does not refer to the general principle of good faith and fair dealing either (except for a reference in Article 7 on the interpretation of the CISG). The concern underlying the preference of the drafters of the CISG was to not exclude the common law perspective from uniform law.[1341]

It is true that it is unnecessary to draft a rule on the principle of good faith as it applies to the rules of interpretation in the texts of uniform law which include detailed provisions on the issue and which refer to the principle of good faith and fair dealing as a general rule. Nevertheless, uniform law texts of the EU place this principle among the elements of interpretation to be taken into account.[1342]

[E] (Non)interpretation Rules

Another issue of debate is whether or not the rules that restrict the interpretation of contracts can be considered as principles. The views on this issue are motivated by the concern for legal security on one side and the rules of logic on the other.

A judge can only reach the conclusion that a contractual clause is "clear" through the interpretation process. Therefore, rules that prohibit the interpretation of "clear" contract clauses appear to be logically inconsistent. Moreover, they bear the risk of leading to different meanings than the ones commonly intended by the parties. For this reason, such restrictive rules as the *in claris non fit interpretatio* rule, the *doctrine de clauses claires et précises* in its strict sense, and the plain meaning rule are not generally recognized in comparative and uniform law.

Nevertheless, some authors propose moderate interpretations of these restrictive rules in various jurisdictions, converting them into reasonable rules of interpretation. For instance, although the *in claris non fit interpretatio* rule has been generally adopted

1340. *See*, section §3.02[B][6][d] Article 1366 of the CC. It., *supra*.
1341. Section §4.02[E] Rules of Interpretation not Covered by the CISG.
1342. *See*, sections §4.04[A][2][b] Article 5:102 of the PECL; §4.04[B][2][b] Article II—8:102 of the DCFR; §4.04[C][2][b] Article 59 of the CESL, *supra*.

in Italian case law and literature, it is not considered to be a rule that prohibits the interpretation of a contractual clause whose meaning is clear. According to an opinion, this rule requires the termination of the interpretation process once a meaning has been obtained through the application of the rules of interpretation in their hierarchical order. This rule is a consequence of the hierarchy between the rules of interpretation, and it is by virtue of this rule that when a judge determines the common intent of the parties through subjective interpretation, he can no longer have recourse to objective interpretation.[1343]

Likewise, the French doctrine of *clauses claires et précises* does not function as a rule that prohibits the interpretation of clear contractual clauses, as the name suggests. On the contrary, according to this doctrine, if a court inaccurately characterizes a contractual clause as "clear and precise," it is grounds for review on appeal. Therefore, this doctrine functions as a means of making decisions relating to the interpretation of contracts reviewable on appeal, although interpretation is considered a question of fact in principle.[1344]

In common law jurisdictions, the rules restricting the interpretation of contracts are found among the procedural rules of evidentiary law. Restrictive rules such as the parol evidence rule, the four corners rule, and the plain meaning rule have been challenged, and there is a question as to whether these could still be considered to be "rules."[1345]

According to a moderate interpretation of the parol evidence rule in English law, this rule requires a written contract, if the parties have one, to be used as the primary tool of interpretation for the determination of the intent of the parties.[1346]

The rules that restrict the interpretation of contracts are generally not recognized in comparative and uniform law. Moderate approaches to these rules have developed in individual legal systems, deviating from their traditional meanings. These rules are not even mentioned in uniform law, except for criticisms directed at them in scholarly literature.

[F] Scope of Application of the *Contra Proferentem* or *Contra Stipulatorem* Rule

This principle directs the interpretation of an ambiguous clause against the party that wrote or supplied it. Although this principle emerged in Roman law in relation to *stipulatio* transactions and was originally named *contra stipulatorem*, it is referred to as the *contra proferentem* rule, especially in uniform law, the name given to it by Bartolus

1343. Sacco, *supra* n. 7, at 257; *see*, section §3.02[B][2] The Discussion on the *In Claris Non Fit Interpretatio* Rule, *supra*.
1344. *See*, section §3.02[A][4][e] Article 1192 of the CC. Fr., *supra*.
1345. *See*, sections §3.04[A][3] The Parol Evidence Rule and Merger Clauses (English Law); §3.04[B][4][a] (Non)interpretation Rules: The Parol Evidence Rule, the Plain Meaning Rule, and the Four Corners Rule, *supra*.
1346. Calnan, *supra* n. 737, at 27.

de Saxoferrato in the fourteenth century.[1347] Bartolus also suggested the *contra creditorem* rule, which directs interpretation against the creditor. This rule has not been adopted as a principle (except for the new Article 1190 of the CC. Fr.), because it is based on erroneous presumptions that there is a clear distinction between the creditor and the debtor and that the debtor is the weaker party.

Nevertheless, some jurisdictions set certain limitations on the *contra stipulatorem* rule. Article 1370 of the CC. It. provides that this rule applies only to standard conditions of a contract.[1348] Likewise, Article 23 of the TBK only addresses the issue with regard to standard conditions.[1349] Romano-Germanic law systems tend to interpret this rule narrowly.[1350]

However, the general tendency in comparative and uniform law has been to recognize the *contra stipulatorem* or *contra proferentem* rule as a general principle which is based on the principle of good faith and fair dealing and which applies to all types of contracts.[1351] This approach is more accurate, considering the Roman basis of this rule and its connection to the principle of good faith and fair dealing. The reason for the tendency for a narrow interpretation of this rule in some jurisdictions must be sought in the *contra creditorem* principle suggested by Bartolus in the Middle Ages, not in the *contra stipulatorem* rule of Roman law.[1352]

There is a legitimate concern for the protection of consumers or weaker parties that accept nonnegotiable conditions supplied by the other party, and as a result, consumer protection regulations commonly include rules for this purpose. These are special rules of consumer protection, and they cannot limit a well-established, general principle of Roman law, which also constitutes the basis of these special rules.

§5.02 SEARCH FOR BALANCE BETWEEN OBJECTIVE AND SUBJECTIVE APPROACHES AND THE PENDULUM METHOD

[A] Generally

The debate regarding the interpretation of contracts has not been limited to the issues mentioned above. On the contrary, these debates focus on such important questions as whether to base interpretation on the subjective intent of the parties or the objective meaning of the terms, whether or not there is a hierarchy between the rules of

1347. *See*, section §2.01[B][2][b] The Emergence of Principles of Objective Interpretation in the Classical Period, *supra*.
1348. *See*, section §3.02[B][6][h] Article 1370 of the CC. It., *supra*.
1349. *See*, section §3.03[C][2][e] Article 23 of the TBK and the *Contra Stipulatorem* Rule (Turkish Law), *supra*.
1350. *See*, sections §3.03[A][3][c] § 157 of the BGB; §3.03[B][5] Principles of Interpretation Developed Through Case Law; §3.03[C][2][e] Article 23 of the TBK and the *Contra Stipulatorem* Rule, *supra*.
1351. *See*, sections §4.03[B][6] Article 4.6 of the UPICC; §4.04[A][2][c] Article 5:103 of the PECL; §4.04[B][2][c] Article II—8:103 of the DCFR; §4.04[C][2][h] Article 65 of the CESL; §4.05[B][4] Trans-Lex Principle No. IV.5.4, *supra*.
1352. *See*, section §2.01[B][2][b], The Emergence of Principles of Objective Interpretation in the Classical Period, *supra*.

interpretation, how to avoid the excessive consequences of purely subjective or purely objective interpretation, where to begin interpretation, and which methods to apply. These questions and their answers are interconnected. For this reason, it is more appropriate to provide observations relating to these discussions in their entirety.

Most domestic legislation and uniform law texts acknowledge a hierarchy and an order of priority between the rules of contractual interpretation. The Latin,[1353] Swiss,[1354] Turkish,[1355] and certain texts of the U.S. legal systems[1356] include rules which provide that if the intent of the parties can be determined, it will prevail over the objective meaning of a contract or a term. Objective interpretation only applies when the meaning of a contract or a term cannot be ascertained through subjective interpretation.

In legislation where provisions on the interpretation of contracts are limited to one general rule, as in the Swiss and Turkish codes of obligations, legislators only included the priority of the common intent of the parties with regard to the text of the contract. German legislators, however, included a subjective (§ 133 of the BGB) and an objective (§ 157 of the BGB) rule of interpretation in the BGB, which are of equal weight.[1357] This approach reflects the search for a balance between objective and subjective methods of interpretation in German law.

Nevertheless, the priority of subjective interpretation and the common intent of the parties over the objective method is not absolute. In jurisdictions where the subjective interpretation prevails, case law and literature search for a balance by objectivizing the interpretation and vice versa in jurisdictions where objective interpretation is more prevalent. As a result, a search for balance between the subjective and objective approaches characterizes the general tendency of today's legal systems regarding the interpretation of contracts.

In most legal systems, subjective interpretation gets objectivized through the emphasis put on literal interpretation. In uniform law and individual legal systems, regardless of whether the subjective or objective approach prevails, it is generally acknowledged that the process of interpretation must begin with an examination of the wording of the contract.

The primary tools that are used for objectivizing the subjective approach are the emphasis put on the "common" intent of the parties in Italian law[1358] and the principle of trust in Romano-Germanic legal systems.[1359] The principles of objective interpretation which are not concerned with the intent of the parties, especially the principles of

1353. *See*, sections §3.02[A][4][a] Article 1188 (Former Article 1156) of the CC. Fr.; §3.02[B][6][a] Article 1362 of the CC. It., *supra*.
1354. *See*, section §3.03[B][4] Article 18/1 of the OR, *supra*.
1355. *See*, section §3.03[C][2][a] Article 19(1) of the TBK, *supra*.
1356. *See*, section §3.04[B][3] Subjectivization of the Interpretation of Contracts: The UCC and the Restatement (Second) of Contracts, *supra*.
1357. *See*, section §3.03[A][3][a] Relationship Between the Two Paragraphs, *supra*.
1358. *See*, section §3.02[B][4] Views Pertaining to the Objectivity of the Subjective Interpretation, *supra*.
1359. *See*, sections §3.03[A][3][c] § 157 of the BGB (German Law); §3.03[B][1] Generally (Swiss Law); §3.03[C][2][b] The Will Theory, the Theory of Declaration, and the Trust Theory (Turkish Law), *supra*.

contra stipulatorem, systematic interpretation, *ut res magis valeat quam pereat*, *favor negotii*, and usages are other tools that serve to balance the subjective approach.

Likewise, objective interpretation gets further subjectivized by taking into account certain matters and conditions that affect the contract, such as the time and place of the conclusion of the contract, prior statements, prior and subsequent conduct of the parties, their purpose, the balance of interests between them, and their cultural background.

As regards uniform law, even though uniform law texts unanimously acknowledge the priority of subjective interpretation, it is generally agreed in the literature that the application of subjective interpretation is exceptional because of the difficulty in determining the intent of the parties, and therefore objective interpretation is the rule and not the exception.[1360] In objective interpretation, the understanding of a "reasonable person" is taken as a basis. However, this criterion is usually subjectivized as a reasonable person "of the same kind as and in the same circumstances with the other party."[1361]

Taking all these into account, it is possible to observe that the process of the interpretation of statements and contracts in comparative and uniform law functions in four phases.

[B] The Pendulum Method: Four Phases of the Interpretation

[1] First Objective Phase

The first objective phase includes the rules that only relate to the specific wording of the contract or the statements of the parties.

Individual legal systems agree that the wording of a statement or contract is the starting point of interpretation, regardless of whether the subjective or objective approach prevails. The wording prevails over any other tool of interpretation.[1362]

This is also true for legal systems and uniform law texts where the basic principle of interpretation is the supremacy of the common intent of the parties over the wording. A judge who is in a position to interpret a contract first sees the text of the contract. The meaning understood at first sight is also an outcome of a judge's interpretation of the text. The meaning given to the wording of the statements or contract is an objective meaning, because it is independent from the intent of the

1360. *See*, sections §4.02[D][1] Article 8(1) of the CISG—Subjective Interpretation; §4.03[B][1] Article 4.1 of the UPICC, *supra*.

1361. *See*, sections §4.02[D][2] Article 8(2) of the CISG—Objective Interpretation; §4.03[B][1] Article 4.1 of the UPICC; §4.03[B][2] Article 4.2 of the UPICC; §4.04[A][2][a] Article 5:101 of the PECL; §4.04[C][2][a] Article 58 of the CESL, *supra*.

1362. *See*, sections §3.02[B][6][a] Article 1362 of the CC. It. (Italian Law); §3.03[A][2] Types or Methods of Interpretation in German Law (German Law); §3.03[B][4][a] Subjective Interpretation (Swiss Law); §3.03[C][2][c] Principles of Literal Interpretation (Turkish Law); §3.04[A][3] The Parol Evidence Rule and Merger Clauses (English Law), *supra*.

parties, even if they have a common intent. For this reason, the process of interpretation also begins with an objective phase in jurisdictions that adopt the priority of the common intent of the parties as the most basic principle of interpretation.

The interpretation conducted by a judge for giving a meaning to a statement or a contract is a literal interpretation. The rules and tools of literal interpretation are considerably developed, even in legal systems where subjective interpretation prevails.[1363] One of the rules of the literal interpretation is that the words are to be understood in their natural sense. The exception to this rule is that technical terms are to be explained according to their technical use. These principles were first stated by Hugo Grotius[1364] and have been commonly adopted in most jurisdictions.[1365]

Another principle of the first phase of interpretation is the one according to which a meaning not intended by the parties cannot be applied to a contract, expressed in former Article 1163 of the CC. Fr and Article 1364 of the CC. It. Other rules of the first phase include more special rules of literal interpretation, such as the prohibition on interpreting illustrative examples in a contract in a sense to limit the scope thereof, stated in former Article 1164 of the CC. Fr and Article 1365 of the CC. It.; the rule providing that general expressions cannot be interpreted in a way to include objects that the parties did not intend, expressed in Article 1364 of the CC. It.; and other special rules of literal interpretation mentioned by Pothier.[1366] These rules only relate to the text of a contract and not to any other tool of interpretation and therefore belong to the first objective phase of interpretation.

Common law jurisdictions have demonstrated more interest in literal interpretation than most continental jurisdictions because of the dominance of the objective approach to interpretation in the common law tradition and went so far as to produce some restrictive literal rules of interpretation.[1367] The four corners rule, which provides that the meaning obtained through interpretation must comply with the text of the contract, and the parol evidence rule, which prohibits the use of extrinsic evidence in the interpretation of a contract, are restrictive literal interpretation rules that relate only to the wording of a contract.[1368]

1363. *See*, section §3.03[B][4][b] Objective Interpretation, *supra*.

1364. *See*, section §2.02 Humanist and Naturalist Schools of Law and the Divergence of Approaches among Continental Legal Systems, *supra*.

1365. *See*, sections §3.03[A][2] Types or Methods of Interpretation in German Law (German Law); §3.03[B][4][a] Subjective Interpretation (Swiss Law); §3.03[C][2][c] Principles of Literal Interpretation (Turkish Law); §3.04[A][5] Lord Hoffman's Five Principles of the Interpretation of Contracts (English Law); §3.04[B][2] The Objective Approach and The Restatement (First) of Contracts; §3.04[B][3] Subjectivization of the Interpretation of Contracts: The UCC and the Restatement (Second) of Contracts (US Law), *supra*.

1366. Pothier, *supra* n. 37; *see*, section §2.02 Humanist and Naturalist Schools of Law and the Divergence of Approaches among Continental Legal Systems, *supra*.

1367. *See*, section §3.04[A][2] Objective Approach, *supra*.

1368. *See*, section §3.04[B][4][a] (Non)interpretation Rules: The Parol Evidence Rule, the Plain Meaning Rule, and the Four Corners Rule, *supra*.

[2] First Subjective Phase

The task of a judge in the first objective phase of interpretation is to adhere a meaning to the wording of a contract, but the next task is to examine the true intent of the parties that underlies that wording. This is the first subjective phase. The meaning of a term or a contract does not need to be ambiguous for a judge to perform this task. Even if the wording clearly has an apparent meaning, the true intention of the parties may differ from that meaning.

In the first subjective phase, or the second phase of interpretation, the most basic rule is the superiority of the common intent of the parties over the wording of a contract, which is recognized as the most basic principle in most continental jurisdictions[1369] and uniform law texts.[1370] This principle was first identified by Papinianus in *Dig.* 50, 16, 219 and Ulpianus in *Dig.* 2, 1, 15.[1371] The first subjective phase begins with the application of the rules of subjective interpretation that emanate from this most basic principle. One of these rules is the prohibition on purely literal interpretations, which is recognized by most continental jurisdictions, including the French, Italian, German, and Swiss.[1372]

Another rule of this phase is the principle of *falsa demonstratio non nocet* which provides that a false statement or description does not vitiate a contract if the common intent of the parties can be established. In most continental jurisdictions[1373] and uniform law texts,[1374] this principle is recognized as a consequence of the most basic rule of subjective interpretation. In common law, the doctrine of rectification for common mistake replaces the principle of *falsa demonstratio non nocet* and is the functional equivalent thereof.[1375]

The purpose of the first subjective phase is the determination of the true common intent of the parties pursuant to the abovementioned principles. If the true common intent of the parties can be established, it will prevail over the words they used.

1369. *See*, sections §3.02[A][4][a] Article 1188 (Former Article 1156) of the CC. Fr. (French Law); §3.02[B][6][a] Article 1362 of the CC. It. (Italian Law); §3.03[B][4] Article 18/1 of the OR (Swiss Law); §3.03[C][2][a] Article 19(1) of the TBK (Turkish Law), *supra*.
1370. *See*, sections §4.02[D][1] Article 8(1) of the CISG—Subjective Interpretation; §4.03[B][1] Article 4.1 of the UPICC; §4.03[B][2] Article 4.2 of the UPICC; §4.04[A][2][a] Article 5:101 of the PECL; §4.04[B][2][a] Article II—8:101 of the DCFR; §4.04[C][2][a] Article 58 of the CESL; §4.05[B][1] Trans-Lex Principle No. IV.5.1, *supra*.
1371. *See*, section §2.01[B][2][a], The Emergence of Principles of Subjective Interpretation in the Classical Period, *supra*.
1372. *See*, sections §3.02[A][4][a] Article 1188 (Former Article 1156) of the CC. Fr.; §3.02[B][6][a] Article 1362 of the CC. It.; §3.03[A][3][b] § 133 of the BGB; §3.03[B][5] Principles of Interpretation Developed Through Case Law, *supra*.
1373. *See*, sections §3.02[A][4][a] Article 1188 (Former Article 1156) of the CC. Fr. (French Law); §3.02[B][6][a] Article 1362 of the CC. It. (Italian Law); §3.03[A][3][b] § 133 of the BGB (German Law); §3.03[B][4] Article 18/1 of the OR (Swiss Law); §3.03[C][2][a] Article 19(1) of the TBK (Turkish Law), *supra*.
1374. *See*, sections §4.02[D][1] Article 8(1) of the CISG—Subjective Interpretation; §4.03[B][1] Article 4.1 of the UPICC; §4.04[A][2][a] Article 5:101 of the PECL; §4.04[B][2][a] Article II—8:101 of the DCFR; §4.04[C][2][a] Article 58 of the CESL; §4.05[B][5] Trans-Lex Principle No. IV.5.5, *supra*.
1375. *See*, section §3.04[A][2] Objective Approach, *supra*.

However, some principles of objective interpretation are so important and fundamental that they also apply in this phase. These principles will be treated under the second objective phase.

If it becomes evident that the parties did not have a common intent and agreed upon the same words with different intents, the process of interpretation will proceed to the second objective phase.

[3] Second Objective Phase

The third, or second objective phase of interpretation is necessary when the true common intent of the parties cannot be ascertained. This phase makes use of the rules relating to the determination of what a reasonable third person would understand from a contract or its terms.

Interpretation according to the principle of good faith and fair dealing, first stated by Donellus,[1376] is the primary purpose of this phase. The second objective phase of interpretation is reflected in Romano-Germanic legal systems as the principle of trust, which is based on the principle of good faith and fair dealing.[1377] In Italian law, this phase is expressed with the emphasis placed on the "common" intent of the parties.[1378] This phase is represented in common law jurisdictions by their general objective approach to interpretation based on the understanding of a reasonable third person.[1379] In uniform law texts, the second objective phase of interpretation is expressed more clearly, as the ascertainment of the meaning that a reasonable person would give to a contract or to its terms, when the determination of the intent of the parties is not possible.[1380]

Some principles of objective interpretation, which are independent from the intent of the parties, have an important role in the second objective phase of interpretation. These principles must also apply to the meaning obtained in the first subjective phase. One of these principles is the principle of systematic interpretation, first expressed by Celsus in *Dig.* 1, 3, 24, according to which every expression in a contract must be interpreted in light of the whole transaction.[1381] This principle is

1376. *See*, section §2.02 Humanist and Naturalist Schools of Law and the Divergence of Approaches among Continental Legal Systems, *supra*.
1377. *See*, sections §3.03[A][3][c] § 157 of the BGB (German Law); §3.03[B][1] Generally (Swiss Law); §3.03[C][2][b] The Will Theory, the Theory of Declaration, and the Trust Theory (Turkish Law), *supra*.
1378. *See*, section §3.02[B][4] Views Pertaining to the Objectivity of the Subjective Interpretation, *supra*.
1379. *See*, section §3.04[A][2] Objective Approach, *supra*.
1380. *See*, sections §4.02[D][2] Article 8(2) of the CISG—Objective Interpretation; §4.03[B][1] Article 4.1 of the UPICC; §4.03[B][2] Article 4.2 of the UPICC; §4.04[A][2][a] Article 5:101 of the PECL; §4.04[C][2][a] Article 58 of the CESL; *supra*.
1381. *See*, section §2.01[B][2][b], The Emergence of Principles of Objective Interpretation in the Classical Period, *supra*.

recognized in both continental and common law jurisdictions, along with all uniform law texts.[1382]

Another principle unanimously recognized in comparative and uniform law is the principle of *magis valeat quam pereat*, as expressed by Iulianus in *Dig.* 34, 5, 12 (13),[1383] which provides that an interpretation in favor of the validity of a term or a contract prevails over the one that makes the contract or a term invalid or meaningless.[1384]

The principle of *contra stipulatorem* has also been generally adopted in comparative law and uniform law. This principle has been referred to as *contra proferentem* since the Middle Ages, and it provides for the interpretation of ambiguous expressions in a contract against the party who supplies them. Celsus stated this principle in *Dig.* 34, 5, 26, and Ulpianus confirmed it in *Dig.* 45, 1, 38, 18.[1385] Although this principle has been unanimously recognized, its scope of application may differ from one jurisdiction to another as explained above.

Two other principles of the second objective phase of interpretation provide for the interpretation of ambiguous terms according to usages and to the nature of the contract. The former was expressed by Ulpianus in *Dig.* 50, 17, 34, and the latter by Iulianus in *Dig.* 50, 17, 67.[1386]

[4] Second Subjective Phase

Even though there is a logical order of priority between the phases of interpretation, they cannot be separated with sharp lines. The second objective phase provides for determination of what a reasonable third person would understand, through the application of the rules of objective interpretation, which are unrelated to the intent of the parties. However, the interpretation process does not end there. Interpretation based on an objective meaning obtained in the second objective phase must be completed through examination of the subjective elements that influenced the writing of a contract or a statement.

1382. *See*, sections §3.02[A][4][b] Article 1189 (Former Article 1161) of the CC. Fr. (French Law); §3.02[B][6][b] Article 1363 of the CC. It. (Italian Law); §3.03[A][2] Types or Methods of Interpretation in German Law (German Law); §3.03[B][4][a] Subjective Interpretation (Swiss Law); §3.03[C][2][f] Principles of Interpretation Developed Through Case Law or Recognized in the Literature (Turkish Law); §3.04[A][5] Lord Hoffman's Five Principles of the Interpretation of Contracts (English Law); §3.04[B][4][b] Other Rules of Interpretation Recognized in the Literature (US Law) *supra*.

1383. *See*, section §2.01[B][2][b] The Emergence of Principles of Objective Interpretation in the Classical Period, *supra*.

1384. *See*, sections §3.02[A][4][d] Article 1191 (Former Article 1157) of the CC. Fr. (French Law); §3.02[B][6][e] Article 1367 of the CC. It. (Italian Law); §3.03[A][3][c] § 157 of the BGB (German Law); §3.03[B][5] Principles of Interpretation Developed Through Case Law (Swiss Law); §3.03[C][2][f] Principles of Interpretation Developed Through Case Law or Recognized in the Literature (Turkish Law); §3.04[A][4] Other Principles of Interpretation (English Law); §3.04[B][4][b] Other Rules of Interpretation Recognized in the Literature (US Law), *supra*.

1385. *See*, section §2.01[B][2][b], The Emergence of Principles of Objective Interpretation in the Classical Period, *supra*.

1386. *Ibid*.

Therefore, the fourth phase of interpretation encompasses the evaluation of the relevance of subjective elements or circumstances, of which the parties were or should have been aware, to the meaning that a reasonable third person would understand from a term or a contract. In this phase, the meaning based on the understanding of a reasonable third person obtained in the third phase is developed into a meaning based on the understanding of a reasonable person in the same circumstances as the parties. This phase is a subjective phase because it involves ascertainment of a meaning that was or should have been understood by the parties to a term or a contract based upon an understanding of the circumstances that existed.

In Romano-Germanic legal systems, the principle of trust, which is based on the principle of good faith and fair dealing, requires courts to consider the circumstances in which the parties found themselves when making the term or contract.[1387] In accordance with this requirement, the principle of systematic interpretation is also conceived broadly so as to include not only the consideration of the other terms in a contract but also of all the circumstances of the parties, which existed at the time of the conclusion of a contract.

Article 1362(2) of the CC. It. in Italian law,[1388] § 1-303(b) and (d) of the UCC, and § 202(5) of the Restatement (Second) of Contracts in U.S. law[1389] reflect the second subjective phase of interpretation by directing that course of dealing and course of performance are matters that should be taken into consideration.

As regards uniform law, almost all the codifications examined above reflect the second subjective phase by listing circumstances to be taken into consideration immediately following the provisions on the general rules of subjective and objective interpretation.[1390] These circumstances include subjective elements, such as preliminary negotiations between the parties, practices established between them, and their conduct subsequent to the conclusion of the contract.

The circumstances to be taken into consideration in the interpretation of a contract or a term include, in particular, the time and place of the conclusion of a contract, the cultural and legal background of the parties, their previous agreements, and their statements and conduct before and after the conclusion of the contract. The principle of *protestatio facto contraria non valet* also belongs to the second subjective phase, which was particularly developed in German law and provides that in the event of a discrepancy between a contract and the conduct of the parties in their performance, the latter prevails.[1391]

1387. *See*, sections §3.03[A][3][c] § 157 of the BGB (German Law); §3.03[B][1] Generally (Swiss Law); §3.03[C][2][b] The Will Theory, the Theory of Declaration, and the Trust Theory (Turkish Law), *supra*.
1388. *See*, section §3.02[B][6][a] Article 1362 of the CC. It., *supra*.
1389. *See*, section §3.04[B][3] Subjectivization of the Interpretation of Contracts: The UCC and the Restatement (Second) of Contracts, *supra*.
1390. *See*, sections §4.02[D][3] Article 8(3) of the CISG—Relevant Circumstances of the Case; §4.03[B][3] Article 4.3 of the UPICC; §4.04[A][2][b] Article 5:102 of the PECL; §4.04[B][2][b] Article II—8:102 of the DCFR; §4.04[C][2][b] Article 59 of the CESL; §4.05[B][1] Trans-Lex Principle No. IV.5.1, *supra*.
1391. *See*, section §3.03[A][3][b] § 133 of the BGB, *supra*.

The most controversial tool of interpretation is the consideration of previous statements and agreements between the parties. In most jurisdictions, these are generally accepted as tools of interpretation that courts can take into consideration. The parol evidence rule, which prohibits the admission of this kind of evidence in the interpretation of a contract, is not generally recognized in comparative and uniform law.[1392] This rule, in its strictest traditional meaning, has almost been abandoned, even in common law jurisdictions.[1393]

Nevertheless, parties may agree to a merger clause in their contract stating that their previous statements and agreements are not effective and that their entire contractual agreement consists of one single document. However, comparative and uniform law generally recognize that such clauses cannot prevent the prior statements and agreements of the parties from being used in the interpretation of their contract.[1394]

[C] Final Words

Although the formulation, conception, and application of the rules relating to the interpretation of contracts have differed across time and jurisdictions, it is possible to observe that the rules that emerged in the classical period of Roman law continue to play a significant role in this field. These rules, be they codified or not, are expressed in comparative and uniform law as established principles of law. The contribution of authors to these principles from the Middle Ages to modern times as expressed in modern codifications, common law, and uniform law has remained relatively limited.

Throughout legal history, at times the subjective approach has prevailed and at times the objective approach has prevailed, but there has always been a search for balance between the two. This search for balance also characterizes the approach of today's individual legal systems and uniform law.

Today, this balance is expressed through a systematic method for the interpretation of contracts. This method swings back and forth between objective and subjective interpretation like a pendulum. It starts with the objective interpretation of a text or a statement and swings to subjective interpretation based on the examination of the intent of the parties. If the latter cannot be determined, the pendulum swings back to the application of certain objective rules of interpretation for the determination of an objective meaning that would be understood by a reasonable third party. Finally, the swing of the pendulum ends with the interpretation of that objective meaning through the lens of the subjective conditions and circumstances in which the parties found themselves at the conclusion of an agreement, and in some cases, preceding or following the conclusion of a contract.

1392. *See*, sections §4.02[F] Parol Evidence Rule, Merger Clauses, and Article 8(3) of the CISG; §4.03[B][3] Article 4.3 of the UPICC, *supra*.

1393. *See*, section §3.04[A][3] The Parol Evidence Rule and Merger Clauses; §3.04[B][4][a][i] The Parol Evidence Rule, *supra*.

1394. *See*, sections §3.04[A][3] The Parol Evidence Rule and Merger Clauses; §4.02[F] Parol Evidence Rule, Merger Clauses, and Article 8(3) of the CISG; §4.03[B][3] Article 4.3 of the UPICC; §4.05[B][7] Trans-Lex Principle No. IV.5.7, *infra*.

Bibliography

Aepli, Viktor, *Art. 18 OR*, in Peter Gauch, Viktor Aepli, Hubert Stöckli, *Präjudizienbuch OR—Die Rechtsprechung des Bundesgerichts*, 8th ed., Schulthess, Zurich, 2012.

Akyol, Şener, *Sözleşmenin Yorumu*, Vedat, Istanbul, 2010.

Alpa, Guido, *Istituzioni di Diritto Privato*, UTET, Torino, 2002.

Antalya, Gökhan, *Borçlar Hukuku Genel Hükümler*, Vol. 1, Legal, Istanbul, 2015.

Appelhoff, Bernhard, *Die Revisibilität der Auslegung von typischen Verträgen nach der Rechtsprechung*, PhD Thesis, University of Cologne, 1935.

Armellini, Nicola, *Dizionario di Giurisprudenza per uso del Regno delle due Sicilie*, Vol. 2, Napoli, 1822.

Astone, Francesco, *Art. 1363, Dell'interpretazione del Contratto*, in Emanuela Navarretta, Andrea Orestano (eds.), *Commentario al Codice Civile*, Vol. 2, *Contratti in Generale*, UTET Giuridica, Torino, 452, 2011.

Astone, Francesco, *Art. 1364, Dell'interpretazione del Contratto*, in Emanuela Navarretta, Andrea Orestano (eds.), *Commentario al Codice Civile*, Vol. 2, *Contratti in Generale*, UTET Giuridica, Torino, 467, 2011.

Atiyah, Patrick S., Smith, *Stephen A., Atiyah's Introduction to the Law of Contract*, 6th ed., Clarendon Press, Oxford-New York, 2005.

Avenarius, Martin, *Benignior Interpretatio: Origin and Transformaton of a Rule of Construction in the Law of Succession*, 6 Roman Legal Tradition 1, 2010.

Bachiashvili, Vakhtang, *Contract Interpretations According to the Principles of European Contract Law and Expediency of Implementation of These Principles in Georgian Legislation*, Ivane Javakhishvili Tbilisi State University Faculty of Law Journal of Law, 1, 2013.

von Bar, Christian, Clive, Eric, Schulte-Nölke, Hans, Beale, Hugh, Herre, Johnny, Huet, Jérôme, Storme, Matthias, Swann, Stephen, Varul, Paul, Veneziano, Anna, Zoll, Fryderyk (eds.), *Draft Common Frame of Reference (DCFR) Prepared by the Study Group on a European Civil Code and the Research Group on EC Private Law (Acquis Group) Based in Part on a Revised Version of the Principles of European Contract Law*, Sellier European Law Publishers, Munich, 2009.

Basedow, Jürgen, *Germany*, in M.J. Bonell (ed.), *A New Approach to International Commercial Contracts—The UNIDROIT Principles of International Commercial Contracts*, Kluwer Law International, The Hague-London-Boston, 1999.

Baumann, Antje, *Regeln der Auslegung internationaler Handelsgeschäfte, Eine vergleichende Untersuchung der UNIDROIT Principles, der Principles of European Contract Law, des Uniform Commercial Code und des deutschen Rechts*, V&R Unipress, Osnabrück, 2004.

Beltramo, Mario, Longo, Giovanni E., Merryman, John Henry, *The Italian Civil Code*, Oceana, New York, 1969.

Beltrani, Sergio, *Istituzioni di Diritto Romano*, 4th ed., Simone, Napoli, 2003.

Bénabent, Alain, *Droit des Obligations*, 15th ed., LGDJ, Paris, 2016.

Bianca, C. Massimo, *L'interpretazione*, in *Diritto Civile, Vol. 3, Il Contratto*, 2nd ed., Giuffrè Editore, Milan, 2000.

Bonell, Michael Joachim, *The UNIDROIT Initiative for the Progressive Codification of International Trade Law*, 27 International and Comparative Law Quarterly 413, 1978.

Bonell, Michael Joachim, *An International Restatement of Contract Law—The UNIDROIT Principles of International Commercial Contracts*, Transnational Juris Publications Inc., Irvington, New York, 1994.

Bonell, Michael Joachim, *The UNIDROIT Principles of International Commercial Contracts and the Principles of European Contract Law—Similar Rules for the Same Purposes*, 26 Uniform Law Review 229, 1996.

Bonell, Michael Joachim, *The UNIDROIT Principles and CISG—Sources of Inspiration for English Courts?*, 11 Uniform Law Review 305, 2006.

Brödermann, Eckart J., *UNIDROIT Principles of International Commercial Contracts—An Article-by-Article Commentary*, Nomos, Munich, 2018.

Busche, Jan *§ 133*, in Franz Jürgen Säcker, Rolan Rixecker (eds.), *Münchener Kommentar zum Bürgerlichen Gesetzbuch*, Band 1 Allgemeiner Teil §§ 1-240, ProstG, AGG, 7th ed., Verlag C.H. Beck, Berlin, 2015.

Busche, Jan *§ 157*, in Franz Jürgen Säcker, Rolan Rixecker (eds.), *Münchener Kommentar zum Bürgerlichen Gesetzbuch*, Band 1 Allgemeiner Teil §§ 1-240, ProstG, AGG, 7th ed., Verlag C.H. Beck, Berlin, 2015.

Calnan, Richard, *Principles of Contractual Interpretation*, 2nd ed., Oxford University Press, Croydon, 2017.

Canaris, Claus-Wilhem, Grigoleit, Hans Christoph, *Interpretation of Contracts*, Hartkamp et al. (eds.), *Towards a European Civil Code*, Kluwer Law International, Nijmegen, 2004.

Capobianco, Ernesto, *La determinazione del regolamento—L'interpretazione*, in Giuseppe Vettori, Vincenzo Roppo (eds.), *Trattato del Contratto*, Vol. 2—*Regolamento*, Giuffrè Editore, Milan, 2006.

Chitty, Joseph, Beale, Hugh (eds.), *Chitty on Contracts*, Vol. 1—*General Principles*, 32nd ed., Sweet & Maxwell, London, 2015.

Corbin, Arthur L., *A Comprehensive Treatise on the Rules of Contract Law*, Vol. 3, West Publishing Co., New York, 1960.

Damar, Ceren, *Sözleşmenin Yorumu*, Çankaya Üniversitesi Hukuk Fakültesi Dergisi, C. 1 S. 2, 89, 2016.

Djordjevic, Milena *Article 4*, in Stefan Kröll, Loukas Mistelis, Pilar Perales Viscasillas (eds.), *United Nations Convention on Contracts for the International Sale of Goods (CISG) Commentary*, C.H. Beck/Hart/Nomos, Munich, 62, 2011.

Domat, Jean, *Les lois civiles dans leur ordre naturel*, Vol. 1, Jean Baptiste Coignard, Paris, 1689.

Domat, Jean, *The Civil Law in Its Natural Order*, Vol. 1, Charles C. Little and James Brown, Boston, 1850.

Donellus, Hugo, *Commentarii de iure civili*, Brussels, 1589.

de Douai, Philippe Antoine Merlin, *Répertoire universel et Raisonné de jurisprudence*, 3rd ed., Vol. 3, Garnery, Paris, 1807.

Duxbury, Neil, *Elements of Legislation*, Cambridge University Press, New York, 2013.

Eren, Fikret, *Borçlar Hukuku Genel Hükümler*, 23rd ed., Yetkin, Ankara, 2018.

Fagan, James, *The Legal Phoenix: The Plain Meaning Rule Is Dead, Long Live the Rule*, 29(2) California Western Law Review, 1993.

Farnsworth, E. Allan, *Article 8*, in *Bianca-Bonell Commentary on the International Sales Law*, Giuffrè, Milan, 1987.

Farnsworth, E. Allan, F. Young~~ Jr.,~~ William~~, Sanger, Carol, Cohen, Neil B., Brooks, Richard,~~ *Contracts, Cases, and Materials*~~,~~ 8th ed., Foundation Press—Thomson West, New York, 2013.

Ferrari, Franco, *Article 8*, in Franco Ferrari, Harry Flechtner, Ronald A. Brand (eds.), *The Draft UNCITRAL Digest and Beyond: Cases, Analysis and Unresolved Issues in the U.N. Sales Convention*, Sellier European Law Publishers, Munich, 172, 2004.

Ferreri, S., *Interpretation*, in Luisa Antoniolli, Anna Veneziano (eds.), *Principles of European Contract Law and Italian Law*, Kluwer Law International, The Hague, 251, 2005.

Fontaine, Marcel, de Ly, Filip, *Droit des contrats internationaux—Analyse et rédaction de clauses*, 2nd ed., Bruylant-FEC, Paris-Brussels, 2003.

Furmston, Michael, *United Kingdom*, in Michael Joachim Bonell (ed.), *A New Approach to International Commercial Contracts—The UNIDROIT Principles of International Commercial Contracts*, Kluwer Law International, The Hague-London-Boston, 384, 1999.

Furmston, Michael, Cheshire, *Fifoot & Furmston's Law of Contract*, 17th ed., Oxford University Press, Oxford, 2017.

Gadamer, Hans-Georg, *Classical and Philosophical Hermeneutics*, 23(1) Theory, Culture and Society 29-56, 2006.

Gandolfi, Giuseppe, *Lezioni sull'interpretazione dei negozi giuridici*, La Goliardica, Milan, 1966.

Gauch, Peter, Aepli, Viktor, Casanova, Hugo, *Schweizerisches Obligationenrecht Allgemeiner Teil (Art. 1-183), Rechtsprechung des Bundesgerichts*, 4th ed., Schulthess, Zurich, 1996.

Gauch, Peter, Schluep, Walter R., *Schweizerisches Obligationenrecht Allgemeiner Teil*, 9th ed., Schulthess, Zurich, 2008.

Gentili, Aurelio, *Art. 1362, Dell'interpretazione del Contratto*, in Emanuela Navarretta, Andrea Orestano (eds.), *Commentario al Codice Civile*, Vol. 2—*Contratti in Generale*, UTET Giuridica, Torino, 2011.

Geri, Lina Bigliazzi, *L'interpretazione del Contratto Artt. 1362-1371, Il Codice Civile—Commentario*, Giuffrè Editore, Milan, 2013.

Ghestin, Jacques, Billiau, Marc, *Traité de Droit Civil—Les obligations, les effets du contrat*, 4th ed., Librarie Générale de Droit et de Jurisprudence, Paris, 2001.

Goudsmit, Joel Emanuel, *The Pandects: A Treatise on the Roman Law and upon Its Connection with Modern Legislation*, Longmans, Green, London, 1873.

Grotius, Hugo, *Commentaries on the Roman-Dutch Law* (translated by Simon van Leeuven), Joseph Butterworth and son, Dublin, 1820.

Grotius, Hugo, *De Jure Belli ac Pacis Libris Tres*, Vol. 2, Chapter XVI, Paris, 1625.

Guido, Alpa, *Il controllo giudiziale del contratto e l'interpretazione*, http://www.altalex.com/index.php?idnot=64932#_Toc369871176 (accessed December 7, 2018).

Gülerci, Altan Fahri, Kılınç, Ayşe, *6098 Sayılı Yeni TBK ile Karşılaştırmalı Borçlar Hukuku Genel Hükümler*, Yetkin, Ankara, 2011.

Gür, A. Refik, *Hukuk Tarihi ve Tekeffürü Bakımından Mecelle*, 3rd ed., Sebil, Istanbul, 1993.

Hadžimanović, Nataša, *Auslegung und Ergänzung von Verträgen—Vertragliche Nebenpflichten im englischen und schweizerischen Recht*, PhD Thesis, University of Zurich, Schulthess, Zurich, 2006.

Honnold, John O., *Uniform Law for International Sales under the 1980 United Nations Convention*, 3rd ed., Kluwer Law International, The Hague, 1999.

Huber, Peter, *Some Introductory Remarks on the CISG*, 6 Internationales Handelsrecht, 2006, 228-238; Sellier European Law Publishers, Munich, 2006.

Huber, Peter, Mullis, Alastair, *The CISG: A New Textbook for Students and Practitioners*, Sellier European Law Publishers, Munich, 2007.

İlhan, Cengiz, *Günümüz Türkçesiyle Mecelle*, 2nd ed., Yetkin, Ankara, 2014.

Jäggi, Peter, Gauch, Peter *(Zürcher) Kommentar zum Schweizerischen Zivilgesetzbuch—Obligationenrecht, Allgemeiner Teil, Band V 1b, Kommentar zu Art. 18 OR*, 3rd ed., Zurich, 1980.

Kaplan, İbrahim, *Banka Sözleşmelerinin Yorumu ve Tamamlanması*, Banka ve Ticaret Hukuku Dergisi, C. XIV, S. 2., 1987.

Kaplan, İbrahim, *Hakimin Sözleşmeye Müdahalesi*, 3rd ed., Yetkin, Ankara, 2013.

Kocayusufpaşaoğlu, Necip, Hatemi, Hüseyin, Serozan, Rona, Arpacı, Abdülkadir, *Borçlar Hukuku Genel Bölüm*, Vol. 1, 7th ed., Filiz, Istanbul, 2017.

Kornet, Nicole, *Contract Interpretation and Gap Filling: Comparative and Theoretical Perspectives*, Intersentia, Antwerp, 2006.

Kramer, Ernst A., Schmidlin, Bruno, *Berner Kommentar, Das Obligationenrecht, Band VI,1, Kommentar zu Art. 1-18 OR*, Stämpfli, Bern, 1986.

Lewison, Sir Kim, *The Interpretation of Contracts*, 4th ed., Sweet & Maxwell, London, 2007.

von Lingenthal, Karl Salomo Zachariä, *Versuch einer allgemeinen Hermeneutik des Rechts Erbstein*, Meissen, 1805.

Linzer, Peter, *The Comfort of Certainty: Plain Meaning and the Parol Evidence Rule*, 71 (3) Fordham Law Review, 2002.

Lookofsky, Joseph, *1980 United Nations Convention on Contracts for the International Sale of Goods, Article 8 Interpretation of Statements by Parties*, in J. Herbots (ed.), R. Blanpain (general ed.), *International Encyclopaedia of Laws—Contracts*, Suppl. 29, Kluwer Law International, The Hague, 2000.

Lookofsky, Joseph, *Understanding the CISG, A Compact Guide to the 1980 United Nations Convention on Contracts for the International Sale of Goods*, Kluwer Law International-DJØF, Copenhagen, 2008.

Looschelders, Dirk, *§ 133*, in Thomas Heidel, Rainer Hüßtege, Heinz-Peter Mansel, Ulrich Noack (eds.), *Nomos Kommentar, BGB Allgemeiner Teil,EGBGB, Band 1*, 3rd ed., Nomos, Baden-Baden, 2016.

Looschelders, Dirk, *§ 157*, in Thomas Heidel, Rainer Hüßtege, Heinz-Peter Mansel, Ulrich Noack (eds.), *Nomos Kommentar, BGB Allgemeiner Teil,EGBGB, Band 1*, 3rd ed., Nomos, Baden-Baden, 2016.

Malaurie, Philippe, Aynès, Laurent, *Les Obligations*, 10th ed., LGDJ, Paris, 2018.

McKendrick, Ewan, *Construction of Terms*, in Joseph Chitty, Hugh Beale (eds.), *Chitty on Contracts, General Principles*, Vol. 1, 32nd ed., Sweet & Maxwell, London, 2015.

McMeel, Gerard, Grigoleit, Hans Christoph, *Interpretation of Contracts*, in Gerhard Dannemann, Stefan Vogenauer (eds.), *The Common European Sales Law in Context*, Oxford University Press, Croydon, 2013.

Mercadal, Barthélémy, *Les principes généraux gouvernant l'interprétation du contrat/ The General Principles Behind Contract Interpretation*, 6 IBLJ/RDAI 541, 2017.

Moens, Gabriël A., Cohn, Lisa, Peacock, Darren, *Australia*, in Michael Joachim Bonell (ed.), *A New Approach to International Commercial Contracts—The UNIDROIT Principles of International Commercial Contracts*, Kluwer Law International, The Hague-London-Boston, 1999.

Monateri, Pier Giuseppe, *L'interpretazione del Contratto*, in Pier Giuseppe Monateri, Enrico del Prato, Maria Rosaria Marella, Alessandro Somma, Cristina Costantini (eds.), *Il Nuovo Contratto*, Zanichelli Editore, 5th ed., Bologna, 425, 2010.

Net, Le, *Rules of Interpretation of Contracts under the UNIDROIT Principles and Their Possible Adoption in Vietnamese Law*, 7 Uniform Law Review 1017, 2002.

Neumayer, Karl H., Ming, Catherine, in François Dessemontet (ed.), *Convention de Vienne sur les contrats de vente internationale de marchandises—Commentaire*, CEDIAC, Lausanne, 1993.

Oğuz, Arzu, *Karşılaştırmalı Hukuk*, Yetkin, Ankara, 2003.

Oğuzman, Kemal, Öz, Turgut, *Borçlar Hukuku Genel Hükümler*, Vol. 1, 16th ed., Vedat, Istanbul, 2018.

Oktay (Özdemir), Saibe, *İsimsiz Sözleşmelerin Geçerliliği, Yorumu ve Boşluklarının Tamamlanması*, İÜHFD, 1996, C. LV, S. 1-2, 263-294.

Olmos, Javier M. Rodriguez, *Contexto y construcción de la regla "interpretatio contra proferentem" en la tradición romanista*, Revista de Derecho Privado, N. 14, 78, 2008.

Osman, Filali, *Les principes généraux de la lex mercatoria—contribution à l'étude d'un ordre juridique anational*, LGDJ, Paris, 1992.

Ott, Edward E., *Die Interpretation von Verträgen und Statuten*, Helbing & Lichtenhann, Basel, 2000.

Özel, Çağlar, *Türk Borçlar Kanunu / Turkish Code of Obligations*, 3rd ed., Ankara, 2016.

Perillo, Joseph M., *The Origins of the Objective Theory of Contract Formation and Interpretation*, 69 Fordham Law Review 427, 431 (2000).

Perillo, Joseph M., *Calamari and Perillo on Contracts*, 5th ed., Thomson West, St. Paul, 2003.

Perillo, Joseph M., *Editorial Remarks on the Manner in Which the UNIDROIT Principles May Be Used to Interpret or Supplement CISG Article 8*, http://www.cisg.law.pace.edu/cisg/principles/uni8.html.

Posner, Eric, *The Parol Evidence Rule, the Plain Meaning Rule, and the Principles of Contractual Interpretation*, 146 University of Pennsylvania Law Review 533, 1998.

Posner, Richard, *The Law and Economics of Contract Interpretation*, 83 Texas Law Review 1581, 2005.

Pothier, Robert Joseph, *Pandectæ Justinianæ in novum ordinem digestæ*, Paris, 1748-1752.

Pothier, Robert Joseph, *Traité des obligations*, Orléans, 1761.

Reisoğlu, Safa, *Borçlar Hukuku Genel Hükümler*, 25th ed., Beta, Istanbul, 2014.

Richman, Barak D., Schmelzer, Dennis, *When Money Grew on Trees: The Untold Story of Lucy v. Zehmer*, 61 Duke Law Journal 1511, 2012.

Sacco, Rodolfo, *Dell'interpretazione del contratto*, in Paolo Cendon (ed.), *Commentatio al Codice Civile*, Giuffrè Editore, Milan, 2010.

Sangermano, Francesco, *L'interpretazione del contratto: profili dottrinali e giurisprudenziali*, Giuffrè Editore, Milan, 2007.

von Savigny, Friedrich Karl, *System of the Modern Roman Law*, Vol 1 (translated by William Holloway), J. Higginbotham Publisher, Madras, 1867.

Schlechtriem, Peter, *Uniform Sales Law—The UN-Convention on Contracts for the International Sale of Goods*, Manz, Wien, 1986.

Schmidt-Kessel, Martin, *Article 8*, in Peter Schlechtriem, Ingeborg Schwenzer (eds.), *Commentary on the UN Convention on the International Sale of Goods* (CISG), 2nd (English) ed., C.H. Beck, New York, 2005.

Schröder, Jan, *Recht als Wissenschaft*, C.H. Beck, Munich, 2001.

Schulze, Reiner, Zoll, Frydeyk, *European Contract Law*, C.H. Beck/Hart/Nomos, 2016.

Singer, Reinhard, *§ 133*, in Berg von J. Staudinger (ed.), *J. von Staudingers Kommentar zum Bürgerlichen Gesetzbuch: Staudinger BGB—Buch 1: Allgemeiner Teil*, 15th ed., Sellier-De Gruyter, Munich, 2017.

Stein, Peter, *Interpretation and Legal Reasoning in Roman Law*, 70 Chicago-Kent Law Review 1539, 1995.

Story, Joseph, *Commentaries on the Law of Bailments, with Illustrations from the Civil and the Foreign Law*, Hilliard and Brown, Cambridge, 1832.

Story, Joseph, *Commentaries on the Law of Bills of Exchange, Foreign and Inland (1847)*, The Lawbook Exchange, New Jersey, 2005.

Tekinay, Selahattin Sulhi, Akman, Sermet, Burcuoğlu, Haluk, Altop, Atilla, Tekinay *Borçlar Hukuku Genel Hükümler*, 7th ed., Filiz, Istanbul, 1993.

Tercier, Pierre, Pichonnaz, Pascal, Develioğlu, H. Murat, *Borçlar Hukuku—Genel Hükümler*, On İki Levha, Istanbul, 2016.

Terré, François, Simler, Philippe, Lequette, Yves, *Droit civil—Les obligations*, 11th ed., Dalloz, Paris, 2013.

Tokbaş, Hakan, Tüzüner, Özlem, Milli Şerh *(National Commentary) 6502 Sayılı Tüketicinin Korunması Hakkında Kanun Şerhi (Commentary on the Consumer Protection Law No. 6502)*, Aristo, Istanbul, 2016.

Treitel, Guenter, *The Law of Contract*, Sweet & Maxwell, London, 2011.

Underwood, James M., *Supplemental Serendipity: Congress' Accidental Improvement of Supplemental Jurisdiction*, 37 Akron Law Review 653, 2004.

Vogenauer, Stefan, *Interpretation of Contracts*, in Jürgen Basedow, Klaus J. Hopt, Reinhard Zimmermann, Andreas Stier (eds.), *The Max Planck Encyclopedia of European Private Law*, Vol. 1, 974, Oxford University Press, Croydon, 2012.

Vogenauer, Stefan, *Chapter 4—Interpretation*, in Stefan Vogenauer, Jan Kleinheisterkamp (eds.), *Commentary on the UNIDROIT Principles of International Commercial Contracts (PICC)*, 2nd ed., Oxford University Press, New York, 2015.

Watson, Alan, *Narrow, Rigid and Literal Interpretation in the Later Roman Republic*, 37 Tijdschrift voor Rechtsgeschiedenis 351, 1969.

Wendehorst, Christiane, *Interpretation*, in Reiner Schulze (ed.), *Common European Sales Law (CESL) Commentary*, C.H. Beck/Hart/Nomos, Baden-Baden, 314, 2012.

Werro, Franz, Besler, Eva Maria, *Switzerland*, in M.J. Bonell (ed.), *A New Approach to International Commercial Contracts—The UNIDROIT Principles of International Commercial Contracts*, Kluwer Law International, The Hague-London-Boston, 1999.

White, James J., Summers, Robert S., Hillman, Robert A., *Uniform Commercial Code*, Vol. 1, 6th ed., West, New York, 2012.

Wiegand, Wolfgang, *Art. 18* in Heinrich Honsell, Nedim Peter Vogt, Wolfgang Wiegand, *Basler Kommentar—Obligationenrecht I, Art. 1-529 OR*, 6th ed., Basel, Helbing & Lichtenhahn, 2015.

Williams, James, *Interpretation in Roman Law*, 15 The Law Magazine and Review of All Reported Cases, 5th ser. 223, 1889-1890.

Williston, Samuel, Jaeger, Walter H.E., *A Treatise on the Law of Contracts*, Vol. 4, 3rd ed., Mount Kisco—Baker Voorhis & Co., New York, 1961.

Williston, Samuel, Squillante, Alphonse M., Fonseca, John R. (eds.), *Williston on Sales*, Vol. 1, 4th ed., LCP-BW, New York, California, 1973.

Yeniocak, Umut, *Türk Borçlar Kanunu'nun Getirdiği Yenilikler ve Değişiklikler*, 2nd ed., Seçkin, Ankara, 2013.

Yıldırım, Ahmet Cemil, *Equilibrium in International Commercial Contracts with Particular Regard to UNIDROIT Principles of International Commercial Contracts*, Wolf Legal Publishers, Nijmegen, 2011.

Yıldırım, Ahmet Cemil, *Lack of Uniform Application Regarding Transfer of Property in International Sales Contracts with Particular Regard to Retention of Title Clauses*, in Şükran Şıpka, Ahmet Cemil Yıldırım (eds.), *Yeni Türk Borçlar Kanunu ve CISG'e Göre Satış Sözleşmeleri (Sales Contracts under the New Turkish Code of Obligations and the CISG*, On İki Levha, Istanbul, 189, 2012.

Yıldırım, Ahmet Cemil, *Ottoman Mecelle as a Secular Uniform Law Instrument*, 10 International Journal of Turcologia 19, 27, 2015.

Yıldırım, Ahmet Cemil, *Raisonnable et bonne foi: de nouveaux usages des standards juridiques? / Reasonable and Good Faith: New Usages for Legal Standards?*, 6 IBLJ/RDAI 549, 2017.

Zeller, Bruno, *Determining the Contractual Intent of Parties under the CISG and Common Law—A Comparative Analysis*, 4 (4) European Journal of Law Reform (Kluwer) 629-643, 2002.

Zimmermann, Reinhard, *The Law of Obligations—Roman Foundations of the Civilian Tradition*, 2nd ed., Oxford University Press, New York, 1996.

Zimmermann, Reinhard, *The New German Law of Obligations—Historical and Comparative Perspectives*, 2nd ed., Oxford University Press, New York, 2010.

Zuppi, Alberto, *Article 8*, in Stefan Kröll, Loukas Mistelis, Pilar Perales Viscasillas (eds.), *United Nations Convention on Contracts for the International Sale of Goods (CISG) Commentary*, C.H. Beck/Hart/Nomos, Munich, 142, 2011.

Zweigert, Konrad, Kötz, Hein, *Introduction to Comparative Law*, 3rd ed., Clarendon Press, Oxford, 1998.

Official Documents and Reports

American Law Institute, Restatement of the Law of Contracts, Vol. 1, American Law Institute Publishers, St. Paul, 1932.

American Law Institute, Restatement of the Law, Second, Contracts 2nd, Vol. 2, American Law Institute Publishers, St. Paul—Minnessota, 1981.

American Law Institute & National Conference of Commissioners on Uniform State Laws, Uniform Commercial Code—Official Texts and Comments, Thomson West, New York, 2008.

UK Law Commission 154, 1986, Cmnd. 9700.

Council Directive 93/13/EEC of April 5, 1993 on unfair terms in consumer contracts.

The Commission on European Contract Law, Ole Lando, Hugh Beale (eds.), Principles of European Contract Law Parts I and II, Kluwer Law International, 2000.

European Commission, Proposal for a Regulation of the European Parliament and of the Council on a Common European Sales Law, COM (2011) 635 final, 2011/0284 (COD), Brussels, October 11, 2011.

European Parliament, European Parliament legislative resolution of February 26, 2014 on the proposal for a regulation of the European Parliament and of the Council on a Common European Sales Law.

European Commission, Work Program 2015, COM(2014) 910.

European Commission, Proposal for a Directive of the European Parliament and of the Council on certain aspects concerning contracts for the online and other distance sales of goods, COM (2015) 635 final, 2011/0288 (COD), Brussels, December 09, 2015.

European Commission, Amended proposal for a Directive of the European Parliament and of the Council on certain aspects concerning contracts for the online and other distance sales of goods, amending Regulation (EC) No 2006/2004 of the European Parliament and of the Council and Directive 2009/22/EC of the European Parliament and of the Council and repealing Directive 1999/44/EC of the European Parliament and of the Council, COM (2017) 637 final, 2015/0288 (COD), Brussels, October 31, 2017.

UNCITRAL, Richard Hyland (rapporteur), *CISG Advisory Council Opinion No. 3, Parol Evidence Rule, Plain Meaning Rule, Contractual Merger Clause and the CISG*, October 23, 2004.

UNCITRAL, 2012 Digest of case law on the United Nations Convention on the International Sale of Goods.

UNCITRAL, Guide to CISG Article 8, Secretariat Commentary (closest counterpart to an Official Commentary).

UNIDROIT 1977, Study L—Doc. 12.

UNIDROIT 1978 Study L-Doc 13.

UNIDROIT 1983, Study L—Doc. 25.

UNIDROIT 1991, PC—Misc 15.

Electronic Sources

http://www.adusbef.veneto.it.

http://books.google.com.

http://caselaw.findlaw.com.

http://cisgw3.law.pace.edu/cases.

https://droitromain.univ-grenoble-alpes.fr/Anglica.

http://ec.europa.eu.

http://law.justia.com/cases.

http://openjurist.org.

http://scholarship.law.duke.edu.

http://scocal.stanford.edu.

https://supreme.justia.com/cases.

http://tx.findacase.com.

http://www.ali.org.

http://www.bailii.org/uk/cases.

http://www.bger.ch.

http://www.altalex.com.

http://www.cisg.law.pace.edu.

http://www.foroitaliano.it.

http://www.gesetze-im-internet.de/bgb.

http://www.i-law.com.

http://www.iium.edu.my/deed/lawbase/al_majalle/al_majalleintro.html.

http://www.jus.uio.no/lm/eu.contract.principles.parts.1.to.3.2002.

http://www.jus.unitn.it.
http://www.kazanci.com.
http://www.lawandsea.net.
http://lawcommission.justice.gov.uk.
http://www.law.cornell.edu,ucc.
http://www.legifrance.gouv.fr.
http://www.legifrance.gouv.fr,initRechJuriJudi.do.
http://www.lonang.com.
http://www.mevzuat.gov.tr.
http://www.mindserpent.com.
http://www.resmigazete.gov.tr.
http://www.servat.unibe.ch.
http://swarb.co.uk.
http://www.textes.justice.gouv.fr.
http://www.thelatinlibrary.com.
http://www.trans-lex.org.
http://www.uncitral.org.
http://www.unidroit.org.
http://www.uniformlawcommission.com.
http://www.unilex.info.
http://www.west.net.

Table of Cases

Cases from French Courts

Cases from Italian Courts

Cases from German Courts

Cases from Swiss Courts

Cases from Turkish Courts

Cases from English Courts

Cases from US Courts

Cases from Ukranian Courts

CISG Cases

Arbitral Awards

Index

U

V

W

Y

1. Moshe Hirsch, *The Arbitration Mechanism of the International Center for the Settlement of Investment Disputes*, 1993 (ISBN 07-923-1993-1).
2. Aida B. Avanessian, *Iran-United States Claims Tribunal in Action*, 1993 (ISBN 18-533-3902-4).
3. Isaak I. Dore, *The UNCITRAL Framework for Arbitration in Contemporary Perspective*, 1993 (ISBN 18-533-3573-8).
4. Vesna Lazić, *Insolvency Proceedings and Commercial Arbitration*, 1998 (ISBN 90-411-1115-8).
5. Joachim Frick, *Arbitration in Complex International Contracts*, 2001 (ISBN 90-411-1662-1).
6. Katherine Lynch, *The Forces of Economic Globalization: Challenges to the Regime of International Commercial Arbitration*, 2003 (ISBN 90-411-1994-9).
7. Christoph Liebscher, *The Healthy Award: Challenge in International Commercial Arbitration*, 2003 (ISBN 90-411-2011-4).
8. Hamid G. Gharavi, *The International Effectiveness of the Annulment of an Arbitral Award*, 2003 (ISBN 90-411-1717-2).
9. Abdulhay Sayed, *Corruption in International Trade and Commercial Arbitration*, 2004 (ISBN 90-411-2236-2).
10. Gabrielle Kaufmann-Kohler & Thomas Schultz, *Online Dispute Resolution: Challenges for Contemporary Justice*, 2004 (ISBN 90-411-2318-0).
11. Christopher R. Drahozal & Richard W. Naimark (eds), *Towards a Science of International Arbitration: Collected Empirical Research*, 2005 (ISBN 90-411-2322-9).
12. Ali Yeşilirmak, *Provisional Measures in International Commercial Arbitration*, 2005 (ISBN 90-411-2353-9).
13. Christian Bühring-Uhle, *Arbitration and Mediation in International Business*, second revised edition, 2006 (ISBN 978-9-041-12256-8).
14. Bernard Hanotiau, *Complex Arbitrations: Multiparty, Multicontract, Multiissue and Class Actions*, 2006 (ISBN 978-9-041-12442-5).
15. Loukas A. Mistelis & Julian D.M. Lew (eds), *Pervasive Problems in International Arbitration*, 2006 (ISBN 978-9-041-12450-0).
16. Julian D.M. Lew & Loukas A. Mistelis (eds), *Arbitration Insights – Twenty Years of the Annual Lecture of the School of International Arbitration, Sponsored by Freshfields Bruckhaus Deringer*, 2006 (ISBN 978-9-041-12606-1).
17. Mark Kantor, *Valuation for Arbitration: Compensation Standards, Valuation Methods and Expert Evidence*, 2008 (ISBN 978-9-041-12735-8).
18. Christoph Brunner, *Force Majeure and Hardship under General Contract Principles: Exemption for Non-Performance in International Arbitration*, 2009 (ISBN 978-90-411-2792-1).

19. Loukas A. Mistelis & Stavros L. Brekoulakis (eds), *Arbitrability: International & Comparative Perspectives*, 2009 (ISBN 978-90-411-2730-3).
20. Sam Luttrell, *Bias Challenges in International Commercial Arbitration: The Need for a 'Real Danger' Test*, 2009 (ISBN 978-90-411-3191-1).
21. Monique Sasson, *Substantive Law in Investment Treaty Arbitration: The Unsettled Relationship Between International Law and Municipal Law*, Second Edition, 2017 (ISBN 978-90-411-6103-1).
22. Ileana M. Smeureanu, *Confidentiality in International Commercial Arbitration*, 2011 (ISBN 978-90-411-3226-0).
23. Won Kidane, *China-Africa Dispute Settlement: The Law, Economics and Culture of Arbitration*, 2011 (ISBN 978-90-411-3674-9).
24. Karel Daele, *Challenge and Disqualification of Arbitrators in International Arbitration*, 2012 (ISBN 978-90-411-3799-9).
25. Crina Baltag, *The Energy Charter Treaty: The Notion of Investor*, 2012 (ISBN 978-90-411-3428-8).
26. Alexandra Diehl, *The Core Standard of International Investment Protection: Fair and Equitable Treatment*, 2012 (ISBN 978-90-411-3869-9).
27. Manuel Indlekofer, *International Arbitration and the Permanent Court of Arbitration*, 2013 (ISBN 978-90-411-4766-0).
28. Günther J. Horvath & Stephan Wilske (eds), *Guerrilla Tactics in International Arbitration*, 2013 (ISBN 978-90-411-4002-9).
29. Albert Badia, *Piercing the Veil of State Enterprises in International Arbitration*, 2014 (ISBN 978-90-411-5162-9).
30. Nadja Erk, *Parallel Proceedings in International Arbitration: A Comparative European Perspective*, 2014 (ISBN 978-90-411-5264-0).
31. Simon Vorburger, *International Arbitration and Cross-Border Insolvency: Comparative Perspectives*, 2014 (ISBN 978-90-411-5419-4).
32. Ahmad Ali Ghouri, *Interaction and Conflict of Treaties in Investment Arbitration*, 2015 (ISBN 978-90-411-5417-0).
33. Reto Marghitola, *Document Production in International Arbitration*, 2015 (ISBN 978-90-411-5159-9).
34. Alfonso Gómez-Acebo, *Party-Appointed Arbitrators in International Commercial Arbitration*, 2016 (ISBN 978-90-411-6671-5).
35. Jonas von Goeler, *Third-Party Funding in International Arbitration and Its Impact on Procedure*, 2016 (ISBN 978-90-411-5015-8).
36. Dean Lewis, *The Interpretation and Uniformity of the UNCITRAL Model Law on International Commercial Arbitration: Focusing on Australia, Hong Kong and Singapore*, 2016 (ISBN 978-90-411-6700-2).
37. Stavros Brekoulakis, Julian D.M. Lew & Loukas Mistelis (eds), *The Evolution and Future of International Arbitration*, 2016 (ISBN 978-90-411-7004-0).
38. Rémy Gerbay, *The Functions of Arbitral Institutions*, 2016 (ISBN 978-90-411-6217-5).

39. Maximilian Clasmeier, *Arbitral Awards as Investments: Treaty Interpretation and the Dynamics of International Investment Law*, 2017 (ISBN 978-90-411-8357-6).
40. Tony Cole (ed.), *The Roles of Psychology in International Arbitration*, 2017 (ISBN 978-90-411-5921-2).
41. Pietro Ferrario, *The Adaptation of Long-Term Gas Sale Agreements by Arbitrators*, 2017 (ISBN 978-90-411-8232-6).
42. Jacob B. van de Velden, *Finality in Litigation: The Law and Practice of Preclusion – Res Judicata (Merger and Estoppel), Abuse of Process and Recognition of Foreign Judgments*, 2017 (ISBN 978-90-411-8342-2).
43. Dolores Bentolila, *Arbitrators as Lawmakers*, 2017 (ISBN 978-90-411-8354-5).
44. Giacomo Marchisio, *The Notion of Award in International Commercial Arbitration: A Comparative Analysis of French Law, English Law, and the UNCITRAL Model Law*, 2017 (ISBN 978-90-411-8391-0).
45. Csaba Kovács, *Attribution in International Investment Law*, 2018 (ISBN 978-90-411-9675-0).
46. Mary Mitsi, *The Decision-Making Process of Investor-State Arbitration Tribunals*, 2019 (ISBN 978-90-411-9600-2).
47. Ahmet Cemil Yıldırım, *Interpretation of Contracts in Comparative and Uniform Law*, 2019 (ISBN 978-94-035-1130-6).